The Ethical Consumer

The Ethical Consumer

Rob Harrison
Terry Newholm
Deirdre Shaw

SAGE Publications
London • Thousand Oaks • New Delhi

First published 2005

SAGE Publications Ltd
1 Oliver's Yard
55 City Road
London EC1Y 1SP

SAGE Publications Inc.
2455 Teller Road
Thousand Oaks, California 91320

SAGE Publications India Pvt Ltd
B 42, Panchsheel Enclave
Post Box 4109
New Delhi 110 017

British Library Cataloguing in Publication data

A catalogue record for this book is available from the British Library

ISBN 1-4129-0352-1
ISBN 1-4129-0353-X (pbk)

Library of Congress Control Number: 2004116094

Typeset by Selective Minds Infotech Pvt Ltd, Mohali, India
Printed and bound by The Cromwell Press Ltd, Trowbridge, Wiltshire

Contents

Contents

PART THREE
Understanding Ethical Consumers

PART FOUR
Responding to Ethical Consumers

Notes on Contributors

Contemporary academics are far less inclined to claim independence from the social phenomena they research. Like practitioners and activists they are embroiled in the culture in which they work. In the spirit of reflexivity we have asked our contributors, where possible, to talk a little about themselves as consumers, researchers, practitioners and/or activists, as well as giving some more conventional biographical details. We have also asked contributors, where appropriate, to include a note on their funding sources.

Carol Adams

I am a professor of accounting and Head of School of Accounting, Economics and Finance at Deakin University. I am a former director and council member of the Institute of Social and Ethical AccountAbility and a judge for the ACCA sustainability reporting awards. My research on social and environmental accounting and reporting has been funded by UK professional accounting bodies. For more information about my research please see the website at www.deakin.edu.au/fac_buslaw/sch_aef/.

    I would like to boycott all multinational corporations which violate human rights, mistreat their employees, disregard safety and pollute the environment. But in a fast, increasingly globalised environment, they are hard to avoid and they don't disclose all their negative impacts.

Clive Barnett

I teach in the Faculty of Social Sciences at The Open University. I am currently working on a research project, part of the ESRC/AHRB *Cultures of Consumption* Programme in the UK, which looks at the ways in which ethical consumerism connects with wider campaigns of global solidarity. What I am really interested in are the relationships between popular culture, public life and democracy. My own consumption habits would probably not fare too well if subjected to a rigorous ethical audit, but I'm working on it.

Hannah Berry

I have worked with the Ethical Consumer Research Association (ECRA) since 1998, after my Biology/Spanish degree became a bit overshadowed by activism. It seemed a good job for not compromising my principles whilst leaving time for environmental direct action, social centre squats and the radical political stuff which is more important to me as a strategy than just avoiding certain products and companies (although I do that too). I live in the housing co-op where ECRA is based. My other job with Manchester's Women's Network is broadening my understanding of gender politics and social deprivation in the city, and helping me to think about consumer culture in new ways. I'm learning about methods of community education and would like to address issues of sustainability in that context.

Philip Cafaro

Philip Cafaro is associate professor of philosophy at Colorado State University, Fort Collins, Colorado, USA. His research and writing centres on ethical theory, environmental ethics and land management issues. Phil and his wife Kris try to be ethical consumers, paying particular regard to the environmental impacts of their consumption. Regarding energy use, they buy wind power from their local utility (rather than relying on cheaper coal), use compact fluorescent bulbs, an ultra efficient washing machine and the awesome power of the sun to dry their clothes, bicycle to work each day, and own one fuel efficient car, which they use moderately. So they look pretty good compared to their neigbours – but is that enough?

Hélène Cherrier

I am a young woman, currently teaching consumer behaviour and marketing management at Westminster Business School. I was born in France but live in London, where I have been regularly browsing and shopping for second-hand goods, using local stores, and visiting farmers' markets. I ride my used bicycle to commute to work, foster water saving with short showers, and by no means would I throw away food or goods. I try to encourage energy cutbacks by refusing unnecessary consumption such as elevators, hair dryers, aerosol sprays, and switch off pointless lights, computers, televisions, and heaters at friends' houses, at work and in my home. Needless to say, my growing awareness on ethical issues is not without struggles and culpabilities. I blame myself for flying too much, buying new electric equipment, and welcoming virtual communication into my daily life. Overall, the saying 'live simply so that others can simply live' summarises my daily consumption struggle.

Barry Clavin

I have worked in the financial services sector since 1992 and I joined the Co-operative Bank's Ethical Policy Unit in 1996. I am now Ethical Policies Manager for the Co-operative Financial Services Group.

I have overseen the development of the bank's work on the Ethical Purchasing Index and ethical policy development since that date. I am currently working on the creation of a new ethical policy for the Co-operative Insurance Society. The research presented in this volume reflects the range of issues and organisations that we have worked with to promote understanding of ethical consumer behaviour. Our practice of working with a variety of research organisations has allowed us to continuously bring fresh observations to the issues.

Having two small children makes it difficult to shop – let alone shop ethically. I still haven't managed to get hold of an FSC wooden Teletubby or an organic sherbert dip.

Scott Clouder

I work for the Ethical Consumer Research Association, as Research Manager for the Ethical Consumer Informations Systems (ECIS) project. I also work part-time as information officer for the Vegetarian Society of the UK. I was born in Aberdeen and studied Social Sciences at the University of Bradford, where I drank my first cup of fair trade coffee and started hanging out with the Peace Studies students. After travelling around the USA by train, I completed an MA in Cultural Studies at Leeds Metropolitan University. During this time I discovered the joys of soya milk and adopted a vegan diet. I briefly moved south to the University of Kent and got an MA in Image Studies. I looked at corporate images of nature and completed my dissertation about 'greenwashing'.

I enjoy growing, cooking and eating organic veg and another passion is football. I hate air travel but love going to Jamaica. I boycott Nestlé but miss eating Lion bars.

Andrew Crane

I am a professor in Business Ethics at the International Centre for Corporate Social Responsibility (ICCSR) at Nottingham University. I do not believe that my job is to prove that businesses are ethical, but rather to illustrate how ethics (good and bad) can be used as a lens to understand organisations and their relations with other constituencies.

I joined ICCSR in October 2002 from Cardiff University, where I was involved in setting up the ESRC Centre for Business Relationships, Accountability, Sustainability and Society (BRASS), and the Cardiff Centre for Ethics, Law and Society (CCELS). Given that the centre I now work in was only founded after Nottingham University was donated a considerable amount of money by a tobacco company, I would not have joined were I not thoroughly convinced that I could continue to teach and research with full academic freedom, and that I could do something positive with the funding available. I mention this because the whole issue of my centre's funding was a subject of initial concern to the editors of this volume, and you may be interested in visiting the ICCSR website for more information about the centre's activities and funding protocols, as well as my own research and publications (www.nottingham.ac.uk/business/iccsr).

Jenny Dawkins

I am Head of Corporate Social Responsibility Research at MORI. MORI is a commercial market research company: the research included in this volume was funded by MORI's marketing budget, and the company gets its income from its clients. I conduct social and market research for a variety of clients from the private, public and voluntary sectors. I also lead MORI's community programme, which encourages our employees to volunteer their time in the community.

I try to buy fair trade, free range products in my supermarket shopping, I make use of the great recycling facilities we have locally, and I don't own (or need) a car whilst living in London. But I'm beset by the same confusion that we find a lot of consumers feel in terms of not being clear about the ethical purchase options in a lot of cases. I have just discovered *The Good Gift Catalogue* at www.goodgifts.org, for presents supporting worthy causes!

Roger A. Dickinson and Mary L. Carsky

Roger Dickinson is Professor of Marketing at the University of Texas at Arlington. He has been on the faculties of the University of California, Berkeley, and the Rutgers Graduate School of Business. He has published in many journals, including the *Journal of Business*, the *Journal of Macromarketing*, the *Journal of Retailing*, the *Journal of Marketing*, the *Journal of Consumer Research*, the *Journal of Consumer Affairs*, and *Agribusiness*. He has held many administrative positions.

Mary Carsky is Professor of Marketing at the University of Hartford. She has published in many journals, including the *Academy of Marketing Science*, the *Journal of Macromarketing*, and the *Journal of Consumer Affairs*. She has held many administrative positions and has been a member of the board of directors of the American Council on Consumer Interests (ACCI).

In the USA marketing academics and most prime journals have focused on helping firms make more money. The authors have sought to help change the focus of academic efforts to examine marketing systems through the prisms of the household and society. Two fundamental considerations underly the efforts of the authors to improve the lot of the household and society. First, firms are primarily interested in households as vehicles to enhance the long-term profitability of the firm. Second, consumers can change the dynamics of the marketing place to better the welfare of their particular households and that of society. In these contexts, the authors created systems to improve the household's 'bang for the buck', analysed consumer voting, and suggested a concept of consumer citizenship. In their individual purchasing the authors use elements of the shopping system, primarily heuristics, that they developed in their chapter. These votes are tempered by societal goals when deemed relevant.

Marsha A. Dickson

I am an Associate Professor of apparel and textiles at Kansas State University. My undergraduate and graduate level teaching focuses on global production and trade of apparel, particularly sweatshop issues, consumer behaviour, and product development. I began research in this area thirteen years ago with a focus on alternative trade. In 1994 I shifted focus to the apparel industry and the practices of multinational apparel manufacturers and retailers. I hope to assist these businesses as they make the transition to more socially responsible practices. I am on the board of directors of the Fair Labor Association.

Yiannis Gabriel

Yiannis Gabriel is Professor in Organizational Theory at the Tanaka Business
School, Imperial College. He has a degree in Mechanical Engineering from Imperial
College London, and a PhD in Sociology from the University of California,
Berkeley. His main research interests are in organisational theory (especially leadership, group dynamics and organisational culture), consumer studies, management learning and knowledge, storytelling, folklore and psychoanalysis. Gabriel is
author of *Freud and Society, Working Lives in Catering* (both Routledge), *Organisations
in Depth* (Sage), and *Storytelling in Organisations* (OUP) and co-author of *Organising
and Organisations, The Unmanageable Consumer: Contemporary Consumption and Its
Fragmentation* and *Experiencing Organisations* (all Sage). He has recently edited the
collection *Myths, Stories and Organisations*, published by Oxford University Press.
He has been Editor of *Management Learning* and Associate Editor of *Human
Relations*.

Rob Harrison

Rob Harrison was a founding director of the Ethical Consumer Research
Association (ECRA) in 1987. He studied Law at Manchester University in the early
turbulent Thatcher years of the 1980s. He became involved in a range of campaigns
and protests, but was particularly attracted to the anti-Apartheid movement's
Barclay's Bank boycott. The success of this boycott in 1986 led him to want to
research more deeply into the potential of consumer actions to force social change
across a wider range of issues.

He has been Editor of *Ethical Consumer* magazine since its launch in 1989. It is
individual consumers' subscriptions to ECRA publications which have formed
the bulk of finance received to date. He has contributed to and edited the
Ethical Consumer Guide to Everyday Shopping (1993) and the *Green Building Handbook*
Vols 1 (1998) and 2 (2000). ECRA remains a not-for-profit workers' co-operative.
More information about ECRA appears at www.ethicalconsumer.org.

Tim Lang

Tim Lang is Professor of Food Policy at City University, London. Over thirty years,
he has worked variously as a farmer, lecturer, researcher and campaigner. Since
1994, he has been an academic. He is a fellow of the Faculty of Public Health and
a vice-president of the Chartered Institute of Environmental Health. He is a member of the UK Department of the Environment, Food and Rural Affairs (DEFRA)
Horizon Scanning Team, advising the Chief Scientist. He has been an advisor to
four parliamentary select committee inquiries, and to the WHO and FAO. He is
chair of Sustain, the UK 100+ NGO alliance promoting better food. He is the
author of ten books and over a hundred articles, reports and briefings. With Erik
Millstone he edited the *Atlas of Food* (Earthscan, 2003), winner of the 2004 André
Simon Food Book of the Year award. *Food Wars* (Earthscan), written with Michael
Heasman, was published in October 2004.

Alex Lewis

I graduated in 2002 from Durham University with a degree in Geography. As part of my course, I travelled to India to investigate the role of information and communication technologies in the transfer and use of agricultural information. The subsequent dissertation has since been awarded the W.A. Moyes prize for fieldwork and the Royal Geographic Society's Alfred Steers Undergraduate Dissertation Award in 2003.

In 2002, I began working with some values based consultants in Manchester, where I developed a strong interest in ethical consumerism. Much of my work has focused on looking at new ways in which we can explore the attitudes and values of ethical consumers in order to gain a deeper understanding of their behaviour.

Morven McEachern

I am a lecturer in marketing and consumer behaviour at the University of Salford and my current doctoral research focuses on quality assurance schemes and consumer purchase behaviour. Please visit the University of Salford website at www.som.salford.ac.uk/research/staff/mmceachern.php for my publications and further research interests. Research activities to date have been financially assisted by charitable educational bodies only.

As a consumer, I'm not a vegetarian but rather than buy meat from supermarkets that refuse to provide me with their animal welfare criteria due to 'commercial sensitivity', I buy locally from farm shops or box schemes. I do own a car, but car share for commuting to work.

Terry Newholm

I am a research fellow at the Open University Business School, with an interest in consumer culture. The UK Economic and Social Research Council funded my research presented in this book. I have also undertaken a literature review of business ethics sponsored by leading UK retailers. I think it can be productive for academics researching consumer culture to work with a variety of sponsors including retailers, producers and consumer organisations. Please visit the OUBS website www3.open.ac.uk/oubs/people2/p333.htm for my publications and further research interests.

I have been a vegetarian for thirty years and free from car ownership for a little less. Although consumption is far too complex for me to say this, I am a fairly conventional consumer. For example, I regularly internet shop with a leading supermarket. I harbour doubts about my increasing use of air travel for work and to see my elder son who lives abroad.

Deirdre Shaw

I am a reader in the Division of Marketing, Glasgow Caledonian University. My research has been funded in the main by Glasgow Caledonian University. I feel privileged that my research and teaching directly relate to my own personal interests surrounding ethical and sustainable lifestyle and consumption choices. I enjoyed a 'thrifty' upbringing in the north of Scotland and this trait manifested itself into a questioning of the need for many of the products reflective of an affluent consumer society.

I do not own a car or a mobile phone, I follow a vegan diet and where possible purchase organic and fair trade products seeking to avoid supermarkets. These choices reflect spiritual and ethical beliefs and also a desire for simplicity. Given that such choices are often far from simple, I do acknowledge the problems attached to my increased air travel and the purchase of new clothing produced under questionable conditions.

Robert Worcester

Robert Worcester is the founder and chairman of MORI (Market & Opinion Research International). He is visiting Professor of Government at the London School of Economics and Political Science and a governor at the LSE and on the court of the University of Kent and of Middlesex University. A Fulbright Commission member, he is a special advisor to the House of Commons' Treasury Select Committee. He has authored and co-authored some dozen books, the most recent being *Explaining Labour's Second Landslide* (with Dr Roger Mortimore).

Robert Worcester is also a long-standing, card-carrying eco-nut. American by birth, he is now a dual citizen. He has lived in the UK for thirty-five years, during which time he has been a WWF trustee and now WWF ambassador, vice-president of the Wildlife Trust, current trustee of the Wildfowl and Wetlands Trust, president of ENCAMS and also serves on the advisory board of the Institute of Business Ethics.

Ambika Zutshi

I am a lecturer at the Bowater School of Management and Marketing at Deakin University, Australia. My research interests are currently focused in the areas of triple bottom-line reporting, the role of various stakeholders in the planning and implementation of Environmental Management Systems (EMS), business ethics and supply chain management. Presently I have research funding from the Bowater School and the Faculty of Business and Law, Deakin University to conduct more research into the area of EMS, and the changing forms of managerial ethics in public service organisations, especially in Australia.

On the personal front, I have been a vegetarian for about ten years now and still struggle to find good takeaways! As a consumer of goods and services, I remain surprised to find well-educated people displaying few concerns beyond their selfish day-to-day necessities. I hope the readers of this book will spread the need for sustainability beyond the next decade.

Foreword

Ed Mayo*

There must have been something in the air at the time. The origins of many of the most inspiring examples of ethical action by consumers lie in the 1970s. The first fair trade initiatives started. Ethical banking made an appearance with the first social banks starting up in the USA and Europe. Early ethical investors in the UK stumped up money to put into worker co-operatives. And alternative technology was born, launched by the enthusiastic readers of the *Observer* newspaper.

These pioneers were engaged in the timeless struggle to run ahead of your own era, and to create new possibilities. The boundaries of the day were drawn by ideology and the great clash between communism and capitalism. Their focus instead, reminiscent of the early co-operators in the eighteenth century, was on creating a politics of the everyday. While radical artists such as Joseph Beuys were turning ordinary objects into art, the ethical consumer pioneers were turning them into activism.

The simplicity of their idea – not that you can do everything through what you buy, but that you can do something – was seductive. Even so, mainstream business was slow to adapt to the opportunities of ethical consumers and leadership came from the margins – the ethical minnows – the small firms and social enterprises connected to the consumer communities that sustained them.

The UK's first ethical unit trust, for example, was launched in June 1984. The fund was dubbed the 'Brazil' model, because city analysts thought the idea was 'nuts'. The most optimistic predictions at the time were that the market would peak at only £2 million. Yet today, investment in ethical unit trusts in the UK has surpassed the £4 billion mark. In the USA, screened portfiolios now hold around $214 trillion in assets. In the UK a further £200 billion is invested in pension funds that incorporate some degree of ethical screening into their investment strategies, and the ethical investment 'niche' could well dominate the market within the next decade.

Ten years later, the first products with 'fair trade' labels began to appear on the shelves. The marks guaranteed that what you buy is produced by people in decent conditions, and that they get a fair share of what you pay. I was involved in setting up the fair trade mark in the UK and I remember a supermarket chief saying he wasn't going to stock fair trade goods, because 'only vicars would be mad enough to buy them'. Well, vicars did. But so did many others that are the subject of this book. There are now over 250 retail fair trade products in the UK from 100 companies, including coffee, tea, cocoa, chocolate, snacks and biscuits, sugar, honey, fruit juice and fresh fruit.

From these beginnings, there are many markets in which ethical consumers have had a significant effect – from animal testing and lead in petrol through to organics and animal welfare in farming. Ethical consumerism has grown to be a force to reckon with.

*Ed Mayo is Chief Executive of the UK's National Consumer Council (NCC – www.ncc.org.uk).

But there is no question that the field has to grow up again, if it is to find opportunities for activism that live up to the wild facts of environmental deterioration and global injustice. A new valley of technology has opened up which offers ways to connect people across the long chains of economic exchange. But the same technologies are driving shifts in supply chains designed to squeeze the last drop of margin out in the pursuit of 'everyday, low prices'.

A new swathe of responsible businesses has recognised the potential of ethical consumers, and has played a significant and undeniable role in its advance, in fields as diverse as sustainable forestry and anti-racism. And yet, the discovery by commercial giants is also leading to shallow 'ethics lite' products, stripped of their values and their transformative power, and with the potential to confuse consumers already baffled and bamboozled by an overload of information and assurance.

Perhaps the ultimate test will be the challenge of sustainable consumption. There are many pioneering initiatives in this field, and the successful ones could yet shape tomorrow's society and economy. But when environmental damage rises lock-step with what you spend, what you spend can't save the environment.

In any text on ethical consumers, the usual caveats apply. There is no one view of what is ethical. We are not all rational and our emotional take on issues matters, thus we are rarely consistent. Being ethical is not easy. For many, it can feel as if you need a degree in environmental science, or a doctorate in philosophy, to know what exactly you should or should not be doing.

And yet the claim of the ethical consumer is a universal one. If it is fair to buy fair trade, it is also unfair not to. If it is ethical to use ethical investment, then it is also unethical not to. If it is sustainable to buy greener, environmentally-friendly products, then it is unsustainable not to.

This book is not simply the best book on the remarkable phenomenon of today's ethical consumer. It is a gift of advice and insight, from the people that know best, to the cause of tomorrow. Many of the writers deserve the plaudits of being pioneers of a new consumer movement.

These are the issues of our time.

Acknowledgements

We would first like to thank the contributors who have all prepared original material specifically for this book. It has been rewarding for us to have worked with them. We would next like to thank Lisa Boyne at Glasgow Caledonian University for her work co-ordinating the contributors and their contributions, and Hannah Berry at ECRA for her work compiling the texts and references in an initial layout.

Rob Harrison would like to thank Jim Sinclair at 3CV and Vincent Commenne at Réseau de Consommateurs Responsables. He would also like to thank James Towell for his contributions on secondary boycotts and the team at ECRA for their general and, frequently practical, support. Terry Newholm would like to thank Bob Blanchard, Roger Spear and Alan Thomas for their unswerving academic support, and Sandy for her tolerance and care. Deirdre Shaw would like to thank friends, family and colleagues for their continued support and encouragement, and Blair for listening.

We would also like to express our thanks to the team at SAGE for their hard work in putting the book together. Particular thanks go to Delia Alfonso for her direction, Sharika Sharma for her supervision of the production process and Audrey Scriven for her editing and comments on the drafts.

Introduction

Rob Harrison   Terry Newholm   Deirdre Shaw

We intend our book to be a broad introduction to the notion of 'the ethical consumer' that has arisen around the turn of the twenty-first century. The notion is important because some concept of ethical (and unethical) consumption is current in all market economies.

Our book is not about business ethics; you will find a plethora of such texts. However, our concluding part looks at the business response to ethical consumers. Our book is not a guide on how to consume ethically, although you will find a discussion of such guides in Chapter 5. It is intended as a book *about* the ethical consumer; their behaviour, discourses and narratives as well as the social and political contexts in which they operate and the manner and effectiveness of their actions.

We intend our text primarily to be of interest to business related graduates, undergraduates and their tutors on courses relating to consumption. However, we very much hope it proves of interest to academics in other disciplines, as well as to politicians, producers, practitioners, campaigners, and not least consumers.

We do not intend to tell a coherent story about the ethical consumer. Rather we have invited authors to contribute who have particular experience in an aspect of ethical consumption and, where appropriate, a particular research method. You will, for example, see the research methods as coming from competing epistemological perspectives.

The geographical scope of our invited authors is wide. Chapters, for example, draw on research with consumers from the UK, USA and Australia. Chapter 1 is a collaboration between authors in the USA and UK. Chapter 5 compares ethical consumer information from ten countries. A French born academic who lives in the UK used data on US consumers to write Chapter 11.

The contributing authors are quite deliberately a mixture of academics, activists and practitioners. You should not, however, assume clear boundaries. Activists have degrees and can turn in excellent research, and practitioners and academics have opinions. In the spirit of reflexive scholarship you will find that in most cases our author biographies tell you something about our lifestyles in addition to our occupations, achievements, research and funding sources. Because our book has a number of audiences we expect you to read selectively.

Understandings of what is 'the ethical consumer' are not particularly straight-forward. In this introduction we offer one definition and a typology of purchasing practices. We then explore some of the reasons why we think the notion has become so important at this moment in time. Finally we guide you through our sections and chapters, introducing subjects by the contributing authors.

DEFINING THE ETHICAL CONSUMER

When people go shopping, economists tell us that they will usually buy the best quality products they can afford. For example, Beardshaw's (1992: 59) economics guide for students states that people will normally choose the cheapest product, but only if they are confident that its 'utility' is as good as slightly more expensive options available. This type of buying can be described as 'traditional purchasing' or 'traditional purchase behaviour'.

Sometimes, however, people might boycott a particular brand or company because of a story they have read in the newspapers. They might also choose a 'fair trade'-labelled coffee due to a concern for 'developing' countries or an eco-labelled washing powder because they think environmental issues are important. This type of buying has been described as 'ethical purchase behaviour' (see for example, Smith (1990b) or, alternatively, 'ethical consumption'.

Obviously people will not choose these types of product if they cost half a month's salary or, in the case of foodstuffs, if they taste bad. Ethical consumers are not, therefore, ignoring price and quality, but applying some additional (and sometimes prior) criteria in the decision-making process.

Although the word 'ethical' is discussed in more detail in Chapter 1, it is sufficient to note at this stage that it is used in this book in its broadest possible sense. Ethical purchasers may, therefore, have political, religious, spiritual, environmental, social or other motives for choosing one product over another and, as we will see, they frequently disagree about who is right and who is wrong. The one thing they have in common is that they are concerned with the effects that a purchasing choice has, not only on themselves, but also on the external world around them.

The buying of organic food provides a good example of how motivation is a key element in identifying and labelling an ethical consumer. Surveys show how many people are buying organic food because they fear that pesticide residues may harm them. These are not strictly ethical purchases because the primary concern is (internal) for the buyers' own health. Others choose organic food because of a concern for the effect (external) that pesticide use has on wildlife and the environment where the produce is farmed. These are properly termed ethical purchases. Of course as we show later, real consumers' motivations will be complex and combine many of these different elements at the same time.

'Ethical purchasing' is, therefore, a very broad expression embracing everything from ethical investment (the ethical purchasing of stocks and shares) to the buying of fair trade products, and from consumer boycotts to corporate environmental purchasing policies. Evidence of ethical purchasing appears in every kind of society and it has been observed in Africa and Asia as well as in Europe and America. And far from simply being an obsession of the well-off who can 'afford' the extra cost of ethical products, it appears to have been used by all sorts of marginalised communities as well. For example, there is much evidence of the use of ethical purchasing in pursuit of goals like civil rights and trade union recognition (see Chapter 6).

Types of ethical purchasing

Ethical consumer behaviours are quite a complex and wide-ranging group of phenomena. There are a number of different ways of dividing them up into manageable pieces. One is to break down ethical purchase behaviours into different types according to how the consumer is relating to, or trying to influence, the product or seller.

Table 0.1   Typology of ethical consumer practices

	Product-oriented purchasing	Company-oriented purchasing
Boycotts	Aerosols (UK) Peat (UK) Timber from unsustainable forestry (international)	Nestlé (international) Shell (international) Philip Morris (USA)
Positive buying	Fair trade Mark (in Europe) Blue Angel eco-label (Germany) No Sweat 100 per cent union-made apparel (USA)	British Union for the Abolition of Vivisection Approved Product Guide Body Shop 'against animal testing' (UK and international)
Fully screened (comparative ethical ratings across whole product area)	Green Consumer Guide (Elkington & Hailes) Which? appliance energy consumption tables (UK Consumers' Association)	Ethical Consumer magazine (UK) Shopping for a Better World paperback book (USA) Ethical screening of investments (international)
Relationship purchasing (consumers seek to educate sellers about their ethical needs)	Community Supported Agriculture (Farms in the USA and UK) Seikatsu Club (Japanese consumer co-operative)	Individual cosumer building relationship with shopkeepers
Anti-consumerism or sustainable consumerism	Avoiding unsustainable products (for example, cars) DIY alternatives (for example, mending clothes)	Adbusters – (Canadian 'culture jamming' magazine)

Table 0.1 examines this approach and shows the five main types of ethical purchasing, illustrating how they can be either 'product-oriented' or 'company-oriented'. It also gives examples for each type.

Although Lang and Gabriel demonstrate in Chapter 3 that ethical consumption has a long history, there appears to have been an unprecedented flowering of these kinds of behaviour over the last three decades. In the next section we explore some of the reasons why this might be happening.

Living in a consumer culture

The society within which the contemporary notion of an ethical consumption has primarily arisen is particular. We customarily refer to it as 'consumer culture'. In his seminal work, Alan Durning (1992) developed a powerful critique of consumer cultures. Drawing on a feast of statistics he illustrated the growth in consumerism in affluent countries: increasing per capita consumption of processed frozen foods, restaurant meals, cars, air miles, televisions, mobile phones, DVDs, a proliferation of home-appliances and so on, paralleled by a more or less constant rise in inflation-adjusted consumer expenditure. Here we want to outline some of the phenomena that are associated with consumption in affluent societies.

4

Food, clothing, accommodation, and consumer durables have become familiar commodities. Where it was previously a public provision, we increasingly *buy* or at least want to *choose* education, healthcare, pensions and care when elderly. We can now buy our exercise, our entertainment or our children's party; all previously in the personal domain. This trend is likely to continue into increasingly personal areas of our lives when we are able to buy an introduction to a potential partner or cold storage of our foetal offspring (Wainwright, 1998) until we have a window of opportunity to care for them. It is a feature of our society that commodification of areas of our lives that were previously outside the market progresses apace whilst domestic production declines (Hanson and Schreder, 1997: 443).

Concurrently, consumer products and services differentiate over time (Heiskanen and Pantzar, 1997). At one time, for instance, cats caught and ate small rodents as their staple diet. Since the middle of the twentieth century, as most became 'pets', their diet was first supplemented or supplanted by butcher's offal, then tinned pet food. More recently easy-to-store packets of dried food, single meal sachets, food for old pets, for young pets and pet 'treats' have all been successfully marketed. Many similar evolutionary histories can be constructed. Stephen Brown (1995) relates the bewildered struggle of a customer to select a hair shampoo from a shelf of differentiated formulations. Impossible and probably irrelevant problems arise. The customer not only is unsure how 'oily' their hair has to be to warrant preparations for 'oily' hair, but also is unsure how 'oily' or 'dry' their hair actually is.

In this proliferation, yesterday's luxuries are transformed into necessities (Durning, 1992), refrigerators, televisions, mobile phones and so on. Inter-generationally, these changes seem to be reinforced. Thus for one generation a mobile phone is a novelty and 'eating out' an occasional treat, for the next these become respectively indispensable and a routine event. Durning suggests there is plenty of scope for continuation.

But as Bertell Ollman (1998) notes, our involvement in consumption encompasses more than the acts of purchase and consumption.

> With the explosive expansion of consumerism – of the amount of time, thought, and emotions spent in buying and selling, and in preparing for (including worrying about) and recovering from these activities – the market has become a dominant, if not *the* dominant, influence in how people act and think throughout the rest of their lives. (Ollman, 1998: 82)

It is within this intense consumer culture that we speak of 'ethical consumers'. These are consumers who, as we have seen, care whether a corporation promotes employees from minority ethnicities, plan their consumption to avoid harm to other animals, worry about 'product air miles' and probably a plethora of other concerns.

Why now?

The question that follows from this is why has this notion arisen at this juncture? We reject the idea that people might magically have become more ethical (see for example, Schlegelmilch, 1994). From the consumer's point of view, you might consider a range of theories. Sociologists like Ulrich Beck (1999) and Anthony Giddens (1990) have argued that because proportionately more of our risks are human derived, in consumer societies they are politicised. All consumers are forced to consider the increasing consequences of their existence. In this sense consumption itself becomes a site of political dispute. Additionally, one of this book's editors (Newholm, 2000) has suggested that we increasingly express our ethics through consumption precisely because consumption, and the related construction of self-image, becomes our major time-consuming activity. Lastly, we might revive Abraham Maslow's (1987) 'Hierarchy of Needs'. Because for most people in affluent societies when our basic physical needs are fulfilled, we turn to higher order concerns that include the need to know and self-actualisation. We might try to self-actualise through hedonistic consumption as much as through ethical consumption. Our combined research, however, certainly suggests that in consumer cultures there are compelling impulses driving many consumers to consider ethics.

From a campaigning perspective, another editor (Rob Harrison) has proposed seven external factors influencing the growth of ethical consumer behaviours. These are:

- the globalisation of markets and the weakening of national governments
- the rise of transnational corporations and brands
- the rise of campaigning pressure groups
- the social and environmental effects of technological advance
- a shift in market power towards consumers
- the effectiveness of market campaigning
- the growth of a wider corporate responsibility movement.

These are discussed in more detail in Chapter 4. We might therefore argue that many consumers are simply seeking to maximise their political effectiveness in a rapidly changing global economy. From this perspective, ethical consumption is understood primarily as a collective action. David Murphy and Jem Bendell (2001: 304) have gone so far as to describe consumers as the new 'counterbalancing force to capitalists' in the face of declining power and influence by trade unions.

Introduction to chapters

Our book is divided into four parts: theorising, campaigning, understanding, and responding to ethical consumers.

In theorising the ethical consumer, the first part considers the philosophical and political traditions that are relevant to ethical consumption. The geographer Clive Barnett, philosopher Philip Cafaro and sociologist Terry Newholm look at ethical consumer behaviour through a philosopher's lens. They explore the usefulness of competing philosophical theories in understanding ethical consumption as well as looking at ethical critiques of consumerism itself.

In a provocative second chapter, marketing academics Roger Dickinson and Mary Carsky explore the idea of consumption as voting. They remain unconvinced by some traditional economic ideas such as consumer sovereignty, but go on to argue that societies would be better off if all consumers were educated to consider the common good in their purchasing decisions.

The second part is mostly given to the campaigners. Tim Lang and Yiannis Gabriel open it by revisiting their brief history of consumer activism. They propose four waves of consumerism: 'co-operative', 'value-for-money', 'Naderism' and 'alternative'. Interesting developments are occurring now as earlier movements and institutions are being revitalised by an (re)injection of ethical thinking.

Building on this introduction, Rob Harrison looks at the ethical consumer phenomenon from the perspective of campaigning pressure groups. He argues that consumers are helping campaigners to achieve limited 'civil regulation' of multi-national corporations in a globalised economy, and he explores how pressure groups are entering markets as 'campaigning traders'.

Hannah Berry and Morven McEachern explore the types of information which currently exist to enable consumers to make ethical decisions. They look at governments, campaign groups, specialist ethical consumer publications and the private sector as information providers. After looking at some of the critiques and problems in the field, they conclude by linking the growth of ethical consumption to the rise of new information technologies, and argue that this process is still far from over.

Has all this activism and inspiring consumer voting been effective? It falls to Scott Clouder and Rob Harrison to review the evidence of campaigns to date. They look at how academics have drawn a distinction between 'expressive and instru-mental campaigns', and go on to explore 'secondary effects' of consumer actions (where other companies in the same sector quietly improve their behaviour) and 'unintended consequences'.

Authors report some of the academic and marketing research of ethical con-sumers in the third part of our book. These are organised from the more generalised attempts to understand ethical consumers' lives to focusing on particular issues: fair trade; apparel; the environment; and financial products. In general these chap-ters also move from more qualitative to quantitative research strategies. In each case the authors were encouraged to say something about their research methods as well as reporting their findings. Accordingly you should gain valuable insights into the application of case study, interviewing, modelling, profiling, focus groups and questionnaire surveying.

These chapters are written from different theoretical perspectives. In general they start with more 'constructivist' understandings and move to 'realist' research. The first authors believe that ethical consumers tell stories and engage in practices through which the researcher can interpret their understandings of the world. Because everything is dependent on how it is interpreted, there is no point to seek-ing a single truth or correct understanding. The latter authors believe that ethical consumption is understandable as a set of real behaviours that derive from consumers' attitudes. These behaviours have essential characteristics that can be identified and measured.

This section begins with Terry Newholm's 16 UK case studies. Ethical consumers, he argues, are confronted by a multiplicity of issues. His question is, therefore, how do they maintain their self-identity as an ethical consumer given such an apparently daunting environment? He concludes by suggesting three approaches: 'distancing', 'rationalising' and 'integrating'.

Hélène Cherrier focuses on the USA, exploring how narratives of ethical con-sumption incorporate and depend on a notion of consumption simplicity. She explores how some of her interviewees had experienced 'destabilising life events' and discovered ethical consumption as a means of social integration, or of regaining control, or of seeking 'authenticity'.

Deirdre Shaw's contribution looks at how we can model the decision-making process of UK ethical consumers. Current marketing models do not take sufficient account of consumer ethics. She identifies the additional factors that affect decisions and organises these into the 'revised standard model' in accordance with a large-scale survey of ethical consumers.

Marsha Dickson, an academic and director of the Fair Labour Association, looks at a large-scale questionnaire survey of apparel consumers in the USA which attempted to ascertain the extent to which they were willing to take action on fair labour issues. The results provided some answers, as well as a range of new questions.

In the two chapters following hers commercial practitioners discuss the use of focus groups and large-scale polling. The UK Co-operative Bank has been at the forefront of 'consumer-led, ethically-motivated' commerce since 1991. How do they maintain their contact with the developing ethical views of their customer base? In that chapter Barry Clavin and Alex Lewis reveal details of five pieces of research carried out by the bank between 1999 and 2004.

Similarly, the international pollsters MORI have been surveying the rise of social and environmental attitudes among consumers for many years. Robert Worcester and Jenny Dawkins discuss the results of some of this research as well as looking at some general themes within this field such as 'social desirability bias' – the wish of respondents to appear socially concerned.

The fourth part addresses the response of businesses to the rise of interest in ethical issues amongst consumers. Carol Adams and Ambika Zutshi mainly consider the 'defensive' responses from business and focus on corporate disclosure and social reporting. They also look at codes of conduct addressing workers' rights at supplier companies and conclude that, at present, there is a long way to go before such voluntary disclosures reach a satisfactory standard in most cases.

Andrew Crane's concluding chapter explores some of the ways businesses may be responding more positively to ethical consumers. Although there are new niche and mainstream ethical products appearing on the market, he argues that many companies are opting for safer 'risk-management' and 'cause-related marketing' responses to what seems, after all, a very new movement.

Future direction

We have aimed to include a broad range of issues that are commonly addressed in ethical consumption, such as clothing and labour rights, fair trade, financial services, and environmental attitudes. Because key issues vary between cultures (see Chapter 5 on informing consumers), lists of ethical issues might be considered limitless and we had to agree some curb to our enthusiasm with our publishers. We do not, therefore, claim to have comprehensively covered all aspects of ethical consumption. This will, no doubt, be the role of a future work.

We have not sought to persuade readers to become activists in their own consumption. However, if after reading the book you decide that you are clearer on what you as an academic, member of a community, politician or producer might be able to achieve as a consumer, we would not be displeased. In the same way, while some chapter authors have provided suggestions for action by governments, campaigners, companies or consumers, it is understanding rather than future action which has been the primary focus of this work.

Nevertheless, you do not have to work long in this field to realise that we may be getting a tantalising glimpse of how trade and commerce of the future will look. For despite its at times infuriating complexity, many ethical consumer actions – especially buying from 'trading campaigners' like Cafédirect – implicitly posit alternative models for development (see Chapter 6). And these proliferating alternative models make it harder than ever to argue that 'business as usual' is the only option we have.

Part One
Theorising Ethical Consumption

Philosophy and Ethical Consumption

1

Clive Barnett   Philip Cafaro   Terry Newholm

INTRODUCTION

This chapter introduces some basic philosophical approaches that are useful in understanding and evaluating ethical consumption issues and ethical consumer behaviour. The chapter is divided into three sections. The first section introduces the two main approaches to ethics in moral philosophy, 'consequentialism' and 'deontology', and considers how appropriate they are when applied to questions of consumption. The example of consumer responses to products made using child labour is then explored to show how these two different approaches to ethics can lead to different outcomes.

The second section considers the relevance of another approach, virtue ethics, which it is argued has the advantage of concentrating on the broad contexts in which ethical issues arise. Virtue philosophy focuses on flourishing and living a good life. Empirical evidence suggests that a sense of integrity is more fundamental to the well-being of ethical consumers than either a concern for consequences or rules (though both of these are evident).

In the third section we discuss the distinction between ethical consumption and the ethics of consumption. The former tends to see consumption as a means to express one's moral commitments and the latter tends to be critical of the whole panoply of modern consumerism. We also look at work which has focused on the extent to which all consumers unconsciously consider moral issues in purchasing decisions.

In the conclusion we argue that the future lies in facilitating more widespread public participation in debates about the meaning and purpose of ethical consumption itself.

RULES, CONSEQUENCES AND THE ETHICS OF CONSUMPTION

Moral philosophy often divides ethical theories into two sorts: theories that privilege the *right*, and theories that privilege the *good*. Definitions of the good refer to the properties or outcomes that our actions should endeavour to bring about; definitions of the right refer to what people and organisations ought to do in responding to ethical imperatives. Theories of the good therefore focus upon which outcomes to *promote*, whereas theories of the right focus upon which principles to *honour*, or on questions of duty (Pettit, 1991: 237). Discussions of moral philosophy inevitably distinguish between these two broad positions, if only for heuristic purposes.

Calculating consequences

Theories which privilege questions of the good are often referred to as *consequentialist* – they are concerned with defining ethical conduct by reference to the consequences or outcomes of actions. These approaches are also sometimes called *teleological*, because they start by specifying an end (or 'telos') independent of moral obligations. They then define the right thing to do as acting to maximise the good. For example, utilitarianism advocates practices that maximise the overall sum of happiness.

Peter Singer is an important contemporary philosopher who has employed consequentialist arguments. He is well known for his advocacy of animal welfare and is opposed to the other main approach to moral philosophy – deontology – because he thinks it narrowly defines ethics in terms of a system of rules. He argues that consequentialist approaches are more practical and realistic, insofar as starting with goals means that judgements of actions will always depend on contextual factors. Singer's animal welfare advocacy leads him to condemn most consumer uses of animals, including meat-eating and wearing fur or leather. He advocates an environmental ethics which holds that we should, as far as possible, act to avoid unnecessary harm to the environment and sentient creatures (Singer, 1997: 284–8). In a recent book, he argues that wealthy westerners should forego frivolous consumption that adds little to our lives, and devote the resources saved to helping the world's poor (2002: 180–95). For Singer, all this implies that we should adopt an ethic of frugality and simplicity. High levels of consumption are a major problem in modern societies, an unjustified 'using up the world' (Singer, 1997: 45–64), and a foolish misallocation of resources. Consumption, from this perspective, is associated with the conspicuous and extravagant display of social position (Singer, 1997: 238–9).

Singer's arguments are more complex than this brief summary suggests, but they provide one influential template for understanding the relationship between ethics and consumption. In particular, his argument that there is no good reason to restrict the scope of concern to our nearest and dearest, or indeed only to other people, seems highly appropriate to the field of ethical consumption, in which the fact of being one link in a much wider chain of relationships with strangers in distant locations is often made the basis of appeals to alter one's consumer behaviour in order to bring about more ethical *outcomes*.

Ethical consumption campaigns and policies often rely on consequentialist assumptions and appeals. They tend to assume that ethical decision making works through the rational calculation of ethical obligations, for which the provision of knowledge, advice and information is an essential prerequisite. Existing research on consumption therefore often depends on relatively narrow conceptualisations of ethical decision making by consumers, companies and public organisations. In particular, ethical consumption is understood in both theory and practice to depend on access to information. This leaves aside the questions of how the goals considered worthy of pursuit through consumption are decided upon, and by whom. It also seems to imply that there is a single measure of what 'the good' is, and of what 'acting ethically' should entail, and that the main challenge is to get consumers to adopt the appropriate forms of conduct and behaviour.

Obeying universal rules

In contrast to consequentialist approaches, deontological or duty-based approaches define right action as independent of its contribution to human happiness or other favoured goals. Deontological moral theories have gone through a revival since the publication of John Rawls's (1972) *A Theory of Justice*. Rawls explicitly set about developing an alternative approach to utilitarian theories of ethics and justice. He argued that teleological theories implied that it is justifiable to exploit some people, or limit their rights, in pursuit of a more general utilitarian benefit. Utilitarian theories did not 'take seriously the distinction between persons', tending to assume that collective choices by whole societies were analogous to individual choices. They therefore ignored what Rawls takes to be an inevitable plurality of views regarding what constitutes the good. The plurality of values led him to defend the priority of the right over the good, as a means of ensuring that definitions of the collective good do not come at the cost of basic individual liberties. Rawls's work is important because it highlights the tension between the plurality of personal values and ethical positions on the one hand, and the degree of unity required to pursue collective outcomes and decisions on the other.

Ethical consumption discourses also contain elements of deontological understandings of moral obligation. They often invoke highly universalised arguments about people's responsibilities to care for others – whether this is other people, other creatures, the environment, or future generations, as in the Precautionary Principle. Ethicists who have written about the ethics of global warming, for example, tend to argue along the following lines: 1) current energy consumption patterns are warming the earth, with unknown but potentially disastrous consequences for human life support systems; 2) current humans have a duty to future generations to pass on fully functioning life support systems therefore; 3) current humans have a duty to significantly scale back our energy consumption (Brown, 2002).

The limitations of universal prescriptions

Both consequentialist and deontological approaches are open to two related criticisms that are relevant to ethical consumption. First, both present models of ethical conduct that appear to be far too stringent in the demands they make on the capacities of ordinary people – consequentialist arguments seem to imagine it is possible to collect, collate and calculate all sorts of information and chains of causality prior to, or even after, action. While utilitarian considerations might be relevant in relation to evaluating collective public decisions, they seem rather unrealistic as complete models of personal choice. Similarly, deontological approaches seem to present an implausible picture of actors rationally judging the degree to which each of their actions conforms to a very abstract principle of universalisation. This criticism – of over stringent or unworkable models of ethical conduct – is related to a second problem with both consequentialist and deontological approaches. They end up presenting models of ethical conduct that are rather inflexible, leaving little room for the complexities and ambivalences of ethical decision making. They therefore present a highly abstracted model of the ways in which people are implicated and involved in their actions.

To illustrate the relevance of these concerns to how we approach ethical consumption, consider a couple of examples. First, there is the case of sustainable consumption initiatives which have become increasingly important in the wake of international programmes such as Local Agenda 21. As Hobson (2002, 2003) observes, the assumption of many of these initiatives is that the exposure of the public to scientific knowledge will trigger changes in consumer behaviour. However, this assumption takes no account of the myriad ways in which consumer goods play important symbolic roles in the ordinary lives of people. As Jackson

(2001) observes, material products do more than simply provide basic needs – they also serve to facilitate interpersonal interactions, senses of personal identity and worth, or as means of creativity. To use the vocabulary developed by Amartya Sen and Martha Nussbaum, the value of material consumer goods needs to be understood in terms of the 'functionings' and 'capabilities' they enable people to develop. Jackson's argument is that this tendency for sustainable consumption policies to ignore social aspects of consumption accounts for the difficulty of altering consumer behaviour. Simplistic appeals to reduce or forego consumption are 'tantamount to demanding that we give up certain key capabilities and freedoms as social beings' (Jackson, 2001: 9). The implication of this argument is that ethical consumption cannot depend solely on either consequentialist or deontological approaches, because these fail to register the motivations behind a great deal of consumer behaviour. What may be required, then, is an approach that is more sensitive to the experiential horizons of ordinary consumers, and in particular to the ways in which certain sorts of ethical conduct are already embedded in everyday consumption practice.

A second example of the limitations of abstract models of moral responsibility is the recent emergence of concerted anti-sweatshop campaigns in the USA, especially on university campuses. It is common to think of boycott campaigns in terms of bringing into view the connections between the consumption of particular products, such as Nike sportswear for example, and the perceived oppressive or exploitative working conditions in which these are made. It would be easy to think of these sorts of campaigns in consequentialist terms. They aim at changing individual or collective conduct by providing knowledge of spatially distant contexts and empowering individuals to accept their responsibilities. Consequentialist responsibility is understood to depend on a clear calculation of the relations between our voluntary actions and their consequences. However, the idea that ethical consumption can work simply by bringing to view the chain of consequences and connections between consumers and producers is highly simplistic. As Iris Young (2003) has argued, this notion of responsibility tends to elide important distinctions between being causally responsible for events, being a beneficiary, and being in a position to actually change outcomes. This model of responsibility ends up being overwhelming as well as highly unfair in its ascription of obligations to change things.

Young argues that anti-sweatshop campaigns are, in fact, important because they have developed a non-individualised political sense of responsibility that departs from a wholly individualistic understanding of causality, agency and blame. The success of anti-sweatshop movements depends, she suggests, on campaigners and activists being able to provide frames in which consumers can acknowledge responsibility for distant contexts without being overwhelmed.

Young also argues that people are likely to be moved to change their consumption behaviour by all sorts of different considerations. This is also the implication of empirical research on consumption boycotts which suggests that these are not forms of collective action, but that boycotters are motivated by personal factors such as the emotional expression of individuality, so that boycotting serves as a vehicle for moral self-realisation (Kozinets and Handleman, 1998). This is important because it suggests that ethical consumption is not simply a matter of wholly selfless beneficence, but that successful campaigns will combine appeals to both other-regarding and self-regarding virtues.

One problem, then, with a narrowly consequentialist understanding of moral reasoning is that by implying that we should act in a manner wholly oriented to collective outcomes, it ignores what acting morally actually means to people. As Derek Parfit points out (1984: 27), if we all acted as pure do-gooders, it might actually make things worse rather than better. This is because being a pure do-gooder would involve so much self-sacrifice that it would decrease the overall sum of happiness. Parfit's point is that being wholly selfless would involve acting against many of the motives that we act upon when we love, care, show concern, and so on. The implication of this argument is that changing people's consumption practices is probably not best pursued by simply appealing to people's sense of self-sacrifice or altruism, or by supposing that it requires a wholesale abandonment of self-interested concerns.

We saw above that one advantage of consequentialism is that it is contextually sensitive, so that it does not hold that the value of a particular course of action is determined in advance by a set of rules. However, if this is one charge made against deontological approaches, the counter-argument is that consequentialism can, in principle, lead to indifference to the righteousness of actions – to a privileging of ends over means (Parfit, 1984). We might ask whether it matters if ethical consumption campaigns realise their aims and objectives by actively altering people's sense of what is the best thing to do, or simply by more anonymous changes to consumption patterns. Is ethical consumption simply about aggregate outcomes – reduced pollution, less exploitative work conditions, etc. – or is it also about actually changing the sense of self held by ordinary people? Many advocates of ethical consumption see the adoption of a more conscious approach to consumption as an important objective of their overall strategy.

If neither pure consequentialist nor pure deontological approaches capture the complexity of moral action, perhaps it might be better not to abandon these approaches, but to recast them in less all-or-nothing ways. Amartya Sen distinguishes between consequentialism and consequentialist reasoning. He suggests that consequentialism demands 'that the rightness of actions be judged entirely by the goodness of consequences, and this is a demand not merely of taking consequences into account, but of ignoring everything else' (Sen, 1987: 75). However, he suggests that it is possible to develop what he calls 'consequence-sensitive deontological' arguments (1987: 76). This requires acknowledging that rights – the primary concern of deontologists – have both an *instrumental* and an *intrinsic* value. This means that deontology is itself not immune to consequentialist considerations: rights are not only valuable intrinsically, but also because of the goals they enable people to pursue. What all of this suggests is that it is more appropriate to think of any ethical theory as combining an understanding of the good with an understanding of the right in a distinctive way (Pettit, 1991: 230).

Products made using child labour

To illustrate some of the arguments made above about the complexity of ethical action, let us consider how consequentialism and deontology might be applied to the example of products made by child labour. First, the deontologist might refuse to buy products made using child labour on principle, arguing that this violates a fundamental moral rule against the exploitation of children. After all, she would not wish her own children to labour, less still in exploitative conditions, and must universalise this rule. However, the dilemma arises when one is faced with the argument that the fate of children is worsened by her action – an important source of family income might be reduced (see Meiklejohn, 1998). In contrast, and on these grounds, the utilitarian might buy products made using child labour, since not to do so would cause more harm than good. She might also have a reasonable, but not certain, expectation that in the long term trade conditions would improve. However, this consumer is still faced with the question of when should she withdraw support for iniquitous producer practices?

Forms of consequentialist reasoning can therefore help us to consider our external environment and our effect on the happiness of others. However, we cannot ignore our own moral beliefs in considering these sorts of issues (Norman, 1998). It is not a case of *choosing* between the happiness of the many and our own egoistic morals. Our own unhappiness as ethical consumers is not simply to be weighed in the generality of happiness. That we are concerned *at all* is because we are moral agents. Any capacity for moral agency is indivisible from the sense of personal integrity upon which it is partly based in the first place. We cannot entirely derive our notion of what is the ethical thing to do from an external consideration of effects on others, thereby ignoring our own intuitions of right and wrong.

The deontologist and the consequentialist seem to make cold calculations of what is right to do, based either on a calculation of the outcomes of buying products made by child labour, or by reference to a general rule against ever so doing. Neither approach gives adequate attention to what motivates people to be concerned by this question to begin with. This is the question that virtue theorists do address, and virtue ethics represents the third approach which we consider in relation to ethical consumption. Virtue theorists are concerned with what we should do, but they relate this to the question of what kinds of people we should aim to be, and how this sort of consideration shapes our actions. So, faced with the concern about child labour, our consumer might be advised by a virtue theorist to be compassionate and generous. Clearly she should be concerned with the children's plight, not shrink from paying more for a product if that is appropriate and not overly prioritise her own interest. A generous and compassionate mother might campaign to challenge entrenched interests. Nevertheless she would have to weigh these actions against the needs of her own children. The main focus of this approach then, in our case, would be upon the cultivation of those dispositions that enable consumers to juggle what are often equally compelling ethical imperatives in a reasonable fashion. The ethical issues raised in 'decisions concerning what, whether and how much to consume' (Cafaro, 2001) cannot be reduced to simple calculations of outcomes or rules, but require a more careful consideration of the complexities of ordinary ethical conduct in everyday life.

Summary: restoring the social focus

We have suggested that much of the focus of ethical consumption is on the individual. How and what individuals consume is critical both to the project of ethical consumption and to their understanding of themselves. Both consequentialist and deontological forms of moral reasoning tend to focus on individual conduct. However, it is important to acknowledge that individuals consume within broader networks of social relations and cultural codes. This allows us to recognise that all consumer behaviour, however ordinary and routine, is likely to be shaped by diverse values of caring for other people and concern for fairness. The success of ethical consumption campaigns is likely to be enhanced if they connect up with these ordinary and routine values of care and concern that already subsist in every-day consumption, rather than setting off 'ethical consumption' as a completely different set of activities that requires a wholesale abandonment of self-concern. In the next section, with these thoughts in mind, we turn to consider the relevance of virtue ethics, which has the potential of refocusing our attention on the whole context of social life in which questions of individual responsibility arise and are worked out.

LIVING VIRTUOUSLY AND MOTIVATING ETHICAL CONSUMPTION

Consequentialism and deontology do not exhaust the approaches to ethics that are relevant to ethical consumption. A third approach, virtue ethics, has become increasingly important in recent moral philosophy as an alternative to both out-come-oriented consequentialism and rule-based deontology (MacIntyre, 1984; Swanton, 2003). Virtue theories redefine the overarching question of ethical the-ory away from 'What ought I do?', to 'What sort of person ought I strive to be?'. Virtue ethics makes new sorts of consumption arguments possible. Virtue theories concern themselves less with our duties toward others, and more with specifying personal excellence and societal flourishing, and the best ways to achieve them. While consequentialists and deontologists work to justify altruism against the obstacles of self-interest, virtue ethicists try to awaken us to our enlightened self-interest in caring for others. While the former's main question is 'What are my duties to others and their responsibilities to me?' the latter's is 'What is the good life and how can we go about living it?' Virtue theories work to specify the char-acter traits, or virtues, that lead to human flourishing (Foot, 2001; Hursthouse, 1999). Such virtues include justice, compassion, tolerance, courage, patience, per-sistence, intelligence, imagination and creativity. Virtue, on this approach, is a synonym for human excellence and goodness (Cafaro, 2004; Taylor, 2002).

Virtue theory pays attention to the habits and practices through which virtues are learned. It is thus well placed to discuss which habits and practices might lead us to act in ways that are, for example, more environmentally sustainable. Virtue ethics is appropriate to the analysis of ethical consumption because there is empir-ical evidence to suggest that 'ethical consumers' are motivated primarily by a sense of personal integrity. Kozinets and Handelman (1998) speak of '[boycott] actions that remind and connect the individual to their deeper moral self'. Similarly, respondents to recent research often expressed concern for the consequences of their consumption practices but more fundamentally a desire to respond to their choices with personal integrity (Newholm, 2000; Shaw and Shiu, 2003). Even if consumers rarely feel able to foresee the consequences of their choices, what they seemed sure of was that, as one respondent put it, 'I couldn't bear to do nothing' (Shaw and Newholm, 2003). In this concern we see a merging of the self-interested and altruistic aspects of morality.

From one perspective, virtue ethics allows us to clarify what the problem with consumption is, by asking the question whether consumption as an activity is virtuous or not. There is a long tradition of philosophers arguing that a life devoted to consumption is ignoble and limiting. Thus, Aristotle wrote in his

Nicomachean Ethics: 'The many, the most vulgar, would seem to conceive of the good and happiness as pleasure, and hence they also like the life of gratification. Here they appear completely slavish, since the life they decide on is a life for grazing animals' (1999: 8). This argument sees consumption as primarily about providing pleasure, that is, as an essentially hedonistic practice. It is also assumed that consumption is at heart a passive process, and therefore it contravenes the imperative to actively develop one's capacities upon which virtue theories put considerable emphasis. On these grounds, too much emphasis on consumption could be seen to lead to a passive life that is ultimately unsatisfying.

One problem with virtue ethics, however, is that it can easily lead to a paternalist and censorious judgement of the apparent *vices* of specific social groups. This risk follows from the idea that, as Phillipa Foot puts it, the virtues are 'corrective', that is, that the value of different virtues (such as courage, or temperance, or charity) emerges at 'a point at which there is some temptation to be resisted or deficiency of motivation to be made good' (1978: 8). For example, she continues, 'it is only because fear and the desire for pleasure often operate as temptations that courage and temperance exist as virtues at all' (1978: 9).

The main point that follows from this observation is that any contemporary conceptualisation of virtue needs to be extremely sensitive to the underlying image of human life that determines where 'temptations' and 'deficiencies of motivation' are to be identified. The virtues must not simply reproduce a highly problematic superiority that covers over a whole set of class and gender stereotypes about which sorts of people are susceptible to a relative lack of proper virtue. As Foot observes, it is possible that 'the theory of human nature lying behind the traditional list of the virtues and vices puts too much emphasis on hedonistic and sensual impulses' (1978: 10). This is a particularly telling point with respect to the application of virtue theory to issues of consumption. A virtue ethics approach could easily lead to an analysis that sees the main problem in terms of unchecked hedonism and desire for pleasure by selfish unethical consumers. Such an analysis is likely to alienate the sorts of people with whom ethical consumption campaigns most need to communicate.

The critical question with respect to the relevance of virtue ethics to consumption issues is how to think of the relationship between individual actions, consumption, and broader conceptions of the good life. In this respect, in order to avoid the paternalism noted above, it might be more fruitful to rethink what we understand consumption to be. Rather than thinking of consumption as a set of distinct practices (shopping, eating, and so on) set off from other activities and carried on by a particular sort of social subject (the consumer), who may be more or less virtuous, it might be more beneficial to think of consumption as one aspect of any social practice. This is the approach suggested by the sociologist Alan Warde who defines consumption 'as a process whereby agents engage in appropriation, whether for utilitarian, expressive or contemplative purposes, of goods, services, performances, information or ambience, whether purchased or not, over which the agent has some degree of discretion' (2004: 5). According to this definition, consumption is not understood as a practice as such, but rather as 'a moment in almost every practice' (2004: 6). This shift of emphasis onto the sorts of practices that people are engaged in is consistent with the value that virtue ethics places on thinking about the roles and activities in which people are involved. This practice-based conceptualisation of consumption maintains the emphasis on the roles through which people cultivate different dispositions towards the world and others, but understands these primarily in relation to the collective modes for organising the conduct of everyday life. It enables questions to be asked about the sorts of consumption effects embedded in different practices to which people may feel more or less strongly committed (for example, being a caring parent, a true friend, a loyal supporter of a football team, and so on). And it opens up these questions in such a way that makes it possible to differentiate between actors who may be differentially empowered to change these consumption effects – the key issue identified by Iris Young in developing a fully political sense of responsibility in relation to consumption practices. Being able to make these sorts of differentiations is crucial to developing an effective sense of the sorts of *actors* and the types of *agency* that are required to bring about changes in aggregate patterns of consumption.

Partiality and impartiality in ethics

One important distinction between virtue theory and both consequentialist and deontological approaches is that the latter two are both universalistic in their orientation – morality is understood according to notions of universal benevolence, or as acting in accord with principles that can be universalised to all others. In contrast, virtue theory does not argue that either universal benevolence or duty is the best motive for acting. Virtue theory tends to imply a version of partiality in ethics, in which caring for and acting to benefit some people more than others is morally acceptable. This seems to conflict with some basic principles of ethical consumption, which often call for an extension of the scope of our concern beyond the confines of our nearest and dearest or compatriots, to distant others, to non-human animals, and to the environment. The key challenge presented by virtue ethics, then, is that of finding ways of combining *intimate caring* for particular others with *humanitarian caring* about others in general (Slote, 2000: 337–9). The moral concerns that motivate love, or caring, cannot simply be extended or aggregated across all contexts without undermining the very value of those virtues. Rather than assuming that this justifies according lesser priority to general or universal principles of moral action, we might instead interpret the qualified defence of partiality in virtue ethics as raising the question of how to develop forms of practice which can successfully connect both partial and universalistic motivations. So, for example, it might lead us to acknowledge that concerns over the ethics of food production – evident in campaigns around GM foods, the use of pesticides, the BSE crisis, and the growth of organic food production – are not simply motivated by abstract concerns for 'the environment' or for 'future generations', but are intimately bound up with the forms of care and concern that shape everyday social relations of domestic family life. They are manifest, for example, in a concern over the long-term health risks of the food that parents provide for their kids. While clearly a partial concern in one way, this type of care for others can lead to ways of living that are beneficial for all if it leads to changes in consumer activity on a sufficient scale.

This observation underscores the importance of taking account of the concerns that motivate ordinary consumption practices. Rather than thinking of 'ethical consumption' being set off against 'unethical' consumption, we might do better to recognise the forms of ethical concern always embedded in consumption practices. If 'ethical' is taken, in a Foucauldian sense, to refer to the activity of constructing a life by negotiating practical choices about personal conduct, then the very basics of routine consumption – a concern for value for money, quality, and so on – can be understood to presuppose a set of specific learned ethical competencies. These competencies make up what one might call the habitual dimensions of consumption practice (Hobson, 2003). Daniel Miller's (1998) ethnographic accounts of everyday consumption behaviours in North London illustrate the extent to which shopping is always laden with values, as a means of expressing concern and care for others. It has been argued that Miller's work shows us:

> how far shopping is directed towards others, particularly family members, and how far it is guided by moral sentiments towards them and about how to live. Far from being individualistic, self-indulgent, and narcissistic, much shopping is based on relationships, indeed on love. It often involves considerable thoughtfulness about the particular desires and needs of others, though it may also reflect the aspirations which the shopper has for them, thereby functioning as a way of influencing them. (Sayer, 2003: 353)

Given this sense of the ordinary moral dimensions of shopping and other routine consumption practices, the emergence of ethical consumption as a field of marketing, campaigning, and policy making can be understood in terms of the ways in which the practical moral dispositions of everyday consumption are rearticulated by policy makers, campaigning organisations, academics and businesses. Formal campaigns and policies of ethical consumption involve making the ethical dispositions already implicit in routine consumption the object of explicit strategies in changing people's sense of the scope and quality of their responsibilities.

This same point also implies that certain sorts of consumption, and certain sorts of commodities, might lend themselves better to ethical consumption initiatives than others. This might depend on the degree to which particular commodities are embedded in everyday practices of care that enable the mobilisation of partial modes of concern to be rearticulated with more extended and expansive forms of concern. This section has argued that virtue ethics moves us beyond stringent models of universal rules or the sense that universal benevolence requires the abandonment of self-interest. This approach points towards the importance of finding ways of connecting self-regarding concerns to other-regarding concerns, and with combining partiality and universality in creative ways. As Colin Campbell argues, 'both self-interested and idealistic concerns are involved in consumerism' (1998: 151–2). Consumption, therefore, cannot be divided simply into 'good' and 'bad' or condemned and extricated from our cultures to leave some untainted good society.

Summary: ethical consumption and ordinary consumption

Conventional discourses on ethical consumption tend to polarise arguments: fair trade conjures an unequivocally unfair trade; voluntary simplicity presupposes consumerism; vegetarianism problematises omnivory; veganism problematises vegetarianism; and in the broadest sense ethical consumption conjures unethical consumption. However, not all 'free' trade is necessarily unfair. Consumerism is always wrapped up with morality, as when someone buys a bigger car to take the elderly to church. Pork can be bought by a parent who believes they are doing their best for their offspring, since beef was contaminated with BSE. Thus it is the way that a simply defined ethical consumption creates pejorative dualities that we are questioning here. Social science research on consumption has found that much ordinary consumption is suffused with moral rhetoric and ethical concern. Much of the moralising is localised around family and friends, but can be seen as part of people's self-image, their integrity. Three important points follow from this. First, without this ordinary ethics of consumption there would be no basis upon which to build an ethical consumption agenda. Second, to cast everyday consumption as unequivocally unethical threatens to alienate ordinary people rather than recruit them. And third, ethical consumption should refer to discussions that seek to refine consumption and non-consumption towards more broadly ethical practices. This is not to argue that all ordinary consumption is acceptable. Rather it is to recognise that the basis for an ethical consumption is to be found in the morality of ordinary consumption.

ETHICAL CONSUMPTION OR THE ETHICS OF CONSUMPTION?

The preceding discussion of the pitfalls of moralising in discussions of ethical consumption suggests that it might be useful to distinguish between two senses in which ethics and consumption can be related. On the one hand, there is a set of debates concerning the 'ethics of consumption', where what is at stake is a judgement concerning the morality of a whole system of provisioning, that of capitalist commodity production (see Crocker and Linden, 1998). This is perhaps the dominant sense in discussions of environmental problems, debates about sustainable consumption, and in movements such as voluntary simplicity and the slow food movement. Here, it is 'consumption' itself that is the object of moral evaluation. The objective of these projects is the reduction of levels of aggregate consumption.

On the other hand, ethical consumption also refers to a set of debates and strategies in which consumption is not so much the *object* of moral evaluation, but more a *medium* for moral and political action. This is the dominant sense in the case of consumer boycotts, ethical audits, corporate social responsibility initiatives, and fair trade campaigns. In these cases, there is no *necessary* implication that 'ethical consumption' implies less consumption, quite the reverse. Commodity consumption as a mode of provisioning is taken as given – assumed to be open to some transformation certainly – but not taken as the object of moral evaluation as such. Rather, the fact of commodity consumption as a means of social reproduction is understood as being a potential resource for changing other practices and patterns: consumption as voting.

These two senses of ethics and consumption are not completely separate. Lots of ethical consumption campaigns are geared towards reducing overall levels of consumption. Others also play upon the standard desires and motivations of consumer behaviour, deploying the strategies of advertising, marketing, branding and so on. Many combine elements of both emphases. But the distinction is important to keep in mind for two reasons. First, it raises questions about how these two distinct concerns – consumption as the object and medium of moral action – are connected in different contexts. Second, it raises the question of just what are the moral and political issues most at stake in discussions of ethical consumption.

The moralisation of consumption

One recurring concern of those promoting ethical consumption is the worry that this set of practices is the reserve of a relatively privileged stratum of highly affluent consumers. This niche comprises those able to spend the time, energy, and money to buy organic, drink fair trade, and invest ethically. This sense of ethical consumption as a practice of social distinction, to use Pierre Bourdieu's (1984) idea, is connected to the sense of ethical consumption being associated with highly moralistic forms of discourse. This moralistic stance extends to a great deal of academic, policy and campaigning research and debate about consumption. There is a long tradition of criticising mass commodity consumption as a means of criticising much wider objects such as capitalism, modernity, the materialism of popular culture and planetary destruction.

Danny Miller (1998) argues that the moralistic tone of so many debates about consumption is itself open to criticism. Miller's argument is based on a particular philosophical position, one which is suspicious of the romanticised notions of authenticity that often underlie criticisms of consumption as a realm of social and cultural alienation. Miller holds to a philosophy of subject–object relations, according to which subjectivity and inter-subjectivity is always mediated by material objects. From this perspective, attention is focused upon the symbolic meaning of material objects as mediators of social interaction. As we already noted, Miller has demonstrated in empirical depth the ways in which love and care are mediated by practices of commodity consumption. In the modern world, Miller argues, commodities become the mediums for objectifying and performing values and moral orders, perhaps most obviously through various forms of gift giving. Consumption is a sphere in which people routinely negotiate moral dilemmas. As Robert Wilk observes, 'consumption is in essence a moral matter, since it always and inevitably raises issues of fairness, self *vs* group interests, and immediate *vs* delayed gratification' (2001: 246).

Miller's argument is that, in a world of commodities, consumption *per se* is neither moral nor immoral. The key issue is whether 'people appropriate this plethora of goods in order to enhance and not to detract from our devotion to other people' (1998: 231). And Miller makes the provocative argument that ensuring this appropriation does enhance our relations with others depends on the consumption of more, not less, industrially produced commodities. This runs counter to the general positions of recent movements around consumption, such as the voluntary simplicity movement, which holds that poverty is a product of particular modes of consumption (see Wilk, 2001: 257). Such movements do aim more at reducing consumption levels.

Miller's is very much a conception of consumption as a *medium* of ethical conduct. He is highly critical of traditions of thought and activism that see the ethics of consumption in terms of excess. These are guilty, he suggests, of adopting 'an ascetic repudiation of the need for goods *per se*' (1998: 241). Miller places poverty at the centre of the moral analysis of consumption, with surprising and provocative results. Poverty, he argues, is constituted by a lack of material resources. Arguments about over-consumption, which define the objectives of ethical consumption in terms of the reduction of overall levels of consumption, work against 'an ethics based on the passionate desire to eliminate poverty. We live in a time when most human suffering is the direct result of the lack of goods. What most of humanity desperately needs is more consumption, more pharmaceuticals, more housing, more transport, more books, more computers' (2001: 227–8). The distinction between ethical consumption and the ethics of consumption is, then, a key tension within the whole field of the ethics and politics of consumption. It draws sharply into focus the question of just what are the moral or ethical stakes in consumption, and in particular, whether it is possible to square different moral values such as freedom and sustainability, autonomy and responsibility.

Questioning consumption

Bernard Williams (1985) has argued that what he calls the 'morality system' has led philosophers to focus on abstract models that narrowly define ethics in terms of a chain of relations between agency, obligations and blame. His argument is that a focus on universal, often prescriptive, understandings of moral action excludes from consideration factors that are not easily reduced to obligations, consequences, or rights. Following Williams's argument that the morality system is just one particular frame in which ethical concerns are interpreted, we might return to the observation that consumption has become increasingly politicised as an area of activity with a new critical agenda. As Robert Wilk (2001) suggests, the moralism that pervades discussions of consumption is itself worthy of study. Questions of who makes moral arguments about consumption, about how these arguments are deployed, and about what effects they have on different people, are important if we are to understand the complexities through which changing consumption patterns develop and evolve over time, and the ways in which interventions may be made into these processes.

It is important to recognise that consumption is itself an arena through which people learn the meanings of what it is to act morally (Barnett, Cloke, Clarke and Malpass, 2005). In this respect, the emphasis found in the work of Sen and Nussbaum on the role of material goods in providing a means through which people are able to cultivate certain sorts of competencies and capacities, including those of caring for others and participating in public life, is valuable. It suggests that the ways in which ethics and consumption are related are much more complicated than simply quantifying the extent to which particular practices or products conform or not to a particular measure of 'ethicality'. This is not to undervalue the campaigns that develop accessible discourses to boycott the unethical or promote the ethical and rally collective action. Rather, it is important to acknowledge both the intrinsic and the instrumental value of involving ordinary people in the decisions and debates about what goals and objectives, rights and obligations should guide the ethical evaluation of consumption practices.

Such debates, however, do not take place in a vacuum. As Cafaro argues (2001), affluent cultures are suffused with a discourse of individual self-interest and collective economic growth. Economics abstracts Adam Smith's theory of the good flowing from self-interested action from its moral grounding to produce a mere multiplicity of consumer preferences. Economic growth results and is itself presented as a moral good. In this sense no individual or society need question its preferences. We have argued for the counter position. More open debate, continuing discussion and some introspection about our ordinary consumption are valuable to prevent ossification into the moral or immoral imperatives of others.

CONCLUSION

In this chapter, we have outlined some basic philosophical approaches to ethics that are relevant to the area of ethical consumption. These include deontological approaches and consequentialist approaches which focus on notions of obligation and on good outcomes respectively. We have argued that such formalistic philosophical positions can be too demanding and abstract for application in everyday consumption. Consequentialism would presuppose the individual's capacity to make demanding and overly disinterested calculations about what action would produce the most desired aggregate outcomes. Deontology draws the consumer into a set of universal obligations whose development he or she need not be party to. These approaches are also too demanding in the sense that they imply stringent accounts of what is required to act ethically. Imagine how focused you would have to be on consequential calculations or rule-following to be a comprehensive ethical consumer! Being constrained to act within dictates or calculations also implies that something important about one's own moral motivations would be lost. Nonethless, these two theoretical traditions are indispensable parts of an applied ethical consumption: 1) consequentialist philosophies necessarily draw our attention to the outcomes of our consumer practices, and 2) deontological philosophies cause us to generalise our consumer practices and therefore to think from the position of others.

We have suggested that recent work in the area of virtue ethics is also useful for approaching ethical consumption. This is because it focuses on a broader and more practical array of life's considerations than either deontology or consequentialism. Virtue philosophy focuses us on *flourishing*, and living a good life is within our immediate grasp. Empirical evidence suggests that a sense of moral integrity is more fundamental to the well-being of ethical consumers than either a concern for consequences or rules (though both of these are evident). Virtue theory implies a degree of partiality when having to decide between competing claims. This is a necessary introspection that we think cannot be avoided in ethical consumption. However, this flexibility and self-concern can lead to unwarranted ideas of superiority and inferiority. This tendency can be moderated, we argue, by acknowledging the forms of morality embedded in ordinary consumption practices.

Thus, the mere application of consequentialist, deontological or virtue philosophies does not in itself unravel the conundrums of contemporary consumption. We have illustrated this with examples of the conflicting conclusions that might be drawn from applying them. This divergence of conclusions occurs not least because good consumption practices might have temporally limited applications; what is good at one time might be detrimental later. Since a simple set of unchanging ethical consumer practices is neither possible nor desirable, we conclude that they must be formulated and reformulated in a continuous and open public debate. An important dimension of ethical consumption initiatives therefore becomes that of finding ways not just of enabling people to change their consumption practices, although that is important, but also of facilitating more widespread public participation in debates and decisions about the meanings, objectives and responsibilities involved in contemporary consumption.

The Consumer as Economic Voter

Roger A. Dickinson   Mary L. Carsky

2

Consumers participate in creating the societies of which they are a part by their purchases, just as they may influence their environments by their votes in political elections. This idea is not new, but it has been neglected. Early last century Frank A. Fetter (1907: 394) suggested that 'Every buyer … determines in some degree the direction of industry. The market is a democracy where every penny gives the right to vote.' Later, and from the political right in the UK, Enoch Powell (1969: 33) explained how 'everyone who goes into a shop and chooses one article over another is casting a vote in the economic ballot box'.

The expression 'consumer votes' therefore has been used by economists to describe the ordinary process of aggregating individual product choices made on the basis of price and quality alone. More recently, the idea of consumer voting has been adopted by commentators specifically to describe ethical consumer behaviors such as boycotting or positive buying.

Anwar Fazaz, president of the International Organisation of Consumer Unions, noted in 1986 for example that:

> The act of buying is a vote for an economic and social model, for a particular way of producing goods. We are concerned with the quality of goods and the satisfactions we derive from them. But we cannot ignore the conditions under which products are made – the environmental impact and working conditions. We are linked to them and therefore have a responsibility for them. (Ellwood, 1984: 8)

In this chapter, we adopt Smith's (1990b) term 'ethical purchase behavior' but set it within the theoretical concept of consumption as voting. As mentioned in the introduction to this book, it should be noted that what is perceived as 'ethical' or not is frequently the cause of some controversy. For example, consumers have used ethical purchase behavior both to support and oppose the State of Israel. Indeed, the fact that ethical consumer behavior may be misguided in some circumstances is discussed as one of the disadvantages of consumer voting through ethical purchase behavior later in this chapter.

As important as the concept of consumption as voting may be, studies have not flourished in many educational environments. Part of the reason for this neglect is the perspective of many economists that individuals ought to maximize their utilities. These utilities are typically assumed to be created in the context of individual preferences and to be primarily evaluated in terms of his/her self-interest. As will be indicated later, ethical purchase behavior as reflected in this chapter runs counter to what has been taught in many economics and business curricula. Indeed, the concept of ethical purchase behavior has been developed outside of economic and business theory by societally conscious individuals as a practical alternative for participation in the creation of their societies, outside of political voting.

This chapter also addresses the responsibility of consumers to evaluate the consequences of their individual purchases on society, where the impact of those votes is reasonably and readily ascertainable. This responsibility is not straight-forward. Clearly, there can be many forces. Different consumers have different values. Product issues may conflict and there may be no ideal choice. However, consumers should subject their choices to reasoned scrutiny (Ryan, 2003; Sen, 2003) in the context of the good of the community. It could be argued that the greater the monetary value of the votes, the greater the responsibility. Thus the rich bear a greater burden in the context of economic markets and it becomes not quite one person, one vote. We argue that consumers, particularly rich consumers, should do more than maximize their utilities.

This chapter covers the following: the importance of consumption; consumers maximizing utility; consumer sovereignty; the stakeholder concept; boycotts; ethical purchase behavior; possible benefits of ethical purchase behavior; possible costs of ethical purchase behavior; group perspective; who might be interested; and, finally, the reactions of firms.

IMPORTANCE OF CONSUMPTION

Consumer buying and consumption, and their levels, are important to society for many reasons. Buying by consumers is a key component of the economic system of many countries. In the USA, for example, buying by consumers represents more than two-thirds of spending, and this is the highest level in more than fifty years (Norris, 2003). In Japan consumer spending makes up only 55 per cent of the economy (Belson, 2003). Low levels of consumption have been seen as a key cause of the malaise of the Japanese economy over the last fifteen years.

Consumer buying also influences social and cultural aspects of society. Individuals reflect their values and beliefs by what they do or do not buy (Dickinson and Hollander, 1991). They signal to others their perception of the good life and the bad life. Consumers indicate their perceptions of the strengths and weaknesses of countries by favoring or not favoring goods produced in a particular country. Consumption can fill the hunger for a space in which to construct a sense of self and what is important in life (Kozinets, 2001).

Further, the discipline exercised over the products and actions of the firm is primarily that of the customer (adapted from Adam Smith, 1937 [1776]: Vol. I: 161; Dixon, 1992). Firms have all sorts of objectives, strategies, attitudes, and the like that are reflected in the market-place. But over time, firms must induce enough customers to purchase their goods and services so that at least the bills are paid.

Today consumers are seen as co-creators of the value that they derive from a product or service (Senge and Carstedt, 2003). Firms are increasingly seen as solic-iting the participation of their customers in creating new products or adapting products and services for their consumption. Such interaction between firms and consumers can be seen as integral to most product development processes. Clearly the internet can facilitate such interaction with consumers to more efficiently include the perspectives of varied consumers in the development of the final product or service.

An industry that has for many years, and probably for centuries, put particular emphasis on evaluating consumer behavior is retailing. What is selling clearly dictates what is purchased, what is displayed, the space given to various types of products, and so forth. The retail fashion industry particularly is dominated by the analyses and consideration given to the votes of consumers and the trends of those votes at particular time periods, for example, at the beginning of seasons. In food retailing, substantial niche markets have been created, for example in organic foods, through the consideration of the votes of consumers. Chapter 14 of this book looks in more detail at the niche market as an industry response.

Before discussing ethical purchase behavior, this chapter comments on four related areas: the contention that maximizing utilities (suggested here as greed) is the dominant perspective taught by economists and others; consumer sovereignty; the stakeholder concept; an element of ethical purchase behavior – boycotts. Ethical purchase behavior is then described and analyzed.

CONSUMERS MAXIMIZING UTILITY

Standard economic theory views individuals as maximizers of 'utility' who are rational in that they select the most efficient means of achieving the goal of maximizing utility (Hollis, 1995, as reflected by O'Shaughnessy and O'Shaughnessy, forthcoming). The best known theory of rationality is the rational choice theory of economists that explains consumer behavior in terms of maximizing expected utility (O'Shaughnessy and O'Shaughnessy, forthcoming). Ryan maintains that rational choice in economics has for many years considered rationality as concentrating on either the capacity to choose efficient means to what are presumed to be selfish ends, or even more minimally, consistency in choice. 'What ends we pursue and how we have come to adopt them are widely thought not to be of any of the economist's business' (Ryan, 2003: 43). The ideology of consumer choice is that all wants are, at least in principle, equal (Collini, 2003). Excluding specific commodities like drugs, tobacco, and varied illegal products and/or socially opprobrious items, consumers are admonished to select those items and services that offer the highest utility per unit of cost to them. Thus, in general, self-interest is thought to be enough (Etzioni, 1988; Rhoades, 1985; Wolfe, 1989). For a discussion of self-interest see Dickinson (1988) and Holbrook (1998: 10–11).

Just as there are many kinds of costs a consumer may have to 'pay', clearly there are many kinds of value that a consumer might find of particular interest. Consumer value refers to the evaluation of some object by some subject (Holbrook, 1998: 5). We do not here address different consumer values per se. Rather, the chapter suggests that consumers ought to consider the consequences to others as part of their purchase decision processes. For a discussion of consumer value see the varied authors in Holbrook's *Consumer Value* (1998). It is contended that by and large in the USA, academics teach in business and economics courses that self-interest is the key consideration, and for most purposes the dominant consideration in decision making. Further, several academic scholars have suggested that in teaching this perspective we may be creating individuals who fit the theory, who act in a more self-interested manner than might otherwise be the case (Bloom, 1987; Frank, 1988; Thurow, 1985). And in what some might perceive as support for the perspective that greed is an important perspective in economic courses, economics students have manifested more self-interested behavior than other students (Kahneman et al., 1986; Marwell and Ames, 1981).

In this context, however regrettable, greed can be perceived as a dominant thrust of society (Holbrook, forthcoming). It appears reasonable to label a person acting 'completely' in his/her own best interest as 'greedy'. And we think it is fair to maintain that greed is what is being taught to many students as sufficient for a guide to consumer purchasing.

By contrast, the term 'consumer citizenship' has been used to describe the obligations of consumers to make contributions to the social good through their economic votes (Dickinson, 1996). Citizenship, discussed later in this chapter, can be seen as a mechanism for tempering the greed present in much economics teaching. Some would see consumer sovereignty as a means by which consumers might control the economy. After all, sovereigns generally have some power. And if consumers are sovereigns, maybe they have enough power to institute desired changes.

CONSUMER SOVEREIGNTY

As suggested above, in some sense what consumers purchase, their votes, have always been considered by decision makers of the firm. Consumer demand matters. What firm would produce an item or open a store without some sort of 'evidence' that individuals are going to buy in acceptable volume what will be offered? This was the case in 1400 as much as today. Firms are continuously adjusting their offerings in the context of attracting and maintaining customers and developing profitability for the firm. This is not quite the 'consumer is king' philosophy. But firms are adjusting their offerings in their own best interests, in general to enhance the value of the firm. The interests of the firm and those of the consumer clearly conflict in many dimensions (Dixon, 1992; Smith, 1990b). Smith (1990b: 36) observes that consumer sovereignty is incompatible with the notion of marketing strategy.

The importance of consumption was recognized centuries ago. 'Consumption is the end and aim of all economic action' appeared initially in the third edition of *The Wealth of Nations* (Dixon, 1992, reflecting Smith, 1937). Early American writers suggested that the purpose of marketing was to satisfy human wants (Dixon, 1992). Ludwig von Mises suggested that firms are steersmen bound to unconditionally obey the captain's (consumer's) orders (Greaves, 2003). Indeed, the consumer is ultimately in charge in the sense that it is his or her decision to buy or not to buy. In this view the consumer is king or captain, but again the perspective of the consumer is just one of the considerations of the firm in making consumer related decisions.

Hutt (1934) introduced the phrase 'consumer sovereignty' in a discussion of the concept of market structure. Monopoly was seen as frustrating consumer sovereignty. Von Hayek (1935: 214) describes a centrally planned economy as the 'Abrogation of the Sovereignty of the Consumer.'

Consumer sovereignty may be defined as the power of consumers to determine, from among the offerings of producers of goods and services, what goods and services are and will be offered (produced) and/or created in the economic sphere of society. (See Dixon (1992) for a variety of definitions of consumer sovereignty and a description of the evolution of the concept in the 1930s, including its introduction into economic texts.)

That consumer sovereignty would in some sense maximize overall consumer welfare is, of course, an absurdity. Firms have their needs and desires and produce what is in their best interests to produce. Firms can and do persuade and manipulate consumers. Firms can and do activate latent wants and needs in an effort to increase profitability. Consumers also have their needs and desires, as do governments. The resulting markets are influenced by all kinds of factors including the impact of these three: firms, governments and consumers.

The next section makes it clear that the consumer is just one consideration of the firm. And in general, in the USA at least, while there are exceptions, the consumer is mainly considered through the vehicle of enhancing the long-term profitability of the firm.

THE STAKEHOLDER CONCEPT

The stakeholder concept is often abused as reflected in colleges of business, at least in the USA. (This is also discussed later in this book by Adams and Zutshi in Chapter 13.) Many times it comes down to the proposition that managements should show due consideration to each group that has a stake in the firm. None should be left out of this process. But on this view decisions with respect to each stakeholder should be made in the context of 'maximizing' shareholder value which is seen as dominant. The stakeholder concept defined in this way suggests little more than good management is better than bad management (Dickinson, 1996).

The above definition does not reflect the creation and evolution of the stakeholder concept. Berle and Means (1932), seen as substantial 'promoters' of the stakeholder concept, suggested that top managements and boards did not have very large ownership positions in the firms that they managed. Their legitimacy with respect to running the corporation was thus open to question. Therefore, top management should manage for the benefit of many stakeholders including society. In this view, the shareholder is seen as just one of the stakeholders. Other stakeholders had claims against the decision processes of the firm. As the concept evolved over time, the employee became a particularly important stakeholder, for example in many European countries. (For some perspectives on the stakeholder concept see Varney, 2002: 101.)

It is quite obvious, at least in the USA, that dishonest and/or immoral executives aside, the shareholder concept dominates other considerations. No protection is offered to the consumer by the stakeholder concept if, in fact, the other stakeholders are only considered through the prism of shareholder value. However, it is clear that in most instances it does pay firms to closely study and monitor consumers and their decision processes in an effort to earn profits for the firm over substantial time periods.

Consumers often recognize their individual powerlessness in society and attempt to redress the balance. These efforts are designed to change the inputs into the cost–benefit frameworks of the decision makers of the firm. The efforts are often organized as boycotts, the subject of the next section. Boycotts can both decrease the revenue of the target of the boycott and, as explained below, increase costs such as transportation, labor and the like.

BOYCOTTS

One form of ethical purchase behavior that has a substantial history is boycotting. Boycotts can take many forms and have been used for centuries (Smith, 1998). Boycotts hurt some firms and help others. For example, those firms not boycotted may be helped by a boycott of competitors. Some firms will have values consistent with those of the boycotters. In many instances, those boycotting may only reduce the monetary value of their purchases and not completely discontinue purchases in a product category or with respect to a firm. Friedman (1999a: 33) offers three types of boycotts: those that place obstacles in the way of consumers, for example sit-ins; those that focus on an economic entity, for example a retailer who buys products from a supplier; and those that focus on business firms operating in a designated geographic area. Boycotting is generally seen as a collective act. Little research on boycotting has been conducted from the individual consumer's perspective (Kozinets, 2003), although Kozinets and Handelman (1998) found that individuals engaged in boycotting as a complex emotional expression of their individuality and further that boycotting is a vehicle for moral self-realization.

In boycotting a highly interested group tries to exert pressure on an adversary or enemy, and/or the entire system of marketing and commerce, by inducing consumers to vote by not purchasing (Friedman, 1999a; Garrett, 1987). Boycotts have been brought against all kinds of activities and firms including specific retailers, Coors Beer, prison-made goods, California lettuce and other produce, Polish hams, and goods from South Africa (Dickinson and Hollander, 1991). In 2003 and 2004 many new boycotts of US goods and companies emerged around the world in protest at the policies of the USA in the political and military arenas.

Boycotts focus on the negative aspects of economic votes, although Friedman (1999a: 34) identifies positive boycotts, or 'buycotts', that take the form of a list of recommended products to purchase. These attempt in general to hurt particular firms or areas by creating an emotional response from the larger culture that is translated into economic action by consumers. Frequently they last for relatively short periods of time although the long running Nestlé boycott is an exception. Boycotts and Friedman's analyses of them are covered in more detail by Clouder and Harrison in Chapter 6 of this book.

VOTING THROUGH ETHICAL PURCHASE BEHAVIOR

We have maintained to this point the following: self-interest is a dominant element in the consumer decision process and taught that it should be so; the concept of consumer sovereignty clearly does not maximize consumer welfare; and that the stakeholder concept does not protect the consumer in many parts of the world, at least in the USA. We now discuss how consumers might influence their worlds by their economic votes.

In the USA consumers (almost all of us) consistently criticize one or more groups for their extreme dedication to self-interest. Doctors, lawyers, business people, legislators and so forth are seen as money grubbing opportunists dedicated to short working hours, high compensation, and so forth. To the extent that society is considered at all, it is generally perceived to be an afterthought, a sort of possible constraint. Perhaps the group displaying exciting new levels of greed, possibly not exceeded in history, is the top management-board of director grouping which in essence often sets their own compensation in the context of mutual appreciation and admiration. That some key figures in our economic system have no conscience with respect to the amounts they 'steal' from the system is beyond question in the present environment.

Of course, there are justifications for self-interest and greed. Adam Smith and nineteenth-century classical economists maintained that the competitive market transforms individual actions based on self-interest into the common good (Dixon, 1992). Few, however, would see the labor markets of the groups drawing the harshest criticisms as competitive in the context of controlling such things as compensation. It does not appear that the common good has much to do with the thrusts of the dominant groups of society.

Most of the criticisms come from outsiders to the specific group whose moral values, integrity, and the like are being questioned in a particular situation. But there is something that we almost all do. We buy goods and services. Now what criteria should we use in selecting the goods and services that we buy? Clearly we want whatever we purchase to at least meet functional needs. But in addition to the varied wants that we may desire to fulfill, as suggested earlier, our purchases can impact society. We may be promoting sweatshops in developing countries by our votes. And why not demand of consumers that they consider the ramifications of their actions on the common good, if that impact can be reasonably and readily ascertained? Otherwise consumers may be perceived as no better than the groups which they criticize. This is what the remainder of this chapter is about. In many instances, at least those consumers that are better off economically have, it can be argued, a responsibility to make a bona fide effort to consider the consequences of their votes on the system (Hanson and Schreder, 1997).

Dickinson and Hollander (1991) made a proposal for consumers considering the impact of their economic votes. They suggested that teaching individual members of society that they should be responsible for the consequences of their action, if such consequences could be reasonably and readily ascertained, should be integral to various levels of education. The standards by which individual households measure the consequences of their purchasing activities is left to the individual household to decide. The values and beliefs of human beings are complex, but we believe that many households can deal with the varied and complex elements to be considered. Clearly, however, wealthy individuals have more potential votes than the poor. It is argued that individuals, in general, come to the decision-making process with an intuitive common-sense morality (Seanor and Fotion, 1988). It is also argued that educators should be enlisted in an attempt to change the values and assumptions underlying the dominant approach in the USA and in much of the developed world with respect to consumer purchasing. Those who teach economics would be particularly important in this respect. The proposal with respect to consumer voting may be thought of in four, possibly complementary, ways (see Dickinson and Hollander, 1991):

- as a way to have consumers co-operate to obtain long-term or higher order goals that might be precluded by everyone acting in his/her self-interest;
- as a non-legislative alternative to redress imbalances in the perceived distribution of goods and services to various components of society;

- as a means of promoting private and public discussion with respect to utilities and perhaps their transformations to a higher level;
- as a way to support worthwhile economic institutions, for example, retailers offering outstanding value, seen to better society as a result of these better values offered.

Possible benefits

The four ways just described offer some insights into the kinds of benefits that might be possible if consumer voting through ethical purchase behavior is accepted and promoted to substantial numbers. A key general benefit is that many of the obstacles to obtaining long-term goals might be overcome. Considering communal values might make some opportunities feasible that would not otherwise be possible, at least if some idea of the common good can be engendered. Another key benefit is that ethical purchase behavior offers an alternative course of action to those complaining about the greedy behavior of others. Consumers can select alternatives that do not offer the greatest 'utility' or pay-off to themselves in the hope of bettering society. Some additional benefits might be as follows (see Dickinson and Hollander, 1991):

1) If accepted, the message that considering others should be a key component of purchase decision making can be important in changing society in various ways. It could become a central message in education at many levels. In much economics today the message of greed is enough, euphemistically worded as a central consideration. At some levels ethical purchase behavior, given the strong feeling of consumers about fairness, might be seen as a way to reintroduce it as relevant for consideration in subjects like economics. One would hope that many economic models would change their assumptions.

2) Considerations related to ethical purchase behavior may increase the sense of participation by members of society. Political voting often does not give participants in the election a feeling that they matter. Further, there have been many articles, books and so forth suggesting that we are more frequently 'bowling alone', more isolated, more self-concerned, and the like (Beck, 1999; Giddens, 1990). Conceivably, thinking more about the consequences of our actions on others would give consumers a greater sense of participation in creating a better society. To many observers effective democracies should be more of a participating and less a spectator 'sport', and economic voting through ethical purchase behavior may increase the number who feel that they are taking part.

3) Focussing on the impact of one's actions on others might be a way for individuals to integrate their public and private lives. Bellah et al. (1985) found that individuals were locked into a split between two worlds, their relation to others and their private world.

4) Related to the above, it can be suggested that markets and their consideration can civilize behavior with respect to one another (Le Grand, 2003b). As Montesquieu put it: 'commerce ... polishes and softens barbarian ways,' and perhaps markets can reinforce altruism in the context of ethical purchase behavior.

5) Consumer behavior would not be seen in isolation from other aspects of existence (Belk, 1987).

6) The large number of votes cast by the rich should create particular obligations for them to behave in a more socially oriented manner in their economic

votes and perhaps in other facets of their lives. Indeed, a focus on ethical purchase behavior would clearly open up large value purchases for discussion by the public. And some purchases by rich consumers might rightfully draw ridicule.

7) There is a huge discrepancy in income and wealth between rich and poor in many countries today. The differences have reached record levels in some societies. Perhaps the kind of discussions one would expect with respect to the impact of consumer votes might also go some way to addressing such issues.

Possible costs

The costs of a society strongly adopting consumer voting may be seen as a mirror of the benefits (Dickinson and Hollander, 1991). A possible consequence of consumer votes as described in this chapter is that rich individuals obviously not considering the common good of their purchases would be made to feel shame, or at least one would hope so – the greater the extravagance, the greater the shame. However, is society benefited if individuals feel more shameful? Further, considered consumption might mean less consumption. But many societies have been at varied times plagued by low levels of consumption that could not support desired levels of employment, growth and prosperity. Insufficient consumption has often been seen as an element in the extraordinarily long duration of the Great Depression of the 1930s. If individuals had bought more, the lot of everyone might have been improved. Today under-consumption is seen as a great problem in Japan and other cultures. Thus, increased consumption can have very positive consequences on an economy. In some economic environments, any additional consumption would have the possibility of helping others.

The assumption of much of the analysis with respect to the benefits of ethical purchase behavior is that logic will prevail. But the argument can be made that seldom does logic prevail, particularly in a democracy where votes are constantly sought by those facing elections. Everything is 'spin'. Spinning is the organizing thrust of the messages emanating from individuals, groups and governments of all types. A key purpose of spin is obfuscation by inducing a perspective on the target audience favored by the author of the spin. It can be argued that emotion, often engendered by misrepresentation, is what moves individuals to vote and to change votes. Why should it be any different when exercised in the context of an economic ballot?

For example, Pat Buchanan (2003), occasional presidential candidate in the USA, encouraged a boycott of the products and services of all firms that agreed to advertise on a CBS television network which was critical of the presidency of Ronald Reagan. The programs apparently reflected President Reagan in a deleterious light. There were many complaints and presumably threats of one sort or another, and CBS moved the program to a cable station under the control of CBS's parent, Viacom.

In no sense should one assume that the threat of boycott is necessarily a source for the common good. Threats from important groups can represent coercive power, and one may not assume that such power will be used wisely.

The net impact of extensive analysis of ethical purchase behavior would probably be to reinforce the consumer side of the consumer-firm interface. Many have commented on the increase in consumer power that has occurred as a result of the growth of technological sophistication, the internet and related consumer knowledge. There may be few further benefits to a society by another surge of consumer power. Further, increases in consumer power need not be in the best interests of society. Clearly increased power to any segment of the population, as suggested earlier, may not be used wisely.

Following from this, since the human world is highly varied there would be many reactions to any efforts to change society. Many individuals and groups have radically different beliefs and values. One consumer's good will be another consumer's ill (Dickinson and Hollander, 1991). Thus there may not be a common good for many key issues. Managements may be caught in a cross-fire for which there may be no reasonable resolution. In other words, one possible impact of many varied responses to particular changes might be inaction and/or substantial cost increments of varying types with little pay-off. A preoccupation by managements with political actions may lead to them pursuing, and being consumed by, dynamic inaction and/or counterproductive actions.

Trying to reorient teachings and actions in society at a time that might be seen as at a peak in self-interest in what has been termed a self-interest community cycle, might be over-reacting. (For a discussion of these cycles see Hirschman (1982), Lerner (1988) and Schlesenger (1986).) We may be reacting to the 'thuggery' of some corporations in recent boom times. The cyclical thesis suggests that the USA may now naturally move more toward community behavior.

Futhermore, a substantial risk may be forthcoming if we make great efforts to mitigate greed in our society. However regrettable, greed might be conceded to be a dominant thrust of many affluent societies (Holbrook, forthcoming). Greed, however, may be the glue that holds society together. Indeed, the failure of individuals to realize the necessity of self-interest, and the freedom that flows from it, is seen as frightening and depressing by some (Ayn Rand as reflected by Buckley, 2003). Herbert Simon, Nobel Laureate, once said to one of the authors that if you want to understand a person's actions, look toward his/her motivation. And the assumption of direct household self-interest may provide a reasonable basis for anticipating and predicting the behavior of others. Motivations other than direct household self-interest may be far more difficult to ascertain and understand. For example, the statement has been made that Saudi Arabia's behavior with respect to oil can be readily understood in the context of enhancing the standard of living for the ruling class and/or all the citizens of Saudi Arabia. When other criteria become important, anticipating behavior becomes more difficult.

Perhaps the greatest cost of trying to induce great change is the unintended consequences that are to be expected from any new dramatic thrusts for society (Hirschman, 1989). Hirschman describes the perverse effect where an attempt to set society in one direction often results in its moving in the opposite direction. For example, stopping child labor may substantially impoverish families in underdeveloped countries.

GROUP PERSPECTIVE

To this point we have considered ethical purchase behavior primarily in the context of the individual household. As the boycott variant of voting suggests, group action is likely to be more useful in creating substantial change. Indeed a key element of marketing is that the patronage of an individual consumer, except under the most unusual conditions, is not worth a great deal. There is not enough expenditure to make a difference and a household usually has just one set of votes. But as consumer sovereignty suggests, if many consumers vote the same way, the marketing systems of most societies will have to respond. Thus the common values of consumers voting independently, as suggested by the buying system posed later in this chapter, can induce similar kinds of purchasing that can reward society as 'common' values are advanced.

However, people also influence other people. And there are groups that can effectively disseminate information, values and the like to others. The internet has become a key vehicle through which individuals and groups can be more effective in this. Thus the greatest impact of ethical purchase behavior, if generally accepted, would undoubtedly be through groups, but the sensitivity of the individual to the impact of his/her votes might be an essential precursor to flourishing group frameworks in the context of the common good. (For more information on the role of groups in promoting ethical purchase behavior see Chapter 4.)

Who might be interested?

There appear to be three types of consumers who might be particularly interested in and/or support ethical purchase behavior. First, in most societies there are a substantial number of individuals who are pursuing or would like to pursue the common good. Ethical purchase behavior would fit into their perspective of life or life as it ought to be lived. Such individuals may be interested in integrating various facets of their lives to improve life on the planet.

Second, some individuals may need a little incentive to do what they should do anyway. Thus it can be argued that, in their own best interests, consumers and households should set up a system of shopping to counteract the actions of firms that are continuously trying to manipulate them in one way or another (Carsky et al., 1995). But the creation and implementation of such systems requires substantial effort and thought, including the development of purchasing heuristics. The additional attractiveness of improving society in the context of benefiting one's household should be an added attraction pushing some households into action.

The shopping system alluded to by Carsky et al. (1995) focuses on 'substantive value' as a key consideration in purchases for the household. The results of many households developing systems focussing on substantive value would be, given certain assumptions, to reward those economic institutions focussing on offering the highest 'quality' related to price, presumably to the benefit of most societies. Those retailers and brands that offer the best value for a particular household are rewarded and sustained. Those elements of the marketing system offering poor value would be punished. Of course, retailers and wholesalers that do not offer perceived value of some sort are punished today for the most part (for a description of types of consumer value see Holbrook (1998)). However, the punishment in the context of organized consumer voting might be more direct and immediate than in the present economic environment.

Third, a number of consumers might be embarrassed by being recognized as being manifestly indifferent to the common good. There could be substantial social pressure, particularly if the teaching in society were oriented to understanding consumption as a form of voting as part of consumer citizenship. Indeed, as suggested earlier, much education in the USA has emphasized that greed creates an efficient society, albeit that greed is couched in euphemistic terms.

CONSUMER CITIZENSHIP

Varney (2002: 44) indicates that a consumer citizen acts beyond his or her own interests as a consumer and takes responsibility for the future. Perhaps the most important part of any concept of being a citizen is that something is to be considered beyond oneself, larger than oneself. And central to any definition would be that time is important in the sense that long-term considerations should dominate shorter term considerations. Of course, consumers do much more than just consume. However, integrating the concept of consumer voting into a general concept of citizenship, political and otherwise, is beyond the scope of this chapter and has been addressed by others elsewhere (see for example, Gabriel and Lang, 1995).

REACTIONS OF FIRMS

Professor Lester Thurow (1986) maintained that any important economic action is going to help some groups and hurt others. Undoubtedly, if ethical purchase behavior were to become a focus of a substantial number of household efforts, some firms and industries would be hindered and others would be helped. Firms related to industries disadvantaged by a thrust with respect to ethical purchase behavior by many highly varied individuals and groups seeking the common good would undoubtedly not be pleased. Firms and industries helped by such a thrust would presumably look at ethical purchase behavior positively.

By and large, however, firms and individual executives would do as they always do – adapt to the new environment with the goal of enhancing the value of the firm, or in the context of top management, of increasing their own compensation. Clearly products, services, advertising, and sales promotion would be created or adjusted in the context of the changing environment. To the extent that households in a particular country developed shopping systems that focussed on substantive value, the price of some products would probably decrease, or the substantive quality of the product would increase, as a result of the changed competitive environment. All of this would occur in the context of the firm and/or its executives making the maximum money they can over the long term. Some executives would favor and thrive in the new environment. Others would be disadvantaged and presumably react negatively.

Further, as values within a society change, firms would be expected to anticipate and take advantage of these changes. Whole new markets could be created in the context of consumers desiring different products, services, or value alternatives. (This is covered in more detail in Chapter 14.) Our argument has been precisely that society might be improved if consumers spend more time considering the impact of their decisions. Organic food retailers and organic food sections of 'traditional' retailers can be seen as examples of adaptation to the votes of consumers. Perhaps society might be improved if consumers spent more time considering the impact of all their purchase decisions.

Part Two

Campaigners and Consumers

A Brief History of Consumer Activism

Tim Lang   Yiannis Gabriel

3

Consumption and consumerism are tricky words in the English language. They are replete with positive and negative attributes, implying on the one hand that people are free to vote with their feet, and on the other that they are manipulated by superior market forces. The rich literature on consumers, consumerism and consumption all thrive on this ambiguity. In our book *The Unmanageable Consumer* (Gabriel and Lang, 1995), we set out to explore this ambiguity, trying to make sense of the diverse forms that consumption assumes in modern societies and the variety of meanings assumed by the term 'consumerism'.

In this chapter we reflect and build on the analysis we offered in our book on what we called the active consumer: those people and movements setting out to promote the rights, consciousness and interests of either all or particular groups of consumers. This is what we refer to in this chapter as active consumerism or simply consumerism. In our earlier work, we offered an historical and sociological analysis of consumer movements as emerging in four waves. We posited that each wave proposed not only new forms of organising, but different ways of looking at consumption. All of these waves have left traces which are still visible in the world of consumer organisations today throughout the world. This chapter outlines those four waves of consumer activism and asks what, if anything, has changed in the decade since we outlined our theory. We conclude that some interesting realignments are under way within and across the 'waves' of consumer activism, suggesting considerable dynamism and inventiveness.

THE NEED TO UNDERSTAND ACTIVE CONSUMERS AND CAMPAIGNERS

Consumer activists have been high profile in most reasonably affluent societies for decades – appearing in the media, writing reports, appealing for support, giving government or companies a hard time. Yet, as Winward suggested, consumer activism 'has always been under-theorised' (1993: 77). Reading the academic and historical literature, we were surprised at the relative dearth of plausible analyses of active consumerism. When consumer activists meet socially or in consumer congresses, there is no shortage of reflection or analysis. The consumer movement tends, we concluded, to analyse its own work in private, leaving the theoretical analysis to academics or practitioners who have tended to underplay the importance of activism and to focus on markets, culture and signs. One exception is the study of boycotts, perhaps because they have 'bite', not just heart. Clouder and Harrison review the boycott literature in Chapter 6 in this book, so there is no need to discuss it further here.

Apart from boycotts, the dearth of good analyses of activism is surprising for two reasons. First, consumerism has been enlightened by active attempts to redirect consumer behaviour. The committed attempt to inject ethical and fair trade notions into the otherwise free trade dominated discourse about world economic development is but the most recent example (Lang and Hines, 1993: 108–11; Nader, 1991). Second, we were perplexed at the lack of good analysis of active consumerism because the consumer movement's own history highlights how passionately it has debated which direction it should go. For instance, the world's largest consumer organisation, the US Consumers Union (CU), was born out of a long and bitter struggle in the 1930s in Consumer Research Inc., another organisation which the CU eventually superseded. The fight was over both formal philosophy – particularly attitudes to organised labour – and internal management styles (Herrmann, 1993).

Debating the direction of consumer activism is not new, nor is the attempt to organise disparate individual acts of consumption by appealing to higher moral or political ends. The US non-importation movement of 1764–76 was America's first consumer revolt. Aimed against the import of goods, it was more than a rejection of colonial tax laws, an expression of cultural independence and an assertion of the local over the global. This was echoed in anti-colonial struggles elsewhere, notably by Gandhi's independence movement in India. By signing a declaration in public that they would stop purchasing British goods, his supporters also pledged, *de facto*, to live more frugally from local resources as an assertion of community values (Witkowski, 1989).

The social historian E.P. Thompson showed how the emergence of the new corn markets in eighteenth-century England were 'disinfested of intrusive moral imperatives' (Thompson, 1993: 202). The morality, an amoralised version of Adam Smith's new political economy, had to be imposed on British society. This conveniently ignored Smith's prior theory of moral sentiments (1759). People's expectations and life assumptions had to be re-moulded, in a process which was messy and at times bloody. In his celebrated essay on 'The Moral Economy of the English Crowd in the Eighteenth Century', Thompson (1993) showed how the food riots of that century were the expression of people taking direct action against the imposition of the new free market in grain because they were hungry. More importantly, however, they were reacting to higher food prices, as the paternalism of Tudor economics gave way to the amorality of Smith's market forces. For Forbes, contemporary consumerism is but a version of the same principle, that is the 'organised reaction of individuals to inadequacies, perceived or real, of marketers, the marketplace, market mechanisms, government, government services, and consumer policy' (Forbes, 1987: 4).

Although this chapter explores different manifestations of consumer activism, there are some characteristics that run through all these manifestations:

- organisation – consumption is an organised and coherent set of activities informed by the actions of different organisations, including consumer bodies;
- a desire for change – consumption can be the vehicle of its own transformation and it can, therefore, be imbued with some mission;

- rights – consumers have rights which have to be fought for or else they will (probably) be lost or never gained;
- collectivity – individual actions can be strengthened by acting in concert with others;
- values – consumption is not merely a set of market transactions but has moral messages too and that consuming can be good or bad;
- implications – consuming has effects, on other people, on society or on the environment that go beyond the act, good or service itself.

FIRST WAVE: CO-OPERATIVE CONSUMERS

The first widespread organised consumer movement began as a working-class reaction to excessive prices and poor quality goods, food in particular. The Co-operative Movement took off in its modern form in Rochdale, in north-west England, in 1844, at the height of the industrialisation process. The first co-operatives in fact date from even earlier and were co-operative corn mills established by skilled artisans. These were set up in opposition to local monopolies who in the words of one Co-op historian 'had conspired to supply that most basic of commodities, bread, at very high prices' (Birchall, 1994: 4).

Despite repression in 1834 (Birchall, 1994: 31), such organisations provided practical proof that consumers could exercise power over production. Co-operation rather than Adam Smith's self-interest could function as the basis for meeting consumer needs. The Rochdale co-op built on this idea by setting up a shop – now a museum – to sell goods to those who joined up. Profits, instead of being allowed to be accumulated and ploughed back into manufacture, as in Owen's model, were divided amongst the co-operators (Redfern, 1913: 1–11).

The principle of this new movement, which was extraordinarily successful both in business and ideological terms, was 'self-help by the people'. No distinction was made between people as consumers and as producers. Business, co-operators argued, divided producers from the output of their own hands. Co-operation was the great social alternative to the capitalists' economic armoury which merely divided and ruled the mass of working people (Thompson, 1994). This principle was admirably expressed by Redfern in 1920:

> In our common everyday needs the great industries of the world take their rise. We – the mass of common men and women in all countries – also compose the world's market. To sell to us is the ultimate aim of the world's business. Hence it is ourselves as consumers who stand in a central relation to all the economies of the world, like the king in his kingdom. As producers we go unto a particular factory, farm or mine, but as consumers we are set by nature thus to give leadership, aim and purpose to the whole economic world. That we are not kings, but serfs in the mass, is due to our failure to think and act together as consumers and so to realise our true position and power. (Redfern, 1920: 12)

Co-operation offered a richer, more fulfilled social existence, a chance for working people to build a better world. To allow this mass to participate, a new civic society had to be created, and vice versa. It was a subversive combination of theory and practice, means and ends, which was and still is deeply threatening to prevailing market theory. The co-operator Holyoake parodied the movement's detractors as follows:

> The working class are not considered to be very rich in the quality of self-trust, or mutual trust. The business habit is not thought to be their forte. The art of creating a large concern, and governing all its complications, is not usually supposed to belong to them. (Holyoake, 1872: 1)

The movement prospered and proved these Jeremiahs wrong. The Rochdale Pioneers, for instance, had within six years their own corn mill. The practice of local co-ops spread like wildfire – and its legacy continues to this day (Thompson, 1994). Co-operation from below, rather than Owen's benign vision of production for mutual benefit, put the consumer in charge, probably for the only time ever. In the mid-nineteenth century, the co-operative movement grew into hundreds of societies, but as these began to merge in the next century, the mutuality principle weakened, becoming more like a distant and tiny share holding at the point of sale. Indeed, for most British people in the second half of the twentieth century, co-operation meant a retail store where the customer received a coupon with the bill at the check-out counter – the famous 'divi' or dividend, which before its demise in the 1960s had become a rather weak parallel to the nakedly capitalist savings stamps schemes run by the rival private or stock-holder retailers. The practice of consumer co-operation for mutual benefit had become a trading stamp.

A century and a half after its foundation, the Co-operative movement has spread throughout the world. As Kofi Annan, Secretary-General of the United Nations, wrote in 2003 the co-operative movement:

> is one of the largest organized segments of civil society, and plays a crucial role across a wide spectrum of human aspiration and need. Co-operatives provide vital health, housing and banking services; they promote education and gender equality; they protect the environment and workers' rights ... they help people in more than 100 countries better their lives and those of their communities. (Annan, 2003)

There are 700 million people signed up to co-ops in those 100 countries.

Banks, factories, insurance, farming and retailing companies all reside under the Co-op movement's umbrella, even in the UK. In the 1990s, however, the UK movement began to sell off huge parts of its food industry empire. Vertical integration, owning everything from land to point of sale, for so long a strength of the movement, had by the end of the twentieth century become an economic liability. This was now the era of tough contracts and specifications policed by ruthless retail giants to cut prices (Blythman, 2004; Lawrence, 2004), a far cry from the co-operators' dream of an autonomous empire with everything kept within the co-op 'family'. It was once said that the active consumer could be born, eat, live and die, all serviced from within the movement. With time and scale of operations, the direct control of consumers slipped away and the co-operative societies were forced to retrench, amalgamate and restructure. The Co-op had become associated with old values.

Many began to write it off. Today, however, there is a return of interest. The UK Co-operative Group started growing again in the twenty-first century, after decades of decline before the conventional supermarket giants. A new generation of consumers, as we note below, has emerged unhappy with the corporate giants, and open to what marketing specialists call the 'offer' of Co-ops. The Co-operative Bank, for instance, made a virtue of what it would *not* invest in, and saw its client base increase and rise up the social scale. In other countries, the social class connotations of co-ops has not been so stifling. In Japan, the Seikatsu Clubs, a network of 700 consumer co-ops, prospered from the 1960s (Nelson, 1991). The Seikatsu club movement was started in 1965 by a Tokyo housewife to buy milk more cheaply in bulk. When members join the Seikatsu Club, they made an initial investment of 1,000 yen, and paid a similar sum every month. The Clubs made a virtue of the duty to be harmonious with nature by 'taking action from the home' (Gussow, 1991: 101–3). By the 1990s there were 25,000 local groups turning over an annual £260 million (Ekins, 1992).

In the late twentieth century, food has been a key area of consumer disenchantment with conventional modes of market relationship. Scandals and crises have been experienced around the globe over food quality, safety, information, price, environmental damage and public health. Urban societies with long supply chains rely upon a trust relationship, which if damaged takes time to repair. Not just in Japan, but in the heartlands of capitalism such as the USA and Europe, co-operatives have often been a lifeline for 'alternative' visions, from the wholefood co-ops of the 1970s (Hines, 1976), to community-supported agriculture of the 1990s. Small direct farmer to consumer links such as box schemes and farmers' markets have emerged as highly visible loci of activism. So-called box schemes build links between the consumer who pays a fixed sum each week and the grower who provides a box of fresh food, whatever is in season (Festing, 1993).

These initiatives are small and, in formal economic terms, barely register as irritants to the big supermarket chains which now dwarf food retailing and frame supply chains regionally and globally (Lang and Heasman, 2004). Yet, they have been very successful in capturing attention, offering a critique of conventional production, an appeal to immediacy and an authenticity that the larger chains now also try to offer. In the early 1990s, the Co-operative Group in the UK began to realise the opportunities this shifting consumer consciousness offered and began a slow process of injecting ethical, health, environmental and information advantages to its users (Co-operative Group, 2004). Many within the movement saw this as a return to its roots: a mix of enlightened self-interest and citizenship but above all the Co-op becoming once more an active consumer organisation after decades in retreat. The Co-op is also reconnecting with its social mission, as a voice for the disenfranchised (Birchall, 2003; Co-operative Group, 2004).

The co-op movement now has a big challenge: how simultaneously to address, confront, service and deliver on consumer appetites that are contradictory – damaging ecology and health, yet being bought with apparent free-will and awareness! In the past, the co-operatives had an easier time; associated with decent but low income working people, value-for-money was assumed to be a driver. The hard work, zeal and commitment of the nineteenth-century pioneers who built the local societies, who saved and invested in new shops, factories and land to serve working people, all this brought good quality goods and services to those who hitherto had lacked them. The co-ops made consumerism affordable. But with the arrival of the mass consumer society in the late twentieth century, that rationale for the movement waned.

Others could do it cheaper, faster, with modernity. The co-op's affairs were inevitably conducted by professional managers, whose vision became more pragmatic, though it never collapsed into quite the ethos of other retail organisations. Despite these limitations, the active co-operator/consumer retains its potency even if today's global markets and the international division of labour make it hard to realise. Will co-operatives be able to rebuild the local? Combine ethics with efficiency? Be associated with flair and panache rather than solid respectability – or recapture respectability as more potent than flair and excitement?

SECOND WAVE: VALUE-FOR-MONEY CONSUMERS

The second wave of the consumer movement is today by far the highest profile wave of consumer activism, to such an extent that it is often wrongly regarded as being the entire consumer movement. We term this 'value-for-money' consumerism. This emerged in its modern form in the 1930s, but built upon tentative US consumer initiatives in the late nineteenth and early twentieth centuries.

A Consumers League was formed in New York in 1891. In 1898, the National Consumers League was formed from local groups, and by 1903 had 64 branches in 20 states. The movement took off after a celebrated exposé of wide-scale food adulteration and bad trade. Upton Sinclair, a radical journalist, was sent to write newspaper articles on the insanitary condition at the Chicago stockyards and meat packing plants, and wrote *The Jungle*, a novel published in 1906. A socialist, he hoped to proselytise with the political message that market forces served neither worker nor consumer, he hoped to bring down US capitalism. Instead he changed US food law. 'I aimed at the public's heart and by accident hit it in the stomach,' he wrote, anticipating many a single issue consumer campaign which launches a simple message, from which it generalises (Sinclair, 1985 [1906]). As a result of the reaction to Sinclair's book, legislation was rushed through Congress, the Pure Food and Drug Act of 1906 and the Meat Inspection Act of the same year, an extraordinary impact for a book (Forbes, 1987: 4). The Federal Trade Commission and a variety of anti-monopoly laws were also set up at the turn of the century.

These early US consumer groups placed heavy emphasis on the containment of the emergent powerful corporations. Their writings were full of concerns about the power of the new combines over individuals, both as workers and as consumers. Unlike the first wave of consumerism, these groups were concerned about the threat posed to consumers by increasing concentration and monopoly capital. In the Roaring Twenties with its unprecedented explosion of consumption, *Your Money's Worth* (1927), a best-selling book, tried to show how consumers were being exploited even as they were first tasting the fruits of mass production. A year later, one of the authors, Schlink, founded Consumers Research Inc to carry out consumer product testing on a large scale, its purpose to provide research and information to consumers. This was the first time that consumer activism saw itself as enabling consumers to take best advantage of the market, rather than trying to undermine the market through co-operative action or political agitation and lobbying. In 1936, following a bitter confrontation over Schlink's authoritarian management, a group from Consumers Research Inc split to form the Consumers Union. This is now a huge organisation with around five million subscribers to its magazine *Consumer Reports*, which epitomises the principle of second wave consumerism, namely enabling its members to get best value for money by offering authoritative information. The principle of value-for-money took root in the consumer movement and reached its heyday in President John F. Kennedy's 1962 Consumer Message to Congress (Forbes, 1987: 37).

Some value-for-money organisations have grown into very substantial operations. The UK Consumers' Association's *Which?* magazine had a 700,000 subscriber list by the mid-1990s (down from a million at the start of the decade), while the Dutch Consumentenbond had a 660,000 membership, the highest of any consumer movement in the West proportionate to national population, and the Belgian *Test Achats*, whose own subscriber list is 320,000, has considerable extra weight due to its formal link up with similar Spanish, Portuguese and Italian groups who have 230,000, 150,000 and 350,000 subscribers respectively. Smaller organisations with the same ethos and publishing a regular magazine can be found in many other countries, such as Germany, Denmark, Australia, New Zealand, and even the newly independent Slovenia. These magazines test products for safety, ease of use, price, durability, task effectiveness, in short overall value-for-money. Readers are informed about the 'Best Buy' and warned about cons and bad buys. Large sums of money are spent testing the products, usually in the consumer organisation's own laboratories or test benches.

Unlike the co-operative movement, this second wave of consumer organisations has no pretensions of offering a radically different vision for society. Its adherents see their role as ameliorative, to make the market-place more efficient and to champion the interests of the consumer within it. Their aim is to inform and educate the consumer about the features which will enable them to act effectively as consumers (John, 1994). The value-for-money model places considerable stress on rights to information and labelling and redress if something goes wrong. John Winward, former Director of Research at the UK Consumers' Association, conceived of these non-profit organisations as 'information co-operatives' (Winward, 1993: 76–7).

Currently, second wave consumerism is facing a number of difficulties. On the one hand, post-Fordism and the proliferation of niche markets undermine the possibility of meaningful comparisons between broadly similar products. On the other hand, the number of subscribers of these organisations which had risen alongside rises in disposable income, began to drop from the early 1990s. This happened for a number of reasons.

First, the pace and impact of technological change meant that consumer organisations' capacity to deliver durable consumer information became harder. As producers delivered ever more nuanced 'niche' products into the market-place, product information was almost inevitably out of date almost before consumers got the data. Models of everything from cars to computers were driven by post-Fordist production.

Second, the emergence of retail giants across national borders gave unprecedented buying power to large retail corporations which could then offer consumers bargains that pitched them rather than consumer advocates as the consumers' champion. Retailers usurped the organisations as the consumers' friend.

And third, value-for-money second wave consumerism began to be hoist by its individualist stance. The main criticisms raised of second wave consumerism have been that it fails to address longer-term environmental and social issues; that it has an overwhelmingly middle-class orientation based on the assumption of ever increasing standards of living; that it disregards the plight of poorer consumers; and that it has an inappropriately conservative approach to consumption (Barker, 1994; Nicholson-Lord, 1994). Second wave consumerism has: 'rarely questioned the fundamental premise on which American industrialism is based: the desirability of technical efficiency and of technological and economic growth. Instead, consumerism has focused most of its attention on such problems as the lack of product safety or of adequate consumer information' (Bloom and Stern, 1978).

These criticisms apply to second wave consumerism everywhere, not just in the USA. However, they should not obscure the constraining effect that second wave groups have had on business. Their independence, their unwillingness to accept advertising revenue and their sometimes religious obsession with accuracy has given them an authority which companies and governments can only disregard at their cost.

THIRD WAVE: NADERISM

The third wave of consumer activism, like the second, emerged in the USA. Its figurehead, Ralph Nader, became one of the most admired US citizens in national polls for years, until his presidential campaign in 2000 was blamed by many for allowing George W. Bush to win the presidency; in 2004 he had little impact. Nader initially shot to prominence with the publication of his book *Unsafe At Any Speed* in 1965, his exposé of the car industry (Nader, 1991). The book argued that one automobile model in particular, the Chevrolet Corvair, and automobiles in general were poorly designed and had built-in safety short-cuts. The industry had resisted giving priority to safety, he alleged, a policy which according to Nader resulted in an annual slaughter of Americans: 51,000 in 1965. Highway accidents cost $8.3 billion in property damage, medical expenses, lost wages and insurance overhead expenses (1991: cii). Relying on independent tests, Nader showed how the Corvair easily went out of control at 22 miles per hour, contrasting with its advertising claims of 'easy handling', being 'a family sedan' and a car that 'purrs for the girls' (1991: 27). Yet the car's road-handling on corners meant that it demanded 'more driving skill in order to avoid collision than any other American automobile'. As though that was not bad enough, he catalogued how General Motors had failed to come clean on the Corvair's design faults. In consumer movement terms, what marked Nader's approach as special was not only that he generalised from the particular, documenting how the Corvair may have been an extreme case of consumer safety being a low priority, but that he spelt out at great length how the case was only the tip of an iceberg. His perspective – much expanded and expounded – posited the consumer activist against the corporate giants. In so doing, he brilliantly voiced the interests of mainstream as well as radical consumers emerging in the phenomenally affluent US society of the 1960s.

Nader, a Harvard educated lawyer, set up the Center for Study of Responsive Law and the Project for Corporate Responsibility in 1969. By the end of the 1970s he had spawned a series of organisations, staffed by young professionals, nicknamed 'Nader's Raiders', many of them lawyers like himself. By the 1990s there were 29 organisations with combined revenues of $75–80 million under the Nader umbrella (Brimelow and Spencer, 1990). The common themes of these organisations were a distrust of corporations, a defence of the individual against the giants, a demand that the state protect its citizens and above all, an appeal for Americans to be citizens, not just consumers. Naderism assumed that the consumer is relatively powerless in a world dominated by corporate giants, whether these be automobile or insurance companies, the health sector or the government–industry complex. The nature of commerce is stacked against the customer, unless regulations or standards of conduct are fought for. This is a hard fight, so the consumer organisations have to be tough, well briefed, well organised and able to make optimum use of the mass media.

Nader brought a new punch to consumer politics and tapped a deep well of public unease about the power of large corporations *vis-à-vis* the individual customer. He saw the role of consumer organisations as going beyond getting the consumer the best deal in the market, and confronting the market itself. Writing about the US food industry in 1970, for instance, Nader made a number of charges about what it will do if left to its own devices:

> Making food appear what it is not is an integral part of the $125 billion [US] food industry. The deception ranges from the surface packaging to the integrity of the food products' quality to the very shaping of food tastes ... Company economy very often was the consumer's cost and hazard. As a result, competition became a way of beating one's competitor by racing for the lowest permissible common denominator. (Nader, 1970: v)

The role of the state, in the absence of consumer pressure, is to collude with this downward spiral, which disadvantages good businesses. The consumer activist's role was and is to confront, to expose, to stand up for public rights, to be a citizen. A persistent theme is to bring the corporate state under the control of democratic forces, and away from the grip of big business (Krebs, 1992: 440–3).

Like the second wave of the consumer movement, Naderism is adamant on the role of information and that it should be free and fair. If the first wave saw capitalism as something to be stepped away from (co-ops are non-profit organisations that share out rather than accumulate or privatise profits), the second wave sees its own role as that of providing information for the consumer to be able to operate more effectively in the market-place. And the third wave, Naderism, sees capitalism as something to be accepted but which has to be worked hard on to prevent its excesses becoming its norms.

Naderism places great emphasis on information from consumer bodies as debunking the misinformation systematically disseminated by companies. Nader has described the situation thus: 'It is time for consumers to have information that will provide them with an effective understanding of the secrecy-clouded situation' (Nader, 1970: vii). Freedom of information – rather than product information or mere labelling on a packet – has been a persistent theme for Nader. Indeed, he helped inspire the UK Campaign for Freedom of Information in its uphill task to reform the British state's reflex for secrecy. For Nader, secrecy is often a collusion between state and commercial interests, and it is the duty of the consumer activist to break that collusion, or else she or he become an accomplice to it. Only vigilant consumers can break the pact, said Nader:

> Major corporations like their consumers to remain without a capacity for group purchasing action, group legal action, group participating action before regulatory agencies ... The possibility that consumers banding together can muster their organised intelligence to play a major role in shaping economic policy and the future of our political economy is an unsettling one for the mega corporations that play much of the world's economy. So too would be an organised consumer initiative to assess the hazards of technology or forestall the marketing of products which use consumers as test subjects or guinea pigs. (quoted in Beishon, 1994: 9)

Nader's views have fed on the deep apprehension of American consumers, and the public in general, towards anything big and unfettered corporate power in particular. Unlike second wave organisations, Nader and his colleagues believe that only active involvement by citizens at the local level can counteract these forces. Whereas second wave groups are reformist and 'top-down' in their strategies, preferring lobbies to rallies, Naderism has been equally content to lobby and rally, priding itself upon building up grassroots citizen action. In the market-place, the message is to be frugal, to get wise in 'the vital art of self defense' to 'protect yourself in the market-place', whether buying a car, health insurance, food or a house (Nader and Smith, 1992). These are terms which echo the early American nonimportation movement (Witkowski, 1989).

Unlike second wave consumerism, Naderism, though admired, has not easily been grafted onto the consumer cultures of other countries. Neither the political culture nor the legal system or the scale of consumption in other countries has until recently favoured the growth of Nader-like organisations. But with global de-regulation in the 1990s, and the emergence of regional trade blocs such as the European Union and the North American Free Trade Agreement (NAFTA), Naderism's persistent charge at the collusion of big business and the state has found new allies. These have included environmental groups, animal welfare groups, trades unions, as well as other consumer groups (Lang and Hines, 1993).

Consumers' International, formerly the International Organisation of Consumers Unions (IOCU), is a global network founded in 1960, which has over 250 affiliated organisations from 115 countries (Consumers International, 2004). These vary in size and wealth, with the larger and wealthier tending to be in affluent Western countries, but activists are strong in developing countries too and the Western groups have funded consumer activism in new markets of the South and, for instance, in the former Eastern bloc after the USSR collapsed in the late 1980s. Developing countries have produced a new generation of consumer activists such as Anwar Fazal, Martin Khor, and others, who not only have applied the lessons of Naderism in their own countries but have taken on corporations outside their national boundaries. They have been particularly active in the anti-globalisation movement from the 1990s. Developing countries, they argue, are particularly vulnerable to the globalisation of capital, equally for the well-being of their consumers, as for their workers. Consumers International members believe that developing and protecting consumers' rights and their awareness of their responsibilities are integral to the eradication of poverty, good governance, social justice and respect for human rights, fair and effective market economies and the protection of the environment (Consumers International, 2004).

FOURTH WAVE: ALTERNATIVE CONSUMERS

A new wave of consumer organisations emerged slowly in the 1970s and accelerated in the 1980s, which in 1995 we termed 'alternative consumerism'. A decade ago, we sensed that while this fourth wave had many elements – green, ethical, Third World solidarity and fair trade orientations – it as yet lacked any overall coherence. In the last decade of the twentieth century, that coherence, we believe began to emerge.

Of the strands we outlined, at the end of the 1980s the most influential was green consumerism. This stemmed from a new environmental consciousness to consume wisely in a manner that did not damage the capacity of future generations to consume at all. Green consumers should protect the environment in a number of ways, from purchasing more environmentally-friendly products to resisting consumption altogether. For the first time since the early Co-operative movement, consumers were offered a message to influence production directly: buy this rather than that product and you can help 'good' producers to out-compete 'bad' producers. 'Good' and 'bad' were defined in environmental terms. Suddenly, the environment movement shifted from being oppositional to staking a claim in the market-place. The impact was significant, although right from its onset, some argued that it would be temporary (Cairncross, 1991: 153).

The green consumer movement began in Europe and spread west to North America. As Cairncross noted 'the sheer speed with which green consumerism erupted in some countries will also leave its mark' (1991: 189). Seemingly overnight, aerosols with CFCs and apples with pesticide residues became no-go areas in the supermarket. The green consumer movement forced companies to listen to them and spawned new ranges of products such as phosphate-free detergents and cars with recyclable components which gave consumers the option of choosing 'green'. Often these products, however, remained at the margins of mainstream consumption. Perhaps the more important role of green consumerism was to question market supremacy that had dominated the 1980s. Green consumerism represented a significant shift from the rampant individualism, short-termism and venality of the Reagan–Thatcher years, assuming the role of primary opposition to the New Right.

One effect of pressure from green consumer groups was that companies started to undertake environmental audits as a way of gaining competitive advantage over their competitors, and fending off criticism (see Chapter 13 in this book). One branch of green consumer activism monitored companies and pursued an approach akin to that of second wave consumerism by comparing products for their environmental soundness and the green credentials of the company that produced them (Elkington and Hailes, 1988). Its fundamental message was less apocalyptic than it was in the early 1970s and more accommodating to productionism. 'Consume carefully' it proclaimed rather than 'don't consume' or 'consume less'.

By the early twenty-first century, environmentalism had fragmented, with green consumerism a niche in the mainstream. A whole new category of green businesses and green product ranges had consolidated ranging from cosmetics to electrical goods and even cars, leading to a green producer–consumer nexus, where environmentalists began to act as referees of corporate behaviour. Green consumer activism had generated another niche in the product mix on offer. It is up to the consumer to chose whether to save or destroy the planet. (Chapters 6, 11 and 14 provide further details of the growth of green consumer markets.)

But the tension between the reformists and radicals continued. In one camp, lay the proponents of a more caring, considerate capitalism: use purchasing power to reduce energy use (von Weizacher et al., 1998). In the other, those who argued that the thrust of green consumers should be to consume less altogether (Irvine,1989). In some respects, the first camp was charged by the latter with coming to the rescue of consumer capitalism and giving it new opportunities for niche products, at the very moment when traditional markets were being saturated.

Like earlier generations of reformers, green activists have been victims of their own success, a process recognised by activists themselves, many of whom have harboured no illusions about the limitations of green activism when restricted to consumption. As a result, radical segments within the movement advocated the case for more structural change (Irvine, 1989).

If green consumerism became mainstream by the early 1990s, by the early 2000s, another previously fringe strand had become the high profile new entrant: ethical consumption. Reaffirming the moral dimension of consumer choice, ethical consumerism initially seemed doomed to the margins (much as these authors willed it to succeed). Who would push its case? Who would fund the necessary organisations? Yet that funding and support emerged. In the UK, the fair trade-oriented New Consumer organisation rose and fell, but the Ethical Consumer Research Association (ECRA) consolidated and thrived. In the USA, the Council on Economic Priorities introduced a guide which rated 1,300 US brands thus: 'Every time you step up to a cash register, you vote. When you switch from one brand to another, companies hear you clearly. You can help make America's companies socially responsible by using this guide' (Will et al., 1989: 143). Ethical consumer groups grade products and companies on criteria such as nuclear power, factory farming and genetic engineering, and have been covered in more detail in Chapter 5 in this book.

These criteria have altered and deepened since the 1990s (Adams, R. et al., 1991; ECRA, 1993). When the Ethical Consumer Research Association was founded in Manchester, close to Rochdale of pioneer fame, in the late 1980s, it was advised not to use the word 'consumer' in its title 'because the word is too narrow a definition of what people do' (Rob Harrison, personal interview with the authors, February 1994). The word 'consumer' places an emphasis on only one aspect of people's behaviour, one which tends to deny the political and moral goals the organisation had come into existence to promote. By the mid-1990s, Rob Harrison of Ethical Consumer argued that the organisation's goal is really to change culture and to promote a consumer awareness of the global implications of Western consumption. Issues such as fair trade, aid and exploitation of Third World workers far from being marginal to the ethics and politics of Western consumption lie at its very heart (Wells and Jetter, 1991).

The fair trade movement has sought to encourage links between the producers and workers of the South and the consumers of the North, by delivering products from developing countries directly to rich consumer markets. It asks consumers to buy these products in part because they return more money to the original producer than does conventional trade and in part as a way of supporting non-exploitative firms operating in the South. In this way they hope to revitalise the old co-operators' goal of bringing the consumer and producer into closer relationship (Barratt Brown, 1993: 184–6).

One particularly successful product in Europe, for instance, has been a coffee branded as Cafédirect in the UK and as Max Havelaar in the Netherlands, named after a famous Dutch novel of the same name, published in 1860, which denounced the use of slaves in the coffee trade, an early appeal to consumers (Mulatuli, 1987). This coffee was adopted by the European Parliament as its official brand. The Cafédirect brand sold its millionth packet in 1994, just two years after its launch. By 2004, fair trade was an important force in 17 affluent food countries, particularly for product sectors such as tea, confectionary and coffee, linking 350 commodity producers, representing 4.5 million farmers in developing countries, to developed world markets (Fairtrade Foundation, 2004b).

THE FUTURE: CONVERGENCE OR CONTINUED DIVERGENCE?

Since we outlined our waves of consumer activism, a number of important changes have occurred all of which point to some convergence and cross-fertilisation across the waves of activism.

First, the fourth wave's ethical and environmental values began to be absorbed by the dominant and powerful second wave or value-for-money consumer groups. Corporate social responsibility advocates became influential in auditing company behaviour. The crises and bankruptcies of giant firms such as Enron in the USA and Parmalat in Italy encouraged financiers to see the economic value of viewing companies through an ethical and longer-term filter (Harrison, 2003). CSR has been a response to consumer activists whose legitimacy grew with the crises.

Second, co-operatives, the first wave, took note of, helped and began to adopt the vitality and appeal of the fourth wave by making new commitments to position co-operatives as more trustworthy sources of the necessities of life. The Co-operative Bank's pioneering return to ethics-led banking had been proven to be good business as well as ethical. Co-op food retailing followed suit launching its Responsible Retailing campaign in 1995 and consolidating this in 2004 (Co-operative Group, 2004).

Third, in December 1999, the disparate strands of consumer activism came together in Seattle in opposition to the proposed revision of the World Trade Organisation's General Agreement on Tariffs and Trade. In the 1990s, the single issue groups had learned that they shared a more common agenda than had been realised. Anti-globalisation became part of consumer activism (Klein, 2000; Vidal, 1997).

Fourth, as we argued in our notion of the 'twilight of consumerism', a certain *s* set in within consumer society. As Alan Durning asked: How much is enough? (Durning, 1992). How much can one consume? There are no signs of an end to consumption – far from it – but the activists began to feel the law of diminishing returns. Ethical consumption began to experience what green consumerism had undergone a decade earlier. Might the activists burn themselves out or, worse, win the publicity war but not alter mass consumer behaviour? Cheap airfares and cheap food still win more consumer 'votes' than the social issues, however much the polls suggest consumers want to act honourably.

One of the most effective globally organised consumer activist campaigns, the International Baby Foods Action Network (IBFAN) has been struggling for over three decades to achieve its ends. This heroic campaign has much to teach consumer activists (Gabriel and Lang, 1995). Is the consumer as activist doomed to struggle endlessly against the odds, only achieving 'success' if it is narrowly defined? (Clouder and Harrison review the effectiveness generally of consumer actions in Chapter 6.)

The consumer as activist struggles daily to redefine the notion of progress and quality of life, to pursue happiness by consumption and to promote or create debate. Crucially, it is the consumer as activist who confronts consumption, explicitly seeking to alter its meaning and to redefine the cultural dynamic of goods by reintroducing the validity of the idea of needs and wants. Few movements apart from the feminist and gay movements have had such a discernible effect in truly remoulding culture. And yet the consumer as activist seems to be the great absentee from many celebrations of contemporary consumer culture. This absence has left discussions on the subject seriously impoverished.

CONCLUSION

From this short review, very different strands of consumer activism emerge. Some are summarised in Table 3.1.

Consumer activists' efforts and successes constitute a stubborn rejection of the anarchism of the market, by persistently stressing that right and wrong, damaging and beneficial, useless and useful, needs and wants are concepts which cannot be written out of consumption. The vast majority of consumers recognise these terms even as they continue to be driven heavily but not exclusively by price, to be tempted by advertising and to be seduced by images. Ironically, consumer activists today perhaps achieve influence less in the market-place and more via public relations departments of companies which are now so finely tuned to neutralise or reduce any potential shocks such as activists can deliver.

Many activists acknowledge that consumer capitalism can redefine itself in ways which accommodate many of their demands. This may take the form of creating niche markets for ethical or green products (see Chapter 14) or by accepting a degree of regulation as a necessity for its continuing legitimation. Some consumer activists recognise this as an inevitable limitation of much reformist activity. This in no way annihilates the value of their efforts or undermines the objectives, but does mean that there is a ceaseless process of incorporation and accommodation, as ideas are 'cherry-picked' and modifications are made to products and processes, ranging from slight to significant. Cynics might argue that this relegates ethical consumption and other progressive movements to a process of being unpaid revisionists of advanced capitalism. In some respects, this might be true, and is inevitable, but in important ways their contribution lies in acting as the moral conscience of the existing system, a set of principles that is above price or minor product amelioration and diversification. Others go further and view palliative reform as inadequate in stopping the ruinous path of consumer capitalism. For them, the concept of the consumer must now be itself overcome, having

Table 3.1 Some dimensions of consumer activism

Dimension of activism	Ranges from	To
Organisational form	Individual consumerist 'heroes'	Collectivist
Size of organisation	Small	Large
Range of action	Single issue	Entire consumer culture
Focus of action	The state	Corporations
Nature of activism	Direct action	Sentiment
Values	Reform markets	Constrain or reduce markets

become fatally flawed and compromised. Only by redefining how they think and act as consumers, can individuals today individually and collectively recover some of the control which they have lost to the organisations and objects which now dominate their lives and through which they express themselves.

In this important sense, ethical consumption maps one clear path for consumers, a route for translating consumerism into citizenship, consumer/citizen being one conventional ideological contrast. Much as we would like consumers to take the 'high' road, evidence suggests that there are powerful forces pushing and pulling consumers in different and 'low' roads too. Ethical consumption, by internalising otherwise externalised social, environmental and human costs, almost inevitably adds to the price of goods and services. Ultimately, we feel, ethical consumption has to be open about this fact. If humanity wants a decent society, it has to be paid for. If it doesn't, or enough don't, society and the biosphere will pay anyway. The stakes are high.

Pressure Groups, Campaigns and Consumers

4

Rob Harrison

INTRODUCTION

Although ethical purchase behaviour has been observed for centuries (see for example, Smith, 1990b), the flowering of ethical consumer activity around the world over the last twenty years appears to be unprecedented. In order to understand why this is happening it is necessary to examine the political context in which these developments are taking place.

In the first part of this chapter, seven key political trends driving this growth are identified. The main proposition here is that the growth of ethical purchase behaviour is not just a spontaneous maturing of individual consumer awareness, but is also a phenomenon deliberately driven by pressure groups seeking to achieve a variety of specific campaign goals in a globalised world. Many groups have discovered that campaigning for change by seeking to manipulate or influence markets can be a quick and effective way of addressing particular social and environmental problems, and are therefore campaigning in this way more frequently. In other words, it is argued that ethical consumer behaviours are, in many cases, a form of collective action.

The second part of this chapter looks at the idea of the 'market campaign'. It explains how persuading consumers to act ethically is often just one element of a broader campaign which may involve other activities such as shareholder actions, political lobbying, pickets and non-violent direct action. Four case studies which illustrate the variety of approaches are discussed – two are primarily boycotts and two are primarily positive buying campaigns.

The third part looks at how the growth of market campaigning has created a blurring at the edges of what it means to be a campaign group and a commercial company respectively. It is suggested that, with companies like the Body Shop campaigning against animal testing, and with development charities forming fair trade subsidiaries, the separate worlds of trading and campaigning are beginning to merge.

The final part looks at how the growth of market campaigning is affecting some broader ideas. Perhaps the most significant of these are the ideas of 'civil regulation' and 'citizen consumers'. In the conclusion it is argued that should the seven political trends continue, then further growth of ethical purchase behaviour should be expected as a wider variety of pressure groups discover the efficacy of market campaigning.

PART 1: FACTORS INFLUENCING THE GROWTH OF ETHICAL CONSUMER BEHAVIOURS

To some extent it is possible to look at a list of ethical consumer actions (such as those outlined in Chapter 6) and to observe that they tend to have elements in common. They often address global issues, like whaling or deforestation, or the consequences of technological innovation such as GM food. They are commonly orchestrated by single-issue pressure groups and directed at prominent brands of transnational corporations. From observations such as these it is possible to derive a hypothesis of potential causal factors behind the growth of ethical consumer behaviours, and this is the broad approach used to identify the seven trends discussed below. Of course it should be noted that many of these trends are highly complex and interlinking, and it is only possible to address each very briefly in a chapter of this length.

Globalisation of markets and the weakening of national governments

There has been a rapid globalisation of markets in the second half of the twentieth century. One consequence of this is that the ability of national governments to regulate company behaviour has weakened. This weakening is occurring:

a) directly – through the ceding of rights to regulate markets to supranational institutions such as the WTO, EU or NAFTA, and
b) indirectly – through competitive pressures. It is commonly recognised that governments offering less regulation are able to attract greater levels of capital investment (for example see Korten, 1995).

It is argued below that, to some extent, citizens appear to be stepping in to attempt 'civil regulation' of company behaviour in some circumstances. And in many cases, campaigners have explicitly pointed to failure to regulate as a reason to launch a market campaign. For example, Friends of the Earth UK cited the lack of success by the official conference on the Convention on International Trade in Endangered Species (CITES) to protect mahogany, as increasing the pressure for a consumer boycott (ECRA, 1995a: 24). Part 2 of this chapter on market campaigning also observes lack of regulation as a spur to action in the cases of peat extraction in the UK and FSC timber labelling.

Other commentators have also commented on this process. Brass and Koziell for example have noted how people:

> ...feel that public institutions and the Government are too busy trying to compete in the global market economy to actually listen to the needs and ideas of...individuals and communities...many of them have tried conventional channels for change, but have got so fed up with the lack of response that they have decided to take matters into their own hands. And it is not just a question of having to wait too long for things to get better, increasing numbers of people are coming to the conclusion that their needs will never be addressed by those in power. (1997: 7)

The rise of transnational corporations

Profit-seeking businesses, such as Nestlé and Citigroup, have grown to become dominant global institutions, with financial resources far exceeding those of national governments in many instances (Korten, 1995). There are three factors particularly worthy of note here.

First, much has been written about how corporations appear to have 'captured' many regulatory processes through lobbying, and are intensifying the pressure to free them from government interference (see for example, Greider, 1992; Monbiot, 2000). Second, the pursuit of profit in competitive markets has the tendency to reward those companies which can externalise (or pass on to society) costs most effectively (see for example, Daly and Cobb, 1989: 51). In other words, companies without costly emissions controls or workers' rights may be able to produce cheaper products than those which have sought to act more responsibly. Third, despite their great financial power, those companies with brands in consumer markets are both highly visible and vulnerable to attack from organisations objecting to particular activities (see for example, Klein, 2000). These three factors all contribute to make market campaigning more, rather than less, likely.

The rise of single-issue pressure groups

In the past, political analysts viewed pressure groups as seeking primarily to promote their members interests. Groups fitting this description would include the National Farmers Union and the Confederation of British Industry. However, the 1960s, 1970s and 1980s saw the proliferation of a more altruistic type of group. Such groups have been described using a variety of terms including 'cause groups' (Grant, 2000), 'public interest groups' (Libby, 1998), 'promotional pressure groups' (Smith, 1990b), 'NGOs' (Murphy and Bendell, 2001), and 'expressive interest groups' (Libby, 1998). The rather dated expression 'single-issue pressure groups' has been used here, partly because it allows comparisons with private interest groups later in the chapter.

Groups fitting the description of this newer type would include Friends of the Earth, People for the Ethical Treatment of Animals, and Amnesty International. One UK study in 1998 (Grant, 2000: 3) found that membership of environmental organisations had quadrupled since 1970. Another study in the USA (Berry, 1989: 34) found that half of expressive groups surveyed were established between 1972 and 1986.

Some have argued that such groups have emerged because new levels of economic security after World War II made possible the pursuit of postmaterial or quality-of-life concerns (Inglehart, 1977). Although this may be true to some extent, it is also clear that many groups have been formed specifically to address new issues resulting from some of the trends discussed here such as globalisation and technological change. In addition, some goals like environmental sustainability are quite legitimately seen as enlightened (or long-termist) self-interest rather than as a purely ethical position. It is further recognised that the communications revolutions – fax and internet – have enhanced the ability of pressure groups to mobilise public support for their cause (Berry, 1977: 280). The falling cost of computing power, and with it enhanced organisational capacity, are also likely to have helped the expansion of this sector in the last two decades.

Lastly, it is worth noting that many analysts of pressure group activity have discussed how the ideas of cause groups and social movements are interlinked (Byrne, 1997; Grant, 2000: 10; Jordan, 1998; Libby, 1998: 7). Civil rights, feminism and environmentalism are all examples of social movements. In many cases over the last thirty years, political change is commonly attributed to broad social movements rather than to individual cause groups (Grant, 2000: 10). According to Rucht (1996) key characteristics of social movements are:

a) they are not formally organised or hierarchically controlled
b) they comprise a network of cause groups
c) they have a well of individual grassroots supporters.

It is almost exclusively these cause groups and/or social movements which have begun to use and develop market campaigns and ethical consumer behaviour to further their goals. We discuss below how the drive for corporate social responsibility can itself be viewed as a social movement.

Technological change

The fourth factor driving ethical consumer behaviour is technological change, which is moving at its own pace, independent of other factors. The introduction of powerful new technologies can bring enormous benefits and, at the same time, threaten social relationships, environments, animal welfare and human health. In democratic societies it is quite right that public debate should focus on the extent to which new technologies benefit the common good. And where technologies – such as human cloning – are found to be generally unacceptable, it is inevitable that societies will reject and prohibit their use.

The classic example of social movements using consumer pressure to respond to a new technology occurred during the development of genetically modified organisms (GMOs). According to Lasley and Bultena: 'Biotechnology is the third wave of technology, after the mechanical revolutions of the nineteenth century and the petrochemical revolution that began in the 1940s and reached its zenith during the 1970s' (1986). Biotechnology therefore appeared at the very time when globalisation of markets and regulatory capture made prohibition so difficult. It is for this reason that market campaigns against GM food became the logical approach of cause groups opposed to their introduction.

Other technological advances which brought market campaign responses include nuclear power and the Siemens boycott in Germany (ECRA, 1994: 6), nuclear weapons and the INFACT boycotts (INFACTa, 2004), and BST (bovine growth hormone) and various associated campaigns (Libby, 1998: 49). It is also worth noting that some animal welfare campaigns – such as the free range egg response to battery hens – are also, in some senses, a response to technological change.

Of course, not all market campaigns are a response to technological changes. For example, a whole host of campaigns addressing workers' rights in low wage economies are responding not to technological change but to globalisation itself.

A shift in market power towards consumers

It has been commonly recognised that there has been 'a tilt in market power from producer to consumer...[over]...the last thirty or so years' (Scammell, 2003). Ironically, perhaps, the very forces of economic globalisation and de-regulation which are disempowering national governments, have significantly increased choice and competition, which in turn is shifting the balance of power away from companies and towards consumers. Digital technology is also playing a part in accelerating this power shift by providing consumers with comprehensive and instantly available information about products, companies and prices. This 'democratisation of the information environment' is discussed elsewhere by Philip Kotler amongst others (Kotler et al., 2002).

The effectiveness of market campaigns

One reason for the increase in market campaigning has been its demonstrable effectiveness in achieving campaign goals. Pressure groups can observe other groups wresting significant concessions from corporations and can identify the potential for similar actions in their own spheres of interest. (The effectiveness of ethical consumer behaviour is addressed in Chapter 6, and so is not considered further here.) A number of successful campaigns are also reviewed in the next section below.

The corporate accountability movement

Vogel (1978) in 'Lobbying the corporation: citizen challenges to business authority' is one of the earliest writers to propose the existence of a corporate accountability movement. He suggests that many of its origins lie in the civil rights protests and boycotts of the mid-1950s, as well as in the later protests against businesses involved in the Vietnam war (1978: 23). Of course more that twenty-five years have passed since Vogel's seminal work, and the movement itself has increased considerably in sophistication and size (Bendell, 2004). The corporate accountability movement has not only been able to share information quickly on specific campaigns against specific companies, but also to marshal and develop powerful intellectual arguments for corporate responsibility generally.

At the core of the corporate accountability movement are institutions concerned with ethical investment or socially responsibly investment – such as the Social Investment Forums in the UK and USA, and the Interfaith Centre on Corporate Responsibility in the USA. They co-ordinate shareholder actions as well as publish research on issues such as the performance of screened investments. In the UK, institutions involved in the corporate accountability movement, such as Friends of the Earth, have set up a campaign specifically to lobby the UK government for new regulatory requirements on companies to disclose social and environmental impacts as part of their annual public reporting requirements (Friends of the Earth, 2004).

All these activities within the corporate accountability movement therefore help to provide an intellectual framework for ethical consumer action and further help to encourage its use. In the next part of this chapter, we will also see how the corporate accountability movement can help simultaneously to bring different types of pressure against companies in a concerted market campaign.

PART TWO: THE MARKET CAMPAIGN

In one of the most analysed corporate campaigns of recent years (see for example, Rose, 1998), in 1995 Greenpeace activists occupied the Brent Spar oil storage facility to prevent it being sunk in the North Atlantic as part of a low-cost disposal strategy. Spontaneous consumer boycotts of Shell petrol around the world saw sales fall by 70 per cent in some German outlets and led to a spectacular change in policy by the company (ECRA, 1995b: 3). Although this campaign illustrates how non-violent direct action can bring sufficient publicity for a campaign to have a serious impact in consumer markets it is, in many ways, atypical of the slower, more deliberate, market campaigns that have come to characterise the movement.

In this section, four brief case studies provide an illustration of how a typical market campaign will seek and encourage consumer participation. Two cases concern, primarily, consumer boycotts and two concern, primarily, positive buying. They also illustrate how contemporary pressure groups can bring a sophisticated scientific analysis of markets, companies and issues to the design strategies which will best achieve their political goals.

The Campbell's Soup boycott 1979–86

The campaign began as a route to improve working conditions for the mainly Hispanic migrant farmworkers who harvested crops in Ohio. In the 1970s, employment of child labour was rife, as were 12-hour working days, hazardous working conditions and low pay (ECRA, 1989a: 10). In 1978 the local Farm Labour Organising Committee (FLOC) began a series of strikes which failed to draw the multinational food processors who bought the crops into an agreement to improve conditions. Impressed by the successful boycotts of Californian grapes in the late 1960s, FLOC called for a boycott of the Campbell Soup Company's products in 1979.

By 1981 the boycott was receiving support from trades unions around the world as well as widespread media coverage – including a BBC TV programme about the problem of child labour (ECRA, 1989a: 11). In July 1983, FLOC used a 540-mile month-long march from Ohio to the Campbell's Soup HQ to bring publicity to its cause, and engaged a group of specialist campaign consultants who organised advertising for the boycott in the *New York Times*. Church groups across the USA were also becoming involved, and in 1984 sponsored a shareholders' resolution on the issue at Campbell's AGM.

By 1985 the National Council of Churches (representing 41 million members) became involved and their threat to join the boycott brought Campbell's to the negotiating table. On 21 February 1986, Campbell's signed an agreement with FLOC which guaranteed minimum standards for working conditions at its suppliers. On the same day, Heinz announced a willingness to enter into a similar agreement. A Campbell's spokesman at the time of the agreement denied that sales had been affected by the boycott, but that they were concerned that the corporate image had suffered (ECRA, 1989a: 11).

This early corporate campaign illustrates how a number of complementary strategies – including shareholder actions, marches and boycotts – contributed sufficient pressure to create the changes desired.

WWF and the FSC – the classic partnership approach

In the early 1990s, the conservation pressure group the World Wildlife Fund (WWF) was becoming disillusioned in the UK with the potential of international negotiation to deliver real change in the rate of destruction of the world's forests. Murphy and Bendell (2001: 295) quoted Francis Sullivan, the WWF Forests Officer: 'You cannot just sit back and wait for governments to agree, because this could take forever.'

At the same time, UK timber retailers were coming under increasing pressure from direct action campaigners. In 1991, both Friends of the Earth UK (FoE) and autonomous rainforest action groups were staging 'Chainsaw massacres' outside home improvement and furniture stores. A group of businesses joined with WWF to seek a solution to the issue, and soon realised that a credible system for certifying sustainably sourced timber was required. In 1993 the Forest Stewardship Council (FSC) was launched with both NGO and business support, and by 1996 the FSC had offered the first global mechanism for guaranteeing good forest management with its independent accreditation of four certifying bodies (Murphy and Bendell, 2001: 295). During this period, other NGOs were continuing to put pressure on industry bodies, with FoE calling a boycott of all mahogany in February 1995 (Friends of the Earth, 1995).

The FSC logo now appears on hundreds of different consumer products and is widely recognised as one of the most dramatic success stories for ethical purchasing campaigns. It accounts for over 20 per cent of all wood products sold in the UK (WWF UK, 2004), and through a network of similar national initiatives in more than 30 countries, 42 million hectares of forest have been certified (FSC, 2004). According to Murphy and Bendell, 'the case of deforestation and the timber trade illustrates the three key ways NGOs are influencing business: forcing change, facilitating change and sustaining change' (2001: 296). In order to sustain this change, environmental campaign groups even now continue to urge their supporters to select FSC products.

Peat extraction in the UK – 1990 to the present

Peat is a growing medium popular with gardeners but it is being extracted unsustainably from delicate habitats across northern Europe. The campaign to end extraction in the UK is highly complex and can only be discussed briefly here. At the core of the campaign has been FoE UK which in the early stages of the campaign openly admitted that it had three targets (ECRA, 1990b: 18): consumers – who should avoid peat products; industry – which should produce peat alternatives; government – which should ban commercial extraction.

The campaign has involved calls for consumer boycotts, both of peat itself and of the companies supplying it (ECRA, 2002e). It has also encouraged organisational purchasers to join the campaign both by targeting them directly and by producing extensive product and technical guides. It involved one of the earliest shareholder actions in the UK when some local authority pension funds, co-ordinated by Pensions Investment Research Consultants, forced a response from peat-extractor Fisons plc at the company's 1990 AGM (Sparkes et al., 1995: 80). In February 2002, the campaign also employed non-violent direct action when protestors occupied seven offices, factories or extraction sites of the offending company (Scotts) in a National Day of Action (ECRA, 2002e).

From the beginning of the campaign, the Peatlands Campaign Consortium provided a networking and co-ordinating role for the other wildlife, environmental and archaeological groups involved in the campaign. Members of the consortium included the Royal Society for the Protection of Birds, WWF, Plantlife, Butterfly Conservation and the Wildfowl and Wetlands Trust (Friends of the Earth, 1997). Although the campaign is still ongoing, the most scientifically sensitive areas were saved through the purchase of sites by the government (ECRA, 2002e). It is worth noting that in Germany, where planning permission for peat cutting was revoked without compensation in the 1970s, no similar grassroots campaign emerged (ECRA, 1990b).

Cafédirect

Cafédirect is the most successful fair trade brand in the UK, and its widespread distribution through mainstream supermarkets has provided millions of consumers with the opportunity to purchase ethically. It was founded in 1991 by four partner organisations:

- Oxfam – the UK's biggest development charity;
- Traidcraft – a Christian not-for-profit company and the largest importer of fair trade craft products;
- Equal exchange – a workers' co-operative and one of the first groups to import solidarity coffees from Nicaragua and Tanzania into the UK;
- Twin Trading – a not-for-profit company helping groups in developing countries to reach UK markets.

Although it now has a large range of tea, coffee and cocoa products its initial purpose was to address problems for coffee producers in developing countries following the collapse of the International Coffee Agreement in 1989 (Cafédirect, 2004). Its aim was to introduce a fairly traded coffee from multiple smallholders available through mainstream supermarkets.

After oil, coffee is the most important internationally traded commodity, with 75 per cent of production exported. Coffee farmers had become exposed to financial insecurity, and many were becoming desperate when prices fell to a thirty-year low that year. In 1992 its first product, a ground coffee, was trialled in Co-operative and Safeway supermarkets in Scotland. The trials were successful and in 1993 the products gained nationwide distribution in those stores. It launched its first instant coffee in 1994 which grew to take 3.7 per cent of the total UK market in ten years (Cafédirect, 2004). Cafédirect is now the sixth largest coffee brand in the UK and with sales of around £20 million, accounts for about 20 per cent of all UK fair trade sales. Its partnership programmes with more than 30 farmers' co-operatives in 11 countries have had positive impacts on the lives of more than 250,000 growers worldwide (Cafédirect, 2004).

The roots of its success lie in its focus on traditional commercial values like product quality, branding and marketing. According to Zadek et al. 'Cafédirect seems to be having a knock-on effect on the behaviour of multinationals selling coffee, which maybe is its most important contribution to human development' (1998b). In 2004, it was also apparent that the two largest coffee multinationals, Nestlé and Kraft, were experimenting with their own 'fair trade' products (Cafédirect, 2004; Global Exchange, 2003). Oxfam has continued to address issues in the coffee market generally through publications such as *Mugged: Poverty in Your Coffee Cup* (Oxfam, 2002). Cafédirect has also continued to provide a positive ethical alternative for consumers concerned with other problems in the behaviour of coffee companies – such as Nestlé's controversial sale of baby milk substitutes and Kraft's connection to the tobacco manufacturer Philip Morris.

PART 3: TRADING CAMPAIGNERS AND CAMPAIGNING TRADERS

At this stage it makes sense to consider how the growth of market campaigning is beginning to create a blurring at the edges of what it means to be a campaign group on the one hand, and what it means to be a trader on the other. This could, to some extent, compliment another trend among more mainstream businesses to reconsider their core purposes and to adopt more holistic goals such as the 'triple bottom line' (Sustainability, 2004). And if the trends driving market campaigning continue, then we can predict that this blurring is also likely to grow in significance in the future.

For example, in the case of Cafédirect above, is the organisation best described as a company or a campaign group? Its formal structure is an ordinary company limited by shares, but its shareholders are not-for-profit organisations. Quite rightly it seeks to generate a profit or surplus from its trading to reinvest in the growth of the business, but then this growth must also mean a greater pace of social change. Nevertheless, it could also be described as a successful campaign organisation for human welfare in the global coffee industry.

Clearly Cafédirect has aspects of both types of organisation and could therefore be described as something else, such as a campaigning trader. From a consumer's point of view buying a product from a campaigning trader could be described as one of the newest forms of political participation, adding to campaign group or party membership, and financial support for parties or cause groups, in the traditional way. Of course, Cafédirect is not a typical organisation, and in most cases an organisation falls more generally into one or other camp as described here as trading campaigners or campaigning traders.

Trading campaigners

On 15 March 1993 the first 'green fridges' using the naturally occurring gasses propane and butane, were launched by Foron in Germany (ECRA, 1993: 3). German Greenpeace instigated their production by finding a manufacturer in East

Germany which was willing to develop a model based on a Greenpeace design. It also funded it by taking advance orders from its supporters' network.

Within a few weeks of the launch other manufacturers were getting in on the act, despite having claimed the manufacturing process to be technically impossible only a month previous to the launch ... Models from Bosch, Siemens, and Liebherr are now also to be launched in the UK ... Greenpeace now plans to promote the propane/butane technology in countries such as China and India. (ECRA, 1993: 3)

In 1997 Greenpeace received a prestigious award from the United Nations Environment Programme (UNEP) for its work in producing this climate-friendly (or 'greenfreeze') refrigeration. Greenfreeze technology quickly moved to gain 40 per cent of the domestic fridge market in Europe by 1995 (Greenpeace, 1997), and by 2003 accounted for more than 100 million fridges worldwide (Greenpeace, 2004).

Although Greenpeace remains very much a campaigning organisation, the success of the greenfreeze technology intervention brought about a formal 're-orientation of its operating strategy' to take up 'solutions interventions: in which Greenpeace tries, through technical and mainly market mechanisms, to force the development and uptake of innovative, usually suppressed, technologies which contribute significantly to reducing or eliminating environmental problems' (Rose, 1997: 81). Other later 'solutions interventions' would include the Smile eco-car and the Juice offshore wind energy brand.

Oxfam is a useful second trading campaigner to consider because it allows the distinction to be made between trading to raise funds and trading as part of market campaigns which directly bring about social change. As well as having helped to form Cafédirect (see above), Oxfam has long sold a wide range of fair trade goods which directly help Oxfam projects in the developing world. At the same time Oxfam also runs a nationwide network of second-hand clothes shops run largely by volunteers as a fundraising strategy. Although this latter example is trading by a campaigner, it is not designed to bring about change directly in markets.

Campaigning traders

There are a wide range of businesses around the world (often small) which could be described as campaigning traders. Indeed, it is difficult to sell a fair trade or organically labelled product without implicitly commenting negatively on other non-labelled offerings in the same market sector. And although there is a huge variety of approaches, from the reluctant multinational displaying an organic label to outspoken campaigners like those considered below, each of these companies is in some sense an ally with campaigners in their field. The two best known such business in the UK are the Body Shop and the Co-operative Bank, and their activities will be the focus of brief discussion here.

Body Shop International plc describes itself as a 'values driven retailer' and that 'activism has been part of the DNA of the Body Shop' (Body Shop, 2004). In its mission statement it claims to 'passionately campaign for the protection of the environment, human and civil rights, and against animal testing within the cosmetics and toiletries industry' (Body Shop, 2004). Although the company has not been without its critics, its history as a campaigner is both significant and documented. It has campaigned with Greenpeace on banning whaling in the 1980s; on the burning of rainforests in 1989; on Shell's activities in Nigeria in the 1990s; on prohibiting animal testing in the UK and Europe; and on the merits of renewable energy in 2002 (Body Shop, 2004). To a lesser, but still significant, extent the Co-operative Bank chooses to openly campaign on a range of current issues. It has campaigned with WWF and Greenpeace on banning toxic chemicals; with Oxfam and others on restricting the arms trade and landmines; and with War on Want on eradicating Third World debt (Co-operative Bank, 2004b).

Although their outward campaigning behaviour is the most visible campaigning element for these two companies, perhaps more significant in terms of social change are the effects that their ordinary product marketing and successful trading have on the markets they operate in. In 1992, the Co-operative Bank's advertising was the subject of a complaint to the UK advertising regulator by the Chemical Industries Association and the Cosmetics Association (Co-operative Bank, 1997). The complaint was not upheld, but it indicates the concern with which sections of industry viewed their stance.

By claiming that banking or bodycare products retail can be ethical, they place the question in consumers' minds as to what kinds of banking or retail might be unethical and why. As mentioned above, this process also occurs within the markets where organic and fair trade products prosper. As Clouder and Harrison mention in Chapter 6 of this volume when discussing secondary effects of ethical consumer behaviour, successful ethical traders also posit an 'alternative model for development' which makes it hard for unreformed traders to argue that such a position is economically or practically impossible.

PART 4: DEVELOPING CONCEPTS

The trends driving the growth of market campaigning and ethical consumer behaviour are in turn leading observers to look for new concepts to understand and describe what is happening. Two such concepts are briefly explored below: civil regulation and citizen consumers.

Both of these ideas relate to the notion of civil society: 'a public space between the state and individual citizens where the latter can develop autonomous, organised and collective activities of the most varied nature' (Hadeniuus and Uggla, 1996). It is possible that the improved understanding of ethical consumer behaviour which such concepts bring will, in turn, lead to the further growth and development of these two behaviours.

Civil regulation

An early appearance of the idea of civil regulation occurred in a work by Zadek and others (1998b). Drawing upon Ivan Illich's idea of 'tools for conviviality' (1973), the authors suggested that market campaigns could be viewed as either civil tools (persuasive) or civil instruments (coercive). The idea has undergone considerable development in the hands of Bendell and Murphy.

> We are witnessing the emergence of a different model of business regulation which we could call civil regulation. Civil regulation is defined as a situation

where organisations of civil society, such as NGOs, set the standards for business behaviour … Whereas government fines for pollution violations now rarely affect company value, consumer politics brings greater financial risks. Although governments may have the purported monopoly on force … in reality, the ability of NGOs to regulate business behaviour through carrot and stick is rapidly becoming more powerful. (Murphy and Bendell, 2001: 305)

The new standards or rules for business behaviour occur in the detailed requirements of, for example, an organic or FSC label, or in the codes of conduct for workers' rights at supplier companies discussed in Chapter 13. In the same study, Murphy and Bendell (2001) provided extensive and detailed examples of how such regulatory behaviours were not exclusively occurring in developed countries.

They also drew parallels between the new political ideas which emerged in tandem with the growth of trades unions during the last century, and the new ideas emerging with the 'countervailing power' of consumers occurring now. 'Whereas producer politics gained its power through controlling access to labour, consumer politics gains its power by controlling access to customers' (Murphy and Bendell, 2001: 304). Jem Bendell has expanded his analysis of the idea of civil regulation or 'soft law' in other works such as *Terms for Endearment* (2000).

It has also been argued that many forward-thinking businesses now actually favour civil regulation because its alternative – no regulation and constant competitive pressures to externalise social and environmental costs – can act to undermine long-term business legitimacy (Harrison, 2003: 130).

Citizen consumers

Typically, 'citizen' and 'consumer' are considered opposite categories, the first, outward-looking, embracing the public interest, the second, self-interested, inward-looking and private. In fact, as Lizabeth Cohen (2001: 203) notes in respect of the USA, no such simple distinction has held true historically. Citizens and consumers were 'ever shifting categories that sometimes overlapped, other times were in tension, but always reflected the permeability of the political and economic' (Scammell, 2003).

Both Cohen (2001) and Gabriel and Lang (1995), amongst others, have charted and analysed in some detail changing ideas of the consumer and citizenship. It is sufficient here to note that the contemporary notion of citizen consumers has two distinct elements: an ethical consumer element and the notion of a consumer of public services. The rise of market campaigning and ethical purchase behaviour has brought with it notions of a consumer responsibility. Since responsibility is traditionally an idea belonging more to citizenship, it has helped restore to consumption the idea of citizenship.

The ideas of consumer responsibility and consumer citizenship are also explored in Chapter 2, where Dickinson and Carsky argue that responsible consumption should be taught. This argument has also been taken up in the UK (ECRA, 2001; McGregor, 1999), and in 2004 the UK Department for Education and Skills published its 'Objectives For Citizenship at Key Stage 4 (Year 10–11)', with Unit 09 looking at consumer rights and responsibilities and Section 6 looking at fair trade (DFES, 2004).

The idea of citizens as consumers of public services has different roots and occurs when governments encourage citizens to bring 'a consumer mentality to their relations with government, judging state services much like other purchased goods, by the personal benefit they derive from them' (Cohen, 2001: 220). Just as global markets are learning how to treat consumers as citizens, it appears that political 'markets' are trying to treat citizens as consumers. It would also appear that, at least in terms of openly seeking to further the common good, this latter development is a regressive step. It has been observed in both Labour and Conservative Party literature, as well as within the Clinton administration (Scammell, 2003).

CONCLUSIONS

In this chapter, an attempt has been made to place individual ethical consumer behaviours in their broader political context. In many cases, with profound economic changes sweeping the globe, contemporary pressure groups and networks are choosing to use consumer pressure as one of the few effective political channels available to them. Pressure groups are seeking to achieve campaign goals by providing information about corporate malpractice or by supporting the development of alternative products. By facilitating collective actions in this way, they are shaping the environment in which individual ethical consumers operate. (Their role in information provision is explored further in Chapter 5 and their part in the development of alternative products in Chapter 14.) Having identified seven trends which appear to be driving the shift towards market campaigning, it can be proposed that ethical consumer behaviours are likely to increase in frequency should these trends continue.

It should also be noted that the potential for a significant growth of market campaigning exists as a growing variety of pressure groups discover its efficacy. It is already becoming unusual to discover a cause group addressing global issues which does not have some kind of market element to its campaigning. However, the potential to achieve political goals through market campaigns does not stop with cause groups and many powerful private or sectional groups could turn to this type of activity in greater numbers in the future.

First, one recurring theme in ECRA's ongoing analysis of campaigning is that trades unions in the USA are culturally much more predisposed to market campaigning than their European counterparts. The US trades union federation AFL-CIO has both a 'union-label' for products and a boycott list for companies opposing unionisation (AFL-CIO, 2004). Second, although individual politicians will sometimes initiate or publicly support boycotts, it is very unusual to see political parties seeking change through market campaigns. Those that do tend to be smaller parties with clear positions on global issues such as the Greens (see for example, US Green Party, 2001), or governments providing information to consumers on sustainable consumption issues (see Chapter 5). With the potential to drive social change at a national level being progressively eroded, it is arguably only a matter of time before larger political parties – both in power and in opposition – see that market campaigning can operate effectively beside more traditional regulatory projects. Such developments would open up a whole raft of potential new campaign areas for citizen consumers to support.

Informing Ethical Consumers

5

Hannah Berry   Morven McEachern

INTRODUCTION

It is generally accepted that awareness of environmental and social issues is rising, driven by a growing volume of easily accessible information, in which the advent of the internet, and increased media engagement with the issues, have played an important role (Beck, 1999: 102; Langerak et al., 1998; Nicholls, 2002; Peattie, 1992; Thøgersen, 1999). Prior awareness of ethical issues in turn affects a consumer's response to product information: 'The main mechanism for labels (or brands) to work is not to change or make up the mind of the consumer in a shop, but to confirm an earlier decision made outside the market place influenced by marketing, the media, and crucially, civil processes' (Zadek et al., 1998a: 35).

But while studies stress the importance of awareness as a prerequisite for action (Duncombe and Heeks, 2002; Tallontire et al., 2001), one of the recurring themes of this book is the fact that awareness does not necessarily translate into action. Some UK polls show that recently the number of dedicated ethical consumers, or 'CSR activists' as defined in Chapter 7, has stayed fairly constant. One key question is, therefore, to what extent is inadequate information provision inhibiting the translation of professed concern about ethical issues into ethical consumption?

A review of the survey literature suggests that it is certainly a factor. 'Lack of effective communication of ethical issues to mass consumer audiences' is seen as a 'key barrier' by Worcester and Dawkins in Chapter 12. The National Consumer Council (NCC) identified a solid core of willing environmental consumers who could find 'neither the products nor the accurate information to guide their behaviour' (NCC, 1996). In another study, 60 per cent of interviewees said they had insufficient information on company social and environmental behaviour to make an informed purchasing decision (MORI, 2000) and 73 per cent of shoppers in a 2003 poll felt unable to judge the ethical position of companies, due to lack of information (BITC, 2003). Consequently, this discussion about 'informing the ethical consumer' inevitably strays into discussing provision of information to the public in general who are all potential ethical consumers.

This chapter is, however, primarily concerned with the types of information which currently exist to enable consumers to make ethical decisions. These are viewed through the four main types of information provider:

- governments;
- campaign groups;
- specialist ethical consumer publications;
- private sector.

Of course this typology can blur the fact that many mechanisms designed to inform the ethical consumer, such as the organic food label, are collaborations involving more than one of these providers, and the effectiveness of such multi-stakeholder approaches is also discussed. It should also be noted that to some extent the specialist information providers also 'aggregate' and redesign the information from the other three providers for consumer markets.

After these four providers are examined, this chapter goes on to look briefly at two other key areas: the impact of new technology on the provision of ethical consumer information, and specific problems encountered in this field. In the conclusion we note the potential for new technology to deliver still further innovations and argue that government action to encourage ethical consumer actions could be greatly increased. A brief discussion of two key types of information influencing the ethical consumer is appropriate before analysis of the four main information providers begins.

Product data and background data

For the purposes of this chapter, it is useful to distinguish 'product' data, from 'background' data. 'Product' data would include point-of-sale information such as product labels, as well as non-point-of-sale information such as lists of products meeting certain environmental criteria.

'Background' data – such as information discussing the problems of climate change – leads to awareness of broader ethical issues. It can be assimilated by the individual and potentially influence his or her purchase decisions, or act as a spur to seek out product data. Since awareness is what creates the ethical consumer, this type of information is crucial but, for reasons of space, is not given specific consideration here.

It should be noted, however, that product data can sometimes act as an introduction to a background issue. For example, a survey of attitudes to fair trade found that many consumers were first introduced to ideas of fair trade in the supermarket (Eurobarometer, 1997). It has also been noted that some campaign groups may deliberately use product data to introduce consumers to complex political issues (see Chapter 6).

Market research about how people respond to product data on ethical issues has also influenced how product and background data are presented. For example, Langeland (1998) found that people with good awareness of fair trade responded to messages highlighting the problems a product was seeking to address (such as poverty wages), while those less familiar with the concept responded better to messages highlighting the positive impact of their purchase (such as direct finance for schools).

GOVERNMENT DATA

The official aspirations of the international policy community enshrined in Agenda 21 (Rio, 1992), Kyoto (1997) and other global agreements, accord with what might be a typical ethical consumer's hopes for an economic system founded on sustainable production and consumption. Improved animal welfare, environmental protection and the eradication of human exploitation and poverty are the stated long-term objectives of most nation states, and of the United Nations.

Governments are tasked with shaping markets in order to achieve these positive outcomes for society and the environment. As well as direct intervention via taxes, regulation, law and fiscal incentives, it is in their power to strengthen the 'business case' for responsible company behaviour by widening ethical consumer practices through better information provision.

In practice, however, governments are not always so eager to regulate the market relationship between consumers and producers. This can be for fear of damaging national competitiveness or due to constraints placed on them by trade rules which many see as running counter to the principles of global equity (DTI, 2003, and see also Chapter 4 in this book). National politics, powerful corporate lobbies and the agendas of neo-liberal bodies like the World Trade Organisation mean that governments vary considerably in their effectiveness as enablers of ethical consumption.

Despite all this, there is a considerable amount of government activity which directly and indirectly informs the ethical consumer. The regulation of product labelling is probably one of the most important of these, and this is discussed first.

Product labelling

Corporate accountability information does not automatically filter down to the consumer unless he or she is an avid reader of newspapers or uses ethical consumer guides which pre-digest such data and 'rate' companies accordingly. Product-related data, especially when it can be communicated via a simple label, is potentially more accessible.

In a 2002 survey, older consumers believed improved labelling was key to enabling their ethical purchasing. However, they 'did not consider government intervention to be the solution to improving their ability to shop ethically' (Carrigan et al., 2003: 33). In a 2003 YouGov poll, 64 per cent of respondents thought companies should use clearer product labelling, but only 37 per cent believed government should pass specific legislation to compel more responsible corporate behaviour (BITC, 2003). Given that self-certified company labels are widely mistrusted (Cowe and Williams, 2001; Shaw and Clarke, 1999; Tallontire et al., 2001), the role of government in ensuring effective consumer signposting, as well as in supporting business efforts to be more responsible, is possibly being underestimated here. While governments can compel business to act responsibly via legislation, they often favour the less confrontational market-based approach. Enabling the public to choose between 'good' and 'bad' companies or products, via labelling, is key to such an approach.

With regard to labelling, governments have a range of interventions at their disposal. They can:

• initiate mandatory or voluntary labelling schemes;
• increase take-up of existing schemes via publicity and promotion;
• harmonise different initiatives, providing greater clarity;
• support private labelling schemes by endorsing them at international level;
• facilitate partnerships between corporations, consumer groups and campaigners;
• use public procurement policies to support labelling schemes.

Mandatory labelling initiatives

Some compulsory labels can be of accidental value to the ethical consumer. For example, UK food labelling regulations, which require ingredients and country of origin data to be shown, are useful to vegetarians and vegans and those boycotting particular countries or trying to avoid air miles. The labelling of footwear similarly aids those wishing to avoid leather or PVC.

Other compulsory labelling has developed in direct response to an ethical consumer lobby, such as EU legislation on GM ingredients (Boyle and Simms, 2001) or is specifically designed to promote corporate responsibility or sustainability. The EU Energy Label uses a simple A to G index of efficiency to rate energy consumption and performance, and must be displayed on all new domestic appliances and light bulbs. The Energy Label is said to have had as great an impact on company behaviour as on that of consumers, since manufacturers faced with mandatory labelling improved the energy efficiency of their appliances, and retailers found it helped decide which models to stock (Gill, 2003). Similar graded labels have been proposed by the UK's Advisory Committee on Consumer Products and the Environment (ACCPE) for homes, cars and domestic equipment. This would create a coherent 'family' of labels for goods that account for about 90 per cent of a household's direct activities involving carbon dioxide emissions (ACCPE, 2001).

Voluntary labelling initiatives

'Energy Star' is a global standard for electronic equipment, awarded for low standby power consumption. It was created by the US Environment Protection Agency (EPA) in 1992 and is said to partly owe its international take-up to support from the US government (Childs and Whiting, 1998). Another, not insignificant, reason for its success is the fact that it is in the consumer's financial interest to save energy.

There are at least 24 official national eco-label schemes worldwide (Childs and Whiting, 1998). Eco-labels were developed to encourage business to market greener products and help consumers pinpoint the best environmental options. They are usually based on Life Cycle Assessments and awarded on a pass/fail basis, via third party verification. Germany's Blue Angel, the first strictly environmental labelling scheme, was developed in 1977 and is said to enjoy 80 per cent recognition among German consumers (ACCPE, 2001). There is no home-grown equivalent in Britain, but since 1992 the EU Flower Eco-label has been managed in the UK by the Department of Environment, Farming and Rural Affairs (DEFRA). Experience with the EU scheme suggests that the criteria-setting process can drive up standards across the whole sector, as seen with the Energy Label. However, many environmental labels, including the Blue Angel, have remained concentrated in relatively few product areas and they have often struggled to achieve significant market impact (ACCPE, 2001).

The complexities of ethical product labelling, which often means reconciling conflicting sets of concerns, are exemplified by statutory eco-label-type schemes. Australia scrapped its national scheme after two years, deciding to attempt to reach the same objectives through environmental management systems instead (Childs and Whiting, 1998). Protracted negotiations around standards frustrate all parties and can result in the benchmarking of out-of-date technology, while companies complain at disproportionate costs and have in some cases been reluctant to apply for eco-labels even when their products meet the criteria. It was alleged, for example, that low-energy light bulb manufacturers declined to apply for the European eco-label in the 1990s, because they also produced traditional, short-life bulbs and had an interest in the continued flourishing of that, more lucrative, market (ECRA, 1995a).

The logos themselves can be slow to achieve recognition, possibly partly because, as symbols on packaging, they provide no details of the production standards that have been attained. According to Childs and Whiting 'Unless the consumer has been educated about their meaning, they remain a simple picture on the packaging and as such are likely to be ignored' (1998: 7). The issue of effective on-pack information is discussed further in the section on private sector labelling below.

Endorsement, support, promotion and harmonisation of existing schemes

Governments can play a useful role in the harmonisation of labelling schemes that have originated outside of their statutory control. An example is the regulation by the United Kingdom Register of Organic Food Standards (UKROFS), an independent board sponsored by DEFRA, of the UK's 11 different organic certifying bodies. UKROFS ensures that the term 'organic', as defined by EU legislation, is properly applied, and makes each certifier identifiable by a code on product packaging, whether or not its actual logo is present.

The German government has introduced a single organic label for all German products that meet EU organic standards, due to evidence that consumers were confused by a multiplicity of standards (Wright, 2001). As in Germany, it is a goal of the UK's Soil Association to reduce the number of British certifiers, but here the motivation is partly the perceived risk of standards being dumbed down to legal minimums if there are too many schemes (Wright, 2001). In the USA, the government's National Organic Programme (NOP) prevents certifiers from telling consumers they have set their own standards at a 'higher' level than those set by the NOP – illustrating that government involvement in harmonisation can also be problematic.

National or international controls on labelling schemes can also cut both ways. They can be positive when they prevent disadvantage to small businesses or developing country producers, but negative when a rich country's government mounts a legal challenge to an ethical labelling scheme out of national self-interest, on the grounds that it presents a barrier to trade. Under pressure from the USA, the EU forced cosmetics companies to remove 'against animal testing' slogans from packaging, in direct contradiction of its policies for greater transparency and consumer information (Boyle and Simms, 2001) and, more recently, the US government has tried to use WTO free trade rules to outlaw the EU's policies on GM food labelling (Genewatch UK, 2004).

Publishing information

Governments are increasingly using the internet to provide consumer information. The Energy Saving Trust (www.est.org.uk) was part of the UK government's response to the 1992 Earth Summit, providing free energy efficiency advice to householders. In the USA, a 1989 federal law mandated public access to the country's Toxic Release Inventory, and two different portals, the Right to Know Network (www.rtknet.org) and Environmental Defense League (www.scorecard.org) present this data in a format searchable by area or by company group. Naming and shaming worst in sector companies, usually in terms of environmental performance, is another way government agencies can increase public scrutiny of corporations. For example, the Pesticide Residue Committee (www.pesticides.gov.uk) has a policy of identifying manufacturers and retailers who exceed the maximum residue levels of pesticides found in food products. Table 5.1 also includes some other examples of statutory information provision.

Increasing corporate disclosure

Self-regulation of business, mediated by market pressure, can be more attractive to some governments than direct legislation to control company behaviour. However, to work, it requires public availability of comparative information on company practices.

This was the impulse behind the requirement in the UK Pension Act 2000 that British pension fund companies disclose their environmental and social impacts, as described in Chapter 13. Other recent UK legislation forced directors of quoted companies to disclose full details of their pay and other benefits – information previously not in the public domain. However, the British government ducked a 2004 bill drafted by a coalition of NGOs, which was calling for companies to be required to disclose the origins of imported commodities. This would have facilitated supply chain monitoring of products such as palm oil, which is associated with destructive and illegal land use in South East Asia, and allowed consumers to apply pressure on the companies.

In France, any company which produces an annual report is obliged to include a summary of the social and environmental impact of its business and to detail its co-operation with trades unions, civil society and local communities (Hutton, 2002). A group of European parliamentarians is pressing for mandatory EU-wide corporate responsibility reporting along French lines, and the core coalition, including Friends of the Earth, Christian Aid and other NGOs, are campaigning for international standardisation of such reporting (Osborn, 2003).

Monitoring product claims

In the mid-1980s, as producers and retailers realised the sales potential of 'green' labelling, environmental labels and marketing strategies proliferated. Since many were meaningless, they left lots of consumers bemused and cynical about ethical product claims (Burns and Blowfield, 1999).

The UK government responded in 1998 with a 'Green Claims Code' to help producers to communicate honestly and clearly. In 2001 it was made compatible

Table 5.1 Seventeen types of website providing information for the ethical consumer

Type of site	Examples
'Traditional media' websites	www.money.guardian.co.uk/ethicalmoney/
	www.bbc.co.uk/radio4/science/costingtheearth.shtml
	www.ft.com
Specific anti-company sites	www.kfccruelty.com
	www.stopesso.com/
Online buyers' guides	www.greenpeace.org.uk/Products/Toxics/chemicalhouse.cfm
	www.thegreenconsumerguide.com
	www.foe.org.uk/campaigns/climate/press_for _change/
	choose_green_energy/#league_table
Online ethical shopping portals	www.getethical.com
	www.greenguideonline.com
	www.naturalcollection.co.uk
	www.ethicaljunction.org
Online searchable product databases	www.idealswork.com
	www.responsibleshopper.org
	www.ethicalconsumer.org
Online searchable company information	www.transnationale.org
	www.scorecard.org
	www.corporatecritic.org
Online single-issue campaign sites	www.risingtide.org.uk
	www.boycottbush.net
	www.sweatshopwatch.org
	www.fairtrade.org.uk
DIY research opportunities for the ethical consumer	www.corporatewatch.org.uk
	www.corpwatch.org
	www.shareholderaction.org
	www.prwatch.org
	www.multinationalmonitor.org
Online alternative news networks	www.indymedia.org
	www.zmag.org
'Conscious' web hosting	www.oneworld.net
	www.gn.apc.org
NGO sites	www.amnesty.org
	www.tourismconcern.org.uk
	www.peta.org
Second-hand shopping sites	www.ebay.com
	www.abebooks.com
Ethical think-tanks	www.neweconomics.org
	www.thecornerhouse.org.uk
Governmental information sites	www.epa.gov/opptintr/epp
	www.est.org.uk
	www.eco-label.com
Online ethical services/ mail order companies	www.graigfarm.co.uk
	www.greenstat.co.uk
	www.vegetarian-shoes.co.uk
	www.smile.co.uk
Trades unions websites	www.icftu.org
Culture jamming sites	www.adbusters.org.uk
	www.uhc-collective.org.uk

with a new international standard on green claims, ISO 14021, and is accompanied by a leaflet ('Hi, I'm green') which outlines the standard of information consumers should expect and explains how to challenge unhelpful claims. However, there is little financial penalty in the UK for companies who regularly mislead consumers through 'green' labelling – something which, we would argue, should be addressed by legislation. Another legal change that would improve information provision to the ethical consumer would be permitting UK campaign groups to advertise on television. The current lack of a 'right of reply' to consumer-related issues results in a strong cultural bias in favour of the corporate voice (ECRA, 2001).

Creating the cultural climate

The UK's National Consumer Council (NCC) argues that it is not enough for consumers to be provided with information. It wants government to implement a national education strategy to promote life-long skills that will enable consumers to analyse and make use of the information (NCC, 2001). Governments have long used the education system, media messages, media regulation, as well as labelling to try and persuade people to consume differently (Jackson and Michaelis, 2003), but this on its own may still be insufficient to change behaviour. In particular, it has been shown that information may be discounted when the source is not trusted, for example, because it does not follow its own advice (Stern, 1986). When the health of the economy is judged on consumer spending, or best practice is routinely ignored in public sector purchasing, it sends out ambiguous signals about government priorities.

This point is made in a report by the Oxford Commission on Sustainable Consumption (Jackson and Michaelis, 2003), which finds that 'sustainable consumption' has become almost universally framed as 'the production and sale of more sustainable products', in contrast to the original Agenda 21 vision of 'new concepts of wealth and prosperity which allow higher standards of living through changed lifestyles' (Jackson and Michaelis, 2003). The authors describe consumers as being 'locked in to current consumption patterns' and believe the vital task for governments lies in 'shaping the cultural context within which individual choice is negotiated, through its influence on technology, market design, institutional structures, the media, and the moral framing of social goods' (Jackson and Michaelis, 2003).

CAMPAIGN GROUP DATA

Probably the majority of the 'background' awareness-raising data referred to in the introduction to this chapter arises through the work of campaign groups, NGOs and other civil society organisations. Such groups have grown significantly in political and cultural influence over the last quarter century. Their 'moral arbiter' status is self-assumed, but it is probably fair to assert that, on the whole, they seek to uphold agreed societal values and standards. Many can be shown to have emerged out of moral frameworks.

Campaigns can target companies or legislators directly, but informing and stimulating citizens to change their patterns of consumption is another vital route to positive change. 'What is often referred to as consumer pressure is usually political pressure from civil society, orchestrated by NGOs, which use the threat of consumer action to achieve this end' (Duncombe and Heeks, 2002). Such campaigning is reinforced by the growing availability of specialist ethical products, some of which, such as fair trade goods, NGOs have themselves entered the market to produce (see also Chapter 4 in this book on 'Trading Campaigners').

Information generated (through research) and/or disseminated (directly or indirectly) by campaigners, trades unions and other civil society actors interacts with available product data to create informed ethical purchase choices. Direct means of communication with consumers include groups' own media and publicity materials, seminars, information stalls and the fielding of media spokespersons. Indirect intermediaries for the information include coverage by mainstream media, religious or secular discussion forums, workplace initiatives, conversation with family and peers, and the education system. Mintel's 1991 finding that television programmes and documentaries were the main source of knowledge for 70 per cent of ethical consumers, with 63 per cent sourcing information from newspapers, books and magazines, illustrates the significance of these indirect communication channels (Anonymous, 1991). So does the fact that 64 per cent of teachers questioned in one survey said that fair trade was taught on their school curriculum (Comic Relief, 2003).

Campaign group 'buyers' guides' are covered later in this chapter. Other activities through which campaigners generate information for the ethical consumer, as their primary or secondary intention, include co-ordination of national 'awareness days'; research to highlight problems or develop alternatives; political lobbying, including for greater regulation and disclosure; engagement and dialogue with business and policy makers; and the co-ordination of local activists. They also include direct targeting of irresponsible companies via monitoring and public 'naming and shaming'; boycott calls (see Chapter 4); shareholder actions; and direct action. Awareness-raising public protest ranges from mass anti-globalisation demonstrations to localised protests evolved independently of any pre-existing structure in reaction to a specific set of events. Examples of localised protests might include Not-In-My-Back-Yard (NIMBY) anti-supermarket campaigns, or Merseyside's spontaneous boycott of the *Sun* newspaper following its insensitive coverage of the 1989 Hillsborough football stadium disaster.

Finally, NGOs also play a crucial role in providing 'point-of-sale' data to consumers via involvement in labelling schemes, while some, as already mentioned, are spearheading alternative enterprise by entering the market with their own ethical products.

Campaign groups and labelling

Labelling schemes can be single issue and involve one campaign group, as in the UK Vegetarian Society's 'V' symbol or the British Union for the Abolition of Vivisection (BUAV's) not-tested-on-animals 'bunny' logo. Others, such as the Forestry Stewardship Council (FSC) and Marine Stewardship Council (MSC) take a multilateral approach. Here, NGOs have worked in partnership with industry and government to achieve benchmarked standards for the sustainable management of forests and fisheries, respectively, with products from accredited operations displaying an internationally recognised logo. The success of the FSC, in particular, has led to a sense that schemes operated by civil society groups within a framework backed by the public sector is the most assured route to effective labelling (Boyle and Simms, 2001). The Apparel Industry Partnership, which was convened in 1996 by the US government, was set back in its attempt to create a 'No Sweat' label when several trade unions and NGOs pulled out, due to failure to include a living wage as part of the standard (Burns and Blowfield, 1999). Such a conflict might not have arisen, perhaps, in a civil society-led partnership.

SPECIALIST ETHICAL CONSUMER PUBLICATIONS

Campaign group publications

As we have just seen, environmental campaign groups are important providers of advice and information to people who want to minimize the ecological impact of their lifestyles. Social justice movements have also long sought to influence peoples' life choices towards a 'greater good'. However, it was mainly during the 1980s that single-issue campaign groups and NGOs began to publish a range of specific shopping guides, offering 'positive' (what to buy) or 'negative' (what not to buy) information, or a combination of the two.

In the early 1980s BUAV produced its first 'Approved Products Guide' to help consumers locate brands not tested on animals. *The Good Wood Guide* (Friends of the Earth, 1998) directed consumers to sustainable sources of timber whilst naming those companies involved in rainforest logging. *The Green Pages*, an independently compiled directory of natural products and services in the UK, saw the light of day in 1989. It was modelled on the *Whole Earth Catalogue* which became popular in the USA in the 1970s. At around the same time, the South Africa Boycott Campaign was putting out lists of companies and products, such as Barclays Bank and Outspan oranges, from which anyone seeking an end to the apartheid regime could choose to withhold their custom.

Specialist ethical consumer organisations

The ethical investment research group Council on Economic Priorities was the first organisation to publish a shoppers' guide systematically assessing company performance across a spectrum of ethical issues in 1986. *Ethical Consumer* magazine was launched in the UK in 1989, in response to a perceived need of politically motivated consumers for a data source taking a combined product-orientated and company-based approach. Its format, involving company rating tables and recommended 'Best Buys', was modelled on *Which?*, the magazine and the new name of the British Consumers' Association.

Over the last fifteen years, across the world, the number of specialist groups dedicated to providing 'fully-screened' company and brand information to consumers has been steadily rising. Several of these were reviewed in a report in *Ethical Consumer* magazine in 2002 (ECRA, 2002c) and this section updates that article. What unites these 'practitioner' groups and their publications is their comparative analyses of company behaviour. It is also what distinguishes them from organisations which are primarily concerned with directing consumers to ethical products and services (such as www.GetEthical.com in the UK), or which have a narrow area of concern, such as the Vegan Society's 'Animal-free Shopper'. The kinds of organisation involved, their size, methods of data collection and means of presenting the information to the public currently vary from country to country, or occupy different niches within the same country. As groups and their information handling systems mature, there is scope for greater international cross-pollination and collaboration, leading, we expect, to the provision of an increasingly higher quality of information to the public. Most work on the basis of providing unbiased information, through which consumers are able to exercise their own priorities. As Newholm suggests in Chapter 11, many ethical consumers are 'selectively ethical', having their own personal hierarchy of ethical concerns. Countries with specialist ethical consumer publishing, at various stages of development, include Australia, Austria, Belgium, Canada, Denmark, Finland, France, Germany, Hungary, Italy, Japan, the Netherlands, Norway, Poland, Spain, UK and the USA.

The UK's Ethical Consumer Research Association (www.ethicalconsumer.org), rates companies across a range of ethical criteria as mentioned above and illustrated in Figure 5.1. It draws mainly on secondary information such as campaign group publications, commercial reference volumes such as *Jane's International Defence Directory*, and public records on pollution prosecutions, though policies and reports are also requested directly from the companies. Online subscribers can access ECRA's Corporate Critic database, containing more than 30,000 abstracts. Since 2002, ECRA reports have found an audience beyond the bi-monthly magazine's readership of 15,000, having been republished in book format as *The Good Shopping Guide*.

The free online information service www.responsibleshopper.org combines the rating systems of two US organisations. The Center for Responsibility in Business

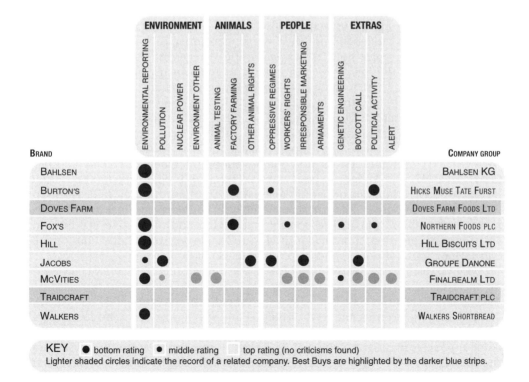

Figure 5.1 Ethical Consumer company rating table

(formerly CEP), grades mostly large corporations on overall performance, gathering data via company-completed surveys as well as secondary sources, in a similar manner to ECRA. It grades companies A–D for each issue area, with F as the lowest possible rating, reserved for companies which do not disclose the information. The categories differ quite markedly from ECRA's, however. They include Women's Advancement, Minority Advancement, Family Benefits, Workplace, Environment, Charitable Giving and Disclosure. The Workplace rating does not include working conditions for a company's contractors or suppliers. The other source of data for www.responsibleshopper.org is Co-op America (www.cepaa.org), which evaluates the social and environmental performance of smaller companies. It makes use of industry-specific questionnaires, as well as other information obtained through secondary research. The questionnaires attempt to find out about environmental policies and practices, workplace and labour issues and charity/community involvement, as well as the level of disclosure. There are three levels of rating, with a fourth – 'poor' – assigned to companies that fail to respond to the survey.

Le Guide Éthique du Consommateur – Acheter Pour un Monde Meilleur (The Ethical Consumer Guide – Shopping For a Better World) was first published in 2001 by L'Observatoire de l'Éthique (www.ode-asso.com). Seventy-five sectors and seven hundred brand names were investigated in order to 'reveal the hidden face of the firms that produce 80 per cent of household purchases'. Commercial strategy, salaries, ecological impact, customer service, transparency, humanitarian considerations, sponsoring and citizenship are all dealt with. Some French organisations have expressed reservations, believing that the questionnaire approach is not, on its own, an effective means of discrimination. It depends too much, they argue, on what proportion of their 'hidden faces' the firms choose to unveil.

The Institut für Markt-Umwelt-Gesellschaft E.V. (www.imug.de) has produced a series of paperback guidebooks for the German consumer, called *Der Unternehmenstester*. They cover topics such as cosmetics and detergents, food companies and household electrical appliances, each looking at mainstream companies under 12 category headings. These include environment, animal welfare, workers' rights and genetic engineering. Like the *Guide Éthique*, IMUG acquires the majority of its data direct from companies by questionnaire. Those that fail to respond are not penalised by receiving the worst rating, which could be said to cause a measure of distortion.

Centro Nuovo Modello di Sviluppo (Centre for New Models of Development, www.cnms.it) brought out its first Italian shopping guide, *Guida al Consumo Critico*, in 1997. The A5-format book covers a range of food, drink and household products and contains information on major multinationals, as well as lots of Italian-based companies. The criteria by which the companies were tested included not only the environment, irresponsible marketing and oppressive regimes, but also a number of issues of particular interest to Italian consumers, including fraud, corruption, abuse of power, and the corporate use of tax havens.

Opcions was the first Spanish responsible consumption guide, launched in 2002, by the Centre de Reserca i Informació en Consum (CRIC) (www.opcions.org). Available in Catalan or Castilian, each issue provides an in-depth guide to a particular product area, covering the environmental and social impacts of production and profiling the top-selling brands in Catalonia along with several 'alternatives'. The company tables highlight ownership and classify companies according to size and the markets in which they operate. Issues such as criticism of irresponsible marketing, membership of lobby groups or involvement in genetic engineering are presented discursively.

Goede Waar & Co. (www.goedewaar.nl), in the Netherlands, produces a magazine called *Kritisch Consumeren* which carries articles of interest to ethical consumers, such as interviews, company investigations and fair trade updates. In 1999 a separate consumer guide was published in book form: *Eerlijk en Groen Boodschappen Doen* (Honest and Green Shopping). The 20 reports, covering goods such as coffee, computers, paint and vitamins, deal with production issues and corporate responsibility, and each end in a table with the category headings: Transparency, Environment, Social, Animal Welfare, Gene Technology, Fair trade and Organic.

Mainstream consumers' associations

The Netherlands' mainstream consumers' association Consumentenbond has begun to include information for the ethical consumer. Following the example of VKI Austria (www.konsument.at), the first consumers' association to depart from considering only price, quality and less controversial product-related environmental data such as energy efficiency, Consumentenbond has undertaken to incorporate ethical ratings into half of all its product tests by 2005 and has committed to substantial research and development in this area. VKI's magazine *Konsument* included an ethical rating of sports shoes in October 2000, since when the 'Ethik-test' has become a regular feature. The data are largely compiled from questionnaires sent to the firms under review, although one on jeans was produced in conjunction with consumers' associations in Denmark, Finland, Norway, Sweden and Iceland.

In June 2003, Europe's largest consumer association joined the trend when the UK's *Which?* magazine published its first ever comparative rating of the ethical performance of a group of manufacturers. In the future, many such ratings may be co-ordinated internationally through the International Consumer Research and Testing (ICRT) (Newholm, 2000).

Belgium's Centre de Recherche et d'Information des Organisations de Consommateurs (www.oivo-crioc.org) is in some ways the missing link between the specialist ethical consumer organisations like ECRA and the national consumers' associations. It is a government-funded body that offers technical support to Belgium's consumer organisations, deals with the protection of consumer rights and product safety, and analyses consumption patterns. However, it also promotes ethical consumption, and to this end has produced several briefings and buyers' guides. *Comment Consommer pour un Monde Meilleur* is an A5 colour booklet containing six product reports. The tables are divided into product information and producer information, basing the latter on data from ECRA and AKB's *Eerlijk en Groen Boodschappen Doen*.

PRIVATE SECTOR

Alternative companies

By their very existence, specialist ethical companies inform consumers about the ethical issues surrounding the products or practices of their mainstream competitors. As well as through on-pack declarations such as 'not tested on animals' or

'100 per cent organic hemp', many such 'ethical niche' companies engage and educate consumers through leaflets, catalogues and in-store displays. The UK's 'Out of this World' supermarket chain produces a regular newsletter for customers, which is also downloadable from the web (www.ootw.co.uk). The Co-operative Bank researches ethical consumers themselves, in order to better understand and promote ethical consumerism. Other examples of niche companies also appear in Table 5.1.

The Body Shop is a company that has been willing to make compromises in certain ethical areas in order to meet the demands of a mainstream audience. However, it has, from the outset, embraced principles of partnership with suppliers and used its store fronts to promote public awareness of issues of environmental and human rights concern. Most famously, it moulded the wider market with regard to animal testing, with its once innovative stance now the industry standard among mid-range cosmetics (Burns and Blowfield, 1999).

The term 'Alternative Trading Organisation' (ATO) refers to the non-profit fair trade companies, most of which have direct links to trade justice NGOs. They benefit from the fact that NGOs enjoy a much higher degree of trust than either government or business (see for example, Crane in Chapter 14).

Communicating the issues is a big part of the ATO marketing strategy: Cafédirect, for example, channels a substantial proportion of its fast-growing profits into promotion of the fair trade concept not only to consumers but to manufacturers and retailers, in an attempt to promote the adoption of fair trade principles by mainstream companies.

However, as fair trade brands reach out increasingly to a mainstream audience, beyond a small base of 'solidarity' consumers, point-of-sale information has to be increasingly concerned with communicating product quality. The Dutch NGO Solidaridad promotes its organic, fair trade 'Kyuchi' jeans like any other fashion product, so that buyers may only discover the fair trade aspects of their new clothes when they get home. The rationale, according to the company is that 'the civilian in us knows the benefits of fair trade, but when we enter a shop, we become a consumer with different priorities – price, quality and image.' The Kyuchi campaign 'tries to focus on the consciousness of a consumer rather than the consciousness of a civilian' (Dempsey, 2002).

Mainstream companies

Chapters 13 and 14 address the incentives for mainstream companies to respond to ethical consumerist concerns. They include public pressure, with ethical investment as an additional lever, legislation, and the direct business case, through effects on resource efficiency or on staff morale and productivity. In terms of informing consumers, general reputational issues can filter down to consumers from CSR reports via the media and the kinds of specialist guides covered in the next section. But apart from advertising, which we would argue is underused as a means of promoting CSR, product labelling is the most direct means of communication.

Standardised labelling schemes, evolved by NGOs and/or government have been discussed. However, self-declared claims made by individual businesses about the environmental or social performance of their products account for the majority of market-place 'product sustainability' information (ACCPE, 2001). Clear and informative private sector labels make an important contribution to guiding the public towards more sustainable consumption. According to Tallontire et al. (2001: 23), 'the communication role of a product on a shelf cannot be under-estimated'. However, others question 'the efficacy of relatively distant and imper-sonal product labels' (Duncombe and Heeks, 2002) and, while many shoppers may be introduced to ethical issues via store shelves, there is a general distrust of infor-mation from companies among ethical consumers, including on-pack information (Shaw and Clarke, 1999; Tallontire et al., 2001).

At the heart of the mistrust is the persistent problem of companies making deliberately vague or misleading statements. Private sector food labelling is partic-ularly notorious for confusing claims, with consumers often unable to differentiate between officially approved logos and marketing symbols (Boulstridge and Carrigan, 2000; McEachern and Schroder, 2002). The Little Red Tractor meat label, for example, proclaims 'Kind to Animals', when its underpinning welfare standards are generally no higher than minimum legal requirements. Research has shown that consumers also overestimate 'Quality Assured' and 'Farm Assured' meat labels, partly due to the lack of access to an explanation of what is being guaranteed. Almost 80 per cent of customers interviewed for the study wished to know more about the underpinning standards of these labels (McEachern and Warnaby, 2004).

All labelling schemes are faced with the problem of determining a socially efficient level of information: how to summarise ethical data without over-simplifying it, while maintaining a simple recognisable design so that it can be an effective symbol. Too much explanatory detail creates information overload, while logos are meaningless if no one knows what they mean, or how they can find out. One solution is to refer to a standard to which a product conforms, or to namecheck an accompanying website, but demanding more work from consumers is not necessarily a solution to their lack of engagement with labels.

Conversely, companies will sometimes choose not to highlight a product's ethical credentials. Several popular toilet paper brands are 100 per cent recycled, but this information, deemed unappealing to the average consumer, is not revealed (ECRA, 2003: 18).

Reluctance to badge products as socially or environmentally responsible can sometimes stem from the lack of management tools to provide proper guarantees, or the fact that it may raise questions about the products which are not thus adver-tised. ACCPE believes government should encourage companies to make sustain-ability more of a mainstream element in their marketing, raising the quality of the communication by harnessing the skills of the advertising industry for the purpose (ACCPE, 2001). Similarly, in Chapter 14 of this book, Crane states that 'the future integration of ethical messages into mainstream communication channels' is posited as the information strategy with perhaps the greatest potential to raise the profile of ethical consumerism.

Some mainstream companies actively 'seek to differentiate themselves along ethical lines' (Crane, Chapter 14). The Co-operative Group has blazed a trail with regard to fair trade retail and by 2003 the company had switched all of its own-label chocolate, tea and coffee to fair trade. DIY chain B&Q decided to stock only FSC certified (or soon-to-be certified) wood products and has also developed its own graded eco-label for the paints, stains and varnishes sold in its stores, focusing on levels of volatile organic compounds. As well as being of use to customers, this innovation focused industry minds, since three years after the introduction of the label there had been a 21 per cent fall in the VOC content in paints stocked by B&Q (Gill, 2003).

The Co-operative is keen to publicise its ethical initiatives, but B&Q's approach is more low key, for a number of reasons. One is that broadcasting green or ethical credentials opens a company to scrutiny and criticism. This will be especially so when certain areas of the business have not been 'ethically' overhauled. The Body Shop has famously taken more flak from ethical consumers than equivalent cosmetics companies with no ethical credentials whatsoever (ECRA, 1998: 5).

Committed ethical consumers are often sceptical of corporate self-promotion, but a massive budget and expert PR team does potentially enable a big company to project a 'responsible face', or to alter public perception of issues in which it is implicated. Oil companies Shell and BP, for example, have quite successfully re-branded themselves in the public mind as alternative energy pioneers, despite ongoing petroleum activities that grossly overshadow any renewables investment and the installation of a few solar-powered petrol pumps (Rising Tide, 2003).

Cause-related marketing is one means of communicating a positive image to consumers, potentially distracting attention from systemic unethical practices. Another phenomenon is the company which publicly champions ethical measures, whilst lobbying behind the scenes, via an industry association, to maintain the status quo or water down or delay progressive legislation. However, there can be serious reputational consequences when ethical claims are made and then found wanting. The biotech giant Monsanto never recovered after its attempts to educate the public on the issues of GM, as it saw them, backfired on the company when factual errors in the propaganda were exposed (Arlidge, 1999).

Committed ethical consumers can be wise to whitewash, or 'greenwash', and may suspect a company has not willingly embraced its new professed ethos. In fact, it can be difficult to win back the trust of ethical consumers – a bad reputation will tend to stick. Even when genuine progress on key issues is made, ethical consumers may have permanently removed their custom, having identified alternative providers whose values they feel they can trust.

IMPACT OF NEW TECHNOLOGY

The role of the internet in empowering the consumer is well documented (Seybold et al., 2001). As already discussed, the media, campaign groups and informal communication networks are some of the most important sources of background information for the ethical consumer, and new technologies not only extend their reach but deliver new dimensions and potential. Information technology helps wannabe ethical shoppers locate 'alternative' products and services, as well as second-hand goods. It brings environmental, social justice and animal rights campaign issues to a wider global audience at minimum cost. Campaign group profiles are raised via their own sites (often well registered with search engines) while email campaign lists and discussion forums create and reinforce 'communities of interest'. Political activists, north and south, can forge international links, and can mobilise mass protests that may in turn bring greater public attention to their issues of concern.

When the first shopping sites appeared, online retailers rarely bothered to publish even statutory product data, such as EU energy ratings. 'Not tested on animals' logos, displayed on packaging, were unavailable to the online customer. In coming years, there is likely to be increasing pressure on producers and retailers to disclose corporate responsibility and product credentials on both shopping portals and company websites, as clued-up consumers make use of the ample scope of the internet to hold them to account. It is even conceivable that exchange of information will take place in real time, allowing a potential customer to directly observe production, or receive oral testimonies from workers on the ground (Duncombe and Heeks, 2002).

The internet enables product and company searches prior to purchase, and there are an increasing number of online databases to aid the process. Some, such as www.scorecard.org, www.idealswork.com, www.ethicalconsumer.org and www.transnationale.org provide product and company information. Other databases, in contrast, focus on product parameters. In Britain, ACCPE believes that, instead of a national eco-labelling scheme, the government should fund a comprehensive 'consumer platform' explaining the environmental, social and ethical impacts of consumer goods. Hosted by an independent consumer organisation, it would guide people to third-party advice and information on the best products to buy, and on their use and disposal. According to ACCPE 'searchable databases are a powerful tool for market transformation, because they combine the transparency of "rating" with the opportunities offered by IT communications, to make environmental factors a competitive issue and apply pressure across a whole product sector' (ACCPE, 2001).

Other new technologies might soon come to the aid of the ethical consumer. Hand-held barcode scanners, used in combination with mobile phones or palm-top devices, are being explored as a means of providing point-of-sale information on company practices. Other teams are exploring text messaging and 3G technology to similar ends. Configurability is important to both concepts – the ability of the individual to program the software to reflect his or her ethical values. A small prototype can be see seen at Doncaster Earth Centre in the UK, where shop visitors can discover the social and environmental impact of the goods on sale by scanning barcodes into a computer. The technology exists – the limiting factor at the moment is the data infrastructure. However, a number of organisations are developing and maintaining just the sort of database that might one day make such gadgets as commonplace as the mobile phone.

PROBLEMS WITH INFORMING ETHICAL CONSUMERS

Credibility and complexity

Trust and credibility will be a major issue so long as there are different interests and motives at work. Point-of-sale labelling is beset by tensions between the interpretative and rational characteristics of data – the conflict between the label as symbol and as stand-alone information source. There is also the risk of oversimplification in information systems, leading to benefits of perception rather than real benefits for people, animals or the environment.

Clearly there are shortcomings in the amount and quality of data currently available, but it is obvious also that there can be no easy answers when there are so many players, interests, complexities, and credibility issues involved, and when it is known that consumers themselves respond subjectively to the messages they receive, according to habit, lifestyle and beliefs (Newholm, 1999a; Shaw and Clarke, 1999).

Strategic criticisms

Perhaps surprisingly, some of the most outspoken critics of seeking change through informing consumers are campaign groups themselves. As a consequence, some have initiated industry partnerships which, instead of labelling, are geared at building 'the toolkit of standards, professional capacity and auditing and reporting processes' needed to permit genuine stakeholder accountability of companies (Burns and Blowfield, 1999: 17). They include systems for reporting performance against codes of conduct along the supply chain (such as the Ethical Trading Initiative (ETI) and SA8000) and on company operations (such as AA1000).

The ETI was established in the UK in 1998 as a tripartite forum of NGOs, companies and trades unions, with the aim of encouraging companies to implement codes of conduct embodying internationally agreed labour standards, and to develop new methods of monitoring and independent verification. The ETI has deliberately steered clear of developing a consumer label, fearing that labelling would reward 'quick fixes' and penalise companies which opted for longer-term but more sustainable solutions to work-place problems. In theory, capital-rich corporations could squeeze out smaller companies which, due to tighter financial margins, might be slower to make the grade. In addition, in seeking to 'get labelled', campaigners are concerned that companies might withdraw trade from countries with structural problems such as restrictions on freedom of association or very low wage levels, risking putting suppliers out of business, and vulnerable workers out of a job. For similar reasons, labour justice groups, such as the Clean Clothes Campaign, tend to caution against company boycotts, unless called by the workers themselves. The knee-jerk response of many companies to consumer concern about child labour in East Asian clothing factories illustrates the dangers of over-simplifying the issues, since many child workers lost their factory jobs, only to end up in more dangerous occupations on the streets (King and Marcus, 2000).

It is important that consumers recognise the complexities of supply chains. Sometimes the case must be made for consumer support for long-term goals rather than immediate achievements (Tallontire, 2001).

With respect to fair trade, consumers need to appreciate that it differs from other ethical monitoring and certification systems in being concerned not only with the site of production, but with altering power relations in trade. As more mainstream supply chains undergo independent monitoring and reporting, it is important consumers remain conscious of the distinction, not least because, unlike with sustainable forest management where the producer pays for accreditation, fair trade is about supporting and nurturing producers, and it's the consumer who pays up front (Tallontire, 2001).

CONCLUSION

This chapter has attempted to show how government, campaign groups, specialist organisations and the private sector contribute to awareness-raising and the provision of information to the ethical consumer, including how they interact to create systems to guarantee that data. It has also looked briefly at some of the problems of informing ethical consumers and at the impact of information technology on this sector.

To some extent, it is probably not coincidental that the rise of ethical consumerism has coincided with the information technology revolution. The complexity of rating competing global products and companies against ethical issues is such that it is difficult to imagine how this would have been acheived without the processing and communication power delivered through new technologies. And as discussed earlier, such technologies are still developing and further potentially significant innovations for the spread of ethical consumer behaviour may be just around the corner. For example, data from specialist ethical consumer organisations could in future be summoned at the point of sale, through the intermediary of a mobile phone. However, the need to ensure credible neutral information will tax the specialist organisations as much as any other information provider. To some extent, greater international co-operation in researching and providing information – again enhanced through technological developments – is likely to have a very significant effect on addressing these issues.

In the introduction, the question 'to what extent is inadequate information provision inhibiting the translation of professed concern about ethical issues into ethical consumption?' was raised. To some extent it is likely to be answered better in subsequent chapters which explore the responses of actual consumers to this and other issues. This chapter has demonstrated that there is not a lack of information on ethical issues, but that its quality and complexity may be of concern in some areas. There are of course many other issues which will affect the 'translation of professed concern' – not least the lack of availablity of hiqh quality competitively priced ethical products in every market sector. It should also be noted that, with the general focus of mainstream product marketing on issues like style, celebrity, fashion and price, it is very easy for consumers to simply overlook the ethical dimension to purchasing amidst all the noise and haste. Goverments clearly do have the potential to change this by their intervention in markets but, in terms of them developing policies to endorse, support and promote ethical products and labelling, the only obvious problem is their persistent underuse of this mechanism.

The Effectiveness of Ethical Consumer Behaviour

6

Scott Clouder   Rob Harrison

If consumers judge that companies are behaving badly, they can and will bring them to their knees ... there has never been such a sudden turn-around in policy as Shell has undertaken these past few days. A social movement that dates back to the consumer boycotts of Nestlé and Barclays is now coming of age.

The Independent, 21 June 1995 (the day after the Brent Spar climbdown)

INTRODUCTION

This chapter aims to examine the effectiveness of ethical consumer action in achieving social and political goals. It also seeks to identify some successes that both historical and current campaigns have enjoyed. As the editors' introduction to this book suggests, such a task is made difficult by virtue of the complex nature of the ethical consumerism concept and by the varied results that may constitute successful outcomes for different campaigns. Indeed, surveying and communicating the outcomes of individual shopping choices as they relate to corporate behaviour appears to be a lower priority for many campaign groups than the initial push to boycott or purchase differently. In addition, the way that some companies respond to consumer demands in an almost secretive manner (because to publicise a consumer-driven change would be tantamount to admitting there was a problem in the first place), means campaign objectives are often quietly implemented without the fanfare that accompanied the original criticism.

Furthermore, the context in which most consumer campaigns operate usually makes it impossible to be certain whether it was the campaign or other factors which caused a change in policy. As Harrison explained in Chapter 4, most consumer campaigns comprise only a small part of a broader political or corporate campaign. In such circumstances it may be that campaign publicity generated by other actions like shareholder campaigns, protests or pickets served to tip the company into action. It may even be that the company was poised to change anyway for other reasons, and that the timing was genuinely incidental.

Despite these difficulties, there has been a growing number of attempts to analyse the effectiveness of ethical purchase behaviour and campaigns, and this chapter considers them below, looking first at boycotts and then at positive buying. It then considers the relatively uncharted territory of secondary effects. If a consumer campaign targets one company, concessions are frequently matched by other companies in the same sector – not wishing to be singled out in a second wave of campaigning. We would argue that this clearly occurred in the sports shoe sector following criticisms of Nike for poor working conditions at its supplier companies in the 1990s. It is further argued that secondary effects may be substantial in comparison with primary effects on the original campaign target.

Of course consumer campaigns may also have unintended or negative consequences and these are briefly discussed. Finally there is an attempt to identify some of the key factors in a successful campaign. In the conclusion it is suggested that, whatever the short-term outcomes of consumer campaigns, they can serve to politicise and activate people who have become disillusioned with other political channels of action.

CONSUMER BOYCOTTS

Effectiveness and success

In 1990, N. Craig Smith (Smith, 1990b) published an original and comprehensive study of the effectiveness of ethical consumer behaviour and particularly of boycott actions. His approach, which made a distinction between boycott effectiveness and boycott success, has helped define the key themes in this chapter. He described boycott effectiveness as attaining a reduction of sales of the boycotted product, and distinguished it from boycott success, which is the achievement of the boycott's political objectives. In this way he explained that boycotts do not need to be effective in order to be successful or vice versa. He cited US sanctions against Cuba as a boycott that was effective but not necessarily successful in its wider aims. This scenario may have occurred less in the instance of consumer-led product boycotts but, according to Smith, it was still significant. So, sometimes a boycott will work but the underlying aims will not be realised, and sometimes a boycott won't be effective but the surrounding publicity will mean the objectives are met after all.

Expressive and instrumental boycotts

The second key point to note about boycotts is that some of them do not primarily seek a short-term goal of a change in company policy. Monroe Friedman (1999a), in the next major study of boycott behaviour, made a distinction between expressive and instrumental boycotts. An instrumental boycott aims to coerce the target to change its behaviour in a specific way, or to alter a disputed company policy. Expressive boycotts are more a form of generalised protest that demonstrates a consumer's antipathy towards the company or product as a whole. So, under this definition, joining a boycott of a clothes shop until it stopped selling fur coats would be an instrumental act, and simply refusing to buy fur generally would be more expressive.

Smith (1990b: 258) also discussed in detail how, in many cases, the boycott was essentially a moral act; an expression by the consumer of disapproval of the firms activities and disassociation from them. In such circumstances, he explained that it may not even be appropriate to refer to effectiveness at all. In particular, he likened such boycotts to a sense of moral duty, and cited participants in the anti-apartheid boycotts of South Africa in the 1980s as being individuals with a sense of morality that told them not to tarnish themselves with the hypocrisy of apartheid. From a business point of view, it is difficult if not impossible to counter such conceptions, save from complying to a boycott's demands.

In 1990, *Ethical Consumer* magazine (ECRA, 1990a) came to a similar conclusion by making a distinction between 'strategic boycotts' and 're-directive boycotts'. Whilst a strategic boycott aims for a specific change in company policy, a re-directive boycott may not expect to succeed but is content with highlighting a company's activities in the minds of consumers and redirecting some funds towards more ethical competitors.

It should be noted that Monroe Friedman's substantial work on consumer boycotts (1999a), also discussed a variety of different typologies of boycott which there is not sufficient space to discuss here. These included 'obstructionist boycotts' (perhaps using sit-ins or pickets) or 'surrogate boycotts' (targeting a third party). Friedman would probably describe StopEsso as a surrogate boycott since its demands related to Exxon Mobil's influence on the US government, regarding the latter's stance on climate change.

It is also worth noting that both Smith and Friedman provided much detailed evidence, both empirical and secondary, showing how boycotts were frequently used by both trades unions and poorer and marginal communities to protect their interests. Whilst there is evidence that positive buying tends to be practised more frequently by higher income groups (Cowe and Williams, 2001), this is definitely not the case with this form of ethical purchase behaviour.

Successful boycotts

The table of successful boycotts (Table 6.1) was compiled from two feature articles and the 'Boycott News' pages published in *Ethical Consumer* magazine over a fifteen-year span. It is not intended to be comprehensive, but simply serves to illustrate the range of issues upon which the boycott has been used with success. The source column indicates the issue number of the magazine in which the news story appeared. It is designed to complement a similar table in Smiths book (1990b) showing 23 successful boycotts in a list of 65 campaigns studied, and the very substantial number of successful campaigns discussed in Friedman's work (1999a).

It should be noted that the list also contains some instances where the threat of a boycott was sufficient for a change of direction by the company. For example, in 1989 Survival International threatened Scott Paper with a boycott because its plans for a eucalyptus plantation and paper mill in Indonesia threatened the survival of tribal peoples. In a letter to Scott Paper, Survival International wrote, 'if we call a boycott, we will mobilize our 20,000 members, and it will also be endorsed by the Sierra Club which has two million members'. In response, Scott Paper abandoned its plans (Murtagh and Lukehart, 2001: 7).

Other measures of the effectiveness and success of boycotts

Clearly a public change of direction by the boycott target company is the surest measure of success; however, we suggest four other potentially illuminating areas worthy of brief discussion. These include survey data, financial data, corporate responses and recruitment issues.

Table 6.1 Some successful consumer boycott campaigns 1986–2004

Year	Boycott issue and outcome	Co-ordinating group	Source
2004	Office depot concedes to recycled paper policy	Forest Ethics/Dogwood Alliance USA	EC89
2004	Price Waterhouse Coopers leaves Burma	Burma Campaign UK	EC87
2003	Focus DIY ceases sale of all pets	Animal Aid UK	EC84
2003	Kuoni stops selling tours to Burma	Burma Campaign UK	EC83
2003	Kookai Clothing pulls out of Burma	Burma Campaign UK	EC83
2003	Staples Office Supplies concedes to recycled paper campaign	Forest Ethics/Dogwood Alliance USA	EC83
2002	Premier Oil pulls out of Burma	Burma Campaign USA/UK	EC79
2002	Triumph pulls out of Burma	Burma campaign UK	EC79
2001	John Lewis ends employees' shooting trips	Animal Aid UK	EC79
2000	Mitsubishi makes concessions to rainforest campaigners	Rainforest Action Network USA	EC64
1999	Burger King closes West Bank outlet	Palestinian Solidarity Campaign UK	EC61
1998	Ford signs McBride principles on employment in Northern Ireland	Irish National Caucus USA	
1998	Texaco leaves Burma	Burma Campaign USA/UK	EC51
1997	Holiday Inn leaves Tibet	Free Tibet Campaign USA/UK	EC49
1997	P&O stops live animal transport	Respect for Animals/CIWF UK	EC48
1997	Pepsi and Apple leave Burma	Burma Campaign USA/UK	EC48
1997	Gillette announces moratorium on animal testing	PETA (International)	EC48
1996	BHS leaves Burma	Burma Campaign UK	EC44
1996	French nuclear testing halted	CND (International)	EC40
1995	Shell disposes of Brent Spar oil platform on land	Greenpeace (International)	EC39
1994	Big Six DIY firms agree to stop selling mahogany	FoE UK	EC39
1994	Selfridges stops selling fur	London Anti-Fur Campaign UK	EC39
1994	Some major supermarkets stop selling Faroese fish due to whaling, other supermarkets agree to label the produce	Pilot Whale Campaign UK	EC39
1994	Scott Paper cancels clear-cutting at Claquot Sound	Greenpeace (International)	EC39
1993	South African apartheid regime ends and boycott of South African produce ceases	Anti-Apartheid (International)	EC39
1993	British Midland ceases transporting live monkeys, some other airlines follow	BUAV UK	EC39

1993	Jack Daniels and Grolsch-Ruddles amongst others stops sponsoring angling competitions	Pisces UK	EC39
1993	General Motors stops using animals for crash tests	PET/BUAV USA	EC39
1991	Philip Morris diverts cash to redress balance of its financial support for homophobic senator	ACT-UP USA	EC39
1990	Ratners divest from South Africa before boycott is officially launched	Anti-Apartheid UK	EC11
1989	Scott Paper pulls out of Indonesian plantation over threat to tribal peoples	Survival International USA/UK	EC11
1989	Bird's Eye and Tesco stop selling Icelandic fish due to whaling	Greenpeace UK	EC11
1989	Avon stops animal testing	PETA etc. (International)	EC11
1988	Benetton stops animal testing	BUAV/PETA etc. UK	EC11
1988	Leading UK retailers stop using CFCs in packaging, as well as eight leading aerosol companies	FoE UK	EC11
1986	Eight leading sports shoe companies capitulate to threat of boycott if they use kangaroo skin – some later renege	Greenpeace (International)	EC11
1986	Barclays Bank pulls out of South Africa	Anti-Apartheid (International)	EC11

Survey data

Consumer surveys often ask questions about boycotts, and some have reported very high levels of people claiming boycott activity. One survey in 2001 revealed that 'two thirds of UK consumers in their thirties and forties – with a weekly spending power of nearly £4.5 billion – had boycotted brands because of their unethical behaviour' (ECRA, 2002d: 33). In Chapter 12 of this book Worcester and Dawkins note, however, the tendency for over-reporting in this type of survey.

Other surveys ask more specific questions, and one conducted by the National Consumer Council (1996) asked about three boycotts current at the time. They reported that 62 per cent of people had not participated; 6 per cent had supported the boycott of Shell over Brent Spar; 15 per cent had supported boycotts of French products over nuclear testing; and 24 per cent had supported campaigns over live animal exports.

The Co-operative Bank's consumer panel (2003) revealed 52 per cent of people claiming to have boycotted at least one product over the last 12 months, with two-thirds of them claiming not to return to a brand once they have boycotted it. This same survey also generated calculations of the financial value of boycotts which we discuss below. It is also covered briefly in Chapter 8.

Financial data

> Most people think that you've got to reduce sales a lot, but if you reduce any company's sales from [between] two to five percent you've won. Having said that, it is very hard to reduce a company's sales by 5 per cent because it takes a massive degree of organisation.
>
> Ralph Nader (*Co-op America*, 1989)

Very occasionally, financial data from within a company can reveal in detail the impact of a particular boycott. In a classic example, an internal Barclays Bank document was leaked to the Anti-Apartheid Movement revealing that the company considered its share of the UK student market to have fallen from 27 per cent to 17 per cent between 1983 and 1985 following a particularly successful boycott campaign (Smith, 1990b: 241). In a similar way, it was revealed that the boycott of Montgomery City Line buses over racial segregation in the USA in 1955 cost the bus company more than $7,000 a day in lost revenue. The outcome, apart from the near bankruptcy of the bus company, was an end to bus segregation in Montgomery and other cities of the South (Smith, 1990b: 214).

A company's share price can also be an indicator of successful pressure. One study (Pruitt and Friedman, 1986) found that announcements of consumer boycotts (in the USA) were followed by statistically significant decreases in stock prices over the following two months (that is, before much of a drop in sales was likely to occur).

The Co-operative Bank consumer panel (2003) asked a representative survey sample to save receipts as evidence of their ethical purchases. The project then extrapolated a monetary value for relevant sales if these patterns were repeated across the UK. They concluded that, in 2002, £2.6 billion of consumer spending had been redirected because of boycotts. £232 million was responding to clothing boycotts, £787 million to grocery boycotts and £454 million to transport boycotts (primarily the StopEsso petrol boycott over climate change lobbying).

Corporate responses to boycotts

It is not possible to study consumer boycott effectiveness without studying the target's reaction to the protest. How firms react will obviously have a direct impact on the boycott's success, but also on its effectiveness, as the firm's response to the challenge may incite more publicity on the subject. A satisfactory response, complying to a campaign's demands, can stop a boycott before it has even got under way, whereas a reaction that is deemed inadequate or insulting could potentially recruit new members to the campaign. Smith identified four key types of management response: ignore, fight, fudge/explain or comply (1990b: 254).

Ignore

Companies which choose to ignore consumer pressure leave their destiny to the 'will' of market forces – on the face of it, a risky strategy. However, some business publications suggest that companies that enter into dialogue with activist groups and NGOs may add publicity to the original complaint and also send signals to activist groups that they are ready to comply to all demands (*The Economist*, 2003).

Fight

An aggressive reaction towards an organising group can take one of two paths: to discredit the allegations of misconduct made by the boycott group, or to simply attack and attempt to discredit the boycotting group.

Some companies have tried to address campaigners' allegations by suing for libel. The most well-known example in the UK involved McDonald's in the 1990s. The 'McLibel' trial, as it has become known, saw the company trying to silence and punish two London Greenpeace activists for distributing leaflets containing allegations about the fast food chain's effects on animals, the environment and human health. The case made history not only because it was the longest running civil trial recorded in the UK but because the company, with all its corporate might, was forced to attempt to substantiate some of its claims that the activists were spreading untruths. Despite the best lawyers and PR firms money could buy, McDonald's was forced to concede on some points, and won a hollow victory (Vidal, 1997).

As part of this 'aggressive response' to boycotters, some corporate strategists and PR gurus have initiated an attempt to routinely discredit NGOs through websites such as Activistcash.com. In 2003 the American Enterprise Institute set up a website called NGOWatch to 'bring clarity and accountability to the burgeoning world of NGOs' (*The Economist*, 2003).

Fudge/explain

It is a central thesis of this book that pressure from radicalised consumers is having a general effect of promoting greater transparency by corporations. Adams and Zutshi in Chapter 13 consider this 'defensive response' in some detail, looking particularly at environmental reporting and supplier codes of conduct. Esso's response to the StopEsso campaign has largely been of this type. It has been described, for example, as 'a PR counter-offensive against what it calls the "highly misleading" arguments of Stop Esso' (Pratley, 2003).

Comply

As even *The Economist* states (*The Economist*, 2003): 'Where brand matters, it may be better to talk than fight. That was Nike's response: its brand was the key to the value of its shoes.'

The Nestlé boycott

Nestlé is a company that has been boycotted since the 1970s because of its approach to the marketing of breast-milk substitutes. This longstanding boycott has seen Nestlé try all the boycott-combating options available to it. After initially ignoring the boycott, Nestlé attacked the boycott organisers in 1974 with legal action. This followed a War on Want publication that branded the company as a 'baby killer'. It succeeded with the libel action but it attracted much adverse publicity, with even the case judge attacking the company's practices.

Currently it is focusing on a PR-based (fudge/explain) approach that includes a carefully controlled presence on university campuses to sell the Nestlé line to students. In 1999 the UK Advertising Standards Authority upheld all of Baby Milk Action's complaints about a Nestlé anti-boycott advertisement, where the company claimed that it markets infant formula 'ethically and responsibly' (Baby Milk Action, 1999).

Recruitment

Although attention to the initial reason for a boycott may be deflected by a company response, our experience suggests that it will never completely go away, and the publicity is liable to engender a negative image that penetrates not just consumers' minds but those of current and prospective company staff. According to *The Economist*, the country's brightest graduate chemical engineers are shunning the likes of BP and accepting job offers from the computer software sector, because it is seen as a greener industry than petroleum.

> You have problems with employee morale. Employees don't like working for a company that is being attacked. You have problems with recruiting the top students from colleges and universities because they don't want to get involved with a company in that kind of problem. Also you'll find that top level executives spend an inordinate amount of time on the issue when they should be doing other things. (Monogoven in Murtagh and Lukehart, 2001: 8)

Nestlé has also admitted being worried about its recruitment of high-quality graduates, as evidenced by an interview with Peter Blackburn, Nestlé UK's CEO (*Guardian*, 2001).

POSITIVE BUYING

In many ways tracking the effectiveness of positive buying is much more straight-forward than tracking the effectiveness of boycotts. A fair trade product or organic vegetable can be traced back to its producing farm and the impact of chemical reduction or wage rises can be studied in detail. Before we look briefly at its effectiveness at achieving political goals, it is first worth examining some attempts to measure the size and extent of this type of behaviour. One project in particular, the Co-operative Bank's Ethical Purchasing Index, is attempting to do this in a systematic way in the UK, and we will look at this first.

The Ethical Purchasing Index

The Co-operative Bank's Ethical Purchasing Initiative project is designed to measure the trends and UK market share of various ethical consumer goods and services. Designed in conjunction with the UK NGO New Economics Foundation, its methodology consists of defining an 'ethical shopping basket', tracking consumption in food, energy, housing, household goods, cosmetics and toiletries, transport, charity and leisure. The bank published its fourth annual EPI Report in December 2003. Copies are distributed to government agencies, business and consumer organisations,

Table 6.2 Ethical Purchasing Index UK spending calculations 2002

Description	Spending (£m)
Household	
Food (including fair trade and organics)	1,770
Green household goods	1,473
Personal items (including cosmetics not tested on animals)	187
Responsible tourism	107
Green housing spend (including green energy)	33
Green transport spend	21
Charitable donations	3,309
Invisibles	
Buying second-hand	1,255
Ethical boycotts	2,582
Local shopping	1,568
Public transport	162
Finance	
Ethical banking	3,886
Ethical investment	3,510
TOTAL FOR 2002	19,863

and the bank claims that: 'All used the Index to evidence growth in the ethical market and to help make the case for expanding the market in order to create more opportunity for consumers to choose ethical products' (Evans, 2003).

The current report informs us that from a baseline of 100 in 1999, the UK Ethical Purchasing Index has increased 30 points to 130 in 2002 (Co-operative Bank, 2003: 7). The actual figures from the 2003 report are reproduced in Table 6.2.

The inclusion of 'ethical invisibles' was a new move for the 2003 report, and was measured by way of a consumer panel (see also Chapter 8 of this book). It relied on analysing product choice from the point of view of consumer motivation. Using this method it identified, for example, that 4 per cent of respondents used the bus expressly for environmental reasons. It could then project an actual value of sales if this pattern were to be repeated across the country. Boycotts of products were also accounted for under the heading of ethical invisibles (see Boycotts: Financial Data above). 'For the majority of consumers ethics do indeed play a role in their purchasing choices. It's just that their behaviours do not conform to traditional definitions of ethical consumption. Rather, they are engaged in what we have termed "ethical invisibles" (such as shopping locally in support of their communities)' (S. Williams, in Co-operative Bank, 2003: 4).

OTHER FINANCIAL DATA

Table 6.3 is now four years old and market shares in all these sectors have grown considerably. Nevertheless it is still useful in that it demonstrates how geographically diverse the phenomenon of ethical purchasing is. It has been compiled from two sources, Commenne (2001) and the European Fair Trade Association (2001).

Although in most cases total market shares remain below 5 per cent, we know that the potential for very significant growth remains. For example, the Co-operative Bank estimates that A-rated household appliances (more energy efficient) in the UK have a 41 per cent market share and that free range eggs have a 40 per cent retail market share (Co-operative Bank, 2003: 9).

Table 6.3 Ethical products market shares 2000

Country	Market share (%)			
	Fair trade coffee	Fair trade bananas	Organic food	Organic food sales
Germany	1	<1	2.5	2,355
France	0.1		1	1,165
Netherlands	2.7	4.2	1	1,041
Italy	0.13	1.2	3	868
Switzerland	3	15	1	793
UK	1.5	<1	3.2	744
Denmark	1.8	2	1.5	570
Austria	0.7		3.5	397
Sweden	0.8	1.8	1.2	347
Belgium	1	0.6	1	149
Total Europe				8,899
USA			1.75	7,536
Japan				2,058
Total world				18,493

Size of ethical companies

There are some companies which have decided to adopt a public-facing ethical position and, when these companies are successful financially, observing their growth and relative market position allows us to further develop our picture of the effectiveness of ethical purchasing. For example, in the UK the Co-operative Bank and the Body Shop are the two most frequently quoted examples of this type of company. In 2003 the Co-operative Bank reported pre-tax profits of £130.1 million for 2003, up 6.2 per cent (£7.6 million) on the previous year (Co-operative Bank, 2004a). In 2003 the Body Shop had global sales of $711 million (Hoovers, 2004).

Positive buying and political goals

As we mentioned above, measuring the effectiveness of positive buying does not usually have the causal problems associated with boycott campaigns. We know, for example, that in 2003 there were around 4,000 organic farms in the UK (Soil Association, 2003). This represented 726,400 hectares, roughly 4 per cent of the total. Issues of local pesticide impact, sustainability and animal welfare will all have been more substantially addressed in these neighbourhoods than in other localities. In the same way, we know that around 800,000 families of farmers and workers (around five million people) coming from over 45 countries in Africa, Asia and Latin America have benefited from the fair trade movement (Fairtrade Foundation, 2004a).

It should be noted that the fair trade movement itself is not without criticism. Burns and Blowfield (1999: 20) have, for example, discussed how:

a) fair trade does not always benefit poor people, and
b) where it does so, it is often in more complicated ways than are portrayed in fair trade advertising.

Thus, 'a search of the available literature on ethical trade reveals very little evidence but a lot of wishful thinking about the impacts of ethical trade on its intended beneficiaries' (Burns and Blowfield, 1999: 20).

SECONDARY EFFECTS

Secondary effects of boycotts

Although boycotts invariably have stated targets and aims, their effects are likely to be felt more widely. It is these secondary effects that concern us in this section.

Sector clean-ups

Sometimes ethical boycotts of one brand may act as a catalyst to 'clean up' an entire business sector. This can be achieved by media/consumer attention being drawn to one company and then the simple logic of the ethical information learnt being extrapolated to all other companies in a sector. To some extent, the boycotts of Nike over working conditions in the footwear industry in the Far East can be said to have led to improvements at key competitors – such as Adidas and Reebok – as well (Harrison, 2003: 128). Adidas executives will have observed the targeting of its competitor and been careful not to draw attention to its own activities by failing to address the issues raised.

In the same way, it is likely that the lesson meted out to Shell during the Brent Spar boycott has set the scene for all other oil companies thinking of deep sea disposal of their redundant extraction equipment. They may, however, vary in the way they address them.

It has been argued that because companies may be reluctant to change as the result of hostile pressure and that competitor companies may be able to move discreetly without 'loss of face', secondary effects could be greater than primary ones in many circumstances (Towell, 1998). Although this is potentially a very significant effect of boycotts, it is an area of study which still awaits substantial analysis.

Government responses

Governments may seek to move in to regulate a sector that has been plagued by boycott actions. To some extent this can be observed in the clothing and footwear sectors in the White House-sponsored Fair Labor Association (FLA) and the UK government-supported Ethical Trading Initiative. In both these cases the governments involved established voluntary frameworks to deal with these issues.

Corporate disclosure

The publication and distribution of environment and/or social responsibility reports to customers and investors by many of today's largest companies is one obvious secondary effect of boycotts. This response has also been discussed under Corporate Responses to Boycotts above, and in Chapter 13 in this book.

Secondary effects of positive buying

> Although it is difficult to attribute causality, it is certainly possible to argue that fair-trade has influenced the behaviour of mainstream beverage companies, and the increased profile of organic agricultural produce has affected the development of integrated crop management systems. Ethical trade can also help to raise support for public policies. (Burns and Blowfield 1999: 20)

As well as beverage companies, the presence of the Co-operative Bank in the retail banking sector in the UK has arguably led to a faster rate of ethical policy development at other banks than in other comparable countries.

Another thing that successful ethical businesses do is to posit an alternative model for development. It is possible to envisage, for example, a future where the model of the organic farm has become the dominant type of food production organisation rather than a niche concern as at present. New entrepreneurs and owners of existing businesses can observe a working company model which is both successful and different from the mainstream and purely financially focused organisation.

UNINTENDED CONSEQUENCES

Disinvestment

Perhaps the simplest example of an unexpectedly negative effect of ethical consumer action, particularly a brand boycott, is that of disinvestment as discussed here by Burns and Blowfield (1999: 21).

Southern activists, in particular, are concerned that well-meaning ethical trade policies may in fact have negative impacts on workers in particular areas, for example through:

- contracts cancelled due to boycotts;
- relocation to other countries if improved conditions lead to cost increases locally;
- codes used to replace and thereby undermine collective bargaining;
- voluntary processes used to undermine public regulation.

The demands of ethical trade may be most easily and profitably met by multinational companies. Indeed, they go on to argue how ethical trade may strengthen the economic power of multinational corporations thus squeezing out small and medium sized enterprises and small producers. This remains a key dilemma for all those involved in ethical trading initiatives. For example, in the case of football stitching in Sialkot, Pakistan, homeworkers have lost out as work has been centralised in factories which are easier to monitor and verify.

In the same way Heeks and Duncombe have discussed some outcomes that, for practical reasons ('design-reality gaps') have proved unsuccessful in implementing a trade system that benefits workers in the majority world:

> Designs mismatched to the socio-economic realities of poor livelihoods: so that blunt-instrument bans on child labour cause more problems than they solve. Designs mismatched to the socio-politics of the workplace: so that audits are

seen by workers as a management initiative, causing them to paint a partial or falsely-positive picture to auditors ... These design-reality mismatches undermine the crucial audit process by producing audit data that falls short on some of the key data criteria. (2003: 20)

Company group restructuring to avoid pressure

The classic example of this kind of effect occurred following a boycott by US corporate campaign specialists INFACT against General Electric over its production of nuclear weapons and its influence over US government weapons policy. The boycott was launched in 1986 and by 1991 had still not forced significant concessions from the company. A short film entitled *Deadly Deception* was then released depicting the grassroots campaign. In 1992 the film unexpectedly won an Oscar, the campaign gained momentum as a result and attracted 4 million supporters in 14 countries (Friedman, 1999a: 177).

INFACT stated that 'after years of pressure, on April 2, 1993, General Electric took a dramatic step out of nuclear weapons by selling its Aerospace Division, removing one of the most powerful forces influencing nuclear weapons policy-making' (INFACT, 2004a). INFACT called off the boycott of General Electric but this was not the end of the story. Friedman discussed both General Electric and AT&T (another boycott target for its nuclear activities) as the companies activities took parallel turns.

> ... the weapons activities continued under other corporate auspices, and, interestingly, the new owners were companies immune to boycott threats because they neither manufactured nor sold consumer goods. Nonetheless, the acts of dissociation with the weapons activities ... were heralded as victories by the boycott groups. By the criteria here, it would be a micro-success and not a macro-success since the boycotts did not result in the discontinuance of military activity. (Friedman, 1999a: 18)

There is also published discussion of Union Carbide's divestment of consumer brands after the company's Bhopal factory tragedy. This evasion manoeuvre was designed to reduce the likelihood of a consumer backlash (Zadek et al., 1998b: 33).

Poorly designed campaigns

A poorly designed consumer boycott campaign may of course have harmful unintended consequences. For example, the outcry against '"French" fries by pro-Bush supporters in the USA following France's opposition to the Iraq invasion had, apparently, more of an economic impact on Idaho potato farmers than on the French government's policies' (US Chamber of Commerce, 2003: 1).

KEY FACTORS IN EFFECTIVENESS AND SUCCESS

Instrumental or strategic boycotts – which seek changes in corporate policy – can be either effective or ineffective depending on factors such as the choice of target and the efficiency of the organisers. There is insufficient space to discuss this fully here, but it is worth noting that the subject has been covered in some detail in the core boycott texts.

Monroe Friedman (1999a: 21) has written a whole chapter on the subject looking at how different tactics can be appropriate to different types of campaign. N. Craig Smith (1990b: 260) has also analysed the area. Central to both reviews are three obvious factors:

- cause – consumers must care about the cause or issue at the heart of the campaign;
- candidate – the boycott target must be visible, image conscious and likely to comply;
- co-ordination – the campaign group must have the resources to run the campaign (although these need not be financial).

CONCLUSIONS

Boycotts

Despite the problems of causation, many writers agree that there is compelling and widespread evidence of boycott actions delivering on social/environmental goals. Examples from Heeks and Duncombe (2003: 15) include reductions in child labour in Central American garment manufacture; workers being reinstated and allowed to unionise in garment factories in Central America; improvements in health and safety conditions in footwear factories in South-East Asia; reductions in water and air pollution emissions from factories in Asia and Central America. Our own table (Table 6.1) of boycott successes also identified substantial progress in areas such as: animal welfare and testing; forest destruction; corporate support for oppressive regimes.

Obviously consumer boycotts cannot effectively address the full range of social and environmental issues, because they require choice and competitive markets to function. Nevertheless, as discussed by Harrison in Chapter 4, ethical purchase behaviour is particularly useful at addressing global issues where national governments are reluctant to regulate. And unlike positive buying which tends to require surplus income, we have argued that boycotts also provide a useful mechanism for poorer marginalised or disempowered communities to defend their interests.

Positive buying

Many commentators have noted the small market share for many ethical products and used this to downplay its significance. For example, Lazzarini and de Mello note that 89 per cent of UK consumers report concern about social/ethical issues, but less than 5 per cent make active purchasing decisions on these factors most of the time: 'The result – when motivation and willingness to pay are added to factors like brand loyalty, switching costs, lack of alternative products, and information asymmetries – is that consumers will generally not switch in large numbers from goods that rank poorly on ethical criteria to goods that rank well (Lazzarini and de Mello, 2001).

In the same way the share of ethical goods and services in the UK as defined by the Ethical Purchasing Index (EPI) is at less than 2 per cent. According to the *Guardian* newspaper's calculations, the £2.6 billion figure of UK boycott expenditure works out at a mere four pence for every £10 spent by British households (Pratley, 2003). Alison Benjamin summed this up: '... the EPI shows that ethical consumers still command only a 1.6 percent share of the marketplace across seven sectors. This consumption is a fraction of the spending power of three-quarters of consumers who tell pollsters that they care about issues enough to sometimes purchase ethical products' (Benjamin, 2002).

The Co-operative Bank itself admits in the report that: 'Whilst ethical consumers can act as innovators in getting new products to the market, for real progress to be made supply side influences or government intervention may be required for some products and services to achieve mass market adoption (Co-operative Bank, 2003: 6).

Nevertheless some more mature ethical markets – such as free range eggs – have reached close to majority support, and this remains a realistic long-term goal for many campaigners.

Spontaneous and expressive activity

Studies of boycotts have shown that there are a whole class of boycotts that are primarily expressive: they seek to express disapproval but do not particularly seek to change company policy. Campaign groups know that boycotts can provide an excellent focus for grassroots public awareness raising which has to be the bedrock of any long-term social change. Boycotts of familiar products also allow campaigners to raise complex social issues in a way which has immediate relevance to a sometimes cynical and disillusioned public.

In addition, spontaneous ethical consumer behaviour is widespread. A survey in the UK in 1989 revealed that almost half of those questioned were operating some kind of personal boycott of products in the market-place (ECRA, 1989b: 1). These ranged from the expected, such as the avoidance of environmentally damaging products, to the unexpected, such as boycotts by older consumers of products from Japan because of the part the country played in the Second World War.

Spontaneous motivations may also be complex and multifaceted. Some vegetarians may choose their diet for religious reasons, others for health benefits and yet others in 'instrumental' protest at factory farming. Many others may have voluntarily reduced meat consumption for some of these reasons but would not be identified as vegetarian in the normal course of events.

Although spontaneous and expressive activity may not be immediately 'effective' in moving markets, it should not be denigrated or used as a reason for doubting the effectiveness of ethical purchasing generally. Given that product choice is a widely recognised route for many types of self-expression for contemporary consumers, it is laudable that many consumers have chosen to express social concerns through their purchases. Consumption is a legitimate and important venue for public discourse about right and wrong in contemporary societies. Indeed, Dickinson and Carsky in Chapter 2 have gone so far as to argue that governments should encourage this kind of behaviour because the public interest will be a long-term beneficiary.

Belief in effectiveness

There are at least two consumer surveys which have shown that a lack of belief in the ability of individual consumers to make a difference is a key deterrent for people thinking of adopting ethical purchase behaviours. The first looked at ecological purchasing in the USA in 1974 (Smith, 1990b: 229), and the second at green purchasing in the UK in 1996 (National Consumer Council, 1996). To some extent, discussions such as those in this chapter can help address uncertainly over effectiveness by distinguishing expressive and instrumental activity. Also effective in challenging this belief will be a further growth of market share for ethical products and continued evidence of demonstrably successful boycott campaigns.

The boycott tactic provides people with a form of political action that is cheap, immediate, non-time consuming and not requiring of any special skill. What better way could there be to allow people who feel politically disempowered to start feeling they can have some influence? Considering only 59 per cent of those eligible voted in the UK's last general election, it is encouraging to see that, according to the EPI above, roughly the same proportion of citizens made a political statement with their shopping basket in the same year.

Part Three

Understanding Ethical Consumers

Case Studying Ethical Consumers' Projects and Strategies

7

Terry Newholm

I begin this chapter with an outline of my understanding of the restless consumer culture and the consumer research within which my work was set. The second section is a brief review of the approaches to case study, as these are associated to particular theoretical perspectives. I indicate appropriate further reading and raise some of the issues with which a researcher is confronted.

My multiple case study of 16 'ethical consumers' in the UK during the late 1990s is presented in the third section. Their projects to distance themselves from unethical consumption, to rationalise consumer culture and/or become integrated into its struggles are my contribution to our understanding of such consumers. I intend this also as an illustration of case study practice and refer back occasionally to the issues raised in the methodological section.

The quality of this type of analysis depends on the openness and logic of the process (Thomas, 1998) but there is insufficient space here to include the full development of the analysis. However, the complete thesis (Newholm, 2000) and data are available. In this chapter, I have been selective in my use of comparative tables and participants' quotations and have abbreviated arguments. Do not be surprised to find me saying that my thinking has changed since completing this research – I consider that a good outcome. Please skip the second section on 'case study' if you are not interested in the methodology.

CONSUMER CULTURE AND CONSUMER RESEARCH

Consumption as an aspect of most people's lives in affluent societies is widely acknowledged as having become increasingly important. As Alan Durning (1992) documented, we consume more and consume more often than previous generations. Increasingly personal areas of our lives are commodified, but as Bertell Ollman (1998) notes our involvement encompasses more than the acts of purchase and consumption. We prepare for, worry about and recover from consumption.

Much has been written about people as consumers, about the apparent rise of ethical attitudes and the lack of corresponding change in consumer practices: the so-called 'words/deeds inconsistency'. Ölander and Thøgersen (1995) review approaches to this perceived phenomenon. This leaves the very notion of an 'ethical consumer' as a contested debate and the subject of competing political interpretations (Newholm, 1999b; Chapters 1 and 2). I have assumed that to have a concern for the culturally specific consumption issues (see this book's introduction) is, *prima facie*, legitimate and therefore that some notion of an ethical consumer is valid. I would, however, suggest that it is better to think of our widening consumption as attracting our ethical consideration than of any increasing morality amongst consumers.

The central question addressed by the study I am reporting here has been, in the cases where consumers describe themselves as ethical, how can they do so in so potentially daunting an environment? Three theoretical features of the ethical consumers' environment are apparent:

- all purchases exhibit ethical dimensions and therefore the potential scope of concern is as wide as an individual's consumption itself;
- the issues arising from consumption acts are at best complex and in some moral respects irresolvable;
- in a continually changing global market, for example where businesses change hands and products change specifications, decisions can only be contingent.

However, specific consumer practices should not be seen in isolation. Animal welfare, human rights, environmental sustainability and corporate responsibility combine, overlap, conflict and vie for attention. There are, therefore, social and contextual questions concerning the way consumers sustain their notion of themselves as ethical, the attention they give and importance they attribute to ethical consumption and what, if anything, stops them from changing their consumer practices further.

Consumer research

Outside the marketing discipline, there has been a belated academic interest in consumers, as Miller (1995) says, rescued from the abstractions of polemic politics. This interest has reinvigorated research that otherwise has tended to be extensive and providing thin abstracted and decontextualised data. However, new debates often engage at an entirely theoretical level as reviewed by Gabriel and Lang (1995). Representations of consumers in sufficient depth to suggest the complexity of their life worlds are only relatively recent. For instance, I would give examples of Lunt and Livingstone's (1992) general survey of consumers; Burgess et al., (1995) and their cross cultural comparative study of environmental attitudes; Miller et al., (1998) and their study of everyday shopping; and Thompson's (2003) narratives of alternative therapy users.

Nevertheless extensive survey research, including market research, has highlighted important issues. Market research has, for instance, charted the widening of consumer interest from only environmental to a broad spectrum of social concerns, especially among the higher socio-economic groups, and among more women than men (Mintel, 1994). From this, however, apparently irresolvable debates have arisen around the so-called 'words/deeds inconsistency' (Wong et al., 1995) or 'attitude behaviour gap' (Carrigan and Attalla, 2001; Roberts, 1996), questions of product quality and price and, within the sustainability debate, conflicting concepts of communication aimed at modifying behaviour (Ölander and Thøgersen, 1995). Following Berke et al. (1993), who found consumers willing to discuss inconsistencies, my approach seeks to redefine these debates by showing the limitations of individual action and by employing a more rounded conceptualisation of the consumer.

I have chosen to view ethical consumers as seeking integrity in a complex and contradictory environment constrained by what they might achieve. I understand such actions to be taken within market relationships where, as Hirschman (1979) observed, consumers may exit from products and voice their opinions with some effect. However, in accordance with Smith's (1990a) seminal work on ethical consumers, I suggest consumers are not sovereign (see Chapter 2 in this book).

CASE STUDY

Case study strategy is used widely to gain an in-depth understanding of one or more consumers, neo-tribes, organisations, phenomena and so on. Indeed N. Craig Smith (1990a) who conducted one of the earliest studies of consumer boycott is a strong advocate of case study. It is generally accepted as a good approach for exploring 'how' and 'why' questions, as you will see in the research I present. However, there is a deep division between modernists whose primary concern is to ensure that the research processes used are rigorous, and pre-structured to deliver internal validity and reliability (see for example, Riege, 2003) and poststructuralists who primarily concern themselves with creating opportunities for understanding, researcher reflexivity and case representation (see Stake, 1995).

This issue of theoretical perspective cannot be avoided since particular research methods and concerns will imply their own perspective. Your ontology, how you believe the world to be, will inform your epistemology, how you believe you might gain knowledge of it, and vice versa. Like many academics, after much reading and consideration I have shifted to a more constructivist position. I now view this research as being a little too concerned with how the participants fitted into the world (as I see it) and not sufficiently how they constructed their realities.

Unlike Riege (2003: 76) who recommends suiting your theoretical perspective to the disciplinary purpose, I think is it better to be broadly comfortable with a theoretical position and then seek consistent methodologies. If you decide to uncover a single reality then Robert Yin (2003) is acknowledged as having provided the most comprehensive approach to social scientific case study. Yin demonstrates how case studies can be pre-structured to maximise researcher objectivity and to answer specific prefigured questions.

If, alternatively, you believe the flux of events to be rendered comprehensible through our stories and practices as humans then realities become relative and researcher objectivity evaporates. Rather you might read Robert Stake (1995) and reflect on your part in the research while you construct opportunities to explore the meanings others hold about events.

Case study does not necessarily imply any particular methods. Accordingly positivists advocate employing some quantitative methods (Reige, 2003; Yin, 2003) whilst constructivists sometimes admit that quantitative methods might, where appropriate, have a limited role to play (Smith, 1990b) in this essentially qualitative approach.

The divergence I have been describing does not mean that there are not points of agreement or that both perspectives are internally coherent. For example, Yin insists that the integrity of each case should be maintained while we make any comparisons. I agree and have presented 16 case outlines to try to ensure the reader can relate extracts to each consumer story. Within constructivism there is disagreement as to whether all human stories are entirely relative or whether some are more adequate than others (see Sayer, 1999; Williams, 2000). I have presented the poles as more or less coherent and distinct for pedagogic purposes.

Sampling and exampling

It is considered quite legitimate to research a single case because it is an exemplar or a revelatory case (see for example, Kozinets, 2002). In multiple case study deciding on what cases to include is again related to theoretical perspective. A positivistic approach demands that you select cases as representative of what is considered to be a 'population' in our example of ethical consumers. Again Yin gives excellent advice on selection. Strauss and Corbin (1998) recommended theoretical sampling where the researcher seeks cases deliberately in order to test developing ideas.

However, if we construct and transform competing concepts of what is 'ethical' through our consumption practices, then our 'population' becomes more nebulous. In such exploratory studies variety is important (Stake, 1995) to afford a broad review of meanings. I have referred to my varied participants as 'examples of …' to distinguish them from a (scientific) sample. I should, strictly, describe my participants as examples of people who would respond to an invitation to contribute to a study as an ethical consumer.

Setting and boundary issues

At an early stage in case study research, a decision has to be made about primary focus. In the case of ethical consumption, for example, is it best to look at the meta-narratives that orientate us to the idea of 'ethical consumption', a specific product group such as green electricity, individual issues such as fair trade or consumers themselves. I chose consumers but still had to make a decision about the boundary. Would I be interested in, say, the discourses of collectivities that frequent wholefood shops, families and their internal tensions, individual consumer lifestyle or perhaps specific 'ethical decisions'? I chose individual consumers without restricting issues because, at the time, I wanted to explore the complexity of their lives.

Multiple cases

From the point that I settled on multiple case study of ethical consumers as my research strategy the question of how many cases to include was a recurrent discussion. There seemed to be some trade-off to be made between depth of investigation and number of cases. If I conceived my participants as having been recruited from different habitats and potentially exhibiting real differences, I might follow Yin (2003) and construct a comparative matrix of say three churchgoers, three academics, three alternatives and three protesters. Comparison might then be made through literal similarities within 'groups' and contrast between 'groups' through theoretical replications (Yin, 2003). Such structure, Yin argues, must be held against 'slippage'.

However, I grew to think of my work as more exploratory and less structured. An influential theory advocates adding cases until nothing further is being learnt (Znaniecki, 1934) but the approach has been criticised (Williams, 2000), and pragmatically this was unlikely to appeal to a funding body. Some years later I was presenting sets of 10 to 12 consumer cases to retail practitioners. They made the important point that a reader would loose track if more than this number of cases were presented. In this sense the representation of consumers to readers becomes an important consideration. You might, therefore, find the 16 presented here to be too many!

Generalising

Generalisation from qualitative research is very different from quantitative work such as market surveys and experimental designs. Where quantitative research intends to generate 'facts' (see Chapter 10 in this book), qualitative work seeks understanding grounded in empirical data. Williams (2000) offers a valuable review of competing theories of generalisability and recommends moderation and rigour. I think that in the following extract Thomas offers a pragmatic and moderating approach to generalising from qualitative research:

> Either the case studies will confirm your ideas so that you are more confident about generalizing on their basis or else the case studies will throw doubt on the applicability of your ideas in different circumstances, in which case you should be able to reconceptualize and generalize on the basis of changed or new ideas. (1998: 323)

Thus results always return to theory (Yin, 2003). However, as Stake (1995) argues, the primary focus of poststructural research is understanding; generalisation is secondary.

ETHICAL CONSUMERS: A MULTIPLE CASE STUDY APPROACH

In order to explore the 'attitudes', meanings and practices of ethical consumers in a limiting environment it is necessary to use methods that reveal considerable depth. Additionally whilst studies of particular issues like fair trade, child labour, and so on are valuable, consumers live in a complex world of competing considerations. Therefore, I adopted a multiple case study approach. Fieldwork was carried out in the UK during 1997 and 1998.

Excepting the pilot study, the individuals contributing to my research were self-selecting 'ethical consumers'. They were all located in one of four cultural 'habitats': church groups, academic settings, alternative venues and protests. No attempt was made to construct a sample. Rather, what follows are examples of ethical consumers drawn deliberately from a variety of possible habitats. Equally, whether or not it might be possible, they should not be considered to be representative of all 'types' of ethical consumer. The 16 participants were, however, selected to give an even number of women and men with at least two being drawn from each habitat.

The data collection methods were additionally designed to examine influences, concepts of ethical consuming, and participants' other interests. I designed data collection and analysis to have sequential stages to build a cumulative under-standing of each consumer. As a first stage each participant filled in a short ques-tionnaire, recorded narratives about their ethical consumption and collected receipts of purchase. I transcribed the audiotape narratives and categorised the text. Along with my analysis of the receipts and the questionnaires, this provided the basis on which I formulated my questions for the semi-structured interview at the second stage.

In these interviews I predominately used non-directive questions because they 'are less likely to result in the omission of factors of which the researcher has not thought' (Hammersley and Atkinson, 1995: 152). Additionally, I often quoted back to the respondent things that they had said. I asked for clarification or expansion especially of any apparent inconsistencies. We discussed relationships, friendships, activities and perceptions and, briefly, their life histories. Their philosophy and attitude towards consumerist lifestyles were explored towards the end of the inter-view. No recordings were made but immediately following the interview, I wrote a full recollection from notes. In all cases my participants approved my account of the interview (for member checking see Stake, 1995) often with minor amend-ments. Since this research I have always recorded research interviews to preserve the participants' words.

In the third stage I checked on information about which I had any doubt and wrote a synopsis of approximately 400 words of each case. In order to strengthen validity participants were sent a copy and invited to comment. The narratives and interviews were stored on a qualitative analytical database. This software facili-tated categorisation based on *my* assessment of their importance and allowed a wide range of functions in sorting, ordering and arranging qualitative data. The database functioned additionally as a discipline since the claims I made in analysing the text were referenced to specific 'text units'. Thus 'most participants said ...' required reference to more than eight examples. Finally, I combined the developing themes to offer my understanding of the broad projects and specific strategies my participants had adopted with regard to ethical consumption.

Exploring 'how' participants consume ethically

Each of my participants reported attitudes and behaviour that would lead a market researcher to categorise them as an ethical consumer. I have set out some key lifestyle indicators in Table 7.1 as an introduction to the cases. This may be taken to represent a considerable variation in lifestyle from affluent relative convention-ality to deliberately restricted income and consumption.

Trust appears as an important factor in enabling many consumers to circum-vent complex decisions. For instance, Bob trusted his business partner's choice of ethical banking services and Alan, his friend's choice of non-leather belt. Ethical consumers can, on occasions, be shown to be satisficers, searching for and buying something that only reasonably met their ethical criteria. By contrast some relied on what Robert happily referred to as prejudice, to enable a quick decision. There was ample evidence of participants being influenced, sometimes strongly, either towards or against the dominant ethical consumption discourse by their family and peers.

Table 7.1   Participants' key lifestyle indicators

Pseudonym	Occupation	Income	Location Dwelling	Transport	Diet	Shopping
Alan	lecturer	above av.	urban semi-det	pedestrian	vegan	wholefood
Anthony	director/performer	below av.	urban rent[3] terr	car/public	vegetarian	supermarket
Belinda	laboratory technician	above av.	suburban semi-det	car/public	omnivore	supermarket
Bob	marketing consultant	below av.[1]	urban terr	car/public	piscarian	supermarket
Elaine	tax consultant	above av.	suburban det	car/public	vegetarian	supermarket
Felicity	solicitor	above av.	urban terr	car/public	omnivore[2]	supermarket
James	baker/bicycle repairer	below av.	urban flat rent[3]	bicycle	vegan	wholefood
Janice	health promotion trainer	above av.	suburban det	car	omnivore[2]	supermarket
Jewel	retired teacher	average	suburban det	car/public	vegetarian	co-operative supermarket
Louise	primary teacher	average	suburban semi-det	car/bicycle	omnivore	supermarket
Lucy	chef	average	suburban semi-det	public/car	omnivore[2]	supermarket
Misha	doctoral student	average[1]	urban rent[3] terr	bicycle/car[4]	omnivore[2]	supermarket
Natasha	shop assistant (student)	below av.	urban terr	public	vegan	supermarket/wholefood
Patrick	not employed for financial gain	below av.	urban flat	bicycle/public	vegetarian	supermarket/wholefood
Peter	management consultant	above av.	urban semi-det	car/public	omnivore	supermarket
Robert	inspector of schools	above av.	urban semi-det	bicycle/public	omnivore[2]	local/supermarket

[1] Expectation of higher income
[2] Omnivores buying free range or reporting reduced meat diet
[3] Rented property (otherwise dwellings are owner-occupied)
[4] Intention to buy car

Participants employed a number of heuristics, loose rules, albeit not applied in any strictly coherent pattern. These suggest a division between those looking for 'alternative' paths to ethical consuming and reformists seeking to modify mainstream economies.

The data suggest that the role of the ethical entrepreneur or company (the Body Shop, Co-operative Bank, Ben & Jerry's and so on) should be thought of as precarious. Whilst I am not denying the success of some such enterprises, individual ethical consumers bring markedly differing analysis to corporate communications. For instance, the same information about a seemingly ethical product was approved by one participant and strongly criticised by another. Although participants seemed generally receptive to new ideas this was sometimes only in quite specific issue areas with which they had a concern. However, new information was not always welcome or indeed necessary, as we will see with Robert's swift prejudice.

Some participants derived information from relatively wide networks whilst others were quite restricted. Many responded to particular or selected activist discourses, for example animal welfare, fair trade, anarchism, Christianity. Some opt out and others adopt a particular strategy of active involvement. In each case there seemed to be a clear limit to their active engagement in ethical consumption. Thus, my examples of ethical consumers found remarkably individual ways ('projects') of living in their society and practising ethical consumption. However, a notion of individual preferences is unhelpful. Additionally, attitudes cannot be 'read off' behaviour or vice versa, not least because of social mediation and the varied meanings associated with particular practices. Without knowing the dominating views of her husband, we might, for example, wrongly understand Belinda to be anti-organic food simply because she does not buy it.

Exploring 'why' they consumed ethically

Among participants there was a strong, but not universal, concern with the beneficial consequences of ethical consumption. Even James, who believed he was only able to change his own practices, lamented what he saw as the present irresponsibility of multinationals. However, such concern with potential change does not fully explain ethical practices especially considering the pessimism often expressed. Some sophisticated philosophical reasoning emerged. One was of a virtuous consumer disassociating herself or himself from unethical practices. Another that there is a duty to consider consumer action given we have a choice (see Chapter 2). My sense of the most pressing motivation, however, was that each participant needed, as Anthony put it, to 'feel comfortable' with themselves; it was a case of integrity. I have presented my understanding of these ethical consumers' projects below. In spite of the seeming complexity and variety of approaches, I suggest that in the main they have been able to achieve their aims. Unresolved philosophical tensions in their integrity remain but for largely explicable reasons: political compromises, social necessities, balancing commitments and so on.

However, most people do not simply strive to be virtuous. The difficulty here is to present important features of people's lives succinctly but in sufficient enough detail to enlarge the picture. I have picked out three instances that seem to be 'out of virtuous character': Robert's passion for (non-fair traded) chocolate; Patrick's cigarettes, biscuits and vinyl records, and Elaine's partially controlled passion for shoes. In some instances my participant has specifically acknowledged that, say, their passion is in conflict with their notion of consumer restraint and/or ethical consumption.

To the extent that one would consider these people's lives to be full, we might characterise any of their activities as concerns competing with matters of ethical consumption. However, voluntary work is important, not only because it is almost certainly one of the ways participants are exposed to, and possibly contribute to, ethical consumer discourse but also because voluntary activities require attention in their own right. In some cases, particularly for Robert's involvement in church and the local community association, Jewel's RSPCA and church work, Anthony's voluntary association with arts funding, Bob's contribution to co-operative sector associations and Janice through Tear Fund, Christian Aid, and pastoral work, I suggest such activity seems to take up a very significant proportion of their busy lives. I found evidence that to give attention to one concern results in the diminution of that given to another. These examples of passions and interests, which my participants have, should be taken as indicative rather than comprehensive. They are simply instances that arose in the study.

Changes dramatic and gradual

Changes in buying patterns towards ethical consuming can develop as people are exposed to new discourses. Conversely, a drift away from some practices occurs. Quite abrupt changes in practice were noted in some of the examples of ethical consumers in this study. Although these changes may follow related events, it may equally be an unrelated occurrence that triggers latent attitudes.

I questioned participants about early decisions to buy ethical products. This elicited vignettes of change of which I will illustrate three: two abrupt examples moving towards ethical consumption by Robert and Elaine and one from Natasha reducing her involvement with the same.

In Robert's audiotape he said 'but certainly my ... er ... shopping behaviour has changed over the last year.' In the semi-structured interview I invited him to expand on this change and we agreed my record of his account as follows: Robert attributed his recent change in shopping habit to perhaps two triggering events. The first was the reopening of a local shop which could supply many of their needs (basically bread and, for a while, vegetables) and the second was starting to play tennis on a Saturday morning. The tennis, he said, forced a change in shopping habit; his attitudes towards local shopping were formed and the reopening of the local shop made his preferred change possible. Robert recalled an argument about the relevant efficiency of local versus supermarket shopping. But this he thought post dated the change in shopping pattern and only served to reinforce his ideas. However triggered, Robert asserted, the change was a specifically conscious shift. At least in part, Robert's change to patronise smaller shops occurred because of an independent event. By contrast, Elaine's conversion to vegetarianism, just as sudden, was undoubtedly triggered by a relevant event.

Elaine recalled that it was some twenty years ago that she had started buying cruelty free cosmetics. A few years later she had tried some vegetarian meals but not found them very appetising. She had not eaten much meat during this period and for much of the time had not eaten chickens, because of their treatment. She had become vegetarian about six years previously in a sudden response to an article in the Animal Aid magazine *Outrage*, about the treatment of calves. Elaine emphasised the finality of this decision in that she imposed her belief on her willing family and arranged for the meat they had in stock to be taken away by relatives.

Elaine's vegetarian consumption followed exposure to a variety of ethical consumer discourses through animal rights magazines. These also gave her some knowledge of fair trade, but whilst she has some sympathy here, she has not acted on the latter issue.

The third case relates to a change in occupation that took Natasha reluctantly away from ethical consumption. It is probable that a propensity to return to buying the ethical products she mentions will remain to be taken up again when

Natasha considers herself better off and other factors allow. Our agreed account records that whilst she had been employed in the wholefood shop she had bought BioD 'vegan' cleaning products. Now that she was temporarily unemployed, she said she was unable to afford this and bought the cheapest cleaner Netto could provide. The price comparison was, she recalled, something in the order of four times.

Such ethical consumer behaviour and changing behaviour are mediated within a range of personal and situational contexts in ways that are unique to each individual. However, common themes, for instance around the range and intensity of familial relationships, are apparent. Additionally, in some cases concurrence or conflict with other interests and commitments to voluntary work were important. The metaphors employed by participants suggest that some see themselves as engaged in a struggle. Robert, Anthony and James referred to particular aspects of ethical consuming, like fair trade or banking, as a 'front'. Here, for example, Robert worries about buying fruit:

> I can't think of any occasion within the last year when I have er ... really thought about ... erm ... the ethical implications of buying fruit from a particular country ... erm ... and er ... whether I'm seriously breaching some of my principles. I ... I just don't know on this front but as I am conscious that it's ... erm ... it is a very difficult area; all sorts of ... erm ... yeah, not only political but ecological and environmental issues er ... come into to play here, some of which I ... I recall I mentioned earlier on in this tape. I suspect there may even be contradictions in my behaviour.

Whilst some like Bob agonise at length over contradictions in behaviour, others, and Felicity is the best example, seem to celebrate their inconsistencies. It is part of what makes life rich and funny for Felicity that she will often buy organic food with a passion and other times not consider it.

PROJECTS AND STRATEGIES

In a similar way to the philosopher Bernard Williams (1973) I want to suggest that participants might be best understood as having a life project. These projects are unique and as I have suggested above are pursued in unique circumstances. By knowing ethical consumers in sufficiently full depth and breadth it would seem possible to express their 'projects' in rational terms and to render their remaining tensions understandable. I now outline the strategies I see each participant as pursuing.

Alan's approach is a carefully worked out balance.

He balances his enjoyment of life, which includes motorcycling, mountain biking, travel and music, with adaptations to accommodate his ethical beliefs. Alan acknowledges there are environmentally damaging elements to his leisure activities. This balance is mostly satisfied by specific adaptations such as veganism and pedestrianism but also by reasoning out complex issues where he believes this to be possible. Alan has, for instance, carefully configured his domestic heating installation to deliver moderated warmth, efficiently and with consideration of long service. He will sometimes devote considerable time to get a particular purchase item right but even he says it is possible to go too far. He sees the Vegan Society, for example, as too serious for him.

There appear to be few tensions except a little in terms of his consumption level. He illustrates this by reference to his lone occupation of a moderately sized house.

Anthony lives a proactive, campaigning lifestyle.

His work in radical theatre shapes his living in both financial and temporal terms. Ethical consumption is a significant part of this but complements campaigns and does not dominate. For instance, Anthony's recent research on abattoirs for a critical documentary is coupled almost essentially with a primarily vegan diet. Yet this considerable self-imposed work commitment prevents him from shopping at his preferred small shops and compounds compromises of diet when he is away from home.

Any achievement of more free time and higher income would, Anthony asserts, alter this equation in favour of smaller shops and more environmentally sound products. If there is tension here, therefore, it is between ethics and ethics.

For Belinda ethical consuming is only necessary at the extreme.

This is because in general she considers consumer capitalism to have delivered goods to the masses. It pleases Belinda, for instance, that the more efficient production of food has meant that ordinary people are, for the most part, better fed than ever before. Consumption, in a limited anthropomorphic sense, is therefore not inherently unethical. Action, however, should be taken when scientifically proven to be necessary, when insufficient knowledge has been gathered or in cases of extreme injustice.

There seem to me to be two tensions in Belinda's project. The first is an apparent inconsistency between her embrace of progressive industrial processes and her desire to retain traditional practices. The second derives from the increasing misgivings Belinda expresses about contemporary food production. By her own criteria Belinda might be expected to act as a consumer to avoid new products that she sees as having undergone insufficient scientific scrutiny. However, her husband's scepticism about organic produce, the possible alternative, seems to be significant in precluding this.

Much of Bob's effort is directed at working within the social economy.

He is both activist and businessperson. This imposes time and money restrictions that at present constrain his ethical consumption. Within these constraints, he likes to think he limits action to those things that have a good chance of being effective, but is mostly pessimistic about the prospects for change. In accord with his support for the social economy, he is interested in what he sees as ethical processes more than outcomes. Bob expresses many concerns about his consumption more in terms of what he buys than the amount. He may see himself as only partially successful as an ethical consumer. He would clearly prefer to be more at ease but pressure of work and complications with family commitments predominate.

Elaine prioritises multiple concerns.

She is somewhat concerned about fair trading, more so about the environment, but crucially she becomes passionately involved at what she sees as the mistreatment of animals. Whilst Elaine sees herself as having deliberately moderated her consumption, compromises on fair trading and her environmental concerns are routine. With animal welfare issues, potential conflicts are the cause of considerable concern. Elaine is an ethical consumer primarily, though by no means exclusively, to the extent that she sees herself as disengaged from animal cruelty. Occasionally the animal rights discourse contradicts her perception. When a problem is so high-lighted, it is 'doing her bit' to respond.

Elaine is a little uneasy with her consumption, for instance in the necessary purchase of a second car by her partner and herself. She would also prefer that her job were in accord with her beliefs. But for the above reasons and because she has demonstrated to herself she can, on occasions, act strictly in accord with her beliefs, her unease, I argue, should not be taken as constituting very significant tensions.

Felicity does not approach ethical consumerism in an organised way.

To do so would be to reduce the spontaneity of life. Although Felicity is whimsical, she will react in all aspects of her life with strong emotion and commitment particularly to what she perceives as injustice. Thus, Felicity's work as a solicitor and her leisure activities address social issues. Her ethical consumption is more likely to be directed towards specific targets than to form a comprehensive strategy. So, in spite of enjoying some of their foods, she adamantly boycotts McDonald's. She equally resolutely patronises the Body Shop.

Life seems to have too great an interpersonal content to admit much materialism in Felicity's life. Contradictions are therefore rife but are a matter of amusement and not tension.

James convincingly says he has deliberately restricted his income.

His ethical consumer decisions have become manageable and his social contacts provide the required discourses to address those remaining. James wants to be sure he discharges his responsibility, especially spending money, in a socially enhancing way and to this extent is working towards doing the right thing. The more he can see a process with which he involves himself is good, the more satisfied he is. Small scale is therefore essential to his project. This is as true of his expenditure as of his paid and unpaid work and leisure.

Tensions seem few and of little substance. He may occasionally wonder what to do, for instance, when his father offers to buy him some shoes.

Janice lives in a world where consumer action can have effect.

What is important, I think therefore, is for her to be active within the structure her church designates. The church selects and designates suitable activities. She achieves ethical consumerism in the areas where she has familial jurisdiction and to the extent that changes in consumption are not difficult to incorporate. As a result, commercial products sometimes coexist with ethical ones. Within this church setting Janice is highly motivated and therefore derives a sense of achievement.

Where there is an underlying tension is that Janice reasons, as a development of the church discourse, that we all go along with cheap products without wondering how their cheapness is being achieved. At base she is therefore uncomfortable.

Jewel is a long-standing Christian socialist.

She attends to the traditional Labour concerns that invariably coincide with her religious beliefs. To the extent that she addresses these imperatives – co-operation, international fraternity and equality – she is content. Through her political and religious activities she picks up on and subscribes to the major ethical consumer discourses.

Tensions arise in two ways. First, when Jewel lapses into comfort and thinks she is doing things she isn't. She originally, for example, spoke as if she bought only fair trade coffee; she did not at the time but because of the study she says that she does now. Second, through her religious work she has an appreciation of the relatively high material comfort of her lifestyle. She therefore has a heightened sense of inequality.

Louise is content to be thrifty.

Much of what she owns is quite deliberately second-hand. Only a small proportion of her regular purchases are consciously ethical and she says these will only be in cases where she wants and likes the product. Ethical consumerism, she says, is good to the extent that it produces any small positive effect but she has only recently been introduced to the notion. To what extent she will consider it worthwhile to extend the project is uncertain.

Louise might wish to show more foresight when making purchases. However, to consume ethically may carry a lower imperative when consumption is in any case very moderate. In this sense no significant tensions seem to me to arise in Louise's lifestyle.

For Lucy, life is to be affirmed and enjoyed.

She should, and does, react to calls to action both in terms of particular products and services and in being active in voluntary groups but does not, and should not, seek to be perfect. She has sufficient information sources to alert her to a range of campaigns, including major ethical consumer discourses. She will take part in these, but will rationalise if they impinge on her celebration of life. Mostly Lucy believes ethical consuming will coincide with improvements to her life in accord with good karma.

Insofar as Lucy has misgivings about increased consumption they are minor. She would prefer her husband not to use a car, for instance, but will not seriously take issue since enjoying life is an overriding imperative.

Misha has accepted compromise.

He is not going to live absolutely in accord with his concerns for the environment. What he does do, including his ethical consumption, is significant and I therefore think of him as pragmatic. Hobbies, travel and other enjoyable pastimes sometimes fall outside ethical consumption but occasionally coincide with his ethical actions. His concerns for human justice are tempered by the difficulty of resolving some issues and circumscribed by his belief in scientifically underpinned progress (which includes scientific research performed on other animals) but again this does not prevent him taking positive action.

Misha's project's success resides in his willingness to respond to most, though not all, of those matters which he sees as important. It is not about comprehensive lifestyle changes. Only in his relationship with his partner, whom he sees as more inclined to act on her ethical beliefs, are slight tensions apparent.

Natasha seriously sets herself high standards.

For instance, she added many concerns to those set out by me in the original questionnaire. With exceptional access to ethical consumer discourses, she seems to aim to meet these in all aspects of her life including her consumption. Partly this is achieved by set-piece approaches such as her vegan diet and non-use of a car, but also by exercising choice. Rarely do practicalities or frivolity intervene, but both are seen as necessary. Practicalities such as temporary lack of money dictate that she cannot buy, for instance, expensive (vegan) household cleaners, but any tension is alleviated by a presumption that she will return to better habits when income permits. So for Natasha her ethical consumption is achieved with few lapses.

Because Natasha does not see herself as materialistic her lifestyle project seems to her attainable. Tensions, insofar as they exist, therefore seem to be superficial.

Patrick says he has deliberately restrained his income.

His ethical consumerism is sometimes a residue from when such decisions were more significant to him. Patrick believes that he could not untangle the complexities inherent in production to be able to consume ethically. For this reason and because he wishes to conserve tradition, low consumption is for him the only rational response. Having said that, Patrick says he would use any increased income to shop more often at wholefood stores. Ethical consumption is therefore a secondary consideration not requiring great deliberation.

If there is a tension it is between Patrick and the profligate society which he sees around him destroying tradition.

For Peter, ethical consumerism should enhance life.

He chooses to do those things that also improve the quality of his life like buying organic produce. Because good actions should be self-enhancing Peter maintains his concept of himself as an ethical consumer. He sees his partner as a good influence in this respect. Peter's work as a management consultant accords with these views when he works for organisations such as Friends of the Earth and the Quakers, but he also works with commercial companies and toys with the notion that bringing ethical ideas even to arms manufacturers would have positive value.

However, Peter speaks of tensions between some of his pleasures and his wish to live carefully. Such activities as rock climbing and skiing that involve environmentally damaging travel worry him but they are pleasures with which he will not easily part.

Robert tends towards Puritanism.

Robert can make decisions, I would suggest, more or less in isolation from conventional ethical consumer discourse by applying principles more probably to the big picture than to the details of his consumption. Robert will be more concerned, for instance, with shopping locally and frugally than to buy a specific, say fair traded or environmentally sound, product and especially not to spend inordinate time and/or money on such detail. Time and money are better deployed, he believes, charitably.

This project sets up underlying tensions not least with his family as he makes efforts to limit and simplify his consumption. That he does not make use of a car is an instance of such a situation. Being convinced of the correlation between poverty and wealth increasingly bothers Robert.

THEORISING: 'DISTANCING', 'INTEGRATING' AND 'RATIONALISING'

Whilst a striking feature of the data is the variety of projects in a small number of examples, I propose these examples exhibit three theoretical ethical consumer strategies: 'distancing', 'integrating' and 'rationalising'. In Figure 7.1 have located my examples of ethical consumers within this tripartite framework, noting resolutions by the use of spheres and tensions by using arrows. Thus some projects seem more stable and predictable but others more contingent.

I must emphasise two things with respect to the diagram. First, since I have worked with sixteen ethical consumers located in four of many possible habitats, the three strategies I suggest are unlikely to be comprehensive. Second, this analysis is not intended to confer value by the use of particular words. Rather, I hope to consider consumers' relationships to a society that exhibits discourses of ethical consumption.

The ethical consumer strategies discussed, 'distancing', 'integrating' and 'rationalising', are in effect Weberian 'ideal types'. I have represented these in Figure 7.1 by overlapping concentric circles to correspond to the possibility of combining two or more strategies. Additionally the circles are progressively shaded. This is intended to avoid the inference that these are quantifiable categories and to represent a notion of core and peripheral strategies.

I have indicated my assessment of each participant's project as a position on this 'fuzzy Venn diagram'. These projects were discussed in some detail in my thesis (Newholm, 2000), but here I shall outline each of the strategies and give examples from among my participants.

'Distancing'

I suggest 'distancing' is exemplified by some of the practices of James, Patrick, Natasha and Alan. All eschew cars in favour of walking, cycling and/or public transport. They opt out of the meat trade and, to differing extents, new durable goods in general. I am not arguing that there is a clear boundary between those who adopt a consumerist lifestyle and others who reject it. Louise who, for example, is omnivorous and owns a car also accumulates mostly second-hand durables. Additionally, among those who I did not feel confident in describing as 'downshifters' (see Chapter 11), commitments to materialism were often tempered. For example, Felicity saw little use for luxuries and Peter often preferred hand-made products.

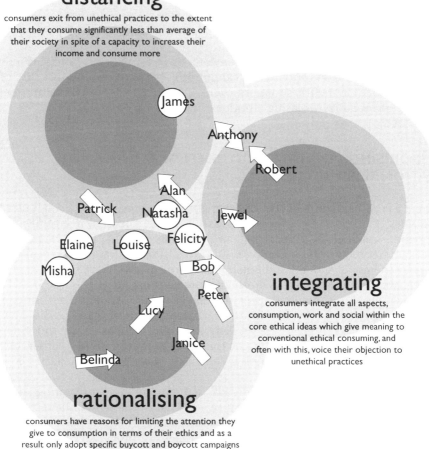

Figure 7.1   Ethical consumer strategies: ideal types

'Distancing' retains an element of consumption since most exits lead to complementary consumption patterns. Vegetable food production, cycle makers, public transport suppliers, second-hand dealers and so on, all benefit from particular 'distancing' strategies.

'Integrating'

I have suggested a further response to the challenges of ethics in consumption as 'integrating'. By this I mean that the consumer attempts to integrate, and perhaps make sense of, elements of his or her life around the core ideas that also give meaning to ethical consumption in their culture. In archetypal cases we might expect boundaries between consumption, work and leisure to be very blurred.

I offer the example of Anthony who when working late at a stage production (often of a political nature) is sometimes hard pressed to find a place to eat. Our agreed text illustrates how in such situations ethics can be compromised.

Later at university he had been made aware of the many ethical issues surrounding McDonald's and was, he said, probably handed one of the original 'McLibel' leaflets. When working difficult hours away from home, Anthony said he would sometimes use Burger King (Anthony added 'as a last resort'). Unlike McDonald's, Burger King he said had always offered a vegetarian burger. He saw McDonald's as dishonest both in relation to their denials of involvement in rainforest destruction and in their late response to the 'green pound'. He preferred an unknown quantity [in this case Burger King] to dishonesty.

'Rationalising'

Belinda, Janice and Lucy are among those I have described as 'rationalisers'. They each give different reasons for accepting or celebrating consumer capitalism. Belinda for the good life it has provided for most of the working class, Janice for the comfort it has brought her and her family, and Lucy because she believes that she should celebrate the material things the earth provides.

At the same time they all consider it to be their duty to act ethically as consumers where there are significant perceived injustices. Lucy said: 'I am concerned about cruelty to animals but do not find it a problem, nowadays, to buy cruelty-free cosmetics – some major outlets make it a policy'. The level of injustices beyond which participants will act differs according to their beliefs and situation. However, each of them has acted according to their conscience: Lucy, for instance, boycotts Nestlé products; Janice has recently heard from her church about the boycott and is likely to join; Belinda is knowledgeable about Nestlé but will only act if the activities are particularly repugnant to her as was the case with apartheid.

CONCLUSION

I have sought to reverse the concept of a words/deeds inconsistency. Rather than asking why people who report strong beliefs concerning the environment, animal welfare, corporate responsibility and other moral issues act inconsistently as consumers, I have considered, given the difficulty of meaningful action, how they act at all.

It seems from my research that more or less coherent stories of ethical consumption can be constructed in daunting circumstances. However, in each case the strategy or strategies adopted limit the necessary engagement. This is achieved variously because few problems are perceived (by rationalisers), or the scope of necessary consumer action is reduced (by distancing) or because a compromise is reached by which time is seen (by integrators) as better spent directly on one or more of the issues relevant to their concept of ethical consumption than on perfecting personal consumption patterns. In all cases there is evidence that active ethical consumption is limited.

It was shown that information is mediated by cultural and contextual situations. The provision of information does not necessarily, therefore, produce commensurate action. Additionally, the fine judgements made and the volatile nature of some projects mean that ethical consumerism, as a political project, is unpredictable. This conclusion is similar to Gabriel and Lang's more general (1995) conclusion of consumer 'unmanageability'. Consequently, although peoples' individual strategies as ethical consumers can be shown to limit their market intervention in various ways, its quest for integrity and very unpredictability means that as a semi-organised project the political phenomenon of ethical consumption remains significant.

Using Existential-Phenomenological Interviewing to Explore Meanings of Consumption

8

Hélène Cherrier

The characteristics of the population that practices ethical consumption behavior are difficult to determine and efforts to delineate this group have been controversial (Al-Khatib et al., 1997; Buchholz, 1998; Carrigan and Attalla, 2001; Shaw, 2000; Shaw and Newholm, 2002; Shaw and Shiu, 2003). One barrier to adequately describing ethical consumers is that ethical decision processes refer to subjective moral judgments. Thus, morality is 'concerned with the norms, values, and beliefs embedded in social processes which define right and wrong for an individual or community' (Crane and Matten, 2004: 11). Even though some moral judgments such as 'do not harm' or 'tell the truth' are invariably seen as universal and enduring and can be theorized into rules and principals (Crane and Matten, 2004: 11), those that delineate the ethics of consumption are not (see Chapter 1 in this book). They are neither universal nor enduring for three main reasons.

First, the ethics of consumption are contextual. The rightness or wrongness of consumption is dependent upon the time and place in which one lives. The importance of the context is evident when comparing today's consumer culture with the American recession of the 1950s, when the societal benefits of consumption were emphasized by a need for economic growth. When the US President Dwight D. Eisenhower asked US citizens to 'buy more' for the good of America and a reporter asked him 'buy what?' Eisenhower replied, 'Anything'. Americans were then exposed to slogans like 'Buy and be happy' , 'Buy, buy, buy, it is a patriotic duty' , and 'Buy your way to economic prosperity' (Pusey, 1956). To be a good American citizen was to strive for more consumption. Then, it was an ethical duty to consume. Through consumption, the economy would flourish and the state would provide security, certainty, and order for its 'good' consumers.

In contrast, today's dark side of consumer behavior (for example, consumer terrorism, addictive and compulsive consumption, theft, credit abuse, road rage, prostitution, and so on), environmental uncertainty, ecological crisis, and increasing social inequality cast a shadow on consumption (Bauman, 1998; Beck, 2000; Harper, 1996; Hearn et al., 1999; Schor and Holt, 2000). According to Beck (1999), the uncontrolled consumption currently endorsed by the richest countries directs the world to a stage where no one can either control global corporations or predict the consequences of unrestrained consumerism. For him, we live in a 'world risk society' in which the distribution of goods coincides inevitably with the distribution of hazards, risk and uncertainty.

Second, the ethics of consumption depends on the consumers' subjective view on ethics, and to some extend their individual concerns. Ethical consumers are reflexive (Giddens, 1991; Murray and Ozanne, 1991) or emancipated individuals (Kozinets, 2001) who question their consumption choices (Shaw and Newholm, 2002) based on various humane, religious, personal, or environmental concerns. For instance, buying a shirt from the Gap store can be perceived as an unethical purchase for a number of diverse subjective judgments including human rights issues, environmental concerns, or resistance to globalization. This variety of ethical consumers' concerns is clearly reflected by a wide selection of activist organizations (see Chapter 3 in this book), which range from consumer protection (Ackerman and Heinzerling, 2004) to social, environmental, cultural, political and economical responsibilities (Antil, 1984; Caruana, 2003). Relevant to the heterogeneity, multiplicity, and subjectivity of ethical consumers' concerns, there is no agreement on the sole ethics of consumption on which all people or philosophers agree.

Third, consumers convey their ethical concerns in varied individuals' actions. Broadly speaking, ethical consumption behaviors are explicit and intentional actions, or body movements, that consumers do in a context and for a purpose. They combine a wide assortment of physical goods, services, events, ideas, people, organizations, and retail outlets. Given such diversity of actions, ethical consumers integrate a multiplicity of sub-cultures that might or might not include voluntary simplicity, co-housing movements, permaculture villages, environmental conservation and recycling, urban co-operatives, boycotts, cyberdemocracy, or anti-nuclear demonstrations, and their ethical message is temporal and contextual.

Implicit to the contextual aspect of the ethics of consumption, the multiplicity of ethical concerns, the fragmentation of ethical consumer behaviors, and the often paradoxical juxtaposition of lifestyles and ethical ideologies is the claim that it becomes impossible to know who belongs to any given ethical constituency and whether all constituents are to be treated as ethical equals. Such an argument questions the possibility of defining a 'valid' ethical consumer with fixed and essential characteristics motivated by ethical concerns and confronted by consumption choices (see the discussion in Chapter 1 in this book).

I am responding to the notions of chaotic and unsystematic consumers' personalities found in the work of Holzner for whom personality is 'a system of relatively enduring behavioral dispositions, which are in part genetically, in part socially determined' (Holzner, 1973: 294). I therefore propose to study the subjective meanings of ethical consumption behavior from the perspective of the ethical consumer. Such an approach recognizes that ethical consumers are forever responding to changes in their environment, perpetually contesting the complexity of consumer culture, and questioning their ethical concerns.

In the following discussion, I propose to study the life experience, rather than the characteristics, of people for whom simplification is narrated as an inextricable part of their ethics of consumption. In so doing, I will present a methodology called 'existential phenomenology' that recognizes the subjective and contextual aspects of life, and in our case, ethical consumers. First, I will define the philosophy of existential phenomenology. Second, I will emphasize the procedures of existential-phenomenological interviewing and hermeneutic analysis. Finally, to clarify how existential phenomenology refines our understanding of ethical consumers' life experiences, I will provide an analysis of six existential-phenomenological interviews completed with consumers who reduced and simplifed their consumption and adopted ethical consumption practices. Ultimately, this chapter provides an understanding of the meanings which some consumers derive from ethical consumption behavior.

THE PHILOSOPHY OF EXISTENTIAL PHENOMENOLOGY AND THE ETHICS OF CONSUMPTION

Existential-phenomenological interviewing is a way to attain a description of everyday experience as it is lived and described by specific individuals in specific situations. It accepts the complexity and ambiguity of human experiences by recognizing that different individuals may be talking about similar experiences using different words or different experiences using similar words. It originates from two distinct philosophies. The first tradition called 'existentialism' suggests that existence precedes essence (Kierkegaard and Auden, 1963; Warnock, 1967). By insisting that existence precedes essence, existentialists decline the notion that there can be a true essence or inherent characteristics of individuals. A consumer becomes an ethical consumer from his/her life experience. It is the moment of choice between what to consume, where to consume, and how to consume that has the potential to orient the consumer toward becoming an ethical consumer. Ultimately, every individual is free to choose between unethical or ethical consumption, and to become an ethical consumer. It is important to note that the existentialist emphasis on individual freedom of choice creates not only excitement and exhilaration for the consumer, but also insecurity, frustration, tension, confusion, and even panic. Indeed, consumers are free to choose among a diversity of products/services, yet the necessity to choose creates conflict over what to choose or what not to choose.

Another important aspect of existential philosophy is that whenever we make a choice for ourselves, we are also making a choice for all of humanity (see Chapter 2). The future as well as our life are contingent upon the choice we make. With this in mind, a study of the ethical consumer requires considering both the negative and the positive aspects of ethical consumption experiences as well as its relation to broader aspects of life.

While existentialism refers to the experience of living, phenomenology refers to the understanding of the structure of the experience. Edmund Husserl (1859–1938) introduced the concept of intentionality to emphasize that human beings are fundamentally related to the contexts in which they live. Thus all human beings are to be understood as being-in-the-world rather than as individuals with independent preferences. For instance, a person choosing to simplify and consume ethically for political considerations is likely to be different from someone who decides to so consume for spiritual or economical reasons. The reference of a certain experience (for example, ethical and simplifying consumption practices) and its alternative meanings (political, spiritual and economical) are never separated from the culture in which we live, talk and act. Understanding the meanings of some experience, in our case ethical consumption, requires describing the situated perspective of the event from the point of view of the experiencing person (first-person description). Therefore, understanding the ethical consumer requires describing the situated perspective of ethical consumption practices from the point of view of the experiencing person.

In the mid-twentieth century, Martin Heidegger (1927–62) combined the philosophies of existentialism and phenomenology into the single project of existential phenomenology to describe everyday human existence (Thompson et al., 1989). As a method, existential-phenomenological interviewing emphasizes that narrative reflects individuals' lived experience and that each narrative story is intertwined with a specific context (Thompson et al., 1989). In the following discussion I refer to the methodology of existential-phenomenological interviewing (see Pollio et al., 1997 and McCracken, 1988b for discussion on method) in the light of consumer research into ethical and simplifying practices.

EXISTENTIAL-PHENOMENOLOGICAL INTERVIEWING AND THE STUDY OF ETHICAL CONSUMERS

In order to scientifically capture the ethical consumer's experience using existential phenomenology, it is important to follow three main methodological tenets. Those tenets direct the researcher's preparation for the interview, the selection of the informants, and the actual format of the interview.

The first step before doing a phenomenological interview is to review related literatures on simplification and ethical consumption practices and to acquire a working knowledge of the major social and historical themes that have been identified as shaping the contemporary cultural situation of ethical consumption (Beckmann and Elliott, 2000; Denzin and Lincoln, 1998, 2003; Thompson, 1996). This process helps to clearly define the research issue relevant to the motivations, processes, and consequences of living simply as an ethical consumer.

Once familiar with the substantive area of interest, the researcher needs to delineate the judgment sample to be considered for the study. Judgment sampling is a procedure used to select the sample that is most appropriate for the study. Although representative sampling rules do not apply for existential-phenomenological interviewing, there are a few rules of thumb. First, respondents should not have theoretical knowledge of the topic being studied. Second, it is best to create a contrast in the respondent pool such as differences in age, gender, status, education, occupation, or a diversity that is relevant given our knowledge of the consumer. The reason for this is to access a broad range of experiences, which in turn provides useful information for finding similarities between consumption experiences. Consumers at various stages of evolving towards a simplified ethical consumption lifestyle should be considered. Also, all the selected informants must have internalized meanings of ethical consumption within their language, discourse and narratives. The idea underlying this selection criterion reflects the need to have respondents whose detailed life history can provide cultural meanings on ethical consumption lifestyles. Finally, due to an emphasis on depth of understanding, the numbers within the respondent pool should range between 3 and 20 (Fournier and Mick, 1998; Thompson, 1997).

After a careful selection of the respondent pool, the next methodological consideration involves the context and format of the interview. The existential-phenomenological paradigm emphasizes that meanings arise from the interaction between individuals and their physical and cultural context. The researcher can seize the consumer's place in the world and his/her understanding of this context by using, if possible, the participant's home as the place of inquiry. As some consumers may not be willing to open their homes for the interview procedures, the researcher nevertheless should find a comfortable quiet place for the interview in which the informants can freely describe their personal experiences in detail.

At the beginning of the interview, the researcher explains the parameters of the study: understanding simplicity and ethical consumption practices and that the interview will be audio-recorded. Each informant is given a pseudonym and is assured of anonymity and confidentiality. Again, the purpose of the interview is to attain the consumer's first-person description of his/her specific experience of ethics and simplicity. Toward this aim, the interview begins with 'small talk' to help the informant become comfortable with speaking into a recording device. Once the respondent appears comfortable and the researcher is certain of the adequacy of the recording device, the discussion begins using grand-tour questions. Grand-tour questions are general and set the direction of the interview toward simplicity and ethical consumption. During the interview, the researcher shares their personal thoughts and feelings with the informant to create a discussion. The informant is indeed the expert on his/her own consumption practices and the role of the researcher is to constantly encourage the respondent to give lengthier and more detailed description. The context of the interview gradually helps to unveil each respondent's subjective meanings of simple and right consumption. A thorough interview should last between one and three hours.

An important aspect of existential-phenomenological interviewing is that questions beginning with 'why' should be avoided. The researcher's interest resides in understanding the consumer's biography and experience, and not his/her reason, rationality, and objectivity. Asking 'why' is only appropriate when seeking to understand the informants' meanings of the consumption experience. For example, rather than asking respondents why they choose to consume ethically, alternative questions are: 'What is your experience as a consumer?' 'How would you describe your lifestyle?' 'Can you tell me about your last Christmas experience?' 'Would you consider that your lifestyle differs from other consumers?' In sum, when conducting existential-phenomenological interviews, every effort is made to keep the informant on track with his/her consumption experience without being too directive, to demonstrate active listening, to watch for key terms in relation to consumption, and to probe the respondent for details that might characterize their simplicity and/or ethics.

It is one thing to interview the consumer using existential phenomenology, it is another to analyze the considerable volume of data generated by the interviews. Some interpretive framework must be applied. Within interpretive consumer research, transcribed interviews and/or videotaped information are analyzed using the hermeneutical framework (Thompson, 1997; Thompson et al., 1989). Hermeneutics is a methodology of interpretation, which articulates the meanings that ethical consumers' stories have in relationship to the broader narrative of simplicity and ethical consumption practices. Thompson (1997) describes three distinct stages of analysis: the intra-case analysis, the inter-case analysis, and the contextualization of the conceptual framework.

The intra-case analysis refers to the study of every case separately. Each ethical consumer's story is read and reread until the researcher understands the *temporal sequencing* of key events. The stories consumers create tell about their personal everyday experiences of simplicity and ethical consumption and represent a constellation of past–present–future relations. The researcher recreates the temporal trajectories of living simply as an ethical consumer in which a present event is understood in relation to past concerns and projected toward an envisioned future.

This temporal ordering emphasizes the relationships between the construction of stories and the cultural understandings of simplicity and ethical consumption.

Having reconstructed the chronological order of key events and organized these in a temporal order directed toward some envisioned future, the researcher analyzes the *narrative framing*. Framing refers to the meanings through which the consumption experience is understood (thematic and symbolic parallels). To analyze narrative framing, the researcher analyzes the pattern of meanings and existential concerns that support the consumer's experience. Once the existential concerns present in participant descriptions are framed in themes and symbolic parallels, the researcher rereads the entire text and writes his/her own interpretation of the text. The task is to say something meaningful that is not to be reduced to the level of objective facts. Rather, it provides a summary of descriptive interpretations noting prominent meanings relations and themes present in the interview.

The second implementation of the hermeneutic is the inter-case analysis. By looking across interviews, the researcher considers a diverse set of consumption experiences. During this process, the researcher looks for common story-lines of simplification and/or ethics between consumers' narratives. These story-lines eventually become overarching themes. Each theme depicts similarities between consumers and is related to a wider cultural context of simplifying and ethical consumption behavior.

Now, one may wonder about the researcher's 'accuracy' when interpreting the informant's everyday experience. Because existential phenomenology seeks to understand the world as lived from the perspective of the first-person, its credibility is not determined by the degree of correspondence between description and reality but rather by the degree of convincing evidence in favor of the aptness of the description. Pollio et al. (1997) defined two ways for evidential support. The first of these is methodological and involves the rigor and suitability of the investigator's procedures. The reader should be able to see what the researcher saw, whether he/she believes it or not. The second aspect is experiential and evaluates if the interpretation provides insight to the reader. Insights are assessed in terms of plausibility and illumination. Plausibility refers to whether the reader is able to see the relation between the data and the interpretation. Illumination allows the reader to see the phenomenon in a different light, to allow for a new understanding.

SIX EXAMPLES OF EXISTENTIAL-PHENOMENOLOGICAL INTERVIEWS

To better appreciate the value of existential phenomenology in understanding the simplifying ethical consumer, I will now provide an analysis of six interviews performed in the Southwestern USA during 2003. The aim of the study was to better understand the meanings of ethical consumption from the insight of consumers who lowered their consumption expectations and expressed ethical concerns. The six consumers were selected in three steps. First, potential respondents were attained via newspaper advertisements saying , 'if you voluntarily changed the way you consume, please contact ...', postings at organizations (environmental organizations, conservation, natural food stores, farmers' markets, etc.), and personal networks. The use of word of mouth was also helpful in contacting individuals who 'voluntarily restrict their consumption practices'. Those respondents were then given an initial telephone interview. This helped select individuals who restrict or control their consumption behavior for ethical concerns and not for dieting or health reasons. The final selection was conducted in face-to-face inter-action. Potential informants were asked to answer semi-structured questionnaires regarding the type and location of their ethical purchases, the style of their house, car and kitchen, as well as questions covering their jobs, travel habits and leisure activities. This last step provided sensitivity to the variance between respondents and their degree of ethical concerns.

The interviews were performed either in the respondent's home or in a quiet coffee shop, in which informants felt comfortable. Each informant was given a pseudonym and was assured of anonymity and confidentiality.

The hermeneutic analysis of the transcribed text resulted in defining the hidden or explicit social and psychological forces that influenced individuals to restrain their consumption practices through ethical concerns. For each informant, this process started with an *uncontrolled and unpredictable event* that occurred in their life. Those events were either abrupt or recurring incidents over which they had no control. Whether they were abrupt events that happened at a specific time and space or recurring events, these events eventually displaced informants' meanings in life. The uncontrollable and unpredictable incident(s) destabilized the 'ontological security' (Giddens, 1990, 1991), or 'protective cocoon' (Goffman, 1956) constructed by others for our own good. With the event, life became uncertain, erratic and chaotic, and plunged informants into intense and confusing feelings including anger, loneliness, fear, powerlessness and anxiety. Confronted with destructive feelings, informants started questioning the meaning of their life. They gradually became sensitive to their external and internal environments, including their values, beliefs, and ethical concerns.

Examples of events that influenced informants to question the way they lead their life or should lead their life were rape (Laila), working in Los Angeles (Jeremy), living with a roommate (Frank), watching terrifying pictures of butchered animals (Philippe), parents' divorce (Vivian), or own divorce (Alexia). Each uncontrollable and unpredictable event destabilized informants' meaning in life.

Explicit examples from the hermeneutic analysis help further articulate uncontrollable and unpredictable events that destabilized informants' meaning in life, which in turn led them to search for control, social integration, or authenticity.

Search for control

Many informants experienced a destabilizing event that led them to search for control in their life. For example, Laila was raped at the age of 14 and immediately after the event she began to exert more control over her life. Although she no longer could choose how and when she would lose her virginity, the abrupt incident made her reflect upon the choices she still could make. She started questioning her religious education and her parents' lifestyle example. While questioning others' ideas of what a good life should be, she became aware of her personal values and ethical concerns. She gradually realized that her parents' lifestyle was unethical toward the natural environment and animal rights. As she no longer was willing to accept choices imposed by others, she decided to relate her consumption practices to her own values on animal rights. At the time of the interview, Laila was twenty-three years old, and over the last ten years she had stopped eating meat, buying leather products, and going to main chain restaurants. She quitted going to church and voluntarily restrained her clothing consumption. She lives in an apartment with her boyfriend, where she creates her own clothing and cooks all her vegetarian meals. Laila's experience of simplifying consumption using ethical judgments clearly reflects a need to be in control of her choices, her appearance, her body, her religion, and above all, her life. What is important to consider in Laila's story is that the abrupt event led her to question her values and ethics. After all, she described it as an 'awakening' that made her conscious of her lifestyle and actions. The relationship she constructed between consumption and ethics reflects her expression of being in control over her choices, her consumption and her lifestyle. Here, ethical consumption behavior serves as a means to achieving control over lifestyle.

Another example that reflects a search for control in the context of ethical consumption is described in Frank's story. For him, the process of questioning consumption practices started after seeing his mother searching for hours for a paper she had misplaced. He recalled seeing his mother living unhappily in a cluttered house and being enslaved by her drive to accumulate objects. Soon after this event, Frank experienced frustration and anger toward material objects. Frank's anxiety and frustration toward material accumulation increased when his parents divorced and fought over their son's affection using material gifts. With the divorce and its consequences, Frank perceived material possessions as a precursor for unhappiness, complexity, anxiety, frustration, and emotional conflict. At the age of 15, Frank sold most of his belongings in garage sales and gave away the objects he did not use. In an emptier room where material objects were 'under control', Frank felt automatically at peace with himself. Frank's ethical consumption behavior started after he moved to a college dormitory and shared his room with an 'average American boy' concerned with fashion and electronic possessions. Confronted with his roommate's materialism, Frank re-experienced the feelings of anxiety and frustration he had felt while living at his mother's cluttered house. In reaction to this new 'uncontrolled' environment, Frank decided to differentiate himself from 'disorganized' individuals and connected his controlled consumption practices with ethical concerns. At the time of the interview, Frank did not buy new objects unless they were thoughtfully and ethically evaluated, and only accepted consumable goods as gifts. For Frank, linking consumption with ethical concern helps him resist the societal pressure for material chaos and complexity.

This need to be in control is fundamental in both Laila's and Frank's consumption behavior. Ethical consumption responds to their need to be in control over their life choices and their space, and helps them reject mainstream governance and resist societal pressures to consume. A second theme relevant to the meanings of ethical consumers I have called 'social integration', and this is presented using the stories of Alexia and Vivian.

Social integration

Once again, all informants experienced abrupt or recurring destabilizing events that gradually displaced their meanings in life. In order to find new meanings in life, some informants reached out for social integration. The story of Alexia's ethical consumption experience clearly depicts a struggle to belong to a community. Alexia's meanings in life were destabilized after she divorced her husband. The painful separation ended with her husband leaving the house with most of their belongings. Single again, Alexia felt sad and depressed. As she could not cope with the new 'empty' space, she used consumption as a self-medication. Little by little she reacquired the same objects she and her husband used to possess together. Still unsatisfied with her life, Alexia met her current boyfriend, an independent video producer for the community access television. With John, Alexia met several local artists, writers and musicians and as a result Alexia discovered the possibility of enjoying life through personal creation rather than consumption.

She also learned that John did not respect the consumer culture, which for him enslaves individuals, destroys individual creativity, and creates social inequalities. In order to stay with John, Alexia adopted his ethical principles and felt compelled to detach herself from objects and the temptation of consuming. Specifically, she stopped consuming the pre-packaged experiences provided by restaurants, movie theaters, or television, and started creating her own movies, making meals at home, and sewing her own clothes. Adopting John's ethical concerns was for Alexia a reaction to her feelings of loneliness. For her, ethical consumption is not simply an act of protecting natural resources and fighting against social inequalities, it is mostly a way to belong to a meaningful community and to 'keep' her boyfriend.

Another valuable example of ethical consumption behavior due to social integration is the story of Vivian. When Vivian was twelve years old, her parents divorced. After this destabilizing event, Vivian moved in with her mother and 'everything was different'. She was a 'child with divorced parents' and could no longer be 'like' her friends who were still living with both parents. In order to hide her difference and belong to the 'cool group of friends', Vivian struggled to acquire the 'best' brands and the most fashionable items. But Vivian did not have the financial means and felt guilty that her mother was working hard to pay the bills. Gradually, Vivian lost the conviction that belonging to 'the cool group of friends' provided meanings in life. She decided to 'shift friends'. During college, Vivian met a new group of friends who were 'more humane' and 'ethically oriented'. In order to belong to the new group, Vivian adopted their ethical views and changed her consumption behavior. She stopped shaving her legs and armpits, ceased caring about brands and fashion trends, started buying second-hand clothes, and became interested in the politics of consumption when boycotting global chain restaurants and big supermarkets. Her consumption now respects her friends' ethical, social and environmental values. Ethical consumption behavior is for Vivian a straight path toward finding meanings in life and a sense of belonging to a community.

Again, informants experienced uncontrollable and unpredictable event(s) that destabilized their idea of what a 'good' life should be. This displacement of meanings in life led informants to seek for new meanings. The theme of social integration depicts ethical consumption as a means of belonging and being part of a community. Another theme found within the practice of ethical consumption was authenticity. In the following discussion, I will present this using the narratives of Jeremy and Philippe.

Authenticity

Authenticity is a most complex theme. It relates to living life in accordance to one's priority and brings ethical consumption behavior to the level of real self or inner self. Jeremy's story is an interesting example of the search for authenticity in ethical consumption behavior which in his case is oriented toward being true to himself and his origins. In his mid-twenties, Jeremy moved to Los Angeles to work as a film technician. Although the job paid well, Jeremy felt different from his co-workers and was missing authenticity in his work. He realized that the film industry was oriented toward profit through mass-commercialism and social exploitation.

After working there for two years, Jeremy suffered from living in what he called 'an inauthentic and meaningless world'. Unable to sustain an inauthentic lifestyle, Jeremy escaped the commercial world, moved to his parents' house in the woods, and began to search for new meanings in life. He read several books on the negative aspects of the consumer culture and adopted an anti-globalization approach to consumption.

Following these new views on the 'dictating capitalist society', he began to engage in political consumption. He stopped eating at food chain restaurants, listening to the radio or watching any television commercials. He also stopped buying global brands, quit eating processed food, and started reading anti-consumption magazines such as *Adbuster*. Adopting an ethical consumption behavior was for Jeremy a matter of psychological survival. He could no longer participate in an unfair system that 'abuses the poor' and 'destroys authenticity'. In order to live an authentic life, Jeremy had to escape the unethical money-driven corporate America and orient his consumption according to what he deliberately wants to hear, see, smell and touch. Clearly, Jeremy's choice to engage in ethical consumption behavior relates to a long process of discovery and a quest for authenticity and fairness.

Another example showing the importance of authenticity when developing ethical consumption behavior is reflected in the story of Philippe. Philippe's ethical consumption behavior started after watching videos on animal cruelty. The 'inhuman' and 'heartless' pictures 'terrified' Philippe. In response to the 'horrifying' videos on animal brutality, Philippe sought information on the food industry. He wanted to better understand how companies contributed to animal cruelty. While studying the food production business, Philippe became aware of unethical production systems and global consumerism. During the interview, Philippe designated affluent consumption as a 'disease' which creates an artificial reality where 'we don't know who's just trying to sell you something and who's really just trying to be human'. It is for him 'scary' to think about the food industry and how it 'kills America' with 'obesity' and 'heart failures'. Philippe identifies himself as an 'industrial kid who just does what he wants to do'. He believes that refusing to participate in 'the things he does not want to contribute to' such as animal cruelty allows him to be true to his real self. Ethical consumption behavior is for Philippe an expression of his inner authentic self.

Here, ethical consumption has the function of helping consumers clarify their conception of self. With this theme, the aspect of commitment is important. Ethical consumers influenced by a search for authenticity appeared more committed than those searching for control or social integration. For instance, those informants changed their physical space and moved to the woods (Jeremy) or completely changed their eating consumption lifestyle to become vegetarian or even vegan (Philippe).

DISCUSSION

Overall, the framing of an ethical lifestyle among these simplifying consumers reflects a search for meanings in life, which starts with implicit human needs including control, social integration, and authenticity. The theme of the *search for control* reflects a need to have power and control over one's life. After the unpredictable and uncontrollable events, informants felt in the grip of forces over which they had no power. With available cultural discourses and the help of others' life examples, they realized that the powerlessness they experienced was not a sign of personal failing, but that it reflected the incapacities of mainstream consumer culture to provide security, order and power. The disillusionment led them to search for more clarity and certainty about consumer culture. Simplified consumption offered a suitable and convincing means of reducing the relative influence of consumer culture, and of improving their social and cultural capital with respect to others. Adopting ethical consumption behavior enabled those informants to claim or reclaim a privileged self-sufficiency and autonomy while resisting social stigmatization.

The theme of *social integration* emphasizes ethical consumption as a system of symbols, signs, tools and beliefs, which allows one to be recognized by others as being part of a community. Through interaction with charismatic locals, those informants developed common interests, ideologies and experiences. I use 'charismatic locals' to depict individuals living in proximity and exercising atypical yet meaningful consumption lifestyles. Thus, ethical consumption behavior emerged from encountering what Foucault calls a critical community, which 'is open to new experiences and ways of being' and 'makes new subjectivities possible' (Weeks, 1995: 80). Through the critical community, ethical consumption behavior was communicated, reproduced, experienced and explored by informants. Here, the group ideology, practice and language were all important in constructing social integration, simplicity and ethical consumption behavior.

The theme of *authenticity* represents a search for the real self in ethical consumption behavior. It holds rights to livelihood through ecological and social consideration as a way to enlarge oneself and embrace more and more possibilities of being. Finding authenticity in ethical consumption behavior enables informants to reshape meanings of consumption to symbolize unique ethical aspects, personal qualities, values and attributes, past experiences and social position (McCracken, 1988a; Miller, 1994, 2001b; Schor, 1999; Schor and Holt, 2000).

CONCLUSION

To date, most studies of simplifying ethical consumers have focussed on defining demographics, socioeconomics, psychographics, pro-social behaviors, ideologies, or beliefs that trigger ethical consumption practices (Rawvas, 2001; Tanner and Kast, 2003; Zhongzhi, 2001). The ontology used in much of this work adheres to a material essentialism, which presupposes that worldly entities, be they people, animals, lakes and the like, have a set of immutable properties that are autonomous from those of other entities (Van Inwagen, 1990; Wiggins, 2001; Williams, 1992). These absolute properties can ultimately be appealed to by researchers to make claims about the 'who' and 'what' of consumer behavior. However, as noted in the introduction, simplicity and ethical consumption behavior are context dependent and subject to the meanings which consumers subjectively experienced and negotiated throughout their temporal activities.

Modelling Consumer Decision Making in Fair Trade

9

Deirdre Shaw

The increase in ethical concerns over the past two to three decades and the resulting growth in ethical consumerism has been well documented, both in the chapters contained in this book and elsewhere. Ethical concerns can be very broad in nature and in some way are applicable to every product and service, including environmental, animal, societal and people issues (see for example, Shaw and Clarke, 1999; Strong, 1997). This chapter is interested in the latter and, as such, will examine the impact of fair trade concerns in ethical consumer food choice.

Fairly traded products can be defined as those purchased under equitable trading agreements, involving co-operative rather than competitive trading principles, ensuring a fair price and fair working conditions for producers and suppliers. The importance of fair trade as a behavioural focus for the research with which this chapter is concerned emerged from an exploratory study of ethical consumers. Shaw and Clarke (1999) found that although many ethical issues were of concern to ethical consumers, concerns surrounding fair trade were deemed to be particularly pertinent at the time of the study. The importance of fair trade among consumers was reflected in the growth and development of fair trade products at that time in the UK market.

Playing an important role was the introduction of Cafédirect, a fair trade coffee brand, to mainstream retail outlets. While ethical consumers place ethical concerns highly on their purchase criteria this is often not at the expense of other more traditional factors important in choice (Shaw and Clarke, 1999). In recognising the importance of traditional product features, including quality and taste, Cafédirect sought to be more than just an ethical brand and also placed importance on product quality and availability in mainstream markets. Indeed, since the research reported in this chapter was first conducted in 1997/8 the increased presence of fair trade products, including coffee, tea and chocolate, in mainstream as well as alternative outlets has improved access, range and availability of these products. In the UK, sales of roast and ground fair trade coffee grew by 27 per cent in 2001, accounting for 10.5 per cent of this total market (Fairtrade Foundation, 2002), and UK sales of fair trade products doubled between 2001 and 2003 (Fairtrade Foundation, 2003). The aim of this chapter, therefore, is to examine the impact of fair trade concerns on decision making through the development of an empirical model of consumer behaviour that will seek to explain ethical consumers' intention to purchase fair trade grocery products.

THEORETICAL FRAMEWORK

In an earlier study the author sought to develop an understanding of ethical consumer intention to purchase fair trade grocery products using an existing model of decision making as a theoretical framework (Shaw et al., 2000). The current chapter seeks to build upon this work further using the data collected by Shaw et al. (2000) to develop an improved model of ethical consumer decision making applicable in this fair trade context. First, however, this earlier work will be outlined to provide a basis upon which to develop subsequent analysis, model development and behavioural explanation.

Theory of planned behaviour

To gain initial insights into the key determinants of intention to purchase fair trade grocery products Shaw et al. (2000) used the well-known and extensively applied behavioural model called the theory of planned behaviour (Ajzen, 1985). The theory of planned behaviour is a theory of attitude-behaviour relationships that seeks to provide an explanation of behaviour, and links attitudes, subjective norms, perceived behavioural control, behavioural intentions and behaviour in a fixed causal sequence. Behaviour is deemed to be a direct function of an individual's intention to conduct the behaviour. For example, in Shaw et al.'s study intention was measured as 'The next time you go grocery shopping how likely are you to purchase a fair trade product.' In turn intention is considered to be a function of attitude, subjective norm and perceived behavioural control. Again, using Shaw et al.'s study as an example, attitude refers to an individual's general attitude (favourable – unfavourable) towards purchasing a fair trade product; subjective norm refers to important social others and whether they think an individual should purchase fair trade grocery products; perceived behavioural control refers to how easy or difficult it is to purchase fair trade grocery products. Each of these measures of attitude, subjective norm and perceived behavioural control seek to provide an explanation of behavioural intention, which in the current study refers to intention to purchase a fair trade grocery product.

Further, in the theory of planned behaviour each of the measures of attitude, subjective norm and perceived behavioural control are deemed to have underlying beliefs. Attitude towards performing the behaviour is deemed to be a summed product of individuals' beliefs and their evaluation of these. Examples of such beliefs in Shaw et al.'s study include the belief that purchasing a fair trade product will result in a fair price and support for fair trade producers. Evaluation of those beliefs will consider an individual's evaluation as to how important these afore-mentioned beliefs are. Subjective norm is considered to be a summed product of individuals' beliefs that important others think that they should or should not perform the behaviour in question, and their motivation to comply with those others. Examples of important others in Shaw et al.'s study included family and friends and control beliefs underlying perceived behavioural control include availability and location of retail outlets. The theory of planned behaviour is diagrammatically represented in Figure 9.1 and is outlined in Ajzen (1985).

Although the theory of planned behaviour has been applied in a variety of behavioural domains, the context of ethical concerns in consumer decision making has been neglected. The theory of planned behaviour in its current form does not

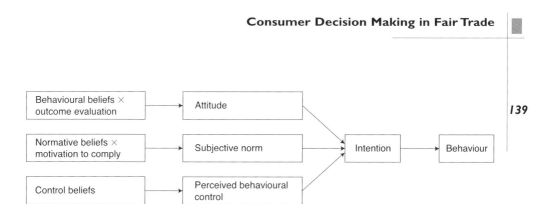

Figure 9.1   Theory of planned behaviour

consider ethical or social issues within its model measures. Indeed, Ajzen invited consideration of additional model measures stating that 'The theory of planned behaviour is, in principle, open to the inclusion of additional predictors if it can be shown that they capture a significant proportion of the variance in intention or behaviour after the theory's current variables have been taken into account' (1991: 199).

Modified theory of planned behaviour: ethical obligation and self-identity

The tendency of the original theory to focus on the self-interested concerns of individuals may be limiting given the more societally centred viewpoint of ethical consumers. Some researchers have argued that a measure of personal 'moral' or 'ethical' obligation be added to the traditional theory of planned behaviour structure (see for example, Eagly and Chaiken, 1993). Such a measure represents an individual's internalised ethical rules, which reflect their personal beliefs about right and wrong. In many instances the addition of such a measure has been found to improve the explanation of intention (see for example, Gorsuch and Ortberg, 1983; Raats et al., 1995). However, it must be noted that ethical consumer concerns have often been neglected in previous research exploring additional ethical/moral variables, where, with few exceptions, the focus has been on areas such as cheating, lying and blood donation. In their study examining the impact of fair trade concerns in consumer decision making Shaw et al. (2000) found the addition of a measure of ethical obligation to be significant in the explanation of behavioural intention to purchase a fair trade grocery product. This supports findings from an earlier exploratory study of ethical consumers which revealed that individuals do hold strong feelings of obligation for others that impact on their purchase choices (Shaw and Clarke, 1999).

Research has also suggested that the theory of planned behaviour be modified to incorporate a measure of self-identity (see for example, Granberg and Holmberg, 1990; Sparks and Guthrie, 1998; Sparks and Shepherd, 1992). The rationale for this argument is that as an issue becomes central to an individual's self-identity, then

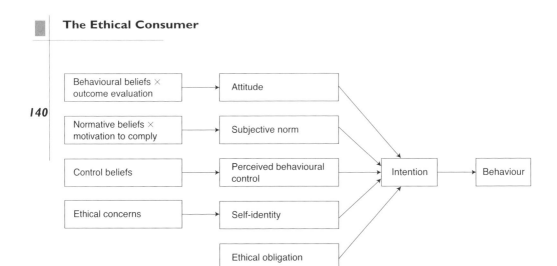

Figure 9.2 Modified theory of planned behaviour

behavioural intention is adjusted accordingly. Indeed, Shaw et al.'s (2000) study supported the notion that ethical consumers make ethical consumption choices because ethical issues have become an important part of their self-identity and as such self-identity was found to be significant in the explanation of intention to purchase a fair trade grocery product. This was also supported by earlier research which found that ethical consumers do not only identify with one ethical issue, but with a range of ethical issues (Shaw and Clarke, 1999). Indeed, in the area of green consumerism, Sparks and Shepherd (1992) found that self-identity contributed to the explanation of intention over and above the contribution made by the other theory of planned behaviour measures.

It has been suggested that some forms of self-identity may involve a moral component (Sparks and Shepherd, 1992). For example, some identities, such as vegetarianism, are generally associated with ethical values. Sparks and Guthrie (1998), however, consider these two constructs, ethical obligation and self-identity, to be conceptually distinct. They argue that neither is reducible to the other and state that independent predictive effects on behavioural intentions should occur in contexts where aspects of self-identity are distinct from ethical concerns. This suggestion has been supported in studies by Sparks and Guthrie (1998) and Sparks et al. (1995) and as such, in the study conducted by Shaw et al. (2000), these variables remained separate.

The modified theory of planned behaviour framework which includes the original model measures of attitude, subjective norm and perceived behavioural control and additionally includes measures of ethical obligation and self-identity is diagrammatically represented in Figure 9.2.

As noted above, findings by Shaw et al. (2000) supported the use of a modified theory of planned behaviour, as outlined in Figure 9.2, to examine ethical consumers' intention to purchase a fair trade grocery product. Due to the novel nature of this behavioural context in the application of a theory of planned behaviour model, Shaw et al.'s (2000) study was concerned with gaining an improved conceptual understanding of the determinants of decision making in this context and, as such, focused on intention only and was not concerned with gaining a measure of actual behaviour.

In their study Shaw et al. found that although attitude played a significant role in the explanation of intention to purchase a fair trade grocery product, of greater significance was the role played by the additional measures of ethical obligation and self-identity. This supports earlier findings which revealed that ethical consumers hold strong feelings of obligation for others that impact on their purchase choices and do not consider ethical issues in isolation, rather the linkages found to exist between issues highlight identification to ethical issues generally (Shaw and Clarke, 1999). Most significant in this modified theory of planned behaviour model was perceived behavioural control. This was not unexpected in the context of ethical consumption where difficulties such as availability and choice can exist in decision making (Shaw and Clarke, 1999). Subjective norm was found to be not significant in the explanation of intention to purchase a fair trade grocery product. The reduced role of subjective norm has been noted and discussed elsewhere. Vallerand et al. (1992), for example, suggest that subjective norm is less pertinent in the explanation of intention because this measure is concerned with a more remote concept, which is what important others think. Remoteness may be particularly relevant in ethical consumption where research has found that individuals often feel isolated in their ethical concerns (Shaw and Clarke, 1999). Indeed, Sparks et al.'s (1995) study examining expectations of eating food produced by gene technology, another area of ethical concern, also found that in a model where measures of ethical obligation and self-identity are added to the theory of planned behaviour structure, 'others' attitudes' makes a non-significant contribution to the explanation of intention.

The pertinence of the additional model measures of ethical obligation and self-identity in a modified theory of planned behaviour highlight, that while many consumers acting in a self-motivated manner may select coffee for example, on the basis of factors such as price and taste, those concerned about ethical issues may be guided by a sense of ethical obligation to others and a self-identification with ethical issues. Although these findings highlight inadequacies in the original theory of planned behaviour in ethical contexts, where behaviour is not purely driven by self-interest, further improvements to Shaw et al.'s (2000) modified theory of planned behaviour model are sought and will form the focus for the remainder of this chapter.

CRITICISMS OF THE MODIFIED THEORY OF PLANNED BEHAVIOUR

Shaw et al.'s (2000) research was important in revealing initial insights into the key explanatory measures of intention to purchase a fair trade grocery product. The modified theory of planned behaviour was better able to explain intention to purchase a fair trade grocery product than the original theory of planned behaviour model, due to the significance of additional measures of ethical obligation and self-identity. It must be noted, however, that approximately 76 per cent of intention remained unexplained. Therefore, the modified theory of planned behaviour as reported in Shaw et al. was able, through the measures of attitude, perceived behavioural control, ethical obligation and self-identity, to explain approximately 24 per cent of intention to purchase a fair trade grocery product. Improvements in explanation can be sought through different methods of analysis.

Shaw et al.'s study was limited by the regression analysis technique adopted. Using this approach, independent measures (namely attitude, subjective norm, perceived behavioural control, ethical obligation and self-identity) are related to a dependent measure (namely intention). Regression analysis is the technique commonly used for the analysis of a theory of planned behaviour model. Limitations in regression analysis include the inability of this technique to allow a full examination of model measures in the explanation of behavioural intention. This is because the technique is commonly applied to the direct measures only, namely attitude, subjective norm, perceived behavioural control, ethical obligation and self-identity. Thus, the beliefs underlying these direct measures are not utilised in regression analysis. Rather, the beliefs underlying these direct measures are elicited and the correlation of the beliefs with their relevant direct measure computed. Even where low correlation results are obtained between beliefs and their direct measures analysis often continues using the direct measures only in the explanation of intention through regression analysis. Therefore, using regression analysis, beliefs relating to intended fair trade purchases such as, 'result in a fair price for fair trade producers' (underlying attitude), are not utilised directly in the explanation of intention to purchase a fair trade grocery product. Research has indeed revealed that beliefs may not always be reflective of their direct measures, as the theory of planned behaviour would assume (Ajzen, 1991; Shaw et al., 2000). This is suggested by research revealing low correlation results between beliefs and the direct measures that they are deemed to underlie. Despite this, however, regression analysis often continues using the direct measures only despite a poor relationship between these and their underlying beliefs.

In light of the often increased complexity of decision making demonstrated in ethical choice (Shaw and Clarke, 1999), it may be deemed more appropriate to use the beliefs underlying each direct measure, as they provide a deeper level of explanation and detail into consumers' motivations than the general direct measure. For example, in terms of attitude, while the beliefs underlying this reveal concerns related to the purchase of a fair trade grocery product, including 'result in a fair price for fair trade producers', 'support fair trade producers' and 'result in non-exploitation of fair trade producers', the direct measure of attitude only reveals in general how favourable an individuals attitude is towards the purchase of a fair trade grocery product. It could be suggested, therefore, that beliefs may aggregate to form latent factors that are different perspectives from the direct measures they are deemed to be a function of, and reveal a greater detail of information in explanation.

Although regression analysis is the most commonly applied method of analysis for this theory, Hankins et al. (2000) and Shiu and Hassan (2002) suggest that structural equation modelling is the preferred analytical technique for analysis of the theory of planned behaviour framework. Structural equation modelling addresses the above concerns in two important respects. First, structural equation modelling allows the specification of a chain of causal links from beliefs, via constructs through to behavioural intention, which is not possible under regression analysis. This allows the use of beliefs more directly in the explanation of intention. Second, structural equation modelling allows the specification of latent factors, enabling the modelling of cognitive constructs underpinning the model. The extraction of only the most pertinent beliefs using an analysis technique called 'reliability analysis' should yield a more appropriate representation than direct measures. This arguably serves to address the possible occurrence of a low correlation between direct measures and their component beliefs and the subsequent non-use of beliefs in explaining intention.

In light of the findings outlined above and the criticisms of the regression analysis technique adopted, this chapter will re-examine the findings from Shaw et al. (2000) through the application of reliability analysis and structural equation modelling as discussed above. The analysis will use the modified theory of planned behaviour as an initial framework and will seek to develop an improved model of ethical consumer decision making in this fair trade context. Using two data sets the model of ethical consumer decision making will be developed using the first set of data and cross-validated using the second set of data. This model will be presented and its implications for understanding consumer choices in the context of purchasing fair trade grocery products will be discussed. First, the methodology adopted in this research will be outlined and discussed.

METHODOLOGY

A quantitative approach to research is traditionally associated with logical positivism (Gill and Johnson, 1991) and, as such, seeks to establish causal relationships among objectively specified variables, testing hypotheses derived from predictive theories (Kerlinger, 1986). Using this approach, variables are precisely measured and data are collected under standardised conditions using an instrument such as a questionnaire. This rests on a clearly different philosophy from qualitative methods that are phenomenological in approach and concerned with gaining an understanding of the unique experiences of the individual. For some researchers the fundamentally different philosophies underlying quantitative and qualitative research are not irreconcilable, since they can serve different purposes. In addressing the aim of the research with which this chapter is concerned, namely the exploration of ethical consumer decision making, the selection of an appropriate methodological approach considered the extent of existing knowledge and appropriate theory.

Although, as detailed previously, a theory of ethical consumer decision making is lacking in literature, the existing modified theory of planned behaviour provided an important context within which to re-examine existing findings in this area (Shaw et al., 2000). This was achieved in two phases: an elicitation questionnaire, designed to elicit the salient beliefs underlying attitude, subjective norm, perceived behavioural control and self-identity as recommended by the theory of planned behaviour approach (Ajzen and Fishbein, 1980) (although it must be noted that in existing literature ethical obligation is represented by one direct measure and, therefore, has no underlying beliefs); and a survey to measure the determinants of intention to purchase a fair trade grocery product. These approaches are detailed below beginning with an outline of the research sample.

Sample

To meet the aim of the research it was necessary to obtain access to a meaningful group of consumers with a strong ethical stance. This was achieved by conducting the research with subscribers to the UK's *Ethical Consumer* magazine, who were selected in a purposive sampling approach. The purpose was to focus on consumers where ethical attitudes are accentuated, rather than overly subtle and harder to detect as in other mainstream consumer groups. Thus, although the study does not attempt to generalise widely, the population size of ethical consumers, and the large sample obtained (see below), cannot be dismissed as trivial or anecdotal. *Ethical Consumer* magazine was selected as the most appropriate source from which to derive the sample, as this specific magazine exists to promote a wide range of ethical issues 'by informing and empowering the consumer' (ECRA, 1998/99: 3).

Questionnaires

First, an elicitation questionnaire was constructed as outlined by Ajzen and Fishbein (1980). This was designed to elicit salient, behavioural, normative, control and identity beliefs associated with the purchase of fair trade grocery products. This questionnaire was sent out in two mailings to subscribers to the UK's *Ethical Consumer* magazine in two UK cities. A total of 55 useable questionnaires were returned. Second, the main postal questionnaire was developed to measure the components of the modified theory of planned behaviour, namely attitude, subjective norm, perceived behavioural control, ethical obligation and self-identity and their respective beliefs as obtained at the elicitation questionnaire stage. In the analysis of the elicitation questionnaire Ajzen and Fishbein (1980) recommend the selection of around 5–9 of the most frequently elicited beliefs for each belief measure, as under most conditions an individual will only be able to attend to that number of beliefs at any given time. These most frequently elicited beliefs are considered to be the most salient and this recommendation was adhered to in the current research.

Questions designed to elicit behavioural intention, behavioural beliefs, attitude, subjective norm, normative beliefs and motivation to comply were structured as suggested by Ajzen and Fishbein (1980), and the measures of perceived behavioural control in accordance with Ajzen (1985). The outcome evaluation measure employed an 'important' to 'unimportant' scale, which reflects the type used by, for example, Manstead et al. (1983) and Raats et al. (1995). The measure of ethical obligation takes on the format suggested by Sparks et al. (1995). Self-identity and an index of ethical concerns followed the structure as outlined by Sparks and Shepherd (1992). Further details of this methodology and research instrument are outlined in Shaw et al. (2000). Questionnaires detailing the purpose of the study along with a prepaid envelope were inserted into the December/January 1997/98 issue of *Ethical Consumer* magazine and mailed to 4,000 UK subscribers. One thousand four hundred and seventy two useable questionnaires (36.8 per cent) were returned within the specified eight-week period.

DEVELOPMENT OF THE MODEL OF ETHICAL CONSUMER DECISION MAKING

This section will firstly give an overview of respondents by outlining the descriptive statistics obtained from the main questionnaire. The stages of development for the model of ethical consumer decision making will be outlined beginning with reliability analysis, a technique necessary to ensure that the elicited salient beliefs form a cohesive grouping under each model measure. Once these belief groupings have been established analysis using structural equation modelling is applied in a two-stage process of model development. To make optimal use of the data obtained, a random sample of the 1,427 total responses (736) was taken for use at the model development stage. Findings from this initial sample selection are detailed in the descriptive statistics, reliability analysis and analysis of model development below. The second sample selection (691) is used in analysis to confirm the developed model.

Descriptive statistics

In the questionnaire, respondents were requested to mark their responses on a seven-point scale, ranging from +3 to –3. Out of the 736 responses, 83 per cent thought they were likely (+1 to +3) to purchase a fair trade product the next time they went grocery shopping, only 9 per cent were unlikely (–3 to –1) to do so. Though 79 per cent held a favourable attitude towards purchasing a fair trade product, no respondents felt unfavourably about this proposition. While 53 per cent thought it likely that their important others would think that they should purchase fair trade grocery products, 20 per cent thought this was unlikely to be the case. Likewise, 53 per cent considered the purchase of fair trade grocery products easy, while 39 per cent considered such purchases difficult. And 96 per cent felt that they had an ethical obligation to purchase fair trade grocery products, with only 1 per cent disagreeing with that stance. Similarly, 99 per cent considered themselves to be someone who was concerned about ethical issues; one respondent disagreed.

These results clearly reveal that this group of ethical consumers held high intentions to purchase fair trade grocery products. Interestingly, it can be seen that while 79 per cent held a favourable attitude towards purchasing a fair trade product, an overwhelming 96 per cent felt an ethical obligation to do so, and 99 per cent identified themselves as someone concerned about ethical issues. These findings point to the importance of the additional measures of ethical obligation and self-identity compared to the traditional attitude measures.

Reliability analysis

Before the application of structural equation modelling reliability analysis was applied to determine cohesive groupings of the elicited beliefs underlying each factor. Reliability analysis generates reliability statistics for multiple item additive scales, aiding the selection of the 'best' scale, which can then be computed (Norusis, 1993). Reliability analysis conducted on the beliefs underlying each of the model direct measures to develop reliable belief groupings is outlined below. The calculation of the reliability scale reveals a figure called an alpha and the closer that the alpha figure is to one, the more cohesive the grouping. The resultant alpha figures in the current study were also analysed in relation to earlier qualitative work (Shaw and Clarke, 1999) to ensure they were socially meaningful in the context of the research.

Attitude

Data exploration based on reliability analysis suggested that attitude consists of two distinct groupings. The division of attitude has been found elsewhere. Giles and Cairns (1995) in a study exploring blood donation behaviour suggested that attitude should consist of a positive and negative belief system. In the context of the current study, the first attitude group, attitude-traditional (alpha = 0.74), comprised the measures closely related to the study focus such as, result in a fair price for fair trade producers and support fair trade producers. The second group, attitude-control (alpha = 0.57), comprised the measures reflective of an individual's attitude towards behavioural control issues namely, 'entail purchasing a product which is not readily available' and 'which is more expensive'. The internal consistency of the items that comprised the attitude-traditional group, as revealed by the alpha result, indicates a strong relationship between the variables. Although the internal consistency for the attitude-control group is not as strong, the distinction between these two attitude groups is clear and conceptually sensible, as attitude-traditional relates very closely to the fair trade focus of the study, while attitude-control reflects behavioural control issues.

The measures contained within the attitude-control group could be considered closely related to the perceived behavioural control belief measures; however, findings from further reliability analysis suggest that attitude-control is distinct from the perceived behavioural control group, and forms a cohesive grouping in its own right (alpha = 0.54, rising to alpha = 0.78 when attitude-control measures are omitted from the perceived behavioural control grouping). This reveals that attitude-control and perceived behavioural control are different, suggesting that attitude-control relates to an individual's attitude to difficulties, and is distinct from perceptions of the actual difficulties themselves.

Subjective norm

Two cohesive groupings were suggested for the measure of subjective norm. The first group, subjective norm-traditional (alpha = 0.60), consisted of the 'traditional' theory of planned behaviour normative others, namely, family and friends. The second group, subjective norm-context (alpha = 0.76) comprised context related normative others, relating specifically to groups associated with fair trade.

Perceived behavioural control

Two distinct cohesive groupings were suggested for perceived behavioural control. Perceived behavioural control-traditional (alpha = 0.82) and perceived behavioural control-context (alpha = 0.55). The division of the perceived behavioural control measure in this way is conceptually desirable, as the measures within the perceived behavioural control-traditional factor could be generally applied to many product categories (for example, availability and limited range), while the component measures of perceived behavioural control-context are difficulties that can be related specifically to fairly traded/ethical products (for example, availability in supermarkets).

Self-identity

One grouping was suggested to exist for self-identity (alpha = 0.83). This supports earlier work which found that important linkages exist between a range of ethical concerns, suggesting that ethical issues have become an important part of respondent's self-identity (Shaw and Clarke, 1999).

As stated previously, ethical obligation is represented in the model by one direct measure and, therefore, does not have corresponding beliefs. Table 9.1 details each of the belief measures underlying the above factors.

Model analysis

Structural equation modelling techniques allow the evaluation of how effectively a conceptual model, which includes observed variables and hypothetical constructs,

Table 9.1   Reliability analysis results

Construct	Factor	Measures	
Attitude	att_traditional	att_a	result in a fair price for fair trade producers
		att_b	support fair trade producers
		att_c	result in non-exploitation of fair trade producers
		att_d	result in my peace of mind
		att_e	encourage retailers to stock fair trade products
		att_f	withdraw support from non-ethical companies
		att_i	entail purchasing a quality product
	att_control	att_g	entail purchasing a product which is not readily available
		att_h	entail purchasing a product which is more expensive
Subjective norm	sn_traditional	sn_a	family
		sn_b	friends
	sn_context	sn_c	fair trade producers
		sn_e	ethical organisations
		sn_g	retailers who stock fair trade products
Perceived behavioural control	pbc_traditional	pbc_a	availability
		pbc_b	limited range
		pbc_c	location of retail outlets
	pbc_context	pbc_e	obtaining information regarding what products are fairly traded
		pbc_f	availability in supermarkets
Self-identity		si_a	fair trade
		si_b	human rights
		si_c	workers' rights
		si_d	company conduct
		si_e	genetic engineering
		si_f	environmental issues
		si_g	animal welfare
		si_h	organic farming
		si_i	country of origin
		si_j	local production
		si_k	health
		si_l	over-consumption

fits the obtained data (Hoyle and Smith, 1994). The structural equation modelling procedure seeks to explain the structure or pattern among a set of latent variables, factors and constructs, where factors are each measured by one or more manifest indicators. The application of structural equation modelling in the current study was two-fold. First, the modified theory of planned behaviour was specified, tested and further developed to seek an improved model of ethical consumer decision making. Second, utilising new data both models were confirmed through cross-validation.

In the present study the data set was randomly divided into two samples of 736 (sample 1) and 691 (sample 2). These sample sizes are consistent with recommendations for structural equation modelling (Hoelter, 1983). It was ensured that the two data sets were similar in terms of representation of categories of respondents (for example, gender), to avoid any bias in the results. The first data set was allocated for use in model development, while the second data set was reserved for validating the resulting models. This process is outlined by Cudeck and Brown (1983).

Within structural equation modelling there is no single statistical test that can best assess the model fit. Rather, an assessment of fit can be best achieved by using a combination of goodness-of-fit measures that can be utilised to assess absolute fit, incremental fit and parsimious fit. In this study a combination of goodness-of-fit index (GFI) (raw and adjusted (AGFI)), comparative fit index (CFI) and parsimonious goodness-of-fit index (PGFI) are used. GFI, CFI and PGFI measures range in value from 0 (poor model fit) to 1 (perfect model fit). The recommended acceptance level for AGFI is a value greater than or equal to 0.90. For further discussion on model fit measures see Hair et al. (1995). The ability of the model to explain behavioural intention is revealed through a R^2 value. The greater the R^2 value the better able the model is to explain behavioural intention. Similarly, paths between model constructs and behavioural intention and correlations between model constructs will be assessed for significance, with higher values revealing stronger relationships. In the model all the path values between model constructs and behavioural intention will be displayed. In terms of correlations results between model constructs only stronger correlations of 0.30 or more will be detailed; this is simply to reduce complexity in presentation.

Model 1 (modified theory of planned behaviour)

Using the groupings, as conceptually defended in the reliability analysis, structural equation modelling analysis was conducted. Model 1 represented the modified theory of planned behaviour framework using the factors defined by reliability analysis. Results revealed a good structural fit within the model (GFI = 0.96; AGFI = 0.93; CFI = 0.96; PGFI = 0.70). However, the ability of this model to explain behavioural intention was poor (R^2 = 0.28). Additionally, problems with this model lie in non-significant paths for constructs attitude-traditional, subjective norm-traditional, perceived behavioural control-context and self-identity (see Figure 9.3: Model 1).

Ethical concerns clearly heighten the complexity of decision making; hence the use of eight factors in Model 1. Bentler and Chou (1987) suggest that in areas where knowledge is limited, models should contain at most 5–6 constructs, each measured by 3–4 indicators. Further, the modified theory of planned behaviour structure, as utilised in Model 1, may be inappropriate for use in the context of

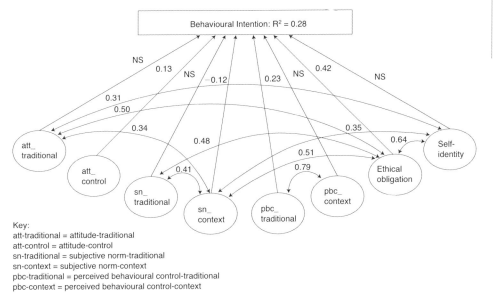

Key:
att-traditional = attitude-traditional
att-control = attitude-control
sn-traditional = subjective norm-traditional
sn-context = subjective norm-context
pbc-traditional = perceived behavioural control-traditional
pbc-context = perceived behavioural control-context

Figure 9.3 Model I

grocery choices, which is often regarded as low involvement behaviour (Foxall and Goldsmith, 1994). This suggests that individuals would not simultaneously consult eight distinct constructs in forming their purchase intention, as this modified theory of planned behaviour structure would propose, and highlights the need to re-examine the model.

The strong correlation results between factors detailed in Model 1 clearly suggest that certain factors, although distinct (given reliability analysis and/or conceptual reasoning), should feed into one common latent variable construct. In the instance of subjective norm it is conceptually sensible that the two factors of subjective norm (subjective norm-traditional and subjective norm-context (correlation = 0.41)) would relate to one latent measure of 'subjective norm', reflecting an overall subjective norm construct. Similarly, the two measures of perceived behavioural control (perceived behavioural control-traditional and perceived behavioural control-context (correlation = 0.79)) should relate to one latent measure of 'external control'.

A strong correlation was also found between ethical obligation and self-identity (correlation = 0.64). Although these factors are distinct, it has been suggested that a degree of commonality may exist between these measures given their centrality to the ethical focus of the study (Sparks and Shepherd, 1992), as such an 'internal ethics' construct is proposed.

Model 1 reveals a strong relationship between attitude-traditional and subjective norm-context (correlation = 0.34), ethical obligation (correlation = 0.50) and self-identity (correlation = 0.31). A new latent meta-construct that is illustrative of an individual's 'internal reflection' is thus specified which considers these relationships. This meta-construct will also take account of the following strong relationships: subjective norm-traditional and subjective norm-context with ethical obligation (correlation = 0.48 and 0.51 respectively) and subjective norm-context and self-identity (correlation = 0.35). The operation of attitude-traditional through the internal reflection latent meta-construct, which includes ethical obligation, may improve the relationship of this factor with behavioural intention.

It is clear that attitude-control does not relate well to attitude-traditional (correlation = 0.10), but relates more readily to perceived behavioural control-traditional (correlation = 0.21) and perceived behavioural control-context (correlation = 0.21). These relationships are not as strong as that between perceived behavioural control-traditional and perceived behavioural control-context. A model is thus proposed which contains external control, as specified above, and a further latent control meta-construct, namely 'behavioural control', which considers both external control and attitude-control. Such a structural specification enables the joining of the control factors, while also recognising the subtle variations between external control and attitude-control. These newly specified relationships are shown in Figure 9.4: Model 2.

Model 2 (model of ethical consumer decision making)

Structural equation modelling analysis results revealed a good structural fit within Model 2 (GFI = 0.96; AGFI = 0.93; CFI = 0.96; PGFI = 0.66). The explanatory ability of this model has increased greatly to $R^2 = 0.52$, compared to $R^2 = 0.28$ previously. Additionally, improvements can be found in the significance of the attitude-traditional, subjective norm-traditional and self-identity paths to behavioural intention, via internal reflection. This suggests that attitude-traditional does

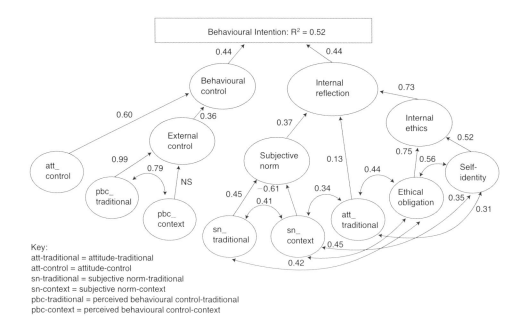

Figure 9.4 Model 2

indeed operate in tandem with subjective norm, ethical obligation and self-identity through internal reflection in the explanation of behavioural intention. The perceived behavioural control-context path to external control remains non-significant. As a group, perceived behavioural control-context has a comparatively low internal consistency (alpha = 0.55) as revealed previously through reliability analysis, suggesting that these variables do not form a very strong grouping, particularly when compared to perceived behavioural control-traditional (alpha = 0.82).

The adoption of a 'layered' model structure is supported in Model 2, as this structure allows constructs and factors to be placed within empirically and conceptually defensible groupings, which are arguably better able to reflect underlying cognitive processing. The explanatory ability of this model is significantly improved (R^2 = 0.52). The contributions towards behavioural intention made by the two meta-constructs of internal reflection (0.55) and behavioural control (0.46) are similar. However, the model is typified by the central role of ethical obligation and self-identity through internal ethics, as well as perceived behavioural control-traditional through external control.

Using the same procedure and analysis technique, the findings for Model 1 and Model 2 were confirmed through cross-validation analyses on the second respondent sample, thus confirming the stability of the resultant models and the improved explanation occurring between Model 1 and Model 2. For recent debate on the structural equation modelling analysis technique utilised please refer to Jarvis et al. (2003).

CONCLUSION

Although moving away from the traditional theory of planned behaviour structure as supported by the literature, the adoption of a conceptually defensible structure for this context has resulted in a model of ethical consumer decision making (Model 2) which is better able to explain behavioural intention to purchase a fair trade grocery product, although it must be noted that one predictor path (perceived behavioural control-context) to behavioural intention remains non-significant. Further, this cross-validated model now contains two meta-constructs, behavioural control reflective of internal and external control factors and internal reflection reflective of internal reasoning, which are specific to ethical consumer decision making. Through consideration of internal reflection, this model takes account of the complexity that ethical concerns can bring to the decision making process through attitude, important others, self-identity and ethical obligation, while also considering the behavioural control issues that can impact on an individual's ability to act in accordance with their ethical concerns.

Developing earlier work in this area, this model further reveals the difficulties posed for consumers in ethical consumption. The significance of ethical obligation in explaining intention to purchase a fair trade grocery product is hardly surprising, given the ethical context of the study where the behaviour is centred on a concern for others. It has been suggested elsewhere, however, that ethics will only matter to consumers when they are directly impacted on by the issue (Carrigan and Attalla, 2001). This can be seen to a degree in organic purchasing where some of the success of this market can be attributed to consumer health concerns. It must be noted, however, that for others organic purchasing centres around a concern for the environment and, therefore, the 'greater good'. This is clearly witnessed in the current study where consumers generally hold a high intention to purchase a fair trade grocery product. Such purchase intentions directly benefit a producer whom the individual consumer is unlikely to ever meet; however, an ethical obligation to such producers strongly influences behavioural intention.

In terms of the important role played by self-identity in explaining behavioural intention in this context, it is apparent that as an ethical issue becomes important to an individual it becomes part of their self-identity, and they form a desire to behave accordingly. The strong impact of behavioural control in explaining intention to purchase a fair trade grocery product suggests the existence of obstacles in decision making for which one would arguably require some self-identity with the issue in order to aspire to overcome such difficulties.

Application of the model of ethical consumer decision making presented in this chapter, and the resulting insights gained, have practical implications for those interested in obtaining an improved understanding of ethical consumers, through information obtained into how consumers *manage* the ethical concerns which impact on their purchase intention behaviour. This serves to provide an improved understanding of the words/deeds inconsistency (see Chapter 7) that can arise from survey data profiles by providing an explanation of behavioural intention.

Further, an understanding of ethical consumers is particularly vital at this time as market evidence reveals that ethical purchasing in some sectors in the UK has outperformed those of 'non-ethical' counterparts (Doane, 2001). The role of the Ethical Purchasing Index recently launched in the UK is to ensure that businesses which act ethically are rewarded at the expense of those who do not respond to ethical imperatives (Doane, 2001). This clearly reveals that many consumers now have the buying power to register considered choices in the market-place, and there is evidence of some who are willing to actively use that power through the purchase of more ethical alternatives (Cowe and Williams, 2001).

Finally, although there is widespread support in the literature for the traditional theory of planned behaviour (Ajzen, 1985) structure, in the context of the present study this model is rejected on the grounds of poor ability to explain behavioural intention and suboptimal representation of model measures (that is, that measures are unidimensional). This model is ineffective in responding to the complexity and interrelationships between factors important in explaining ethical consumer intention to purchase a fair trade grocery product. The adoption of a layered model structure in the model of ethical consumer decision making is considered conceptually sensible and more accurately reflective of true cognitive processing as it is less restrictive in the way it allows beliefs to relate to and explain behavioural intention. The model of ethical consumer decision making as revealed in Model 2 significantly improved the explanatory ability of the model, bringing the R^2 value for behavioural intention in line with much published research (see for example, Reinecke et al., 1996; Taylor and Todd, 1997) and highlighting the important role of behavioural difficulties in combination with internal identity, obligation, attitude and social others in explaining behavioural intention.

My colleagues and myself have tested the generalisability of the model of ethical consumer decision making presented here, with a sample of ethical consumers who were considered more 'mainstream' as they were obtained through a well-known supermarket retailer in the UK. Using the same context and research instrument this model continued to perform effectively in explaining behavioural intention to purchase a fair trade grocery product (Shaw et al., 2004a).

Although the model of ethical consumer decision making has an improved explanatory ability ($R^2 = 0.52$), it must be noted that some information regarding ethical consumer decision making remains unexplained (approximately 48 per cent). It is, therefore, necessary to consider how future research can achieve improvements in understanding. Important links to ethical consumption have been found in areas such as human values (see for example, Shaw et al., 2004b), spirituality (Shaw and Thomson, 2002), voluntary simplicity (Shaw and Newholm, 2002) and information and emotional reaction (Shaw and Clarke, 1999). Further understandings in this and other ethical behavioural contexts may be achieved by considering the development of model measures that represent these areas and others. Such research is important in gaining further understandings in this area as the ethical consumer continues to make an impact on the market-place.

Identifying and Profiling Apparel Label Users

10

Marsha A. Dickson

Marsha A. Dickson

INTRODUCTION

Many labor rights activists, media, politicians, academics and others assume that consumers have a role to play in controlling the action of apparel manufacturers and retailers that have garments assembled around the world. In a noteworthy press conference regarding trade policy, US Senator Howard Metzanbaum stated that it was believed that a majority of consumers would not buy a well-known brand of garment once they know that these were made by children (Federal News Service, 1994). Further, numerous activist groups have surfaced to mobilize consumers against unethical behavior in the apparel industry (Ho et al., 1996) and public opinion polls suggest that many consumers are willing to adopt behaviors supporting more ethical apparel businesses. For consumers to support ethical businesses (also referred to as socially responsible businesses) requires that such businesses do exist, a point that would almost certainly be debated by some consumers and activists, hingeing as it does on how socially responsible business is defined. Littrell and Dickson state that social responsibility in the apparel industry 'involves a system-wide range of practices for conducting business in which [producers], retailers, and consumers make decisions based on how their actions affect others within the marketplace system' (1999: 6).

They further explain that social responsibility is reflected in a continuum of practices that can reflect minimal efforts toward social responsibility, such as attending to fair wages or assuring a safe work-place, to more comprehensive and long-term practices, such as fostering worker empowerment and establishing political and social justice. Thus, companies are not necessarily defined as socially responsible or not, but rather on the extent of their social responsibility. Business practices described by the Fair Labor Association (2003) and a number of scholars (see for example, Hartman and Wokutch, 2003; Hartman et al., 2003; Radin, 2003) indicate that apparel businesses serving mainstream markets are increasingly engaged in socially responsible practices. Despite varying definitions of social responsibility, these opinion polls, because of their measurement techniques, may not accurately reflect the number of consumers willing to take action against unethical businesses. The purpose of this study is to identify and profile ethical apparel consumers, those whose actions are likely to follow their words, and to expand understanding of ethical consumer behavior. Ethical consumers are defined as those who buy products made and sold by companies that do not harm or exploit the environment, people and animals (ECRA, 2002b). This chapter focuses on ethical consumer behavior related to the exploitation of workers in the apparel industry and involves a re-analysis of data that were presented in a previous publication (Dickson, 2001), incorporating qualitative data gathered in the same survey.

GLOBAL ANTI-SWEATSHOP MOVEMENT

Periodically, apparel consumers are reminded that the garments they buy may have been made by exploited workers in sweatshops around the world. The US General Accounting Office defines a sweatshop as 'an employer that violates more than one federal or state labor law governing minimum wage and overtime, child labor, industrial homework, occupational safety and health, workers' compensation, or industry registration' (1994: 1). In the fall of 2003, US rap music artist Sean 'P. Diddy' Combs made news around the world for allegedly having his 'Sean John' line of clothing assembled in a sweatshop in Honduras (Sanger, 2003). A LexisNexis search revealed that news reports about this problem were issued in Australia, Canada, France, Germany, New Zealand, the UK and the USA.

The 'outing' of Sean Combs is one recent event in an over ten-year global campaign focused on organizing consumers against questionable labor practices in the apparel industry. Several events garnered extensive media attention during this period. A federal class action lawsuit was filed against 18 well-known US retailers and manufacturers alleging their garments were manufactured in sweatshops in the US territory of Saipan (Branigin, 1999). Popular television personality Kathie Lee Gifford, and her line of apparel sold by Wal Mart, were linked to sweatshops in the USA and Central America. There was also news of imprisoned Thai immigrants being forced to sew garments in California (Varley, 1998).

Various ethical issues are associated with apparel retailing and manufacturing. The press and activist organizations routinely cite violations of workers' rights, including low wages, excessive hours of work, forced labor, employment of under-aged workers, discrimination, psychological and physical abuse, whether collective bargaining is allowed, and a variety of health and safety concerns (ECRA, 1997; Rosen, 2002; Varley, 1998). These practices are being addressed by a number of different businesses, industries and nongovernmental organizations (ECRA, 1997; ECRA, 2002a). One multi-stakeholder organization, the Fair Labor Association (FLA), anticipated using a label or hangtag on garments to reflect that a company's working conditions were certified by that group's standards (see the FLA charter at www.fairlabor.org). The FLA's initial plans were to use the words 'No Sweat' to indicate that the manufacturer had met minimum standards in an external monitoring of working conditions (*BNA*, 1998; Ramey, 1996).

The labor and working conditions included above form the focus of this study. However, other issues are of concern to apparel consumers as well, including the use and disposal of chemical pesticides and dyes when growing cotton and processing it into apparel products, use of genetically modified cotton, fur and animal-based skin products, animal testing, production in countries with oppressive regimes, and the ethics of many multinational retailers and manufacturers (ECRA, 1997, 2002a; Tomolillo and Shaw, 2003). This research focused on a narrower range of ethical considerations, particularly sweatshop conditions, because of their apparent prevalence in the apparel industry and the substantial media attention these conditions have attracted.

Consumer attitudes about sweatshops

Consumers may be able to pressure multinational apparel businesses to address labor problems and working conditions in global factories assembling their products.

Theoretically, providing information about a company's labor practices would provide consumers with awareness and concern about the issues (Gesser, 1998). Consumers with elevated awareness and concern would then exercise their sovereignty in the market-place, supporting ethical businesses and punishing unethical ones (Titus and Bradford, 1996). As a result, more businesses would have to behave ethically because it would be unprofitable or damaging to the corporate image to do otherwise (Gesser, 1998). One way of providing consumer information would involve a hangtag, such as that initially considered by the FLA. In essence, 'No Sweat' would be marketed to consumers desiring a decline in sweatshop production. If provided by a reliable and trustworthy source, consumers may trust that company actions are 'more than a PR-stunt' (Shaw and Duff, 2002). If these ethical consumers would be willing to pay more to assure that their demands for fair working conditions were met, it would help persuade businesses to participate in such voluntary efforts.

With the ideas of labeling and price difference in mind, the results from a number of public opinion polls have been widely publicized. Polls involving national samples of US consumers have found that 78 per cent claimed to be willing to avoid retailers who sold apparel produced in sweatshops, and would pay as much as 5 per cent more for apparel not manufactured in this way (Marymount University, 1995, 1996), and two-thirds would substitute brands to find others that are associated with a good cause (Cone Communications, 1996). Likewise, research conducted by the Co-operative Bank with a panel of 400 UK consumers found that 52 per cent have joined a boycott or switched to another branded product for reasons of ethics (Co-operative Bank, 2003). The results of these polls have been widely heralded as evidence that consumers will reward businesses that treat workers fairly and sanction those that do not. However, few questions have been raised about whether such a large majority of consumers would truly put their own self-interests behind those of workers typically located in developing countries thousands of miles away.

Beyond opinion polls – accurately predicting consumer behavior

While polls such as those described are valuable for gaining a sense of public sentiment, their measurement of fairly non-specific consumer attitudes diminishes the likelihood that they reflect how consumers would actually behave. The disconnection between attitudes and behaviors parallels the notion of an inconsistency of words and deeds challenged by Terry Newholm in Chapter 7; it was identified by social psychologists decades ago when people's attitudes were found to only match their actions about three out of ten times (LaPiere, 1934).

Since then, considerable research has helped to bridge the attitude-behavior gap, improving correlations between attitudes and behaviors with careful measurement. The concept of behavioral intentions was introduced as an appropriate indicator of actual future behavior (Ajzen and Fishbein, 1980). Additionally, attitudes that are more specific to the behaviors of interest have been found to be better predictors than general attitudes and specific attitudes correspond in target, context, time and action to behaviors of interest (Ajzen and Fishbein, 1980).

Thus, as compared with asking consumers about their attitudes about buying 'clothing not made in sweatshops', attitudes about buying a particular garment, for one's self, within the next two months, from a particular retailer or manufacturer avoiding sweatshops, should better predict whether a similar purchase will actually be made. Furthermore, the decision-making context for purchasing apparel results in information provided by a 'No Sweat' label being weighed against product attributes more typically associated with apparel purchasing, such as quality, price, and style features of the garments involved.

The importance of how attitudes and potential behaviors are measured can be seen in studies of jeans and athletic shoes where product attributes, such as fashionability and uniqueness of jeans and cushioning and durability of shoes, had greater impact on purchase intentions than ethical concerns (Auger et al., 2003; Dickson, 2000). Similarly, Dickson and Littrell's research found that consumers who buy from fair trade organizations (FTOs) that highly prioritize the needs of their producers, were heavily influenced by the quality, style and functionality of the apparel offered by these fair traders (Dickson and Littrell, 1996, 1997; Littrell and Dickson, 1999. In a qualitative study, Tomolillo and Shaw (2003) found that ethical consumers considered the range of styles available from ethical businesses as sometimes too limited and often unsuitable for their functional and aesthetic needs.

All these findings, related to specific attitudes in particular purchase contexts, contrast with those from public opinion polls, where consumers claimed to be far more willing to make sacrifices when shopping for what was vaguely worded as 'clothing'. The divergent findings illustrate the care needed in interpreting the results of polls which would seem to indicate large proportions of consumers behaving in certain ways in the future. Consumers asked to self-report on how they would behave in a very specific situation are likely to respond very differently from those asked about how they would behave in general.

Profiling ethical consumers

Despite the fact that opinion polls have probably over-estimated the numbers of consumers who will buy from ethical apparel manufacturers and retailers, it is likely that at least some consumers shop in altruistic versus self-interested ways. A fairly small body of research examining ethical consumer behaviors related to apparel purchasing has linked these consumers to a variety of attitudes and demographic characteristics. Results from a series of studies focussed on consumers who buy apparel and other products from FTOs have found that their decisions to purchase clothing are primarily influenced by their supportive attitudes toward fair trade. Underlying these attitudes are beliefs and concerns that the producers of FTO products face a variety of social ills (Dickson and Littrell, 1996, 1997; Kim et al., 1999); Littrell and Dickson, 1999.

Similarly, research on consumers of more mainstream apparel offered under well-known brand names by major retailers has found that consumers who are more supportive of socially responsible apparel businesses hold more negative beliefs about the apparel industry, have greater concern and knowledge about issues affecting the industry's workers, and perceive efforts that they take to eliminate industry problems will be effective (Dickson, 2000). The Auger et al. (2003) study found that providing consumers with information about ethical attributes of athletic shoes had a significant impact on likelihood of consideration and purchase intentions. Likewise, qualitative findings show that many consumers feel they need more information about the ethics of particular companies in order to make informed ethical decisions (Mohr and Webb, 2001).

According to a survey of consumers who buy from five major North American fair trade organizations, concrete information about how purchases impact the worker would motivate increased purchases of fair trade products (Littrell et al. 2004). Although consumers can be overwhelmed with information about the ethical or unethical actions of companies, having information condensed onto a simple label from a trustworthy and reliable source would be helpful (Shaw and Duff, 2002). Thus, it follows that consumers who are supportive of socially responsible businesses who are concerned and knowledgeable about apparel industry conditions that they believe are problematic would use the information provided on a 'No Sweat' label to guide their purchasing, if the label were sanctioned by a reputable organization.

Consumers who are most responsive to social labels may represent an ethical market segment with particular demographic characteristics. Using a random sample of US consumers, Roberts identified 32 per cent as socially conscious, and this segment of consumers was different in a number of ways from the general consumer population. As compared with other consumers, the socially conscious consumers were more often married, female, and with slightly lower incomes; their median age was 47 (Roberts, 1995). Similarly, the prime target consumer market for FTO products is comprised of women aged 46 to 49, a little over half of whom are married (Littrell and Dickson, 1999). However, in contrast to the socially conscious consumers identified by Roberts (1995), FTO consumers tend to be more highly educated and have higher incomes (Littrell and Dickson, 1999). Across any population, apparel consumers probably differ in the extents to which they behave ethically. At the very least, some are likely to use a 'No Sweat' label and further prioritize any concerns which they may have about working conditions and labor practices over more typically self-interested preoccupations with price, quality, style, and other garment features.

RESEARCH OBJECTIVES

The purpose of this study is to identify and profile ethical apparel consumers, and to expand understanding of ethical consumer behavior. Ethical consumers were operationally defined as those who would prioritize a 'No Sweat' label over any other product attributes when making purchase decisions. On the basis of the previous research, the following hypotheses were proposed regarding psychographic and demographic characteristics of this segment of consumers:

1 Ethical consumers hold more supportive attitudes toward socially responsible businesses than do self-interested consumers.
2 Ethical consumers have greater concern for sweatshop issues than do self-interested consumers.
3 Ethical consumers have more negative beliefs about conditions in foreign and US apparel factories than do self-interested consumers.
4 Ethical consumers perceive themselves as more knowledgeable about sweatshop issues than do self-interested consumers.
5 Ethical consumers are more likely to be female and married than are self-interested consumers. Ethical consumers are not significantly different in age, income, and educational attainment than self-interested consumers.

The hypotheses listed above were tested with quantitative data. Although past research had identified numerous variables that could influence ethical consumer behavior, it was uncertain whether all relevant variables were being considered. As such, qualitative data were gathered to expand understanding of ethical consumer behavior.

METHOD

Sample and procedure

Survey research was used to reach a representative sample of US apparel consumers. A mailing list of 2000 names and addresses was purchased from Survey Sampling Inc (SSI). SSI draws samples from a database developed from telephone directories and augmented with privately obtained data. Systematic random sampling from the database ordered by state assured that the sample was proportionately distributed by the geographic population. The only restrictions given to SSI for drawing the sample from their database of millions of US residents was that they be 18 years of age or older and that the sample be half male and half female.

A questionnaire was sent to individuals on the mailing list along with a postage-paid return envelope and a letter describing the study and encouraging their response. Two additional follow-up steps, including sending a follow-up reminder/thank you postcard one week after the initial mailing and resending questionnaires to those not responding when a total of three weeks had passed, were used to generate as large a response as possible. A usable response rate of 30 per cent was attained.

Questionnaire

The questionnaire was an eight-page booklet with three sections, similar to that suggested by Dillman (1978). The first section measured consumer likelihood of purchasing 'No Sweat' garments using decompositional conjoint analysis. With the conjoint task, respondents are not asked to provide the weight or importance for each attribute; rather the weights (part worth utilities) are estimated with linear interpolation from the preference ratings of systematically varied products (Green, 1974). As such, this task is thought to better simulate a realistic buying situation where consumers simultaneously consider a range of information about the product. Through analysis, respondents' stated purchase intentions for a variety of products are used to compute a set of part worth utilities that show the relative importance of each level of each attribute to decisions to buy (Green and Srinivasan, 1978).

Respondents indicated how likely they would be to buy a particular garment that had been systematically varied on five attributes with two levels each. A men's dress shirt was selected because most men and many women who shop for their spouses would have purchased these. The five attributes and their levels included 'best quality' or 'good quality'; 'fashion colors (French blue, sage and black)' or 'classic colors (white and light blue)'; '100% cotton' or '50% polyester and 50% cotton'; '$17.99' or '$48'; and '"No Sweat" (guarantees the manufacturing conditions were fair for the workers who made the shirt)' or no label was mentioned. After reading each description, respondents were asked 'How likely would you be to buy this shirt?' and they were offered a response range of 0 = absolutely not, 100 = absolutely. All 32 possible combinations of the 5 attributes with 2 levels were developed and were assigned to 4 blocks of respondents in groups of 8. Thus, each respondent evaluated 8 different shirts.

One attribute, the 'No Sweat' label, was the primary focus of the research. Absence of the label was selected as the alternate attribute level in order to develop product profiles that would equate to 'real' products (that is, there would not be an alternative label proudly claiming the use of sweatshop labor) (Green and Srinivasan, 1978). The other attributes and their levels were selling points used by retailers when advertising dress shirts.

Section 2 of the questionnaire measured beliefs about apparel manufacturing practices in the USA and foreign countries, the extent that respondents felt knowledgeable about the apparel industry and sweatshop issues, concern about issues affecting apparel industry workers, support for socially responsible businesses and potential actions against apparel manufacturers. All items in Section 2 were measured with seven-point Likert-type scales. Items for Section 2 were adopted from a questionnaire developed by Dickson (2000) where attitudinal concepts showed high reliability (Cronbach's alpha = .80 to .89). The 21 items measuring beliefs and attitudes regarding apparel industry issues were reduced to 5 variables using principal components factor analysis. Factor loadings were rotated with varimax rotation to ease interpretation of the resulting variables.

The five variables were created by summing the items with loadings greater than .60 for a factor. The first variable was labeled 'Support' because it included five items related to how supportive respondents are toward socially responsible businesses. The second variable was labeled 'Beliefs about foreign industry' because it included four items related to beliefs about work-place safety, pay, hours worked, and child labor in foreign factories. 'Beliefs about US industry' likewise included respondents' beliefs about these conditions in US factories. The variable 'Knowledge' incorporated four items related to respondents' perceived knowledge about sweatshop issues in clothing factories. Finally, the variable 'Concern' included two items regarding the extent of respondents' concern with sweatshop issues and the situation of factory workers.

Section 3 incorporated two items that would provide further understanding of ethical consumer behavior. The first item forced respondents to indicate whether they did or did not plan to buy clothing for themselves from a socially responsible business in the upcoming year. Immediately following that item, respondents were asked to explain their answers and were provided the remainder of the page to write their responses. The final section of the questionnaire measured demographic characteristics including age, marital status, sex, education and income.

DATA ANALYSIS AND RESULTS

Respondent profile

Of the questionnaires mailed, 1,851 were deliverable and 547 usable questionnaires were returned by respondents for a 30 per cent response rate. Respondents averaged just over fifty-one years of age and 54.2 per cent were female (see the Overall column in Table 10.1). Just fewer than 40 per cent of those surveyed had completed a bachelor's

Table 10.1 Demographic characteristics

| | Consumer group | | |
Characteristic	Overall N = 547	Ethical n = 80	Self-interested n = 467
Age (mean)	51.6	51.9	51.4
17–24	1.7%	2.7%	1.6%
25–40	25.0	22.7	25.6
41–60	43.1	42.7	43.3
61 and over	30.2	32.0	29.6
Sex			
Female	54.2%	71.4%	51.2%
Male	45.8	28.6	48.8
Marital status			
Married	56.9%	40.0%	59.7%
Unmarried	43.1	60.0	40.3
Education			
No high school degree	2.7%	6.5%	2.0%
High school	22.9	28.6	22.0
Some college	34.6	33.8	34.8
College degree	15.3	11.7	15.9
Some post-graduate	9.2	10.4	9.0
Completed graduate degree	15.3	9.1	16.4
Pre-tax household income			
< $10,000	6.0%	8.2%	5.6%
$10,000–$24,999	18.9	19.2	18.8
$25,000–$49,999	36.8	38.4	36.3
$50,000–$74,999	24.4	28.8	23.7
$75,000 and over	14.0	5.5	15.5

degree or higher education. Nearly seven out of ten were employed. More than 61 per cent reported having household incomes in the range of $25,000 to $74,999. Close to 60 per cent were married.

In terms of its representativeness, the sample included a slightly larger proportion of female respondents than the US population (50.4 per cent) (US Bureau of the Census, 1997). Additionally, the sample was more highly educated than the general public. Just under 40 per cent of the respondents had one college degree or more, whereas only 23.9 per cent of the US population had this level of educational attainment (Day and Curry, 1998).

That the sample is skewed toward the more highly educated is supported with an analysis of early and late respondents. This sort of analysis gives clues to the characteristics of nonrespondents (see Churchill, 1991). Early respondents had significantly higher levels of educational attainment than did late respondents. However, there were no differences in the age and income of early and late respondents.

Identification of 'No Sweat' ethical consumers

Multi-step data analysis procedures were used to identify and profile an ethical apparel consumer market segment. In the first step of analysis, each individual's responses regarding her or his likelihood of buying the eight shirts were analyzed with ordinary least squares regression (OLS) to obtain a set of part-worth utilities for each consumer. OLS regression allowed understanding of how the independent variables (product attributes) were related to the dependent variable (the likelihood of buying the various shirts). The magnitude and size of the part-worths (the B-values from the OLS regression) indicated how much and in what direction overall likelihood of buying was influenced by each level of each attribute. Thus, for this study any individual's likelihood of buying shirts would be explained by the following linear equation:

Likelihood of Buying = Constant + Quality (part-worth 1)
+ Color (part-worth 2) + Fabric (part-worth 3)
+ Price (part-worth 4) + Label (part-worth 5)

To develop the equation shown above, the researcher included the ratings of likelihood to buy that were provided by the respondent. A dummy coding scheme was used to indicate which level of each product attribute was described in the shirts that were rated. For example, in this study when the 'No Sweat' label was part of the shirt description, the attribute label was coded with a '1' and when no label was described, the label was coded with a '–1' (see the column descriptions in Table 10.2 for the complete set of dummy codes). OLS regression provided the constant and part-worths (one for each independent variable). By carrying out the math in the equation, it is possible to see how any level of any product attribute increases or decreases likelihood of buying. For example, in the case of shirts described as having the 'No Sweat' label, a positive part-worth would be associated with an increase in the likelihood of buying that shirt – the larger the part-worth, the larger the increase. On the other hand, negative part-worths for the 'No Sweat' label would diminish the likelihood of buying and the larger the part-worth the greater the negative impact. When the researcher uses a 100-point rating scale for the dependent variable, the part-worths can be interpreted like percentages. Thus, a part-worth of 50.0 would indicate a 50 per cent increase or decrease in likelihood of buying the garment depending on the positive or negative coding of the attribute level.

As a next step in data analysis, the part-worth utilities that had been estimated for each respondent were used for classifying them as either ethical consumers or self-interested consumers. Those respondents whose part-worths for the 'No Sweat' label were greater than any other part-worth were classified as ethical consumers (n = 80) and the remaining respondents were typed as self-interested consumers (n = 467). For ethical consumers, the part-worth utility for label ranged from 3.38 to 50.0, indicating that the presence of the 'No Sweat' label increased ethical consumers' intentions to purchase a garment from just over 3 to 50 per cent. There was considerable variation in ethical consumers' responses with some having very low intentions to purchase any garment and some being much more influenced by the 'No Sweat' label than others. While there are probably niche markets of consumers within the ethical consumer segment, the purpose of this research did not support identifying the variations among consumers within this group. Those in the ethical consumers market commonly prioritized the 'No Sweat' label over all other product attributes.

Once respondents were classified into the two groups, OLS regression was rerun on the aggregated data for each group to determine part-worth utilities for ethical consumers as a group and for self-interested consumers as a group. Examining the B-values (part-worths) provided in Table 10.2, and taking into consideration the effects coding for each variable, the strong influence of the 'No Sweat' label

Table 10.2 Regression equations and model statistics for likelihood of buying by consumer group

			Variables									Model statistics	
Cluster	Constant		Quality (1 = Best, −1 = Good)		Color (1 = Fashion, −1 = Classic)		Fabric (1 = Cotton, −1 = 50% Poly/50% cotton)		Price (1 = $48, −1 = $17.99)		Label (1 = 'No Sweat', −1 = no label)	F	R^2
Ethical consumers (n = 80)	50.19[a]	+	2.83[b]	−	0.99	+	1.38	−	4.56[a]	+	23.43[a]	99.15[a]	0.44
Self-interested consumers (n = 467)	42.78[a]	+	2.28[a]	−	3.44[a]	+	1.18[c]	−	16.39[a]	+	2.24[a]	226.48[a]	0.23

[a] p < 0.001
[b] p < 0.01
[c] p < 0.05

on ethical consumers' purchase intentions is clear. Presence of the 'No Sweat' label influenced the purchase intentions of the ethical consumers' group by over 23 per cent, and for garments not carrying the 'No Sweat' label purchase intentions decreased by over 23 per cent. Among the 80 ethical consumers, purchase intentions for the $48 shirt were 4.6 per cent lower than for the $17.99 shirt. Quality was the only other significant product attribute for ethical consumers and the best quality shirt was preferred. In contrast, self-interested consumers were most strongly influenced by lower prices (B = 16.39). All of the product attributes had significant influence, though compared to price, the influences of best quality (B = 2.28), classic colors (B = 3.44), 100 per cent cotton fabrics (B = 1.18) and 'No Sweat' labels (B = 2.24) were minimal.

The part-worth utilities presented here differ somewhat from an earlier analysis of the data where a slightly larger cluster of label users were somewhat less influenced by the label and more affected by price (Dickson, 2001). As compared with the analysis presented in this chapter, the earlier analysis did not so precisely identify ethical consumers. In scanning the data for explanations, it is evident that the earlier cluster analysis technique that was used to identify ethical consumers allowed a few respondents to be categorized as such when the label and another attribute had equivalent sized part-worths. The analysis technique described in this chapter incorporated a more rigorous classification system.

Attitudinal and demographic profile of ethical consumers

In order to test the hypotheses and consider whether it was reasonable to claim that ethical consumers were different from the others in the sample, a discriminant analysis and univariate ANOVA were conducted. With these analysis techniques, it was possible to determine which combination of attitudinal and demographic variables best differentiated the two groups of consumers. Discriminant analysis incorporated the five attitudinal variables (Support, Beliefs about Foreign Industry, Beliefs about US Industry, Knowledge and Concern) and five demographic characteristics (age, sex, marital status, income and education). One significant discriminant function (see Table 10.3) was identified. The discriminant function indicated the linear combination of variables that influenced whether respondents were classified as ethical or self-interested. The value of the discriminant function for classifying respondents was determined with cross-validation. First, the computer used a portion of the sample to develop the discriminant function model and then it tested how well the model worked on the remainder of the sample. The model performed well as 85.4 per cent of cross-validated cases were correctly classified.

There are no rigid guidelines for interpretation of the results of discriminant analysis; thus, the researcher established criteria for doing so. Structure matrix loadings were assessed first and those over .30 were determined to provide good discrimination between ethical consumers and self-interested consumers and were considered for further analysis. Squared loadings represent the amount of variance shared between the discriminant score and the variable (Churchill, 1991); therefore, these variables shared a minimum of 9 per cent of the variance with the discriminant score. Basically, the larger the structure loading, the more helpful it was for differentiating the two groups of consumers.

Standardized discriminant coefficients and output from univariate ANOVAs were also examined. Standardized discriminant coefficients are interpreted like

Table 10.3 Discriminant analysis

| Variable | Means (standard deviations) | | | Function 1 | |
	Ethical consumers ($n = 80$)	Self-interested consumers ($n = 467$)	Univariate F	Discriminant loadings	Standardized discriminant coefficients
Support	6.22 (0.69)	5.66 (0.98)	26.61[a]	0.71	0.63
Marital status (0 = unmarried, 1 = married)	0.40 (0.49)	0.60 (0.49)	11.03[a]	−0.46	−0.41
Sex (0 = male, 1 = female)	0.71 (0.45)	0.52 (0.49)	10.97[a]	0.45	0.23
Knowledge	3.78 (1.25)	3.32 (1.18)	10.29[b]	0.44	0.45
Concern	5.49 (1.22)	5.00 (1.28)	10.11[b]	0.43	0.03
Education	3.19 (1.35)	3.57 (1.37)	5.06[c]	−0.31	−0.24
Beliefs about USA industry	4.54 (1.26)	4.78 (1.28)	1.91	−0.15	−0.11
Income	3.06 (0.98)	3.24 (1.03)	2.26	−0.21	0.15
Beliefs about foreign industry	2.08 (1.29)	2.30 (1.14)	2.44	−0.22	0.02
Age	51.94 (15.32)	51.43 (15.21)	0.08	0.04	−0.10
Variance explained				100%	
Chi-square, df, p				$\chi^2 = 50.02$, $df = 10$, $p = 0.000$	
Wilk's lambda	0.75			0.91	
Group centroid		−0.13			

[a] $p < 0.001$
[b] $p < 0.01$
[c] $p < 0.05$

beta coefficients in regression and they represent the relative contribution of each variable to the discriminant function score (Churchill, 1991). The variable best discriminating between ethical consumers and self-interested consumers was Support, with a standardized discriminant coefficient of .63; next best for discriminating between the two groups were Knowledge and Marital Status, with discriminant coefficients of .45 and −.41 respectively. Finally, education (−.24) and sex (.23) discriminated between the two groups. Interestingly, the variable Concern had a fairly large structure loading but a very low standardized discriminant coefficient (.03). It is likely that variation associated with Concern was shared with the Knowledge and Support variables. The emergence of Knowledge as an important discriminating variable is a notable difference in this analysis, as compared with an earlier analysis of these same data where Concern and not Knowledge was more discriminating (Dickson, 2001).

Combined with the results of the discriminant analysis, univariate ANOVAs can provide further support for determining which variables are most useful for classifying respondents into one group or the other. The two attitudinal variables and three demographic variables identified as most useful for differentiating groups were also significantly different for ethical consumers and self-interested consumers when tested with univariate ANOVA (see Table 10.3). The combined criteria of p < .05 for univariate analysis and discriminant loadings greater than .30 were used for testing the hypotheses. Hypotheses 1 and 4 were supported. Ethical consumers held more supportive attitudes toward socially responsible businesses and were more knowledgeable about sweatshop issues than were self-interested consumers. In contrast, Hypotheses 2, 3a and 3b were not supported. Ethical consumers did not have greater concern for sweatshop issues or more negative beliefs about conditions in foreign and US apparel factories than did self-interested consumers.

Demographically, ethical consumers were more likely to be female and unmarried as compared with self-interested consumers. Ethical consumers also had significantly lower levels of educational attainment as compared with self-interested consumers. Age and income were not significantly different between the two groups. Summarizing the tests of hypotheses, the findings supported the directional hypothesis 5a (sex), differed in direction from hypothesis 5b (marital status), supported the null hypotheses 5c (age) and 5d (income), and did not support the null hypothesis 5e (educational attainment).

Attitudes versus behavioral intentions

Analysis of the single qualitative item asking respondents to explain their intended behaviors provided expanded understanding of ethical consumer behavior and some of the reasons behaviors may differ from attitudes. A grounded theory approach was used to analyze the open-ended responses (Strauss and Corbin, 1990) provided by each consumer (n = 399). Through open coding, 24 conceptual categories were identified. As a final step of analysis, axial coding was used to develop four broader themes, each of which encompassed several related conceptual categories. The four themes and the conceptual categories are presented in Table 10.4.

The first theme, labeled 'Principles for the Workplace', centered on minimum standards for work-place conditions. Under this theme, respondents mentioned specific conditions regarding hours and wages and the need for workers to be

Table 10.4 Qualitative themes and conceptual characteristics

Theme/characteristic
Principles for the Workplace
Morality and Fairness in the Workplace
No Child Labor
Universal Morality and Fairness
Complex Issue
Consumer's Role
Sending Business a Message
Consumer/Personal Responsibility
Self-concerned Peace of Mind
Role of Business and Government
Business Responsibility
Pro-government Assistance
Anti-government Assistance
Consumer Needs
Product Priorities
Need for Information
Assumptions
Awareness

treated with respect and dignity through provisions for a safe and fair workplace. For example, one respondent stated, 'I believe every worker should work under safe conditions, work regular hours, and have a decent living wage.'

Some respondents specifically noted that child labor should not be used for the manufacture of apparel products. Some of the responses seemed fairly emotional. For example, one consumer wrote, 'My heart goes out to the children. I do not want this to be a reality, but since it is, I feel we all need to protect them. I would want someone to help if it were my children.' Yet another respondent was more matter of fact, stating that, 'Child labor is wrong, plain and simple.'

Consumers also mentioned broader universal values that were not specifically associated with the work-place. For example, two respondents explained their willingness to seek out products of socially responsible businesses, 'Because I have nothing but contempt for anyone who would enslave others.' 'I don't like anyone to be taken advantage of whether age, color or sex is concerned.'

Finally, a smaller number discussed the complexity of defining what is 'right' or 'wrong' for business, with many cultural issues to consider in making this assessment. Considering child labor, one respondent explained, 'Sometimes it is necessary for children to work – to put food on the table. This is the way it is.'

A second theme focussed on the responsibility consumers have for influencing business behaviors. Entitled 'The Consumer's Role', under this theme respondents' discussed the messages which consumers send to businesses via their purchasing. Specifically, several mentioned punishing businesses with boycotts. For example, one respondent explained 'I believe that buying clothing from responsible businesses will be rewarding their efforts, thus ensuring further progress. By not buying the unlabeled clothing, the companies will see the loss of income as a sign of the times.'

Others seemed to be motivated by a sense of personal responsibility as a consumer. One respondent stated, 'I believe that in order for practices to change, everyone must do what they can to facilitate that change. It is no hardship on me – nor should it be for the majority of people – to look for labels or to buy from a business who is improving the system.'

Yet others expressed the anguish they would feel in knowing that their purchasing might ultimately support poor working conditions. For example, one respondent shared, 'I would not feel good about myself if I knew I had purchased any garment that had been made by slave labor – especially by children.'

The third theme, entitled 'The Role of Business and Government', focussed on the types of actions that business and government should take to assure business responsibility. These responses contrast with those under the 'Principles for the Workplace' theme that outlined the actual standards. Respondents commented on business obligations to set and follow sourcing guidelines, follow laws, be ethical, and not be greedy. Regarding business responsibility, one consumer argued, 'I believe that companies should follow the laws. Without employees, companies would not exist.'

Other respondents considered whether or not government should be involved. Expressing expectations for government involvement, two respondents stated opposing views. 'I believe that government should regulate this industry as strictly as they regulate chemical plants. There should be routine checks and maybe even a task force to prevent this' and 'I oppose government regulations that interfere with independent businessmen.'

The final theme centered on 'Consumer Needs', and revealed the difficulties consumers encounter when trying to follow through on their attitudes and support ethical businesses. A variety of product-related priorities were discussed and these revealed how self-interest for such things as lower price and convenience can outweigh concerns about workers. Discussing how price might constrain purchasing, one respondent explained, 'With four children and only one income, prices take precedence over the "No Sweat" on the label.'

The availability of information for consumers to know whether or not they were buying from an ethical business was a concern to some respondents. One consumer explained, 'I'd like it if all clothing was marked showing it was made by adults in fair working conditions. Unfortunately, as a consumer it is sometimes hard to tell.'

Other consumers were clearly making assumptions that certain types of information, for example, a 'Made in the USA' label or union label, would assure that a product was made under socially responsible conditions. One respondent explained, 'I attempt to buy only American made goods. The information that I have suggests that most if not all products from overseas are made by people or companies that are only interested in extremely high profit with no regard for the individual.'

Others apologized for being unaware that they could consider social responsibility in their decision making.

DISCUSSION

The purpose of this study was to identify and profile ethical apparel consumers, and to expand understanding of ethical consumer behavior. As anticipated, a potential market segment of consumers demonstrated they would prioritize a guarantee that clothing was not assembled in a sweatshop over price, quality, color, and fiber content attributes when purchasing one type of apparel, men's dress shirts. The market segment represented just fewer than 15 per cent of the sample of consumers studied. The large proportion of consumers unwilling to sacrifice their own product needs for price, quality, color, and fiber content is not surprising and similar to findings from previous research. For most consumers considering an apparel purchase, ethical attributes of a product take a back seat to product features (Auger et al., 2003; Dickson, 2000; Dickson and Littrell, 1996, 1997; Littrell and Dickson, 1999; Tomolillo and Shaw, 2003).

'Ethical consumers' prioritizing 'No Sweat' were more supportive of socially responsible businesses and perceived themselves as more knowledgeable about sweatshop issues than did their 'self-interested' counterparts. These attitudinal characteristics are similar to consumers of FTOs who also tend to be supportive of socially responsible business (Dickson and Littrell, 1996, 1997; Kim et al., 1999; Littrell and Dickson, 1999). As noted by previous researchers (Auger et al., 2003; Dickson, 1999; Mohr and Webb, 2001; Tomolillo and Shaw, 2003), knowledge about the issues is important and those having greater knowledge seem to use it in their purchasing decisions. Providing more information to consumers, as suggested by Dickson (1999a), Littrell et al. (2004) and Mohr and Webb (2001) seems to be an important tool for increasing ethical consumer behavior. This assertion is further supported by the qualitative findings from this study. However, it is important to recognize that consumers can be both overwhelmed with, and distrustful of, this sort of information and that it is probably best that the information be condensed and issued by a trustworthy and reliable source (Shaw and Duff, 2002).

As anticipated, women were more likely to use the label than men, a finding that corresponds with previous literature (Littrell and Dickson, 1999; Roberts, 1995). Nonetheless, four out of ten 'ethical consumers' were men, so men should not be overlooked in efforts to increase ethical consumer behavior. Unlike FTO consumers (Littrell and Dickson, 1999), 'ethical consumers' in this study had lower levels of education than their 'self-interested' counterparts.

In addition to a lack of information mentioned earlier, it is likely that many other reasons exist allowing consumers to not behave ethically. Both quantitative and qualitative findings support the notion that some consumers are more interested in their own needs than the needs of others. Similarly, the qualitative data suggest that some consumers view ethics to be the responsibility of business and government rather than their own responsibility.

CONCLUSION

As with all studies, this one had limitations. In this instance, consumers considered the purchase of men's dress shirts. This level of specificity was needed in order to obtain valid results. Although it is likely that consumers would similarly weigh the 'No Sweat' label in their purchase of other apparel products, further research is necessary to confirm that assumption. Additionally, the research measured behavioral intentions, not the actual behavior itself. The nature of conjoint analysis closely resembles how consumers shop for apparel, allowing them to examine the product attributes they feel are most important, and to ignore those perceived as less important. However, a variety of unforeseen conditions could make actual consumer behavior turn out somewhat differently than predicted.

The role that perceived knowledge plays in influencing ethical consumer behavior is an important finding. Ethical consumers perceive themselves as more knowledgeable about the apparel industry and its issues than do self-interested consumers. Yet, relatively low mean scores for this variable indicate that none of the consumers felt all that knowledgeable. In qualitative findings, consumers expressed a need for information that could be used to assess business practices. If consumers were provided easily accessible, accurate, unbiased information about the apparel industry and particular companies' records regarding labor, in an easy to understand format, there could be some increase in purchasing from ethical companies. A growing number of studies show that consumers desire this sort of information (Dickson, 1999; Mohr and Webb, 2001; Shaw and Duff, 2002; Tomolillo and Shaw, 2003).

Despite its appeal, however, simply providing more information may not be the answer to expanding ethical consumer behavior. Since data were collected for this study in the late 1990s, some significant events have occurred in an effort to reduce sweatshops in the apparel industry. While this research and another study (Auger et al., 2003) were designed with the assumption that ethical attributes could be guaranteed to apparel consumers, this is probably not true. It appears that almost no apparel business can guarantee that their garments were assembled in factories free of sweatshop-like characteristics.

This is evident from the groundbreaking release of reports from external monitoring of factories used by companies participating in the FLA. In their 2003 annual report and the accompanying tracking sheets, the FLA reported a range of violations of its code of conduct (Fair Labor Association, 2003). Although other apparel manufacturers and retailers do not release this information to the public, the violations are undoubtedly similar if not worse. However, FLA participating companies also release how they are attempting to remediate problems that have been found. Even apparel-producing fair trading organizations, long held as a model for ethical business, appear to have shortcomings regarding wages paid (Dickson and Littrell, 2003).

The relevant question then becomes, is there a segment of consumers willing to support companies that are publicly attempting to solve sweatshop problems but cannot guarantee that their products are 'No Sweat'? Likewise, are consumers willing to pay more for garments from apparel retailers and manufacturers who are publicly trying to address the sweatshop problem as compared to what they will pay companies whose labor practices they know nothing about? Further research is warranted since it seems it will be quite some time before apparel consumers can select from a variety of entirely sweatshop-free garments. The topic of ethical consumer behavior is complex as are the likely factors that might expand such behavior.

Focus Groups on Consumers' Ethical Beliefs

11

Barry Clavin   Alex Lewis

INTRODUCTION

This chapter will explore the use of focus groups to investigate consumer attitudes towards ethics. It will provide an insight into the theoretical issues surrounding focus groups, look at their history and development, and outline the methodological considerations that should be taken into account in their commercial application towards ethical issues. It will begin by looking at four case studies of research conducted by the Co-operative Bank between 1999 and 2004. Some other focus group research addressing ethical issues will also be discussed. In this way, it is hoped that experiences at the bank will help illustrate the topics discussed and lend authority to the claims that the bank is making.

FOUR CASE STUDIES

Case study 1: Socially responsible investment research 2004

Background

In 2002, Co-operative Financial Services (CFS) was created to bring together the Co-operative Bank and the Co-operative Insurance Society (CIS), under common leadership. As part of this 'coming together', CFS sought to reconcile the historically different approaches of CIS and the Co-operative Bank to responsible shareholding and ethical investment. This reconciliation was to focus on establishing for CIS a customer mandate for responsible shareholding, much as bank customers currently guide its ethical policy.

Objectives

- To ascertain the level of awareness, appetite and support for a Socially Responsible Investment (SRI) Policy to underpin the product offerings from CIS.
- To understand the way that such a policy should be communicated to customers and how they would wish to engage in its formulation and delivery.

Methodology

A series of 20 focus groups were convened to explore the understanding amongst CIS customers of the role of SRI. The groups were split into three stages to facilitate the acceleration of learning by passing on the feedback from one group of customers in one stage to customers in the next stage. This type of learning is called 'synectics' whereby, through focus groups, you can enhance customer understanding by presenting the views of one set of customers to other customers and test whether the views that you are getting are representative.

Customers were drawn from the age groups 18–35 and 36–55 years, split by gender and socio-economic groupings, that is ABC1 and C1C2.

Outcomes

The outcomes remain incomplete as, at the time of writing, the research is a work in progress. There was almost universal agreement that financial returns cannot come at any cost, social, ethical or environmental. There were, however, inevitable differences about the precise cut-off point for individuals on these issues.

There is common recognition that as investors in companies insurance companies have the opportunity and, for some, the responsibility to use their position as a shareholder to influence the behaviour of the companies whilst seeking to optimise financial performance.

Customer relationships with providers of insurance products are more complex than relationships with other financial service providers. Concerns over performance of individual products will often be of paramount concern to consumers. This has been particularly apparent in the UK, for example, over mortgage endowment shortfalls that, in some cases, have threatened peoples' ability to buy their homes.

Case study 2: Ethical consumer panel research 2003

Background

Since 1999, the Co-operative Bank in partnership with the New Economics Foundation has produced the Ethical Purchasing Index, a measure of the total value of ethical goods and services sold in the UK. As part of this project there was a desire to measure the total financial value of boycotts and other 'invisible' activities.

Objectives

- To generate new insight into, and measurement of, the degree to which consumer purchasing in the UK is affected by broadly 'ethical' concerns.
- To create a reliable methodology that can be repeated annually to track changes in the value of ethical consumption activities over time.

Methodology

The challenge was to devise a methodology that allowed for a large-scale consumer research programme which could also provide extensive and ongoing in-depth data collection. In partnership with the Future Foundation, the bank set up a consumer panel of some 400 individuals. A series of control factors were used to ensure validity.

- An omnibus question was used to provide weighting of the panel to match the ethical profile of consumers across the UK population. If it were the case that the more informed ethical consumers were also more likely to respond to the research invitation, we needed to factor this into the output.
- Consumers were asked to keep receipts or other documentary records as evidence of ethical purchasing.
- Alternative data sources would be used to test the overall veracity of responses (for example, Family Expenditure Survey).
- An economic analyst from the Future Foundation would review and comment on the results.

Outcomes

When faced with having to evidence their 'ethical' choices, consumers inevitably find it difficult. Also, labelling consumers as 'ethical' or otherwise misses out on the range of activities that consumers engage in which have an 'ethical' dimension. For ethical consumers, 'ethics' do not override every other element of the purchasing decision but they are more likely to buy ethically where information and choice exist. Even some long-standing product labelling remains poorly understood by these consumers, for example, green energy and free range meat.

In terms of boycotts, whilst a substantial number of consumers boycott for 'ethical' reasons (most are engaged in long-standing boycotts), only a very small proportion of the public are engaged in reviewing corporate behaviour on a regular basis, and subsequently redefining their relationships with such companies. Furthermore, what constitutes an 'ethical' choice for consumers does not always fit with more widely held definitions of ethics. For example, avoiding companies because of poor customer service or 'buying British' were cited by some consumers as an ethical choice, but not included by ourselves.

What is equally interesting is that consumers who refuse to be labelled as 'ethical' are also engaged in ethical activities. In particular, those consumers who shop locally to support their local communities do not instinctively consider this to be an 'ethical' choice, perhaps in the main because they themselves can benefit directly from their activities. For most, an 'ethical' choice still has to involve some personal price, that is paying more for fair trade or denying choice by boycotting. (Further outcomes of research for the Ethical Purchasing Index are also discussed by Clouder and Harrison in Chapter 6 in this book.)

Case study 3: Ethical policy review April 2001

Background

Focus groups have been a vital component in the bank's development of its ethical policy. Ultimately, this policy is based on large-scale polling of customer attitudes in order that it is as inclusive as possible, and in 2001 the bank polled one million customers. It is, however, only through focus groups that the bank can get to develop refined and subtle positions on what can be complex and sometimes potentially contentious ethical issues. Further, in 2001 the bank was scheduled to

renew the customer mandate for its ethical policy.

Objectives

- To test that the bank's policy was an accurate reflection of customers' views and to identify any issues which should be included in the policy review that the bank was planning to carry out later that year.
- To help develop questions on new issues for the next large-scale poll.

Methodology

A series of four focus groups were held amongst bank current account customers. Recruitment was structured to allow for a balance of age groups (18–35 and 36–55 years), gender and socio-economic profiles (ABC1 and C1C2). MORI conducted the research, facilitated the focus groups sessions and produced the analysis and recommendations.

In the groups customers were divided into sub-groups. Each sub-group was asked to develop their own policies and rationalise their selections to others. The three areas that generated the most debate were the arms trade, animal testing and genetic modification. Interestingly, the arms trade and animal testing are areas where the bank already had a policy, but did not have an absolutist position. Genetic modification was an area where the bank did not have any position, but was keen to explore the issue with customers.

Outcomes

There was consensus on the issue of animal testing with regard to no investment in cosmetic testing but positive support for health-related research. Consensus over animal testing for other applications, in particular household products, was more difficult to achieve. Customers managed to reconcile this issue by agreeing that testing for household products was not acceptable and that investment in the development of alternatives to animal testing would be welcomed.

When the issue of biotechnology and genetic modification were discussed customers' initial responses demonstrated that they were less confident of their knowledge of the subject. Initial responses centred on confusion and suspicion and tended towards the more extreme tabloid expressions of concern, including 'killer tomatoes' and 'designer babies'.

Focus groups can allow consumers to express and debate issues that they may never have had to discuss previously. For example, as part of the bank's review on genetic modification it needed to explore consumer opinions on issues from xenotransplantation to GM patenting – issues on which many consumers have probably not previously needed to publicly express an opinion.

Case study 4: Ethical consumer research 1999

Background

Despite its ethical position, the Co-operative Bank lacked a detailed understanding of what being an ethical consumer meant on an individual level.

Objectives

- The project sought to develop questions for a quantitative research programme designed to map the profile of ethical consumerism in the UK.
- It would seek to identify not only how many people are 'active' consumers, but also what motivates them and what distinguishes different segments within this population.

Methodology

In April 1999, the bank conducted a series of four focus groups across the UK. The research was carried out by MORI and participants were chosen from across the socio-economic spectrum and age groups and split by gender. As part of the recruitment process participants were asked to consider whether they classified themselves as 'ethical' consumers. An even number of participants were then selected based on those who self-defined as 'ethical' consumers and 'non-ethical' consumers. In previous separate quantitative research we had found that the general public responded to this question along the following lines: a great deal 8 per cent; a fair amount 47 per cent; not very much 29 per cent; not at all 11 per cent; don't know 5 per cent.

Outcomes

It was clear from the focus groups that despite the common assumption that younger people are more values-driven, those under 35 were generally less concerned than their elders, especially with corporate involvement. The middle-aged (35–54) appear to be the most active consumers on all issues, possibly reflecting their relative affluence.

Affluence was also evident in analysis by social class. Whilst the lower social group (C2DE) were likely to say ethical issues were very important to them they were less likely to act on this. The more affluent in the ABC1 group were more likely to be influenced by, and act on, ethical issues. A brief list of the five key consumer types identified from this research appears in Table 11.1.

It was also clear from the research that consumers care about ethics large and small – broad company policies as well as detailed product attributes – although some consumers are more interested in one rather than the other. But most consumers seem to judge a company as a whole – a good policy on human rights is no

Table 11.1 Key consumer types (Ethical Consumer research) 1999

Type	Percentage	Characteristics
Global watchdogs	5%	Ethical hardliners
Conscientious consumers	18%	More affluent than 'do what I can' type
'Do what I can'	49%	Older, active recyclers
Brand generation	6%	Younger, less values led
'Look after my own'	22%	Lowest income

good without the right quality and customer service. The research also demonstrated some difficulty with the term 'ethical'. Some people did not want to be dubbed 'ethical consumers' even if they shared the values. The picture that emerges is of most consumers being aware of their power in the market and with widespread concerns, but not always going out of their way to make their point at the checkout.

THE BACKGROUND TO FOCUS GROUPS

As opposed to much of the commercial research discussed in the next chapter, focus groups fall under the domain of qualitative research – that which can be seen as focusing on the understanding and meaning of phenomena, rather than their incidence. However, as we have seen, rather than acting as an alternative to quantitative techniques, very often focus groups and other qualitative forms work in a complimentary manner, shaping the planning of quantitative investigations and vice versa.

As group interviewing in general has made its way into the mainstream of commercial research, 'focus groups' has become an umbrella term. We can define focus groups as a group of individuals selected and assembled by researchers to discuss and comment on a defined topic from their personal experience (Powell and Single, 1996: 499). When discussing their commercial use in order to understand customers' beliefs, it is also useful to refer to Kitzinger's term 'organised discussion' (Kitzinger, 1995).

We should also be aware that focus groups themselves are frequently used to investigate attitudes towards ethics as part of a portfolio of qualitative techniques, with individual interviews, observational methods and interactive workshops acting as the other complimentary methodologies. To further appreciate this theoretical setting, we will now examine the development of focus groups as a research technique.

Focus groups: A short history

The birth of focus groups, and indeed commercial qualitative research at large, is credited to Dr Ernest Dichter, a psychoanalyst working in the USA in the 1950s. He brought his psychology training to the field of marketing, introducing group and depth interviews as ways to elicit more insightful information. His work, which came to be known as 'motivational research', was brought to the UK in

1959 through his colleague Bill Schlackman. At the heart of their work were Freudian ideas of motivation – the need to explore issues that a respondent is aware of but does not care to admit (suppressed motives), as well as more sub-conscious issues that a respondent will not even admit to themselves (repressed motives).

However, through the 1970s this psychoanalytic approach became displaced by more discursive research models that regarded respondents as having everything they needed to express themselves and self-direct their explanations. Thus, whilst the core ideas behind motivational research gradually disappeared, the method-ologies and principles behind it grew from strength to strength as demand for more insightful research exploded. Authors of these studies adopted the term 'qualitative research', a term specifically referring to the methodology itself (primarily focus groups), rather than simply the interpretation of the material that had been the premise of motivational research.

In more recent times, as the industry has evolved and the demands of clients have intensified, two important trends have emerged that have impacted upon the commercial use of focus groups. First, in terms of content itself, there has been a shift away from 'macro issues' concerning the fundamentals of the brand and the market towards a concern with more 'micro issues' dealing with specifics. At the Co-operative Bank, this has manifested itself in focus groups moving from research on 'the brand' or 'the current account market', to much more defined topics, such as exploring customers' views on the insurance industry in light of the bank's ethical policy.

A second change has seen the evolution of the methodology itself, with focus groups becoming much more flexible and interactive with other forms of qualita-tive research. This is particularly true of research techniques that are more ethno-graphically influenced – those that are more observational in their nature, such as video recordings of consumer behaviour. Focus groups have also begun to work in tandem with interactive workshops, individual interviews, qualitative panels and brainstorming sessions. The term 'bricolage' has been attributed to this phenome-non, whereby the qualitative researcher uses the tools of his or her methodological trade, deploying whatever strategies, methods or empirical materials are most suitable for the job in hand (Denzin and Lincoln, 1994: 576).

Adopting the focus groups methodology

With such a range of qualitative techniques each offering distinguishable benefits to the commercial researcher, it is pertinent to ask exactly when and why focus groups should be adopted as a methodology? First and foremost, focus groups are a good methodology with which to explore multiple topics. Their open-ended nature means that the number of variables that can be explored is limited only by time, whilst their interactive attributes allow the group to respond to a variety of stimuli. As such, they can foster a laboratory-type setting where advertising, pack-aging, products, brands, brochures and below-the-line material can be explored.

However, many researchers argue that the real strength of focus groups lies in their ability to highlight a range of behaviors, attitudes and points of view in a relatively short period of time (see for example, Morgan, 1988). With sessions themselves rarely lasting more than a few hours, they represent a time-efficient means of obtaining consumer feedback, and are therefore suited to companies and organisations that want to see results quickly. Indeed, in many cases insights are in real time: the focus group setting lends itself to 'live' research by allowing observers to witness the group discussion through one-way mirrors or television monitors. This offers the further benefit of letting the client experience customer attitudes, responses, reactions, accounts of behavior and perceptions of the market first-hand and, therefore, much more powerfully. This is in contrast to observational techniques that generally require more time to both perform and assess.

The case for using focus groups over individual interviewing centres around what can be seen as the depth-versus-breadth argument. Whilst individual interviews are believed to provide more detailed information of the attitudes and behaviour of the individual, group discussions are seen to provide breadth in terms of the range of behaviours and attitudes attending the group. Unlike one-on-one interviews, focus groups facilitate the gradual building of a range of views and attitudes, as participants feed off each other in expressing similar or opposing experiences, attitudes, thoughts and feelings. This is supported by a group atmosphere that often generates feelings of excitement and energy. Furthermore, the group situation can be seen as a less intimidating setting, whereby the 'safety in numbers' generates a more welcoming and conducive environment in which to express opinions.

Despite these strengths, there are times when there are strong arguments against using focus groups as the sole methodology, most notably when major marketing or budgetary decisions hinge on the results. It is important to remember that whilst they can provide a wealth of consumer ideas, tendencies and perceptions, the sample sizes involved mean that focus groups are usually too small to yield much more than a series of hypotheses on the subject matter, no matter how insightful or enlightening they may seem. As such, there is a large number of both researchers and clients who believe that statistical validity is still of paramount importance when making major decisions.

It is also good practice not to duplicate research by conducting focus groups on issues that have been researched before in the same way. Whilst it is important to add breadth to research to help validate findings, if an equitable amount of focus group-based research has already been done on a particular topic, it is perhaps wise to consider other methodologies. Focus group findings can be expanded upon by the results from quantitative studies – perhaps telephone, internet, mail or on-site surveys. Such research can probe topics that need further analysis, track results over time or test some of the views that came out of the focus groups. The exception to this approach is when consumer opinion on a subject varies over a short space of time, or if external factors influence consumer behaviour and attitudes – such as an environmental disaster or changing economic conditions. This is especially pertinent in the ethical arena, where emotive feelings are particularly subject to local, regional and global changes and events. Under such circumstances, repeated focus groups may be a suitable technique to uncover the changes in consumer attitudes.

THE METHODOLOGY OF FOCUS GROUPS

Having looked at the basics of focus groups and their development, we now move on to examine in more detail their practical application. The most commonly adopted approach to focus group methodology (and the one that this chapter has focused on) has become known as the 'psychodynamic group'. In this model the moderator acts as part of the group and all members are influenced by one another and the interactions of the group. They are actively encouraged to see themselves as part of the group rather than separate from it in order to promote more heart-felt feelings and beliefs. There are three key components to the group itself that we shall look at in turn: structure, content and process.

Structure

The first thing to consider when addressing the structure of a focus group is the participants that will form the make-up of the group itself. Recruitment criteria are ultimately guided by the objectives of the study, which means that the participant sample can range from being random for wider exploratory studies to being shaped by attitudinal, demographic or behavioural criteria for studies focusing on understanding a specific consumer group.

To highlight this, we can look at two of the case studies above. The Co-operative Bank's 2004 research on attitudes to SRI wanted to test, amongst other things, whether people's attitudes to SRI varied according to the type of financial product they held – from life insurance, savings and pensions to motor and home insurance. Recruitment criteria, therefore, included specifications that people representing all types of products held were present.

In the bank's 1999 research on 'ethical' consumers we wanted to understand key differences between 'ethical' and 'non-ethical' consumers. Participants were chosen from across the socio-economic spectrum and age groups and split by gender. Even numbers of participants were then selected based on those who self-defined as 'ethical' consumers and 'non-ethical' consumers.

In recruitment it is also important to consider the demographic make-up of the focus group. If a group is too heterogeneous the differences between participants can make a considerable impact on their contributions, whereas a group that is too homogeneous may not reveal a diversity of opinions and experiences. As Morgan (1988: 40) argues, making sure participants are comfortable with each other is important: meeting with others whom they think of as possessing similar characteristics or levels of understanding about a given topic will be more appealing than meeting with those who are perceived to be different.

Content

Turning now to content, we reflect upon the components that form the subject matter of the group discussion. The most important thing to consider is that both the researcher and the client know in advance of the event what the objectives of the study are and how all the material should be used. Careful attention should be given to the themes and topics of the study and any stimulus material that is going to be utilised. Stimulus materials might include: new products, ethical positioning statements, advertising and promotional material, projective techniques, image boards and so on. Unless understood in advance, these issues can interfere with learning from the group. A good discussion guide that indicates the content to be covered and the stimulus material to be introduced can be particularly helpful in co-ordinating a number of different researchers working on the study or research with an international reach.

The Co-operative Bank's 2001 Ethical Policy Review clearly demonstrates the importance of balance when it comes to the content of focus groups. Reviewing complex issues like arms exports and animal testing necessitated that the moderator was well-briefed and thus capable of developing the dialogue and drawing out issues of concern. Had they been poorly prepared, or overly stringent when following their discussion guide, they would probably have missed important opinions and themes for debate.

By finding the right balance, the focus group allowed the participants to share and explore their own views. For instance, the themes of the arms trade, animal testing and genetic modification generated free and open debate that offered some interesting insights. Participants reached a consensus that the bank should not invest in non-discriminatory weapons, such as landmines, or arms sales to oppressive regimes. However, the legitimate use of arms for self-defence was more contentious as was arms transfer to any other state.

There was much less initial confidence displayed by participants with respect to biotechnology and genetic modification. Again, having internalised the content prior to the groups the moderator was able to explore this apprehension. Further discussion suggested that scientific grounding was important not just for genetic modification, but for other social and environmental issues.

Process

Focus groups on ethical behaviour are likely to be emotive. This is often manifested by one member trying to stamp their 'ethicalness' on others in the group through strong and idiosyncratic statements. This bid for attention can be seen as a way of signaling perceived intellectual superiority and difference from other group members. Another behavioural element observed in ethical consumer groups is often cynical questioning about why or how the research will be used and who the project is for. There is often a reluctance to be seen to be helping companies achieve their corporate goals. Other signs to look out for are members who befriend the moderator, try to dominate the proceedings with their body language or pair off to exclude the rest of the group.

FOCUS GROUP EPISTEMOLOGY

We now discuss epistemology, or in other words, how we can justifiably claim to *know* things from our focus group research. We will examine the analytical procedures involved with focus group research, before going on to highlight some of the arguments against the validity of focus group findings in certain circumstances. We will finally highlight some variations on the conventional focus group that can be adopted to help overcome these.

Analytical procedures

When it comes to the analytical methodology of focus groups, we should begin with a caveat: analysing qualitative material is not an ineffable mysterious process, but neither is it a case of adhering to strict rules of conduct. Whilst there is a wide range of analytical procedures that can be adopted – Tesch (1990: 58) identifies up to 43 'approaches' to qualitative analysis – the typical measures used for focus group research fall into six phases. How these are applied should not be an afterthought, but rather considered in the early stages of research design. We can examine the six stages in more depth using the Co-operative Bank's 1999 Ethical Consumer Research Study to illustrate the procedures involved. The research sought to find out what being an 'ethical' consumer meant on an individual level to consumers, how they went about acting as 'ethical' consumers and what factors encouraged and dissuaded their behaviour.

The first stage, *organizing the data*, is often the most daunting since the data generated by focus groups are relatively voluminous. It quite simply involves re-familiarising oneself with the data. In terms of the bank's Ethical Consumer Research Study this meant becoming intimate with the data through reviewing the transcript, watching the session on video and examining the tasks.

Moving on to *generating categories, themes and patterns*, this phase is often the most difficult, complex and potentially ambiguous, but also the most creative and fun. Identifying themes, recurring ideas and subtle patterns that link people and settings together is certainly the most intellectually challenging phase. It is important to note that whereas quantitative data involve the search for exhaustive and mutually exclusive categories, the same process in focus groups and other qualitative research identifies salient grounded categories of meaning held by the participants. These insights include both those expressed overtly by the members of the focus group and those that are hidden in so much as they exist inherently behind what is articulated. It is worth remembering that as well as the participant's actual words and actions, meaning can be found in the particular times, ways and places they were expressed. A robustness to the analysis is developed through the flexible application of these themes and categories in an iterative process of developing, redefining, categorising and re-categorising all the focus group data. In this way, insights gleaned are coherent and supportable and an idea of the overall findings of the research will emerge.

In the 1999 Ethical Consumer Research Study, generating themes, categories and patterns was invaluable in drawing out meaning from the focus group data. Categorising allowed understanding to emerge of what being 'ethical' actually meant – types of 'ethical' behaviour included upholding human rights (characterised as 'big ethics'), good customer service, and fair pricing and honesty (characterised as 'small ethics'). Identifying patterns also made possible an awareness of the pertinence of age and class in relation to ethics. Finally, generating themes helped to illustrate how the wording and phrasing used in relation to ethical issues was important, with some participants showing an uncomfortableness with being dubbed an 'ethical consumer'.

Coding the data is the formal representation of this analytical thinking. It involves the researcher diligently and thoroughly applying coloured lines and dots, abbreviations of key phrases and perhaps numbers to the data. The codes are not there to be rigidly reproduced, nor to be counted, but rather to act as an aid to the researcher in making sense of the material. Codes provide a means of conceptually organising materials but are not an explanatory framework in themselves. Many researchers make a distinction based on the relationship between the codes and research data (see for example, Pike, 1954). This is between what are know as 'emic codes', which refer to patterns and themes identified or used by the informants themselves, and 'etic codes', which are assigned by the analyst to attribute meanings and patterns. In the 1999 Ethical Consumer Research Study, etic codes were applied to quotes from participants on what ethics meant to them, whilst emic codes were used to highlight the categories that we saw as emerging from these. In this way, the research moved from a series of emic categories towards a more understanding orientated collection of etic codes.

As categories, themes and understanding materialise, the analysis moves into the phase of *testing emergent understandings*, whereby the plausibility of the insights is explored. This can entail a search through the focus group data looking for negative instances of the understandings, but in a commercial setting will often involve further research. For instance, the output from the Ethical Consumer Research was built into a quantitative research programme that was conducted across the UK.

A summary of the five key consumer types that evolved from the whole research programme appears in Table 11.1. A full summary of the final report called 'Who are the ethical consumers?' is available on the Bank's website at www.co-operativebank.co.uk.

Repeat research is particularly common with respect to focus groups on ethics. This is because a wide range of diverse opinions, ideas and beliefs are found and these are constantly evolving. As well as repeated focus groups, it is increasingly common practice to repeat research using quantitative methods or more observational techniques, such as ethnography.

Normally any supplementary research will undergo its own analytical process, meaning the focus group can move on to its next phase of analysis – *searching for alternative explanations*. During this stage, the researcher must search for other plausible explanations of the understandings (Yin, 2003). By identifying these, describing them and then demonstrating why the understandings taken are the most plausible, the explanations and findings are given added validity. For instance, it was possible that during the 1999 Ethical Consumer Research Study that ethical concerns were articulated due to the natural tendency to express concern about such issues. However, by explaining how the subject of ethical consumerism was not introduced until after the participants had set out their personal priorities with regard to the companies, products and services that they used, the analysts were able to demonstrate how the conclusions they had reached with respect to ethical concern were the more viable explanations.

The final stage to the analysis is that of *writing the report*. Having neared the end of such an exhaustive process the temptation may be to simply compile a straightforward list of all the insightful findings that have been generated from the focus groups. However, writing up and presenting the understandings that have been produced is just as important and cannot be separated from the rest of the methodology. It lends the research shape and form and a good writing technique is vital in communicating the findings to the client. Thus, the report must be logically structured and signposted throughout, providing a thorough and deep account of the methodology and clearly presenting the findings and conclusions with justifications as to how they have been reached.

Challenges to focus group understanding

There are a few pertinent challenges to the validity of focus group findings where we are researching consumers' ethical views. As the previous chapter discussed, respondents to quantitative research can have a tendency to over-report the extent to which they behave ethically and this is referred to as 'social desirability bias' (for discussion see Fisher, 1993). Whilst the nature of focus group methodology means it has the ability to delve deeper into the actual actions, motivations and influences behind participants' ethical behaviour rather than quantitative techniques, there is still sometimes a proclivity to conform to an ethical ideal.

A further influence on the behaviour of focus group participants can be when the discussions centre around intimate and personal subject matter, where disclosure can lead to embarrassment in front of the other strangers in the focus group. This is particularly relatable to many of the focus groups conducted by the Co-operative Bank, since financial behaviour and wealth fall into this bracket of 'delicate' discussion material. In terms of groups on ethical beliefs and behaviour, other sensitive topics may also include sexual behaviour, health and religion.

Finally, focus group design should also take into account the fact that findings can be distorted if the participants in the group have different levels of knowledge and understanding. 'Expert' participants, such as specialists in a certain topic area, may intimidate others with less experience and lead to an unbalanced group where they don't truly express their opinions and feelings. However, for certain discussions it may be deemed useful to have such group members in order to provide a fuller, more wide-ranging debate, or if the subject demands informed opinions. Under these circumstances, it can be difficult to recruit some respondents, such as highly paid senior management, selected names from a company, people who travel a great deal, academics or minority groups.

Variants on the focus group

There exist a series of variations on the orthodox focus group methodology that have been developed to help overcome these limitations. Whilst it would be wrong to say that any of them offer some magical answer and absolute understanding, they do provide a solution to some of the restrictions that can exist in the basic focus group, and with it a more colourful picture of the behaviour and attitudes of particular target groups.

The *mini-group* has evolved in light of the challenges posed by embarrassing material, expertise difficulties and recruitment problems. The *extended group* is a longer session that allows further opportunity for participants to take part in tasks and activities such as brand mapping, exploring advertising and promotional material, brand personality exercises, psychodrama and the adoption of extra stimulus material. The extra time also facilitates a longer 'forming' stage to the group, helping create a safe environment in which participants are more likely to disclose feelings and attitudes on potentially sensitive or embarrassing subjects.

Conversely, the *conflict group* has evolved to highlight the differences between people and all the issues that surround them. The moderator makes it clear at the start of the group that the participants have been recruited with very different outlooks and positions and that the group's objective is to explore these differences and their meaning. In groups set up to explore customer attitudes towards ethics, this may take the form of a passionately ethical participant and one driven by less altruistic motivations. The moderator's role is crucial in order for the group to be a productive and insightful generation of ideas, rather than getting locked in conflict and stalemate.

An interesting and innovative variation is to recruit participants for two sessions, separated by one week. The *reconvened group* allows an interim period during which the group can be asked to conduct a series of exercises that help sensitise themselves to the topics that are being discussed. For example, during research conducted into a new range of organic and fairly traded babywear, a group of mothers were asked to write a 'consumption diary' during their week and to collect and take photos of things that had influenced the consumption decisions they made with respect to their child. Entries ranged from baby food packaging to visits to McDonald's and these were then used as stimulus material in the second group session, helping to vividly highlight the key drivers behind their consumer behaviour. This second session was also characterised by a perceptible increase in the energy and involvement of the participants, which lead to willingness to discuss more heartfelt thoughts and feelings (Lewis, 2003).

A similar approach is that of *synectics*, whereby the outcome of one focus group is fed into the next to test whether or not the findings are indeed representative. This method was adopted by Moseley Consulting when they conducted research in 2004 on customer understanding of the role of SRI. The researchers were able to feed the conviction of one group – that financial returns cannot come at any cost – into another group. The consumers in the second group verified this belief. The groups also found that relationships with insurance providers are more complex than those with other financial service providers, with participants exhibiting a range of views on the level of responsibility insurance companies should adopt.

A final variation is that of the *qualitative panel* where a sample of people are recruited due to some sort of behavioural characteristic and asked to attend a focus group, or several groups, on an ongoing basis. (One example of this is discussed in the case study Ethical Consumer Panel Research 2003 above.)

By guaranteeing that the ethical beliefs of the respondents were consistent with national patterns, the use of the panel was able to overcome the problem of social desirability bias and over-reporting. As such, it achieved a more genuine examination of what constitutes ethicalness and allowed greater insight into why the level of people professing to behave ethically does not match actual consumer behaviour. Equally interesting was the finding that most ethical consumers are not ethical in everything they do. Most will make occasional ethical choices when they are informed and the choice exists, but their consumption is multifaceted and complex. Whilst they may buy fair trade coffee and chocolate, their choice of clothing is more likely to be influenced by style, quality and brand. Labeling consumers as 'ethical', we concluded, misses out on the range of activities, ethical or otherwise, in which they engage.

As a footnote, whilst there is not space here to discuss the issues surrounding them, the recent development of *virtual focus groups* should be briefly mentioned. Such methodologies rely on digital technologies to help uncover insights amongst a greater range and wider number of consumers, and in a shorter amount of time. At their simplest level they adopt the use of the internet, email and telephone to survey participants, whilst their recent use in more observational and ethnographic forms represents a more complex application. For those interested in exploring this field further, Sweet's 'Designing and conducting virtual focus groups' (2001) and O'Connor and Madge's 'Focus groups in cyberspace' (2003) both provide a useful introduction to this fast-changing area of focus group research.

CONCLUSION

This chapter has allowed us to explore the issues arising from the commercial use of focus groups to research consumer attitudes towards ethics. We have examined the background and development of focus groups and looked at how they have evolved to become a useful tool to help us understand ethical consumerism. For a more detailed account of this area, Denzin and Lincoln (1994) provide the most comprehensive description around. Moving on to focus group methodology, we looked at how structure, content and process form the three key components to the psychodynamic group, and explored understanding in each of these in relation to groups on ethical behaviour. Gordan (1999) is a good accessible guide to this area, whilst it is also worth consulting the Association of Qualitative Research's website. Finally, we have dealt with focus group epistemology by looking at how we can justifiably take meaning and understanding from our findings. For this, we have considered analytical procedure, challenges to our understanding and variations on the basic focus group methodology that can help overcome these. Marshall and Rossman (1999) offer further insight into this area.

Throughout this discussion we have used examples from the world of banking to illustrate how these principles have manifested themselves in real-life research into ethical attitudes and behaviour. The examples have also illustrated how focus groups can often provide a deeper, more meaningful basis to our understanding of ethical consumers. Nowhere is this more clearly illustrated than in the seemingly simple dichotomy between being an ethical consumer or not. Whilst findings from quantitative research might dictate that a certain proportion of the population deem their consumption to be 'ethical', the focus groups used by the Co-operative Bank as well as research by Shaw and Clarke (1999), illustrate how this fails to uncover the complexity behind this distinction. Instead they show how ethical consumption is a multifaceted activity, with consumers behaving in different ways at different times, and each possessing different opinions as to what being 'ethical' actually means to them.

Finally, it is important to remember that neither the findings from focus groups conducted by the Co-operative Bank nor the other examples discussed in this chapter, nor the theory and methodologies behind them should be seen as prescriptive. Focus group methodology (and to an even greater extent qualitative research in general) is a dynamic process, not a mechanical procedure to be strictly adhered to at all costs. When this is considered, focus groups will continue to be a useful and important tool for helping to understand ethical consumerism in the future.

Surveying Ethical and Environmental Attitudes

12

Robert Worcester   Jenny Dawkins

This chapter provides an outline of the application of systematic and objective market research to determine consumers' views on ethical and environmental issues. Some of the issues arising from the use of market research in this area will also be discussed. This is followed by a summary of the key findings from recent research undertaken by MORI, mainly in Great Britain, while adding an international perspective where possible.

Before discussing some of MORI's recent research findings in this area, we provide some background to our research in this field, both qualitative and quantitative, and discuss some of the theoretical issues arising from the practice of research of this type.

BACKGROUND TO MORI'S RESEARCH ON ETHICAL ISSUES

MORI conducts market and opinion research on the subject of public attitudes towards ethical and environmental issues on behalf of a variety of clients from the private, public and voluntary sectors. These include corporations active in the field of corporate social responsibility (CSR) who wish to consult their stakeholders, government departments and agencies, non-governmental organisations wishing to inform their policy and strategy and a variety of interest groups, consultants and consortia wishing to contribute to issues of public debate.

In particular, we have seen an increase in research for private sector clients in recent years as more companies engage in the corporate responsibility agenda. The objectives of commercial research in this area vary, of course, but there are some common themes: research is often conducted in order to inform future strategy and communications; to ensure they are aligned with public expectations and consumer requirements; to provide internal justification for programmes and campaigns; to monitor the impact of actions and communications on external perceptions; to generate press coverage, or to associate the client organisation with a campaigning stance or cause.

In addition, we have conducted some research in this area for the media, whose end use is to inform, educate and entertain their readers, viewers and listeners, rather than to provide information for their organisations to themselves use to take action. MORI's research in this area includes both one-off investigations into opinions on particular issues, and tracking (or longitudinal) studies, where fieldwork is repeated at regular intervals to establish trends in opinion.

QUANTITATIVE AND QUAIITATIVE RESEARCH

There are two main applications of social and/or market research with different and often complementary applications: quantitative and qualitative research. Quantitative research is used to measure and track opinions, perceptions and behaviour. It uses mostly structured questions asked of purposive samples of relatively large numbers of people, selected by clearly defined sampling procedures, in order to derive percentages and statistics representative of the population under investigation. Some use is made of qualitative questions; for example, the open-ended type ('Why do you say that?') sometimes follow up on answers to 'closed' questions, using scales in order to elicit explanations and more discursive responses explaining earlier answers.

By contrast, qualitative research is used to explore a topic in more depth, usually to determine 'why' views are held. Small numbers of respondents are involved in a less structured interview or group discussion, exploring topics in more detail to generate insight into the motivations and underlying drivers behind stated opinions. Findings are supported by illustrative comments rather than percentages and the selection of respondents is generally more pragmatic; the aim is to generate insights from a range of individuals rather than to be thoroughly representative of the population in question. Frequently the respondents are selected to in fact obtain a 'skewed' group, such as a particular demographic, geographic or attitudinal subset of the population.

We will mainly be discussing findings from quantitative research, informed in places with insights from qualitative research (see Chapter 11 regarding the Co-operative Bank for an extensive discussion of the theory and use of qualitative research carried out for a commercial organisation).

USES AND LIMITATIONS OF QUANTITATIVE RESEARCH

Quantitative research into consumer opinion is an aid to management decision making whether in a commercial company, a non-profit organisation such as a charity, or an advocacy group. It is used to measure and track consumer opinions in a robust and also a cost-effective way. It is effective for providing evidence of people's views on different topics (attitudes, claimed past behaviour and predictions of future behaviour), for measuring changes in opinions over time and for identifying differences in opinion among various groups of people.

The limitations of this sort of research mainly surround financial constraints. Budgetary pressures often mean the research has to take a pragmatic course, and arrive at the most accurate findings available within the budget and time available. Often we are asked to undertake limited studies of attitudes and behaviour to determine responses to specific questions, and not to so-called 'academically rigorous' standards. Furthermore, many of our findings are client-confidential and are not designed to be released into the public domain, especially if they relate to specific companies and were undertaken for strategic objectives. Therefore, such commercially driven information as arrives in the public domain is often fairly generic and 'broad brush' in order to be of interest to a wide range of parties.

Lastly, as we discuss later in the chapter, there is sometimes a mismatch between what people say they think and do, and their actual behaviour. Therefore, survey findings can be potentially misleading if taken at face value. The main issues here are the 'social desirability bias' discussed further below, by which survey respondents are induced to give more socially acceptable answers, and the fallacy that consumers behave rationally and consistently with their stated views (see Chapter 7 in this book).

ENSURING ACCURACY OF RESEARCH

In order to conduct research that is as accurate as possible, there are five main principles that professional market researchers follow, which we will go on to discuss in more detail:

- representative sampling – ensuring that the people participating in the survey reflect the population under investigation;
- consistency of questioning both in phrasing and in positioning within the questionnaire – ensuring a common basis of comparison when comparing the views of different groups of people, or tracking views over time;
- impartial questioning – ensuring the wording and format of questions do not introduce bias into findings or lead respondents to make a particular answer;
- anonymity of respondents – ensuring that respondents are not identified and no answers are attributed to individuals in order to avoid inhibiting response;
- rigorous analysis – ensuring the findings are processed and analysed so that no distortion is introduced into the data.

Representative sampling

Usually in social and market research, a sample of people is surveyed rather than the whole population under consideration. In principle and up to a point, the larger the sample that is surveyed, the closer the finding will be to the result if the whole population were surveyed. For example, on a true random sample of 2,000 people (for example, in 19 cases out of 20), we can be 95 per cent confident that a finding of 50 per cent will be within ±2 per cent of the finding had the whole population been interviewed, whereas with a sample of around 1,000, we would be 95 per cent certain that the response would be within ±3 per cent. MORI generally recommends that at least 1,000 interviews are conducted in the case of a representative sample of the British public.

The statistical confidence in a finding depends on the sample size and proportion of the population that is interviewed (the finding will be considered more 'reliable' as these increase, up to a point), and also on the level of the percentage finding (the statistical confidence decreases as the finding approaches 50 per cent and there is less consensus in opinion). For further detail on statistical reliability of research findings and the formula used to calculate these figures, see the reference section of this book (Chisnall, 2001: Chapters 3 and 4; Kinnear and Taylor, 1995; Worcester and Downham, 1986: 85–110).

In order to ensure the findings are not skewed because an unrepresentative sample of the population is interviewed, quota sampling and data weighting have been employed in many of the surveys we discuss below. Quota sampling involves ensuring a certain number of people with particular demographic characteristics are interviewed so that the sample reflects the make-up of the population. The findings are then weighted on demographic criteria from population sources such as the Census in the UK, up-weighting the answers of groups under-represented in the sample so that it absolutely reflects the actual profile of the population. Tests have shown that if the quotas are carefully chosen and the research carried out to a high standard then quota samples are as accurate as most probability samples, especially on those requiring a quick turnaround which makes the extensive call-backs required of random samples difficult or impossible.

International studies are made up of several nationally representative samples constructed in this way. Particular sampling issues for international studies include the availability of population data in some markets and the consistency of population measures available across different markets. In consequence, international studies sometimes have to use the best sampling information available in each market, which is not necessarily consistent, especially in developing countries.

Consistency of questioning

Moving on to the issue of consistency of questioning, the principle is that if the findings among different groups or from different times are to be compared, then the questions should be asked in exactly the same conditions using exactly the same question wording and response options. Many of the trends outlined in this chapter are taken from annual research studies, which provide a snapshot of opinion and are repeated using consistent sampling and question wording at the same time each year, in order to make the survey methodology as consistent as possible.

Particular issues for international studies include differing interpretations of wording and terminology which is particularly tricky if translation is involved. Local knowledge and thorough translation checking are required to ensure the understanding of questions will be as close as possible in different countries. It is also the case that different survey methodologies are more appropriate in different markets. For example, in the USA the best way to reach a representative cross-section of the public is by telephone. This is because of the high proportion of households which have a telephone, the geographical dispersal of the population, and the security issues involved in face-to-face interviewing in some locations. However, in a developing country where telephone ownership is low, it may be imperative to use face-to-face interviewing in order to obtain a representative sample. Therefore, an international study might of necessity compare findings from telephone interviews with face-to-face survey findings. In this case, questionnaire design must take into account the different constraints of various interviewing methods to ensure questions will be as consistent as possible across the different markets.

Impartial questioning

In terms of impartial questioning, there are standard principles followed by professional market researchers such as using non-leading question wording and balanced response scales (that is, scales with equal numbers of positive and negative response options), for example Likert and Osgood scales. However, there is some debate surrounding issues of question design; for example, some market researchers argue for the inclusion of neutral mid-points in response scales (for example, neither positive nor negative) as this represents a valid point of view, while others feel a neutral mid-point should be excluded in order to encourage respondents to express an opinion one way or the other.

When surveying the public about ethical and environmental issues, some issues can be particularly problematic, such as non-response and social desirability bias. Non-response is problematic where certain groups are less likely to participate in surveys, either due to unavailability or disposition, which might skew the findings. 'Social desirability bias' is a term denoting people's tendency to respond in a socially acceptable way, which can lead to an over-representation of socially 'desirable' attitudes and behaviours and an under-representation of socially 'undesirable' items. Different survey methodologies can counteract these effects in different ways. Methodologies using an interviewer such as face-to-face and telephone interviewing can reduce non-response, since people are more likely to respond positively to a personal invitation to participate in a survey. On the other hand, self-completion methods such as postal and online surveys without the input of an interviewer can reduce social desirability bias since respondents are more likely to be honest through non-personal methodologies.

Managing non-response

The sampling and weighting techniques described above should correct any under-representation of certain demographic groups due to non-response, but it will not be effective for a non-response effect based on attitudinal factors. There are more exhaustive (and therefore more costly) sampling techniques which can reduce non-response, such as pre-selected sampling and non-responder surveys. Pre-selected sampling generates a random sample of addresses for each interviewer, usually on the basis of OA (output areas) from the census. The interviewer can only invite people resident at the addresses on their list to participate in the research and repeated attempts to recruit respondents are often necessary. When pre-selected sampling is used, availability of respondents is less of a factor in the selection of respondents, and therefore non-response is usually reduced. Non-responder surveys use follow-up surveys specifically targeting those who did not respond to the initial survey, to establish whether their opinions are particularly different to the survey sample (see Groves and Couper, 1998).

These techniques are more commonly used in social and academic research where the highest levels of accuracy are required. Commercial market research tends to be more pragmatic and often the additional resources required to refine the accuracy of the survey are not deemed requisite beyond a certain level.

Managing social desirability bias

To counteract social desirability bias, the wording of the question and response options is vital. The less socially 'desirable' response options should be included and given equal weight or prominence to other options and questions should include a mixture of socially 'desirable' and 'undesirable' sentiments wherever possible. In some cases, it may be considered necessary to use a preamble to the question to lead the respondent away from the socially 'desirable' response (Hammersley and Atkinson, 1995), and to allow space for them to voice their honest response to the question.

Preambles are also used to explain the issues underlying apparently simple questions, and this is often necessary in this area of research in order to explain the implications of ethical dilemmas. For example, underlying the apparently simple question of whether companies should communicate their social activities to the public is the issue of how much of their budget for helping the community should be spent on this communications activity. In order to elicit a valid response from the public, a short preamble explaining the issue is read out before the question itself, as follows in the example below. The findings of this question are discussed in the communication section later in this chapter.

Q. Many companies would like to tell the public about the community programmes they run, but don't want to take money away from the programmes for communications. Which of these statements best describes your view of the balance between programmes and communications?

1 It is important we know about companies' programmes, and they should spend significant amounts to tell us.
2 Companies should make an effort to tell us about their programmes, but should not spend significant amounts of money to do it.
3 It is not important for us to know about companies' programmes, and no money should be spent on communication.
4 Don't know/no opinion.

ANONYMITY OF RESPONDENTS

One of the central tenets of professional market research, the anonymity of respondents and the confidentiality of their responses, is an important safeguard in encouraging people both to participate in research and to answer the questions honestly. Nevertheless, despite this and the use of the techniques described above, in some cases one has to accept that there will be some over-claiming of socially 'desirable' attitudes and behaviour, and here the trends in opinion will often be more informative than the absolute figures.

RIGOROUS ANALYSIS

Basic analysis of this sort of data is generally conducted through tabulations showing the amalgamated findings for each question with columns for the overall findings among all those interviewed and then split across different sub-groups, for example, men compared to women, different age groups, social grades and those living in different regions. Thus, tabulations enable comparisons of the opinions of different sub-groups, relative to the population as a whole, and demographic and attitudinal profiling of groups of people holding particular opinions.

In some cases more advanced statistical analysis can be conducted, for example, cluster analysis groups together respondents that answer questions in similar ways so that attitudinal groupings or typologies can be developed. This technique was used on the study for the Co-operative Bank conducted in 2000 to develop typologies of 'ethical' consumers (discussed further in Chapter 11).

IMPACT OF ETHICS ON CONSUMER ATTITUDES

Let us now move on to some key findings from recent market and opinion research about consumers' attitudes towards ethical issues. Most of this research focuses on the influence of ethical considerations on British consumers in terms of a company's responsible behaviour towards its customers, employees, society and the environment. (Please see the technical note at the end of the chapter for details of the methodology of each of these research studies.)

MORI uses several attitudinal measures of the influence of ethical issues on consumers. Most directly, of course, ethics can influence consumer purchase behaviour. This can be measured in relation to past behaviour, or (probably less reliably) in terms of stated importance to current or future purchase decisions. More indirectly, ethical issues can influence consumers' opinions of companies, and corporate reputation can influence a company's relationship with consumers in a wider sense, including trust, license to operate, propensity to recommend, and so on. First we discuss attitudinal measures, such as the stated impact of ethics on consumer purchase and corporate reputation, and then move on to behavioural measures in the following section.

There are signs that worldwide, ethical issues are becoming more important in how people judge companies. In an Environics survey of the public in 23 countries which was conducted at the turn of the millennium using questions derived from MORI studies, for the first time responsibility issues such as treatment of employees, community commitment, ethics and environment were mentioned more often than product and brand quality as important factors in forming an impression of a particular company.

In a MORI study conducted in 2000 on behalf of CSR Europe (a European not-for-profit organisation with member companies, promoting CSR) across 12 European countries, 70 per cent said that a company's commitment to social responsibility is very or fairly important when they are making a purchase decision, and that includes a quarter to whom it is said to be *very* important. Social responsibility is reportedly most important in purchase decisions in Spain, Belgium, Switzerland and Great Britain. Furthermore, around one in five of the public across Europe would be very willing to pay more for products that are socially and environmentally responsible. The balance of opinion in favour of paying more is strongest in Denmark, Spain, Sweden, the Netherlands, Switzerland and Finland.

Focusing on Great Britain, where MORI has explored this issue in more depth, social and environmental issues are not the initial factors on which the majority of consumers judge companies; less than 5 per cent of the British public spontaneously mention environmental responsibility (4 per cent) or social responsibility (3 per cent) as the most important factors they take into account when making judgements about a company. This is in comparison to a quarter of those questioned mentioning the quality of products and services as their foremost concern and around one in five (22 per cent) referring to treatment of customers, while around one in ten (12 per cent) cite treatment of staff.

However, prompting reveals a different picture. While ethical issues are not top-of-mind criteria, when asked directly the public say that their consumer behaviour is influenced by a company's social responsibility. Two in five (38 per cent) of the British public say that it is *very* important when they are making their purchase decisions that a company shows a high degree of social responsibility.

Clearly, this is a broad question which does not specify the type of product or service mentioned, and does not address other discriminating factors on purchase such as price, quality, convenience, and so on. It might also attract a level of over-claiming, whether from social desirability bias or future good intentions. Therefore, the *trend* in attitudes is the more powerful statistic than the absolute values. Over the years there has been a dramatic rise in the proportion saying a company's social responsibility is very important in their purchase decisions, from 24 per cent in 1997 to 46 per cent in 2001 (see Figure 12.1), since when this rapid growth has levelled off. It seemed British consumers were becoming more inclined to take ethical issues into account in their purchasing, from about a quarter to around half of the adult British population by 2001.

Offsetting the long-term upward trend, 2002 and 2003 have seen the stated importance of a company's social activities in purchase decisions slipping back somewhat. In 2003, 38 per cent said it is very important that a company shows a high degree of social responsibility when they are deciding to purchase, as opposed to 46 per cent in 2001 (see Figure 12.1). We interpret this decline since summer 2001 as probably associated with the more difficult economic times experienced since the attack on the World Trade Center in September 2001, compounded by the Enron and WorldCom scandals. It may well be the case that in more difficult economic times ethical criteria are seen as less important by consumers relative to factors such as price and value.

Nevertheless, there are indications that ethical issues remain important to a sizeable proportion of the public, even if somewhat fewer people currently feel moved to act on them in their purchasing behaviour. The perceived importance of a company's social activities to its public reputation has remained stable over the last couple of years. In 2003, 80 per cent said that when forming an opinion of a

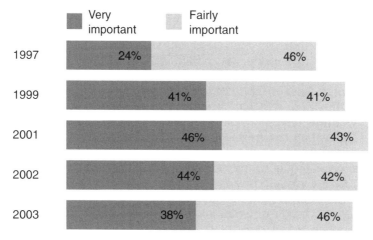

Q   When forming a decision about *buying a product or service* from a particular company or organisation, how important is it that it shows a high degree of social responsibility?

Base: c.1,000 GB adults 16+ each year; 982 July—August 2003

Source: MORI

Figure 12.1 Importance of social responsibility: purchase behaviour trends

company, it is important that it shows a high degree of social responsibility, compared to 82 per cent in 2001, showing a statistically insignificant difference.

The public has a striking view of companies' responsibilities in times of economic difficulty. Despite the evidence discussed above that consumers themselves place less importance on ethical purchasing during tough economic conditions, the public generally feel that it is equally as important, or even more important, for companies to contribute to society in an economic downturn. Two in five (38 per cent) say that it is significantly or slightly more important for companies to show a high degree of social responsibility in difficult economic times, and a similar proportion (44 per cent) say it is of the same importance than at other times. It seems that the public see the community's need for investment as paramount, whether or not companies are experiencing economic constraints. There is also an expectation on companies to deal responsibly with redundancies or site closures which may be more likely in difficult economic times.

Therefore, ethical considerations in terms of a company's responsible behaviour towards its customers, employees, society and the environment influence consumer attitudes in several ways. Ethical considerations are not top-of-mind for the vast majority of consumers, but when asked directly, a company's responsibility is perceived as important to corporate reputation and consumer purchase. Although the stated importance of ethics on purchase decisions tailed off from 2001 to 2003 (probably due to more difficult economic conditions), it is still substantially higher than levels seen prior to 1998. At the same time, corporate responsibility continues to be perceived as an important influence on consumers' opinions of companies.

IMPACT OF ETHICS ON CONSUMER BEHAVIOUR

So how does this high level of stated concern with ethical considerations translate into consumer behaviour? The research covering past consumer behaviour adds another dimension to the picture of the 'ethical consumer'.

Despite the high level of concern expressed by the public on ethical issues in their relationships with companies, half of the British public (53 per cent) agree that they are 'sympathetic to social and environmental issues *but not active*'. In general terms, we find that the propensity for consumers to be concerned about these issues still far outstrips ethical consumer behaviour. This could be partly accounted for by social desirability bias, with people likely to over-claim their propensity to purchase ethically. But we would also expect some over-claiming of ethical purchase behaviour, and the apparent discrepancy between attitudes and behaviour is such as to suggest that there may be other contributory factors at work, which we will discuss later in this chapter.

As indicated in the previous section, two in five of the British public (38 per cent) say that it is very important that a company shows a high degree of social responsibility when they are making purchase decisions. However, only a quarter (24 per cent) would describe themselves as an 'ethical consumer'. Looking at past consumer behaviour, only one in seven (14 per cent) report they have chosen a product in the last year because of a company's ethical reputation and one in six (17 per cent) say they have boycotted a product on ethical grounds. A higher proportion have participated in cause-related marketing; three in ten (29 per cent) have bought a product because of an established charitable link in the last year.

In fact, in a study conducted for the Co-operative Bank in 2000 which looked at both consumer attitudes and, importantly, their behaviours, we found that there is only about 5 per cent of the British population who consistently make purchase decisions based on ethical criteria above all other factors (this group was classified as 'global watchdogs' in the terminology of that study). This increases to around three in ten (31 per cent) who purchase on ethical criteria to some degree (for further details, see Chapter 11 regarding the Co-operative Bank).

This apparent mismatch between stated concern for ethical issues and consumer behaviour is also in evidence internationally. In the MORI/CSR Europe study across 12 European countries in 2000, as we have seen, 70 per cent of the public say that it is important that a company shows a commitment to social responsibility when they are making a purchase decision. Again, a lower proportion (39 per cent) describe themselves as an 'ethical consumer' and 37 per cent say they have participated in cause-related marketing (buying a product or service linked to a particular charity or cause) in the previous year. Participation in cause-related marketing is most common in Belgium, Switzerland and Spain and least common in Italy, Germany and Portugal.

Internationally, consumers are using their purchasing power to punish companies they see as irresponsible, to varying degrees. Across 23 countries worldwide in 1999, an Environics study found that a quarter of the public (23 per cent) had refused to buy the products of an irresponsible company or spoken critically of such a company to others, while a further one in six (17 per cent) had considered doing so. This tendency to boycott and advise others against irresponsible companies is strongest in North America and Oceania, and in Northern Europe, while the public in Eastern Europe, Central Asia and Latin America are least likely to act against companies in this way.

In summary, therefore, consumer behaviour lags behind the stated level of concern about ethical issues. This could be partly due to social desirability bias, but it is likely that other factors are also influencing this apparent disparity. We will go on to discuss a contributory factor to this through failures of communication of ethical company behaviour to consumers. But first we will analyse a niche group of consumers who are more engaged in ethical, social and environmental issues.

THE (INFLUENTIAL) ETHICAL MINORITY

Looking at public behaviour across a range of social, environmental and community activities, it is possible to identify a group of people more engaged in social, environmental and community activities than the population as a whole. This group has done five or more of a list of activities in the last year, ranging from making a charitable donation, to attending a local community event, to boycotting a product on ethical grounds. We term this group 'CSR activists', since they are particularly likely to care about companies' social and environmental responsibilities and they also tend to have higher expectations of companies in this area than the public as a whole.

CSR activists comprise 15 per cent of the British population, and the penetration has hovered around this level for the last five years. Compared to the public

Table 12.1   Characteristics of CSR activists (2003)

Demographic and attitudinal comparisons	CSR activists (296) (%)	British public (2026) (%)
Age		
16–34 years	26	35
35–54 years	45	33
55+ years	30	30
Social Grade		
ABC1	74	49
C2DE	27	51
Newspaper readership		
Broadsheet	34	17
Tabloid	33	48
Level of education		
Below degree level	45	69
Degree level or above	40	17
Attitudinal characteristics		
Agree industry & commerce do not pay enough attention to their responsibilities[1]	84	70
Very important that employer is responsible to society & environment[2]	80	58
Companies should contribute to social issues e.g. healthcare, housing & education in developing countries where they operate[1]	67	50
Very important a company shows a high degree of social responsibility when forming purchase decision[3]	50	38
Describe themselves as 'ethical consumer'	50	24
Have felt guilty about 'unethical' purchase	31	13
Aware of any companies helping the community or society (unprompted)[1]	67	37
Agree most companies do not listen and respond to public concerns on social & environmental issues[1]	60	46

[1] Base: all respondents (asked of half the sample: 147 CSR activists, 1044 British public)
[2] Base: all workers (153 CSR activists, 890 British public)
[3] Base: all respondents (asked of half the sample: 149 CSR activists, 982 British public)

Source: MORI

as a whole (see Table 12.1), CSR activists are more likely to be in the middle age range (35–54 years), of higher social grade, broadsheet (that is, higher quality newspaper) readers and educated to degree level or above. Although a minority, CSR activists are an important group of 'movers and shakers' who could prove influential advocates for a company that can persuade them of its ethical credentials. They could also be a lucrative niche market for ethical products and services, representing as it does around six million consumers, most of whom are in higher socio-economic groups and therefore have a greater spending potential.

This engaged group certainly has higher expectations of companies' ethical behaviour than the public in general. CSR activists are more likely to agree that industry and commerce do not currently pay enough attention to their social responsibilities, compared to the population as a whole. This expectation is reflected in the attitudes of CSR activists as employees as well as consumers and, importantly, this highly educated group would be sought-after in the employment market. The vast majority of CSR activists that are in paid work consider it very important that their employer is responsible to society and the environment. CSR activists are also particularly likely to expect multinational companies to export their responsibility principles to the developing countries in which they operate: two out of three say that companies should contribute to social projects such as healthcare, housing and education in the developing countries in which they operate, regardless of what the law in that country requires.

Among the CSR activist group, corporate responsibility has a stronger influence on purchase compared to the public as a whole, with half saying it is very important that a company shows a high degree of social responsibility when they are forming a purchase decision. They are also more likely to describe themselves as 'ethical consumers' and to have felt guilty about an 'unethical' purchase than the public as a whole.

Unlike the public overall, most CSR activists are aware of specific companies helping the community, and that awareness is rising (from 53 per cent in 2001 to 67 per cent in 2003). It seems CSR activists are more 'tuned in' to the increasing corporate commitment to, and communication of, their responsibility programmes. At the same time and perhaps reflecting their higher expectations of companies, the majority of CSR activists think that most companies do not listen and respond to public concerns on social and environmental issues. Clearly, there is even more need for companies to demonstrate their consideration of ethical issues to this engaged group of CSR activists than to the public as a whole.

The CSR activist group is therefore potentially important as an engaged consumer group, more likely to act on ethical considerations in purchasing and in other relationships with companies, including as potential employees, they become potential advocates of those they consider ethical, and not least potential critics of those companies they perceive to be unethical.

COMMUNICATING ETHICS TO CONSUMERS: THE ISSUE

Moving back to look at the public as a whole rather than just as consumers more engaged in ethical issues, a key barrier inhibiting the translation of public concern with ethical issues into ethical consumer behaviour is potentially the lack of effective communication of ethical issues to mass consumer audiences.

The rise of the corporate responsibility agenda has resulted in many blue chip companies incorporating programmes to improve their responsibility to customers, employees, wider society and the environment through their business strategy. This more ethical approach to business has therefore infiltrated into the boardrooms of some large mainstream corporations which now have ethical messages for consumers (in addition to the conventionally 'ethical' niche players built on ethical product propositions and ethical marketing).

Nevertheless, effective communication remains the missing link in many companies' practice of corporate responsibility, especially to mass consumer audiences. Although nearly nine out of ten of the British public (86 per cent) maintain that the communication of companies' community activities is important, and despite increasing numbers of companies becoming involved in corporate responsibility, awareness of any company's community activities has remained fairly low over the last decade. Without prompting (in this case, that is without suggesting company names or initiatives), only around a third of the British public (37 per cent) can name a particular company that they know is helping society or the community, and this is only very gradually increasing over time (from 30 per cent in 1994). Similarly, only three in ten (30 per cent) can name a company that they consider to be particularly socially, environmentally or ethically responsible. There is clearly a substantial communication gap in evidence here.

A lack of information seems to be contributing to the apparent mismatch discussed previously between the stated level of consumer concern with ethical issues and the lower level of ethical consumer behaviour. It seems that it could be partly a problem of access to information: three-quarters of the public agree that their purchase decisions would be influenced if they had more information on companies' ethical behaviour. Clearly this is a high-level question which does not discriminate between purchasing different product categories, and obviously other factors will come into purchase decisions, such as price, convenience and functionality. Nevertheless, if marketers are to harness consumer concern with ethical issues, or engage a wider group of consumers in ethical purchasing, it seems that this will require better mass communication, not least at the point of sale. We will go on to discuss potential ways of closing this communication gap in the next section.

Responding to demands for transparency, many companies are publishing information on how they fulfil their responsibilities to their various stakeholders, such as customers, employees, the environment and wider society in the form of non-financial reports (see Chapter 13 for a further discussion of non-financial reporting). As we have seen, the extent to which the public are aware of and are accessing these communications is disputable, but the issue does not seem to be primarily a distrust of such company communications. The majority of the public are predisposed to trust social and environmental information from companies (59 per cent say they would trust it a great deal or a fair amount), with around a third displaying a sceptical attitude (37 per cent would not trust it much or at all). This is not far off the 66 per cent who say they would trust such information from non-governmental organisations (NGOs), defined in the questionnaire as 'campaigning organisations and charities such as Amnesty International or Greenpeace'. We would expect trust levels to vary depending on which company or NGO produces the information, of course, as well as on the issues covered and even the medium and style used.

Nevertheless, in the event of a high profile war of words between a company and an NGO on a corporate responsibility issue, this question suggests that the company may find itself at a disadvantage – albeit only a slight disadvantage – in its efforts to win public trust.

Currently, therefore, messages about companies' ethical behaviour are largely not getting through to consumers. Top-of-mind awareness of companies' contributions to society remains fairly low. One barrier in getting consumers to act on their stated ethical concerns in their purchasing seems to be access to information, whereas mistrust of companies' social and environmental information is not a barrier for the majority of the public.

COMMUNICATING ETHICS TO CONSUMERS: WAYS FORWARD?

Currently, the most effective method of communicating companies' social contributions is largely through informal channels rather than through more conventional (and company-controlled) media. Among those aware of individual companies behaving responsibly or contributing to the community, this awareness is most commonly attributed to informal communication channels such as word of mouth (18 per cent), working for the company (17 per cent) or knowing family or friends who work there (11 per cent). Although the public does not always recall sources of information accurately, it seems that in this case informal advocacy of companies based on their responsibility is fairly widespread.

In the last year around a quarter of the British public (26 per cent) report that they have advised someone against using a company because it had not acted responsibly, and a similar proportion (24 per cent) has positively advised someone to use a company because of its responsible actions. A lower proportion recall receiving advice than recall giving it, but still around one in seven (14 per cent) have received advice for or against using a company because of its responsible or irresponsible behaviour. Overall, a significant proportion have been involved in this sort of ethical advocacy of companies in the last year; around three in ten have given or received positive advice and a similar proportion have given or received advice against using a company.

This underlines the potential impact of engaging a company's customers and (not least) its employees in ethical programmes so that their informal communication networks can be used to spread the word. In particular, employees tend to be perceived by external stakeholders as particularly credible commentators on a company's activities; for example, the majority of the British public say that when hearing about a company's contribution to society and the environment, they would be more likely to believe the word of someone who worked for that company than a company brochure or advert. At a time when the internet and email campaigns are increasingly used to publicise and co-ordinate consumer activism, the reach of informal communication networks is ever-expanding.

Therefore, in the communication of ethical issues to consumers, the influence of informal communication networks should not be underestimated. There is a propensity for customers, employees and other stakeholders to act as advocates of those companies they perceive as ethical, and conversely to act as saboteurs of those companies they perceive as unethical.

FUTURE SURVEYING OF CONSUMER ATTITUDES TO ETHICS

Tracking of the influence of ethics in consumer attitudes will continue in order to highlight any changes in consumers' motivations and to help evaluate the business opportunities available in ethical products, cause-related marketing and corporate responsibility. In addition, there are several areas where further research could valuably add to understanding in this area:

- further evaluation of the importance of ethical issues in purchasing decisions, in relation to other criteria and research that is specific to different product categories may be needed in order to fully explore this issue;

- further investigation of the gap between the stated level of concern surrounding ethical purchasing and the level of consumer action, in particular the triggers that are most effective in encouraging consumers to act on their ethical concerns;
- further investigation of the links between different stakeholder groups and the influence opinion formers such as NGOs, government and the media have on consumer attitudes towards ethical issues.

TECHNICAL NOTE

The findings discussed in this chapter are taken from the following surveys:

- MORI Corporate Social Responsibility study, Summer 2003: this survey has been run on behalf of a number of companies annually since 1990. A representative quota sample of 2,026 British adults (aged 16+) was interviewed across 161 sampling points in the UK. Interviewing was conducted face to face, in respondents' homes, between 7 July and 11 August 2003 (Dawkins, 2003).
- Environics Millennium Poll, 1999: a representative quota sample of around 1,000 members of the public was interviewed in each of 23 countries worldwide (Argentina, Australia, Canada, China, Dominican Republic, Germany, Great Britain, India, Indonesia, Italy, Japan, Kazakhstan, Malaysia, Mexico, Nigeria, Poland, Russia, South Africa, Spain, Turkey, United States, Uruguay and Venezuela). Interviewing was conducted by telephone or face-to-face interviewing, as appropriate to each market, in May 1999 (Environics, 1999).
- MORI/CSR Europe European CSR Study, 2000: a representative quota sample of around 1,000 members of the public was interviewed in each of 12 European countries (Belgium, Denmark, France, Finland, Germany, Great Britain, Italy, Netherlands, Portugal, Spain, Sweden and Switzerland). Interviewing was conducted by telephone or face-to-face interviewing, as appropriate to each market, in September 2000 (MORI, 2000).
- MORI/Co-operative Bank Ethical Consumerism Study, 2000: a representative quota sample of 1,970 British adults (aged 15+) was interviewed across 151 sampling points. Interviewing was conducted face to face, in respondents' homes, between 18 and 22 May 2000. Detailed factor and cluster analysis was conducted to formulate typologies of the ethical consumer (Cowe and Williams, 2001).

Part Four

Responding to Ethical Consumers

Corporate Disclosure and Auditing

13

Carol A. Adams   Ambika Zutshi

INTRODUCTION

In Part 2 of this book, entitled 'Campaigners and Consumers', the contributors have outlined how social and economic developments around the world have created a new wave of radical consumer actions against companies. Berry and McEachern (Chapter 5) have explained how a wide variety of organisations are rating companies or their products against social and environmental criteria, whilst Clouder and Harrison (Chapter 6) have gone on to look at how effective this new approach to changing corporate behaviour appears to have been.

Part 3 looks in more detail at attempts to understand the nature and extent of these new behaviours, with surveys and research generating an increasingly detailed picture of consumer response to a range of complex and interlinking issues and demands.

Part 4 seeks to examine some of the ways in which companies – the main target of this raft of new demands – are responding. In their review of boycott literature in Chapter 6, Clouder and Harrison looked at how analyses of specific consumer campaigns have helped develop a typology of corporate responses ranging from 'fight' to 'obfuscate' and 'ignore'. Part 4, however, seeks to put the growth of ethical consumerism into a wider context of general trends and changes in company behaviour. This chapter focuses primarily on the defensive corporate response, and looks in particular at corporate disclosure and social reporting.

There has been a general trend over the last ten years towards greater corporate accountability and transparency. The concept of Corporate Social Responsibility (CSR) has moved to the fore and this chapter begins by looking at this development and at some international codes of behaviour for multinational companies.

The main form of defensive response, the corporate environmental and/or social report, is examined next along with the wide range of standards and guidelines which have emerged to help companies formulate and deliver their reporting policies. There is also a new range of auditing and accreditation mechanisms which are helping to build credibility for some of the better reports. Despite these, there is still much scepticism among social and environmental campaigners over much new reporting, and this and other weaknesses are also discussed below.

It is clear that one driving force behind these developments is the changing pattern of consumer behaviour discussed elsewhere in this book. This chapter discusses some of the other causal factors which include changes to pension fund and investment product legislation, for example in Australia and the UK; industry initiatives; corporate social responsibility and reporting awards and indices; and mandatory disclosure requirements.

The next section looks at the special area of codes of conduct addressing workers' rights issues at supplier companies. These are much more clearly a response to changing consumer demands and are often traceable to very specific campaigns such as the Nike boycott. As with environmental and social reports, however, supplier codes are not without their critics and these are briefly considered before the last section which presents a chapter summary containing future research ideas.

THE GROWTH OF INTEREST AMONG COMPANIES IN CORPORATE SOCIAL RESPONSIBILITY

Smith (2002: 42) defines corporate social responsibility as 'the integration of business operations and values whereby the interests of all stakeholders, including customers, employees, investors, and the environment are reflected in the organisation's policies and actions' (see also Joyner et al., 2002; Kok et al., 2001; Simms, 2002).

Corporate social responsibility is increasingly being seen as essential to the long-term survival of companies. A survey conducted by Pricewaterhouse Coopers in early 2002 found that nearly 70 per cent of global chief executives believed that addressing corporate social responsibility was vital to their companies' profitability (Simms, 2002). More than 60 per cent of executives and managers in Malaysia were supportive of the view that to improve their market share and public image, their business would have to demonstrate that it was socially responsible (Rashid and Ibrahim, 2002).

Organisations which respond to these developments may benefit compared to their competitors according to a study conducted by the Clarkson Centre for Business Ethics and Board Effectiveness, University of Toronto, Canada. The results showed 'that firms that place a premium on ethics and social performance make the most money' (as cited in Svendsen et al., 2001: 30; see also Liedtka, 1999). A study conducted by Feldman et al. (1997) of publicly listed US companies and the adoption of corporate environmental management systems and environmental performance on their bottom-line found a direct and positive relationship between the two, with companies increasing their share price by more than 5 per cent whilst boosting their corporate image and competitive advantage.

Emphasising the growing importance of addressing 'sustainability' issues, William Stavropoulos, president and CEO of Dow Chemical Company said:

> Companies who want to survive and, indeed, thrive in the 21st century will manage for global competitiveness, in large part by reducing wastes, cutting emissions and preventing incidents. In the new world, where all markets are open, inefficient and poorly managed plants will be obsolete ... Sustainable growth recognizes the interdependence of our economy and our ecology. Corporate responsibility is about meeting society's expectations ... Today's competitive reality dictates that corporate responsibility be a key part of any business strategy. Corporate responsibility is about meeting society's expectations. It is also about collaboration. (1996: 29)

Bussell (2003), Liedtka (1999) and Palese and Crane (2002: 285) have also emphasised the importance of collaboration between both internal and external organisational stakeholders. Stakeholders have been rightly labelled as 'gatekeepers' (Svendsen et al., 2001), controlling the organisation's access to resources to continue present and future business successfully.

Codes of conduct for multinational corporations

Producing corporate or company codes of conduct has become one means by which organisations can standardise their directives from the top down, from their board and employees to their suppliers and contractors. A corporate code of conduct is defined as 'a document outlining the basic rights and minimum standards [which] a corporation pledges to respect in its relations with workers, communities and the environment' (Maquila, 2003) (see also Anonymous, 2003).

Three main types of corporate code are generally evident (USCIB, 1998):

- Internal codes – produced by the companies themselves covering specific company codes, statements and policies generally applicable to its internal personnel, suppliers, contractors. These codes address aspects of health, safety and environmental management, employee relations, child labour and general ethical standards (USCIB, 1998).
- Business sectoral codes – a number of business sectors have produced sector-specific codes depicting examples of best practice activities such as the Responsible Care guidelines developed by the chemical industry (Americanchemistry, 2003).
- Multilateral voluntary codes – there are a number of major multilateral voluntary codes that businesses could adopt including the OECD Guidelines for Multinational Enterprises of 1976 (OECD, 2003) and the ILO Tripartite Declaration of Principles Concerning Multinational Enterprises and Social Policy of 1977 (see ILO, 2002). More recently, the adoption of the Global Compact allows companies to demonstrate their commitment towards addressing various issues such as human rights, labour and the environment (Global Compact, 2004). The International Chamber of Commerce (ICC) has also released and supports a number of international codes in areas including environment and energy; taxation; competition; business in society; biosociety; trade and investment policy; and anti-corruption (ICC, 2004).

CORPORATE SOCIAL REPORTING

Corporate social reports are the primary means used by companies to demonstrate their corporate social responsibility. Corporate social reporting or corporate social disclosure can be defined as a medium by which information is 'voluntarily communicated by the organizations about their activities, programs and application of their resources which affect the relevant public image at large to meet social, political and economic demands' (Purushothaman et al., 2000: 103; see also Estes, 1976; Gray et al., 1996; Hackston and Milne, 1996).

Information on environmental and social issues is commonly communicated by companies either as a section within their annual reports or as stand-alone reports which could be either hard copy only, internet-based only or, most commonly, provided in hard copy format as well as being put on the internet (see Adams, 2002; Adams and Frost, 2003). An international survey conducted in 2002 by KPMG on corporate sustainability reporting found that 45 per cent of 250 of the world's largest companies now produce environmental and social reports, a rise from 35 per cent in 1999 (Simms, 2002).

Although time-consuming, developing social and environmental reporting does bring benefits for organisations such as better recruitment and retention of valued employees; improved internal decision making and cost savings; improved corporate image and relations with stakeholders; and improved financial returns (Adams and Zutshi, 2003). Corporate social reporting can also become a pathway for organisations to achieve sustainable competitive advantage, defined as that which is 'long lasting in time and that is not easily matched or surpassed by rivals [while withstanding] the test of imitation and other threats of dissipation' (Ma, 1999: 715; see also Chaharbaghi and Lynch, 1999; Chakraborty, 1997; Flint, 2000). Companies such as Hewlett-Packard (HP) and Royal Dutch Shell have benefited and achieved competitive advantage from practising concepts of sustainability (Rosen, 2001).

Guidelines for reporting

The release of the Rio Declaration and Agenda 21, two major outcomes of the Earth Summit in 1992, reflect the international commitment to achieving sustainability. One of the obstacles identified by companies towards achieving the objective of sustainability has been the absence of a 'specific methodology for incorporating the criteria of sustainability into their policies' (EUROPA, 2003).

The first Global Reporting Initiative (GRI) guidelines were released in 2000 following the 1999 initiative of the Coalition for Environmentally Responsible Economies (CERES) (Cowe, 2001). GRI is probably the best known multi-stakeholder initiative, and it provides comprehensive guidelines on sustainability reporting and on organisations' environmental, economic and social performances. The concept of sustainability reporting has also been popular. Companies with sustainability reporting structures such as that set out in the GRI guidelines are sharing with their shareholders and stakeholders 'an annual account of their environmental, social and economic performance' (Zulch, 2003).

A number of other voluntary guidelines have also been released to assist companies in reporting on their ethical, social and environmental performances. They include those released by the Advisory Committee on Business and Environment (ACBE), the United Nations Environment Programme (UNEP), and ACCA (DETR, 1998) which are assisting companies in reporting their ethical, social and environmental performances (see Zutshi and Adams, 2004, for examples of guidelines for environmental reporting).

In 1999 the Japanese Environmental Agency released the world's first guidelines, 'Grasping Environmental Cost Accounting' (Li, 2001) for calculating and documenting environmental costs. Government agencies in other countries such as Canada, the USA, Germany and Austria are also working towards releasing environmental accounting guidelines in their respective countries (Li, 2001).

John Elkington, chairman of SustainAbility, whilst commenting on the nature of social reports said that 'there is no such thing as a "standard" social report because the nature of each report depends upon the range of stakeholders for whom it is intended, what the reporting organization is trying to achieve and the variety of issues covered' (Anonymous, 2000: 53).

AUDITING AND VERIFICATION OF REPORTS

A senior executive from the oil sector when speaking about the significance of reports being verified by independent parties said that companies now live in a 'prove it world, where investors and society no longer trust a company's word. [Accordingly] information on the environment and society not only needs to be consistent, reliable and measurable against benchmarks, it has to be independently verified' (Plender, 1999: 14; see also Beets and Souther, 1999; DETR, 1998).

Breton (2000) believes that the scope of the social audit as a minimum should incorporate the evaluation of policies on ethics; labour; the environment; human rights; the community; society; and compliance. Dawson (1998) argues that the purpose of social audit should include transparency and accountability of the organisation whilst improving organisational performance and addressing stakeholder interests. Principles that need to be addressed to ensure successful completion of the social audit process include inclusivity; communication; embeddedness; comparability; completeness; regularity and evolution; external verification; and continuous improvement (see Dawson, 1998; Henriques, 2000).

The absence of legislation defining guidelines for verification of reports or for verifiers needs to be addressed by organisations and governments (Scott, 2000). Professor Peter James at the University of Bradford commented that until standardisation of 'performance definitions and measurement techniques is achieved, reports will be unable to deliver what many stakeholders want … reliable and consistent performance data to allow comparisons between companies, especially within the same sector' (James, 1999: 10). Data released in 2003 by SalterBaxter, a design and communication consultancy, and by Context, a corporate social responsibility consultancy, found that only 36 of the 250 FTSE companies' environmental and social reports for year 2001/2 had been externally verified (Maitland, 2002c: 4).

Stakeholder involvement is one of the major components of AA1000 which is concerned with the quality of accounting, reporting and auditing systems and organisational procedures considered essential to achieving improved communication and transparency with their stakeholders (see AccountAbility 2000; EBP, 2003; Todd, 2003).

In relation to the problem of lack of verification guidelines, Svendsen (1998b: 2) commented that senior executives and CEOs of companies are 'looking for new non-financial-based measures of performance' (see also Maitland and Mann, 2002). White, further highlighting the problem of absence of verification of reports, said that the 'hundreds of environmental and sustainability reports has led to an enormous volume of inconsistent and unverified information' (1999: 34). The absence of a report verified externally by an independent third-party assurer/verifier could lead readers to question the commitment to transparency made by those organisations (Swift, 2002; see also Maitland, 2002a, 2002b). Pricewaterhouse Coopers was criticised for lack of verification and failure to address human rights issues in its report produced for Talisman, Canada's energy company (Buchan, 2001). Niall Fitzgerald, chairman of Unilever, commenting on selection and use of external bodies to conduct verification process said that:

> There's a lot of work being done on verification from outside bodies. But I'm not sure that any of these have developed to the point where I could rely on

their judgment rather than my own as to whether our values were being observed. The world, of course, is very much in a 'don't tell me, show me mode', so there's a need for verification. But one has to be very clear that the verification comes from a reputable, knowledgeable, informed source. (Haddock, 1999: 26)

A number of problems have been mentioned when verification of the audit report is undertaken by external parties including:

- lack of clarity as to the scope of the audit and audit reports;
- value for money;
- qualified audit reports can open debate and may prompt negative publicity;
- potential for use in litigation cases; and
- time spent in the verification of the reports and with the verifiers.

(See Dawson, 1998; Knight and Propper, 1999; McCrary, 2002; Monaghan and Beer, 2000; Scott, 2000; Svendsen, 1998a.)

The intended release of new guidelines for verification of social/sustainability reports in 2004 by GRI should assist in solving this problem of absence of standard guidelines. It is expected that FASB will also release guidelines on the auditing and verification of non-financial/non-tangible areas in late 2003 (McCrary, 2002). Currently companies can refer to the guidelines on verification (ISA100) offered by the International Federation of Accountants (McCrary, 2002) or the AA1000 Assurance Standard (AccountAbility, 2003).

Weaknesses in social and environmental reporting

We have argued that the quality of much corporate social reporting is poor and a great deal of it is inadequate as a means of assessing the extent to which companies have acted responsibly (Adams, forthcoming). Adams further argues that the most problematic feature of current reporting on social, ethical and environmental issues is a lack of completeness, an example of which can be seen in the findings of her study of the reporting by a large multinational company. Reports are omitting details of the impact on communities and the environment which are material to key stakeholder groups. This lack of completeness would not be tolerated in financial reporting. Adams discovered a marked shortfall in the portrayal of the company's performance in its own reports when compared with its portrayal in reports by NGOs and in the media.

Voluntary guidelines which specify issues that companies should report on are not solving this incompleteness problem (Adams and Kuasirikun, 2000). In fact, there is a danger they are providing organisations with a legitimising tool and allowing them to get away with omitting material impacts on issues not covered in the guidelines (see Adams, forthcoming). There is general agreement amongst practitioners and academics that a good social, environmental or sustainability report should meet the following key criteria:

- it should be transparent;
- it should demonstrate a genuine attempt to be accountable to all key stakeholders;
- it should cover negative as well as positive impacts on society and the environment;

- it should demonstrate corporate acceptance of its social, ethical and environmental responsibilities; and
- it should be complete, that is, it should incorporate details of impact on communities and the environment which are material to key stakeholder groups.

The Shell Report is one example of a 'good' report. Even though the nature of its business is fundamentally unsustainable, and despite bad press surrounding the Brent Spar incident (Edwards, 2002) and its treatment of the Ogoni people in Nigeria (O'Riordan, 1999), it was joint winner of the first AccountAbility/ACCA Social Reporting awards held in 2002 (ACCA, 2002). Its report provides information on deaths at work, negative environmental impacts, and even negative comments about the company from employees and other stakeholders. It is important to note that good reporting does not necessarily equate to good performance.

FACTORS DRIVING CORPORATE SOCIAL AND ENVIRONMENTAL REPORTING

Academic literature has examined the impact of a range of factors on social and environmental reporting. Adams (2002) grouped these into three categories: corporate characteristics (including size, industry group, financial/economic performance and share trading volume, price and risk); general contextual factors (including country of origin, time, specific events, media pressure, stakeholders and social, political, cultural and economic context); and the internal context (including identity of company chair and existence of a social reporting committee). Few prior studies had examined the internal context and, through a series of interviews with UK and German chemical companies, Adams examined the influence of processes of reporting and attitudes to reporting focusing in particular on organisational constituencies involved in the decision making process; stakeholder involvement; reasons for ethical reporting and its increase; perceived benefits of ethical reporting; perceived costs of ethical reporting; extent to which the company studies other companies' ethical reports and refers to guidelines on environmental reporting; media used to communicate ethical information; attitude to reporting information which might be regarded as bad news; views on reporting in the future; influence of the extent of environmental regulation on reporting; and views on environmental verification.

All of these factors could potentially influence what is reported, its extent and quality. The importance of each factor varies across companies. We consider below two of the factors which are likely to have the most significant impact on general trends in reporting: the extent of mandatory disclosure requirements and changes in shareholder attitudes and values. We also consider a further factor – perceived threat to an organisation's legitimacy – often referred to as its 'licence to operate' which has been shown to have an effect on reporting, albeit often a short-term reactive one.

Mandatory disclosure

Legislation has been found to be a major driving force behind the adoption of corporate sustainability reporting in countries such as Australia, Canada, Denmark, the European Union, Norway, Sweden, the Netherlands and the USA (Nganwa, 2002). Survey results in 2001 from 'The Smart Company', a CSR consultancy, found that three-quarters of the respondents believed that legislation was required to ensure that companies act responsibly (Cowe, 2001).

Since 1996 it has become mandatory for more than 3,000 Danish companies to publish an environmental report following an amendment (s.35a(1)) to the Environmental Protection Act in June 1995 and the release of Ministerial Statutory Order No. 975 (see Adams et al., 2003; Government, 2003a; EPA, 1995). In the Netherlands, the 1997 Environmental Management Act was extended in 1999 (sections 12.1 to 12.10) requiring companies to produce two sets of environmental reports, one for the government and the other for the general public (see Adams et al., 2003; Government, 2003b). Similarly, in Norway following an extension to the 1998 Norwegian Accounting Act, since 1 January 1999 companies are required to disclose environmental information as part of the Director's Report section within the annual report (see Adams et al., 2003; Government, 2003c).

In the USA, the Securities and Exchange Commission (SEC) requires its members to disclose to actual and potential shareholders material information related to environmental performance, compliance and liabilities. Relevant in this context are SEC Regulations S-K, Item 101, Item 103 and Item 303 (see SEC, 2003). These regulations reflect the growing importance placed by companies on disclosure and authenticity of information as data released can be challenged by external parties. This puts added pressure on companies to become more accountable and transparent in their operations and encourages the development of voluntary guidelines.

Pressure from shareholders

In mid-2000 pension funds in Britain totalled more than £800 billion, with only £3 billion ascribed to 'ethical' investment (Smith, 2000). Following the amendments in the Pension Act, from July 2000, British pension fund companies are required to disclose the extent to which their investment policies consider environmental, social and ethical areas (Smith, 2000). Though there are no requirements for fundholders to adopt a socially responsible strategy (Targett, 2000), trustees may be held accountable for a fund's ethical stance and performance (Harrison, 2000). A survey carried out in 2001 by Friends of the Earth (FoE) of the largest top 100 British pension funds found poor disclosure and poor implementation of socially responsible policies by the majority of them (Beatrix, 2001). On the survey finding Simon McRae, FoE's investment campaigner, said that:

> ... standardized wording of paragraphs covering Socially Responsible Investment (SRI) in pension plan statements of investment principles [showed] how little consideration was given to socially responsible investing and [that] most statements [are] aimed simply at complying with the new legislation with the least commitment possible. (Beatrix, 2001: 1)

A survey released in 2001 by the *FTSE4Good Index*, the UK's first index ranking of companies according to their ethical, social and environmental performance, has caught the attention of corporations. The Corporate Environmental Engagement Index measures top UK companies' environmental performance against a number of criteria, from adoption of various standards to publication of reports and relations with their stakeholders (DETR, 1998).

Threats to an organisation's political legitimacy

A number of researchers have found evidence that corporate reporting on social and environmental issues is often influenced by a reaction to perceived threats to organisational legitimacy or a 'licence to operate'. Specific events have been found to increase the extent of reporting as companies respond to stakeholder concerns by attempting to legitimate their activities. For example, Patten (1992) found that companies in the petroleum industry significantly increased their environmental disclosure following the Exxon Valdez oil spill.

Interestingly, Walden and Schwartz (1997) found that increases in disclosure following this event were not limited to the oil industry, concluding that firms report in response to public policy pressure following such events. Brown and Deegan (1998) found a positive association between the levels of environmental disclosure and media coverage of various industries' environmental impacts. Influences of this sort on the reporting of these kinds of events are often short-lived, but longer lasting changes in societal attitudes do impact on reporting trends.

CODES OF CONDUCT ADDRESSING WORKERS' RIGHTS AT SUPPLIER COMPANIES

Multinational companies need to be transparent and accountable for their processes and actions especially in their operations in less developed countries. Compliance with local laws, forced labour, discrimination, child labour, health and safety, hours of work, wages and overtime are the most common areas covered by codes of conduct addressing workers' rights at supplier companies (supplier codes) (Maquila, 2003). Fewer codes incorporate issues such as freedom of association (see Maquila, 2003).

Wal-Mart in 1993 was one of the first companies in the USA to release its 'Standards for Vendor Partner' codes for its retailers and suppliers. Other companies with supplier codes include Sears, Sara Lee, Nike, Reebok, J.C. Penney, Woolworths, Liz Claiborne, The Gap, VF Corporation, Phillips-Van Heusen, C&A, Otto mail and Littlewoods (Anonymous, 2003).

There are a number of driving forces that have influenced organisations in implementing supplier codes including:

- increased public awareness and concern resulting from widely available information from various media sources, including pressure from shareholders (see Harrison, 2003; Todoroki, 2002);
- worker and consumer movements especially in the garment and footwear sectors, for example, a survey of British consumers by CAFOD in 1997 found that 92 per cent supported British companies having some form of minimum standards for their Third World suppliers (Green, 2000);
- an increasing number of multinational companies being indicted for their actions/or lack of commitment towards human rights (McMurray, 2003);

- boycott actions by NGOs which in some instances occur simultaneously across company operations in several countries (see Harrison, 2003; Women Working Worldwide, 2003);

- pressure from competitors with companies not wanting to be left behind, even if it is in the area of 'ethics and ethical trading' (Green, 2000);
- globalisation and blurring of national and international boundaries when trading (see Green, 2000; USCIB, 1998).

The garment and apparel sectors have been particularly active in producing codes. The majority of organisations in this sector have forced their retailers, suppliers, contractors, and in a few instances their subcontractors, to adopt some sort of code if they wish to continue business with them. According to Neil Kearney of International Textiles' Garment and Leather Workers Federation: 'Corporate codes of conduct are not voluntary. There is not a single company anywhere in the world that has adopted a code of conduct without being dragged kicking and screaming' (Maquila, 2003).

CRITICISMS OF SUPPLIER CODES

Critics argue that supplier codes are often nothing more than a public relations exercise by companies. Yanz and Jeffcott (1999) comment that codes provide a medium for organisations 'to deflect public criticism or to hold corporations accountable, to avoid unionization and justify investment in countries with repressive regimes or to increase democratic space for worker organizations'.

A comprehensive code developed by a company is not the same as full implementation across all its retailer, supplier, contractor and subcontractor sites. Sainsbury's, the UK supermarket chain, recently pleaded guilty to 12 charges of employing children without work permits and was fined approximately €10,000 (CSR, 2003a). In another incident more than 250 illegal immigrants were found to be working for Wal-Mart in the USA (CSR, 2003b). In addition, external reports published for companies such as Levi Strauss, Nike, Gap, Reebok and Liz Claiborne all revealed breaches of code in less developed countries (see Women Working Worldwide, 2003).

Codes are primarily written in English, sometimes with vague language limiting their use (see Maquila, 2003). This message was reiterated in the International Codes of Conduct seminar held in Thailand in November 2001. A local garment factory worker from Bangkok commented that: 'We have one company code posted on the factory wall. It is in English. When we workers raise problems to the manager in Thai, he says, "If you are satisfied, stay with us. If you are not satisfied, just leave"' (Schilling, 2003).

There is also a lack of recognition in codes of workplace gender issues. Female workers would like to see greater focus on dealing with problems of harassment and wage inequality due to gender discrimination. Pay below legal minimum rates is also commonly addressed in codes inadequately, as seen in the case of Russell Athletic's code of conduct which reads that: '[Russell Athletic] will only do business with vendors/suppliers who provide reasonable wages and benefits that equal or exceed the prevailing local industry standard' (Maquila, 2003).

Another dilemma facing the adoption of codes by workers is lack of communication as they are often not involved in the formulation process. Lack of education and training within the workforce in less developed countries is another barrier to implementing codes (see Schilling, 2003). There is thus a need for ongoing education, worker training and development. In the majority of instances codes fail to offer choices to workers with regard to trade union membership, although in countries like China where free trades unions are illegal, the problems lie deeper. Barely 5 per cent of Asian garment workers are trade union members (Schilling, 2003).

Companies also face a challenge in implementing codes in areas dominated by small production units or workers involved through home production. There is therefore a need to ascertain that codes are adopted by subcontractors as much as on the factory floor. The founder of the Thai Labour Campaign, Lek, commented that: 'Only the front-line factories are monitored in Thailand. These get monitored all the time, but the work goes out to small sub-contracting shops that never get monitored. And working conditions in the small shops are worse than in the factories' (Schilling, 2003).

Very few corporate codes address the 'rights of home-based workers' (ILO's Convention 177 and Recommendation 184), one exception being the Australian Code of Practice for Home-workers called the Textile, Clothing and Footwear Union of Australia (see Maquila, 2003; Yanz and Jeffcott, 1999).

Even when a failure to follow the codes could result in breakdown of the relationships between organisations and their suppliers, there are few formalised means to measure the extent of compliance with these codes (see Maquila, 2003). Monitoring of suppliers' factories by internal personnel is the most common method employed by companies to ensure implementation (Maquila, 2003). In an attempt to become more accountable and transparent, companies such as Liz Claiborne, Gap, Nike and Adidas-Salomon have engaged external organisations (such as NGOs) to undertake monitoring (Harrison, 2003; Maquila, 2003; Women Working Worldwide, 2003; Yanz and Jeffcott, 1999).

CONCLUSION

Society's expectations of companies are changing rapidly and there are a number of issues which give cause for concern:

- the proliferation of voluntary guidelines and codes of conduct and their limited ability to change behaviour and increase accountability;
- the lack of mandatory legislation and, where it exists, adequate enforcement mechanisms to ensure transparency;
- the lack of completeness in corporate reports on their ethical, social and environmental performance (Adams, forthcoming);
- the lack of appropriate governance structures to ensure that the concerns of key stakeholders with respect to social and environmental impacts of corporate decisions are taken into consideration (Adams, forthcoming);
- verification of reports, particularly of data reported on the internet;
- the limited dialogue between corporations and their stakeholders; and
- limited rigour applied by companies in attempts to influence the responsibilities of their suppliers (Silver, 2002).

Meeting the Ethical Gaze: Challenges for Orienting to the Ethical Market

Andrew Crane

14

Andrew Crane

INTRODUCTION

We have seen thus far that the ethical gaze cast by consumers onto businesses and their practices can be questioning and frequently critical. But for the firms concerned it can also seem inconsistent, ebbing and flowing with personal conscience, determination, and the pull of a good anti-corporate exposé – not to mention the ever-present trade-offs with price, quality and convenience. Nevertheless, the message now seems to be getting through to many organisations that their consumers and other stakeholders increasingly have ethical expectations that they wish to see addressed in one way or another. The question, of course, is how do organisations respond to these expectations?

In the previous chapter, Carol Adams and Ambika Zutshi examined some of the ways that organisations might seek to measure and report on their social performance as a means of maintaining legitimacy in the face of such ethical expectations. We also heard in Chapter 5 about various initiatives to establish labelling schemes and other mechanisms to communicate and certify claims to consumers. In this chapter, I shall take these discussions forward into the specific realm of marketing and strategy, focusing in particular on how organisations might orient themselves in order to appeal to the ethical demands of consumers. This is an important area to consider, not least because it starts us thinking about how (or even whether) ethical concerns might be translated into tangible products and services. But perhaps more importantly, it also starts to focus our attentions on the myriad challenges that ethical consumers might pose for organisations, and in particular, on the difficulties inherent in turning their demands into a viable and sustainable business proposition.

I will begin by establishing the type and range of organisation that might be within the field of vision for ethically concerned consumers – and then put this into the context of other constituencies likely to be casting their ethical gaze at the organisation. I will then go on to look at specific strategic positions that might be adopted, primarily with a view to delineating strategies appropriate to 'ethical niche' and 'mainstream' organisations, before proceeding to outline the challenges and tensions that these postures typically raise. Once I have set out these broad strategic orientations, I will look closer at the types of products, brands, images and programmes that organisations might produce to appeal to ethically concerned consumers, and how we might conceptualise them as 'augmentations' to the basic value proposition but crucially, augmentations that typically have implications well beyond the purview of the marketing department. This will lead us into a consideration of the deeper issues around organisational culture that the ethical gaze might raise for companies, and so in the final section, I will summarise some recent debates about how managers interpret the ethical gaze *within* their organisations. I will conclude with a summary of the main points and a few brief comments on the state of current theory and practice plus prospects for the future.

THE ETHICAL GAZE: LOCATING THE HORIZON

Responding to the ethical demands of consumers is something that all sorts of companies might need to do at some stage – from companies that have been expressly established to pursue particular social goals, such as those in the co-operative or fair trade movements, to huge multinational corporations dedicated to maximising shareholder value, such as Monsanto or BP. Therefore, just as ethical consumers might be from all different walks of life, so too are the companies that might seek to meet (or avoid) their gaze. The horizon, we might say, is an expansive one.

In examining how companies seek to appeal positively to these consumers, it is not unusual to think primarily of those companies at either and of the spectrum, that is, those most in the 'firing line' of boycotters (at one end), or those seeking to capitalise on an explicitly 'ethical' selling proposition (at the other). But even a good deal of those occupying more of a middle ground will need to exercise some kind of strategic decision making, perhaps because they recognise that the firing line isn't fixed, or because they cherish a reputation for being 'good citizens'.

Now, although certain companies might wish to respond to ethically concerned consumers, it needs to be said that there are many companies that do not, and probably even *need* not, consider ethical consumers at all. Although I am not going to discuss these companies here, it is worth remembering that those which do seek to respond to ethical consumers are by no means necessarily in the majority. And, as we shall see, even for many of these, ethical considerations are not always at the heart of their operations.

The first substantive issue to note here is that it is almost impossible to separate out the impact of ethically concerned consumers on organisations from the host of other 'ethical' forces that might confront them. This includes pressure from the media, government, civil society, competitors, or any other relevant constituency. In part, this inability to separate out the impact of ethical consumers is due to lack of research – indeed, I can think of no single study that has as its main focus the impact of consumers' ethical preferences or actions on organisational decision making. But there is also a largely unexamined assumption prevalent in much of the debate around ethical consumption that firms will automatically respond to the demands of consumers – the 'accepted sequence' (Galbraith, 1974) of *consumer sovereignty* that was discussed in Chapter 2. Notwithstanding the theoretical limitations of this assumption, there are also a number of conditions that might influence this purported cause-and-effect relationship, as Clouder and Harrison (Chapter 6) have already shown. Most notably, this includes the amount of concentrated power wielded by consumers, and the vulnerability and visibility of the corporate brand in the market-place.

The relative influence of ethically concerned consumers on firms compared with other 'ethical forces' is not, however, just a matter of establishing empirical fact. There is an extremely important normative question here that is frequently eclipsed by the assumption that firms *will* respond to consumers, namely whether firms *should* respond to the ethical demands of consumers (see also Chapter 1). Now to many advocates of ethical consumption, this probably sounds perverse. But from a normative standpoint, there seems to be no prima facie reason why a firm – even supposing it wanted to act in the best interests of society – should privilege the views of one particular group of consumers, or one particular preference expressed by consumers, however well meaning those consumers might appear to be. Although marketers often assume the primacy of consumer interests, a multi-stakeholder view of the firm would typically regard this as problematic (Jackson, 2001). Moreover, who is to say that answering the demands of ethical consumers is really in the best interests of society? Of course it may be, but then again, it may not. Indeed, determining the 'right thing to do' is inevitably fraught with complexity and uncertainty, especially when firms have a whole range of stakeholders to satisfy. Listening to, and attempting to appeal to, ethically concerned consumers is one possible approach, but there are clearly other approaches that can also be considered (see Crane and Desmond, 2002).

For example, many firms often held up as exemplars of successful social responsibility, such as Ben & Jerry's, Tom's of Maine, and the Body Shop claim to have followed the instincts and drives of their leaders in determining their ethical stance, rather than taking a customer-led approach (see Chappell, 1993; Lager, 1994; Roddick, 1992). This kind of internal drive could be seen as a more stable (though arguably less 'democratic') foundation for responsible business than one that relies on changing market preferences. Similarly, it could be argued that government and civil society organisations have a more legitimate mandate to act in society's best interests than individual consumers, and so companies should primarily determine their ethical priorities in consultation with these parties rather than conducting customer opinion surveys. These propositions are most certainly contestable, but that does not deflect from the issue that the appropriate status of ethical consumers' demands is an often-overlooked issue that almost certainly warrants further debate in the literature. At the very least, I think it is worth considering ethical consumers as just one part of the 'ethical gaze' confronting corporations, albeit one that may well be influential in how firms orient themselves to the 'ethical market'. Let us now turn our attention to the types of strategies that firms may adopt in establishing this orientation.

STRATEGIES FOR ORIENTING TOWARDS THE ETHICAL MARKET: MAINSTREAMING OR ETHICAL NICHE?

In recent years, there has been a growing number of commentators extolling firms to listen and respond to the ethical demands of consumers, to 'sell corporate social responsibility' (Cobb, 2002), to build 'ethical brands' (Mitchell, 1997), and to capitalise on the growing ethical market. The notion of an ethical market is perhaps a rather nebulous one, but what I mean by it here is essentially a demand, either implicit or explicit, for corporate actions, communications, or other artefacts that have a positive and identifiable ethical component to those outside the company. This can mean products with ethical features of one kind or another, such as fair trade or recycled products; it can mean cause-related marketing programmes, employee welfare programmes, or the development of an ethical code; in fact, it can mean a whole host of corporate endeavours that consumers and other stakeholders might demand from corporations for supposedly ethical reasons.

Probably the most straightforward way of thinking about how firms orient towards this ethical market is to conceive of a continuum of focus, from a narrow specialisation in an 'ethical niche' towards an attempt to address ethical concerns within a more 'mainstream' market. Basically, all I'm saying here is that some firms focus exclusively or mainly on promoting their ethical credentials (ethical niche), whilst others primarily stress alternative factors, yet still articulate their ethical credentials as a secondary or additional factor (mainstreaming).

One obvious way of conceptualising this distinction is to consider niche and mainstreaming strategies as the two main manifestations of Porter's (1985) 'differentiation' strategies, whereby firms seek to position themselves as offering superior qualities either across the whole market or in a specific market niche (see Figure 14.1 for a simple depiction). Why should we consider ethical considerations as a 'differentiation'? Well, this is a slightly tricky one, since for many people the whole idea of using ethics or social responsibility to strategically promote firms and products is in fact questionable in itself (for a discussion, see Husted and Allen, 2000). Again, such thinking starts to raise another of the fundamental paradoxes in much of our thinking about firms in relation to ethical consumers. On the one hand, we want firms to *genuinely* and *actively* embrace social responsibility, but at the same time, we extol them to listen and respond to ethical consumers, which suggests a more *instrumental* and *reactive* approach.

Putting such tensions aside for one moment though (we will return to them later), the mere fact that some, perhaps many, consumers are likely to be attracted to firms they perceive to be socially responsible suggests that ethical considerations are a means by which consumers differentiate between firms and their offerings. In this sense, firms promoting their ethical credentials may be seen as supplying 'augmentations' to the basic product offering (Crane, 2001). It is not just a bank account, but a bank account from a 'caring' bank; not just a bar of chocolate, but a bar of chocolate that ensures growers a decent standard of living; not just a trip to the supermarket, but going to a supermarket that gives some of the money you spend back to local schools. There will certainly be other augmentations too, but ethical qualities are part of the bundle of benefits through which firms seek to differentiate themselves in the mind of the consumer.

There are, I should add, considerable limitations to the usefulness of Porter's (1985) model for understanding strategic positioning (see for example, Miller and Dess, 1993). However, as long as we use this model simply to identify the

	Orientation	
	Low cost	Differentiation
Broad	Cost leadership	Mainstream ethical orientation
Narrow	Cost focus	Ethical niche

Figure 14.1 Orientations to the ethical market

basic approaches evident in the ethical market, it seems to be a reasonable conceptualisation, and in so far as it is widely understood and used in strategy theory and practice, it seems to be a useful starting point for thinking about how firms respond to ethical consumers. Let us look now in a little more detail at these main differentiating orientations.

Ethical niche orientation

Firms targeting the ethical niche will see their customers as having strong ethical preferences which drive their product selections and other consumer decisions such as where and how to shop. Hence, such companies will typically position their products as ethical alternatives to conventional competitive offerings. According to marketing logic, these companies' products should therefore offer unique ethical features above and beyond industry standards, and communications should generally concentrate on emphasising these benefits rather than other attributes of the product or firm. Again, conventional marketing logic would tend to dictate that this type of differentiation should provide added value to consumers, and so should command a premium price. Firms occupying the ethical niche might also ordinarily have social, ethical, or environmental goals as an integral part of their espoused mission, coupled with a public commitment to certain principles or practices.

Typical examples of firms targeting the 'ethical niche' include Triodos, the Dutch 'ethical bank', which aims to enable 'money to work for positive social, environmental and cultural change' and markets its corporate banking services to charities and 'social businesses'. Similarly, the UK-based Co-operative Bank has sought to target an ethical niche, as has the Ethical Clothing Company, set up by trade union groups to provide 'sweatshop-free' merchandise for the music industry. Given their commitment to ensuring growers a premium price, many companies marketing certified fair trade products (such as Max Havelaar products in the Netherlands or TransFair in the USA) have also typically targeted a niche of concerned consumers, as have green firms offering more environmentally benign products, such as the Belgium cleaning products company Ecover, or the US toiletries firm Tom's of Maine. The key point is that ethical niche firms see their aims best achieved by satisfying a relatively small group of concerned customers, and as a result, are mainly small specialist firms.

Mainstream orientation

In contrast, a mainstreaming orientation towards the ethical market includes a range of various types of firm with potentially very different values. The ethical considerations of consumers are still important here, and mainstreaming firms may well have ethical codes, or be part of ethical sourcing programmes such as SA8000, or use labels such as eco-labels to certify their credentials. But these will not be the main selling proposition of the products and services on offer, the primary focus of differentiation. This means that it could be that ethical credentials are seen as a fundamental part of doing business, or simply an 'added extra' or even a passing fad, but either way these firms will not principally position their products on this basis.

The reasons why these firms do not seek to invoke ethical criteria as the main selling proposition for their products might stem from a range of factors, including a perceived scepticism or 'backlash' amongst consumers against corporate 'greenwash', and doubts over consumers' willingness to pay a premium for ethical attributes (Crane, 2000). I think it is reasonable to assume though that the basic underlying assumption here is that firms believe that most of their consumers' ethical concerns are secondary to other considerations such as price, quality and convenience – or at least are secondary for more of the time than they are primary. Mainstream firms typically target a larger market than niche firms, and it would appear that there are few if any markets where differentiation primarily on the basis of ethics is a sustainable business proposition beyond a narrow niche. This is not to say that firms will ignore the ethical considerations of their consumers in this context, since we are very much concerned with those firms that do attempt to differentiate at least partly on the basis of ethics. Such ethical differentiation though is typically just one element in a portfolio of differentiating factors that are necessary to gain significant market share in mainstream markets.

This is a relatively broad definition, so naturally there are numerous examples of firms in this category, from those such as the UK home improvements company B&Q, which pioneered the use of the Forest Stewardship Council sustainable timber accreditation programme in the UK, to the oil company BP, which in 2001 rolled out an ambitious high profile $100m ethical rebranding campaign complete with a new name, 'Beyond Petroleum', and a new green logo. The key point though is that mainstream firms see their aims best achieved by satisfying a relatively large group of customers who are concerned about ethical factors, but are unwilling to sacrifice the other aspects they value for those concerns.

A low-cost ethical orientation?

If it then seems reasonable to suggest that firms orienting towards the ethical market have adopted some form of differentiating strategy, we might similarly conjecture that firms adopting Porter's (1985) other main strategic posture – a low-cost strategy – would probably not seek to orient at all towards the ethical market. Indeed, given that attention to ethical considerations and the concomitant needs to certify and communicate ethical credentials are inevitably a costly business, it would seem fairly unlikely that a firm seeking to maintain a strong cost advantage over its competitors would desire, or be able, to appeal very successfully to ethical consumers. For example, in 2003 when the UK clothing retailer Littlewoods experienced a change in ownership, and a reinvigoration of its low-cost strategy, the firm shut down its entire ten-person ethical trading team and pulled out of the flagship Ethical Trading Initiative, despite having been a founding member of the programme (Bowers and Finch, 2003).

Conversely, in the specific area of environmental marketing, a low-cost strategy has been identified as a possible alternative (for example, Peattie, 1995: 146). This might be because firms have opportunities for reducing resource inputs (Peattie, 1995: 146), and/or establishing cost leadership by pre-empting legislative burdens (Porter and van der Linde, 1995). For example, the UK energy supplier Ecotricity offers to match its competitors' prices at the same time as claiming to have 'the greenest tariff in the UK' due to its commitment to wind power.

Whilst issues such as resource utilisation and reuse appear to be particular to environmental considerations, the pre-emptive argument could also be extended perhaps to other 'ethical' issues that are potentially open to legislative change, such as employee rights or social reporting. For instance, moves to implement mandatory social reporting in France may confer cost advantages on those companies that had already advanced along the learning curve and established efficient procedures for auditing and reporting prior to the introduction of legislation. Still, it takes considerable foresight and commitment to be an early adopter of ethical approaches for reasons of cost leadership rather than differentiation, and it is hard to imagine many situations or issues that have clear potential to beget such outcomes. Overall, I would suggest that whilst a low-cost orientation to the ethical market remains a possibility, it is far less common than our two main differentiation approaches.

OPPORTUNITIES AND TENSIONS IN ETHICAL MARKET ORIENTATIONS

Both differentiation approaches offer certain opportunities as well as raising significant tensions for firms choosing to orient to the ethical market. In the case of niche firms, it might be said to be reasonably straightforward to maintain an ethical focus whilst marketing to a fairly committed group of consumers. However, there are often intense competitive pressures from mainstream firms who choose to orient towards the ethical market, and who may be able to replicate (or at least approximate) certain ethical attributes, at the same time as enjoying cost advantages and superior marketing budgets. For instance, many of the groundbreaking green products produced by ethical niche firms in the early 1990s, had by the end of the decade either left the market or been absorbed or copied by mainstream competitors (Crane, 2000; Peattie, 1999). Similarly, many niche firms focusing on organic products now face intense competitive threats from powerful retail multiples who have rapidly expanded their ranges in recent years (Mintel, 2003).

In other instances, ethical niche firms may actually find themselves dissatisfied with miniscule market shares and effectively 'preaching to the converted'. The drive for more mass-market success, firm growth, and a larger audience for the ethical message have therefore led many ethical niche firms to seek opportunities for expansion beyond their existing niche. As Meyer (1999) suggests, this often requires firms to think more in terms of Hamel and Prahalad's (1991) 'expeditionary marketing' approach and 'envision' appropriate mass markets. This means looking towards shaping future markets and going beyond typical niche assumptions and practices that may restrict growth – such as depending on specialist distribution channels and relying on conventional 'ethical' marketing practices.

For instance, many fair trade companies in the UK such as Cafédirect, Day Chocolate, and Traidcraft have moved away from the movement's traditional 'solidarity' approach towards a more market-oriented model in a bid to appeal to a more mainstream market (Davies and Crane, 2003; Nicholls, 2002). This has led to a change in emphasis in product advertising towards product quality and other aspects of consumer self-interest rather than the typical fair trade message that emphasises producer poverty. As Wright (2003) argues, Cafédirect's groundbreaking success in seizing over 8 per cent of the UK roast and ground coffee market by 2002 coincided with a definite shift in communications strategy, from a 'bleeding hearts' message to one reinforcing the 'pleasures of consumerism'. Thus, 'emphasis is placed on the gratification available to the consumers, who can realise their self-worth and display their distinction through treating themselves to a superior coffee' (Wright, 2003: 21).

Such moves, as one might imagine, almost inevitably raise tensions between the need to increase competitiveness and attract more customers whilst at the same time honouring corporate values and maintaining ethical integrity. For example, some ethical nichers seeking to go mainstream may have to face the thorny question of whether they should risk dilution of their ethical values and reputation by either sourcing from, or supplying to, key mainstream companies. For example, major retailers might open the doors to larger markets, but potentially not share the same values as an ethical niche company. Research at the UK fair trade firm Day Chocolate Company, for instance, suggested that the acceptability of various types of relationships with companies such as Sainsbury's, Shell, Body Shop and McDonald's was a matter of quite complex rationalisation and renegotiation amongst managers about who was or was not 'acceptable' to work with (Davies and Crane, 2003). Similarly, ethical nichers risk alienating existing customers and staff alike if the move to the mainstream marks too much of a break with established traditions (Dey, 2002).

At the extreme, ethical nichers may even be purchased by mainstream firms, as was the case with Ben & Jerry's ice cream which was bought by Unilever, and the organic seed supplier Seeds of Change which was bought by the Mars Corporation. Competitive pressures, as well as intense scrutiny from the media and other stakeholders, can challenge the ability of mainstream firms to sustain a convincing ethical differentiation. For example, the Body Shop and Marks and Spencer have found that their attempts to offer 'ethical' differentiation have sometimes been seized upon and condemned by critics, whilst firms such as McDonald's and Nike have struggled even more to convince a sceptical and often hostile public of their ethical credentials.

What these tensions and conflicts suggest is that efforts to target the mainstream with an ethical message have considerable potential to engender strategic confusion or even what we might regard as *dis*orientation towards the ethical market. By this, I mean that firms may well run the risk of either failing to communicate successfully with their stakeholders, or even simply encountering problems in finding the right balance of ethical and other differentiating values to offer their customers. These are significant challenges for all firms faced with some degree of ethical consumption in their markets, and so in the next section I will go on to look closer at the brand building exercises that might be involved in orienting towards the ethical market and to explore the kind of contribution they might make to the overall strategies identified above.

REFLECTIONS OF THE ETHICAL GAZE: BUILDING THE ETHICAL IMAGE THROUGH CAMPAIGNS AND BRANDS

Ethical differentiation or augmentation is essentially a process of creating an 'ethical image', a 'good reputation', or what marketers typically refer to as a 'socially responsible' or 'ethical' brand. The challenge of creating such a brand has given rise to considerable discussion across the business and research communities, especially given growing concerns about falling levels of trust in corporations to behave in an ethical manner (Handy, 2002), coupled with efforts by corporations to use their social responsibility programmes more strategically in order to enhance brand value (Middlemiss, 2003; Mitchell, 1997).

'Ethical' branding in context

Many brands are argued to communicate social or ethical elements of one sort or another, especially values such as trust and honesty, but also increasingly qualities such as 'good citizenship', 'social responsibility' and 'environmental concern' (Lane Keller, 2000). Of course, most firms would like to build brands that customers trust; however, for the most part, what we mean here by trust is typically conceptualised in fairly limited terms, such as trusting the brand to be truthful about its ingredients, deliver consistent quality, or offer value-for-money. Trusting a company to be ethical goes considerably further than this, and it is evident that many brands are facing something of a trust deficit in terms of the public's faith in their commitment to 'doing the right thing'. For example, Wootliff and Deri's (2001) survey shows that rather than businesses, it is non-governmental organisations (NGOs) such as Amnesty International and WWF who are the new 'super brands', particularly in Europe where NGOs apparently enjoy a much higher degree of trust (48 per cent) than either government (36 per cent) or business (32 per cent).

Such problems with the ethical image of corporations are of course something faced mainly by large multinationals, especially as it is typically multinationals that have borne the brunt of the major scandals, media exposés, and boycotts that have accelerated the public's loss of trust. To some extent, the ethical nichers identified in the previous section may have found themselves somewhat insulated from (and possibly even benefiting from) this growing trust deficit of big business. However, it has to be said that the more people distrust business – whether large or small, 'ethical' or otherwise – the more scrutiny business is subjected to, and the harder it becomes for any firm to maintain trust and legitimacy.

In fact, this is likely to impact upon firms seeking to respond in a positive way to the ethical gaze perhaps even more than many others. After all, differentiating on the basis of ethics or social responsibility, even when this is only a minor element in the overall bundle of attributes offered, is somewhat different to many other forms of differentiation. Most notably, in order to be credible 'ethical' differentiation requires a whole company effort (Crane, 2001). Compare, for example, the difference involved in backing up a claim that a company is more 'socially responsible' than a competitor or a product 'more ethical', with the rather more straightforward task of claiming that a sofa is more comfortable, a drink better tasting, or a manufacturer better at designing stylish automotives. Whilst the latter claims can be ascertained by consumers simply by sitting on, tasting, or looking at the products on offer, the former are far more difficult to determine since such claims assume numerous contingencies deep within the operations of the firm and even beyond its boundaries to include the operations of suppliers, advertisers, investors, and so on.

In part, this is because most evaluations of ethical claims, even when very product specific, are likely to involve some broader evaluation of the reputation of the company. After all, any attempt to differentiate a product as an ethical alternative may be assessed by consumers against a backdrop of knowledge about how the company treats its workforce, its environmental record, which companies it has bought from or sold to in the past, and all kinds of other possible factors.

Consumers may not always be very consistent themselves in their purchasing, but they are often quick to denounce a 'cynical' or 'hypocritical' corporation for any observable gap between the socially responsible image projected in advertising campaigns and the 'reality' perceived in the stores and through the media.

Probably the key issue here is one of consistency. I am not sure how realistic it is for firms to attempt to always be completely consistent, not least because they often have such conflicting demands and will project different impressions, identities, even different 'realities' to their various stakeholders (Crane and Livesey, 2003). Nonetheless, marketers often seek to emphasise that in the marketing game 'perception *is* reality', so it is not so much whether firms are consistent that matters, but whether they appear to be. Such a view is popular with brand managers and other advocates of corporate branding, since much of their *raison d'être* is to find and deliver a stable and consistent image of the firm. However, as Cheney and Christensen (2000) argue, there is great potential for self-delusion and self-seduction in such beliefs. In a fragmented and volatile business environment, where corporations are ever more complex, and where some degree of consumer cynicism can be almost taken for granted, the search for a shared understanding about a corporation's values may often be a hopelessly idealistic one.

Indeed, many of the high profile campaigns waged by pressure groups against corporations have involved a hijacking of the carefully nurtured brand image of companies such as Exxon, McDonald's and Nike, in order to take advantage of the brands' immense global leverage to promulgate a radically different message to that intended by the companies. The corporate image, insofar as it is a response to, or reflection of, the ethical gaze of consumers, is open to contestation by those same consumers.

A NEW APPROACH TO 'ETHICAL' BRANDING?

So what can corporations do when faced with such a business environment, where many consumers and other stakeholders seem to be demanding more in ethical terms, but at the same time, are extremely quick to contest the brand image and denounce any efforts they deem to be hypocritical or insufficient? One way to respond could be through better communication to stakeholders. I think it is fair to say that the most risible attempts at corporate 'greenwash' are probably behind us now. The late 1980s and early 1990s were often characterised by researchers and corporate critics as a time when the communications environment was awash with misleading and over-hyped claims about ethical credentials and in particular about purported environmental concerns and benefits (Davis, 1992; National Consumer Council, 1996b).

Firms appear to have now backed away from such an approach, not least because of the cynicism and 'backlash' that it engendered amongst consumers and other stakeholders (Crane, 2000). Although there are of course exceptions, corporations now seem to be more reserved and cautious about the types of claims that they make. As even Robert Wilson, the Chairman of Rio Tinto (a company no stranger to criticism) said on the dangers of not 'walking the talk': 'It's pretty important to get the policies and implementation right before you start spending too much time on the external communications' (Middlemiss, 2003: 358).

For some this has meant taking a more defensive or 'muted' approach (Crane, 2000), whereby specific 'ethical' claims are relegated behind other brand attributes. As we saw earlier, this is consistent with a more mainstream approach to the ethical market, but it also means that social responsibility becomes more of a background quality that isn't necessarily vigorously promoted, but is embedded as part of a broader programme of *reputational risk management* (Middlemiss, 2003). Increasingly, it would appear, the key factor for many companies when orienting towards the mainstream ethical market is not so much the lure of increasing sales, but rather an attempt to prevent their brand being attacked and suffering a similar fate as befell Nike, Shell and others. Here, for example, is David Rice, a BP executive, talking about why he considers it important for firms to address human rights issues: 'In business terms, mitigation of risk is a key component of sound business development. To ignore human rights today in the era of globalisation is to significantly increase the risk of doing business – risk to our markets, risk to the value of our assets, as well as risk to our reputation' (Rice, 2002: 135).

Companies such as Rio Tinto and BP are now all too aware of the dangers inherent in attempting to maintain legitimacy in the face of an ethical gaze by consumers, NGOs, and other potential critics. Therefore, it is perhaps not too surprising that many firms have invested in more defensive approaches to communicating their responsibility, such as social and sustainability reports (see Chapter 13). Similarly, many such companies have also increasingly claimed to have moved from a one-way model of communicating their social responsibility towards a dialoguing model that actually consults with stakeholders to determine their expectations and priorities (Crane and Livesey, 2003).

This is perhaps best encapsulated in the much discussed changearound at Shell following the Brent Spar controversy in the mid-1990s. In the words of its 1998 report, the company decided it had to move from a 'trust me' world to a 'show me' world, meaning that the firm had to learn how to listen before acting. The transformation in its decision processes, the company claimed, went from DAD – decide, announce, deliver – to DDD – dialogue, decide, deliver (Livesey, 2002). It is debatable how many multinationals have actually succeeded in this endeavour, or how far they have actually progressed (or intend to progress) down this path. However, it is fairly clear that the conventional wisdom now is that rather than just undertaking a 'charm offensive' in the foreground of the market-place through advertising and PR, the most effective way to build an ethical brand is to adopt a more holistic, long-term, and some might say conservative, approach that focuses more on communicating with key reality definers in the relative background of the CSR industry.

Of course, this is not to deny that many firms are actively promoting a growing range of ostensibly 'ethical' products to consumers, such as fair trade or organic produce, energy efficient washing machines, and the like. But as we have seen, ethical claims have decreased in emphasis whilst the whole bureaucratic process of backing up and certifying claims, as well as the emphasis on reputational risk management, have rapidly escalated in importance. Similarly, other popular ways of appealing directly to ethical consumers, such as *cause-related marketing*, tend to be rather cautious in their approach to brand building. By cause-related marketing, I mean where consumer purchases are linked to corporate contributions to good causes – essentially a co-alignment of marketing goals with corporate philanthropy (Varadarajan and Menon, 1988). For example, in Tesco's Computers for School's Campaign (in the UK) customers collect vouchers for every £10 they spend in the supermarket and then local schools redeem them for computer equipment.

Such programmes have become increasingly popular with corporations and charities alike (Cobb, 2002; Lewis, 2003). And as far as ethical branding is concerned, although cause-related marketing is one of the most visible aspects of a company's social responsibility programme (Lewis, 2003), it has a relatively narrow remit that tends to focus attention on the specific project rather than the company's broader social role and impacts. As a result, such campaigns are likely to contribute only gradually to the 'ethical' brand image (and for some consumers, arguably not at all) given that the motivations for such 'win–win' initiatives will always be questioned to some extent. Perhaps though, as Cobb (2002: 26) argues, 'even the disillusioned will concede that actions which benefit society are still worthy, whatever the motive'. Hence, providing the project and the partnering are right, cause-related marketing is probably a relatively safe option for companies seeking to 'look good' in the ethical market.

The question of motive that has arisen here in relation to cause-related marketing is something that I raised earlier in the chapter. This is an important issue that in many ways goes to the heart of what exactly consumers expect from corporations in ethical terms – do they just want action that benefits society, or do they also desire firms to be ethical in a deeper sense, perhaps to be motivated by some degree of altruism, or guided by a mission to do good? I will not seek to provide a definitive answer to this question, since my aim in this chapter is not to examine consumers' preferences but to explore how firms respond to them. Therefore, in the final section, I will look more closely at how ethical preferences from consumers are interpreted and made meaningful inside companies – and in so doing, start to unpack the whole motives issue somewhat further.

REFOCUSING THE ETHICAL GAZE?
ACCOMMODATING ETHICAL CONCERNS
IN AND AROUND THE ORGANISATION

So far in this chapter I have spoken of companies as if they were essentially 'black boxes' that responded in certain ways to certain kinds of stimulus from consumers and other stakeholders. This is helpful in some senses, but also somewhat limiting in others. In particular, it seems to me that the ethical gaze on corporations at times begs certain questions about the motives of corporations, and about what we might call the 'ethical essence' of the company – is its commitment to social responsibility genuine, do its managers really believe in what they are doing, is it in the final analysis an 'ethical company'? These are not really questions that it is particularly easy to answer, and many of them rest on fairly shaky anthropomorphic assumptions that a company 'thinks', 'feels', or 'believes' in anything in the first place. But at the very least, they start us thinking about organisational processes that translate the actions or commitments of ethical consumers into tangible products, campaigns, and other corporate artefacts.

I think the first thing to say here is that most companies probably don't have a very clear idea of their consumers' ethical beliefs and values in the first place. Companies such as the UK's Co-operative Bank and the Co-operative Group may have preceded ethical branding initiatives in the mid-1990s with extensive customer surveys ascertaining views on various issues such as animal welfare, the environment, fair trade, and the supply of weapons (CWS, 1995; Kitson, 1996), but these remain the exception. Certainly many ethical niche companies do not tend to go in for (or cannot afford) formal market research. And amongst mainstream firms, the whole idea of canvassing the ethical opinions of the customer base has still not received a wide uptake. Most companies would appear to rely on evidence from more general surveys and market intelligence such as the Ethical Purchase Index (Brock et al., 2001), or MORI polls (see for example, MORI, 2000; also Chapter 12 in this book), as well as the occasional question or two that might make it onto their usual market research instruments.

Regardless though of the factuality of customers' ethical demands, there is little doubt that some sense of the ethical gaze is perceived within companies. Of course, this doesn't necessarily mean that the ethical gaze experienced inside corporations is necessarily recognisable as the same thing that the customer expresses (or intends to express) outside. The corporate decision making process itself often obscures or reconstructs the moral identities of ethical consumers. For a start, most organisations interface with consumers at something of a distance – they canvass opinions through agencies, and with mailshot questionnaires; if they interact with consumers, it is often only at the point of sale; and those making decisions in production, marketing or finance remain physically and psychologically distant from the end consumer. Similarly, because of the bureaucratic nature of most organisations, customers' ethical thoughts and feelings often need to be labelled, aggregated, quantified, and fed into the productive process as inputs and outputs, targets and projections, as objects or units to be plotted onto a chart (Desmond and Crane, 2004). Even if these processes do then lead to 'ethical' corporate behaviour, the paradox is that the moral 'face' of the consumer tends to get removed (Bauman, 1993).

By this, I mean that within the rational decision making process of organisations, the satisfaction of the desires or interests of ethical consumers is often not treated as morally meaningful, or an end in itself, but as the means to an end – namely whatever goals the corporation may have set for itself. Ethical consumers, therefore, can enter this process as moral persons but leave it in pieces, reduced to a series of abstract preferences, variables and averages (Desmond and Crane, 2004). You and I, the thinking feeling moral person becomes simply 'the consumer', or worse, a preference on a questionnaire, a number in a database.

It is probably fair to say that this construction of 'moral indifference' in organisations, and in marketing especially, is not specific to ethical consumers (see Desmond, 1998). However, the paradox is probably more striking in such a context, given that ethical consumers may be hoping to impress a distinctly moralised discourse upon companies from the outside in. Of course, it would probably be misguided to argue that this process happened in the same way, and to the same extent, in all companies. It might also be suggested that I am being a little too pessimistic in my interpretation of the corporate terrain. Some companies may well be more than able to accommodate and sustain some sense of a meaningful moral identity for consumers – especially in smaller, more niche-oriented firms. But I still doubt whether ethical consumers would recognise themselves in how they are constructed within organisations. And as we have seen, the image of themselves that is increasingly reflected back on ethical consumers by advertisers is that of a self-interested indulgent hedonist rather than a concerned citizen troubled by the plight of workers and the environment (Wright, 2003).

Perhaps the most intriguing situation in this respect is when the whole idea of there being ethical consumers 'out there' is surfaced within a firm in order to drive the development of some kind of ethical policy or social responsibility programme. Customer-focused firms consistently invoke 'consumer pressure' as one of the main driving forces behind their attention to social responsibility – a relationship also vigorously supported by many contributors to this book. Regardless of the truth of this claim, or the beneficial outcomes this may ultimately have, the point is that it essentially instrumentalises the consumer to construct a convincing motive of corporate self-interest. In most cases, I would suggest that there are a whole host of reasons and motives used by managers to explain and rationalise social programmes, but the potency of the concept of the 'ethical consumer' is in its power to suggest that failure to act in an ethical manner may bring upon the firm dire reputational consequences. Perhaps in the long run this instrumentalisation doesn't really matter, providing of course that the firm does good deeds and contributes positively to society. But it does give us a clearer conception of the fascinating and at times bewildering paradoxes that surround the whole notion of ethical consumerism when it comes to seeing how exactly it might actually impact upon corporations and managers. Sometimes it seems that the more we try and understand the ethical gaze, the cloudier the picture becomes.

CONCLUSION

The purpose of this chapter was to provide an overview of the issues and challenges for organisations involved in responding to ethical consumers. I first discussed the range of different companies likely to be confronted by such pressures, as well as the strategic postures they might choose to adopt in the face of them – primarily focusing on differentiation strategies of ethical niche versus mainstream orientations. A predominant trend identified here was a move to the mainstream by certain ethical niche firms, although as we saw, such a reorientation raised a number of challenges and tensions. I then reviewed current thinking about ethical 'branding', and in particular, the apparent shift away from explicit ethical branding towards a more conservative reputational risk management approach, as well as narrower, and safer, cause-related marketing initiatives. I then finished with an analysis of what ethical consumerism could or might mean once it had been 'processed' by companies.

Overall, I would say that there is evidence of growing interest in the corporate response to ethical consumers, particularly in terms of how social responsibility issues can be incorporated into organisational practices such as branding, cause-related marketing, and reputational risk management. Of course, consumers are not the only reason that researchers and practitioners are interested in such things, but they are certainly implicated in various ways. That said, there is still a lot of scope for much closer attention to the specific influence of consumers' ethical preferences and values on corporations; it seems to me that too often a simplistic cause-and-effect relation between the two is just automatically assumed rather than rigorously examined. More in-depth in-company research would probably bring to the surface some extremely valuable insights that may well challenge some of our conventional thinking on the subject.

This lack of co-ordination and integration of organisational research with consumer research is part of a broader problem in business research – the two sides too often simply fail to speak to each other. But there is no real reason why this should be replicated by those interested in ethics and business. Indeed, this book is testament to the potential for a closer-knit field of enquiry that isn't just interested in ethical consumers in the abstract, but also in the diverse and complex yet ultimately fascinating relations that they have with corporations and their members.

References

ACCA (2002) ACCA Announces Winners of First Annual Sustainability Awards. www.accaglobal.com/news/releases/413025, accessed 17 April 2002.

AccountAbility (2000) *Social Audit – AA1000*. London: Institute of Social and Accountability.

AccountAbility (2003) *AA1000 Assurance Standard*. London: Institute of Social and Accountability.

ACCPE (2001) *First Report*. 'Choosing Green – towards more sustainable goods and services'. www.defra.gov.uk/environment/consumerprod/accpe, accessed March 2004.

Ackerman, F. and Heinzerling, L. (2004) *Priceless: On Knowing the Price of Everything and the Value of Nothing*. New York: New Press.

Adams, C.A. (2002) 'Internal organisational factors influencing corporate social and ethical reporting: Beyond current theorising', *Accounting, Auditing and Accountability Journal*, 15 (2): 223–50.

Adams, C.A. (forthcoming) 'The ethical, social and environmental reporting-performance portrayal gap', *Accounting, Auditing and Accountability Journal*.

Adams, C.A. and Frost, G. (2003) *Corporate Social Reporting on the Internet*. Research Monograph, Institute of Chartered Accountants of Scotland (ICAS).

Adams, C.A. and Kuasirikun, N. (2000) 'A comparative analysis of corporate reporting on ethical issues by UK and German chemical and pharmaceutical companies', *The European Accounting Review*, 9 (1): 53–79.

Adams, C.A. and Zutshi, A. (2003) 'Corporate social responsibility – why should your business act responsibly?'. Working paper.

Adams, C.A., Frost, G. and Gray, S.J. (2003) 'Corporate Environmental and Social Reporting', in F. Choi (ed.), *International Finance and Accounting Handbook*. Sidney, AU: Wiley & Sons.

Adams, R., Carruthers, J. and Fisher, C. (1991) *Shopping for a Better World: A Quick and Easy Guide to Socially Responsible Shopping*. London: Kogan Page.

AFL-CIO (2004) Union label website at www.unionlabel.org, accessed 10 July 2004.

Ajzen, I. (1985) 'From intentions to actions: A theory of planned behavior', in J. Kuhl and J. Beckman (eds), *Action-control: From cognition to behaviour*. Heidelberg: Springer, pp. 11–39.

Ajzen, I. (1991) 'The theory of planned behavior', *Organizational Behavior and Human Decision Processes*, 50: 179–211.

Ajzen, I. and Fishbein, M. (1980) *Understanding Attitudes and Predicting Social Behavior*. New Jersey: Prentice-Hall.

Al-Khatib, J.A., Vitell, S.J. and Rawwas, M.Y.A. (1997) 'Consumer ethics: A cross-cultural investigation', *European Journal of Marketing*, 31 (11/12): 750–68.

Americanchemistry (2003) Responsible Care Practitioners site, www.americanchemistry.com/rc.nsf/open?OpenForm, accessed 30 October 2003.

Annan, K. (2003) 'Message for International Cooperation Day', 25 June, UN Press Release SG/SM/8762 OBV/359. New York: United Nations.

Anonymous (1991) 'A question of ethics all over the shop', *Marketing*, 15 August: 12.

Anonymous (2000) 'Common grounds for social scrutiny', *Quality Focus*, 4 (1): 52–7.

Anonymous (2003) 'Company codes of conduct: what do they mean for workers in the garment and sportswear industries?', www.poptel.org.uk/women-ww/company_codes_of_conduct.htm, accessed 4 November 2003.

Antil, J.A. (1984) 'Socially responsible consumers: profile and implications for public policy', *Journal of Macromarketing*, 4 (2): 18–39.

Aristotle (1999) *Nicomachean Ethics* (2nd edn). translated by T. Irwin. Indianapolis: Hackett.

Arlidge, J. (1999) 'Watchdog slams Monsanto ads', *Guardian Unlimited*, 28 February.

Association of Qualitative Research, www.aqrp.co.uk.

References

Auger, P., Burke, P., Devinney, T.M. and Louviere, J.J. (2003) 'What will consumers pay for social product features?', *Journal of Business Ethics*, 42: 281–304.

Baby Milk Action (1999) 'Advertising Standards Authority warns Nestlé about ethical claims', press release 12 May 1999, www.babymilkaction.org.

Barker, P. (1994) 'Is Which? still best buy?', *The Times*, 8 June, 15.

Barnett, C., Cloke, P., Clarke, N., and Malpass, A. (2005) 'Consuming ethics: articulating the subjects and spaces of ethical consumption', *Antipode*. In press.

Barratt Brown, M. (1993) *Fair Trade: Reform and Realities in the International Trading System*. London: Zed.

Bauman, Z. (1993) *Postmodern Ethics*. London: Blackwell.

Bauman, Z. (1998) *Work, Consumerism and the New Poor*. Buckingham: Open University Press.

Beardshaw, S (1992) *Economics: A Student's Guide*. London: Pitman.

Beatrix, P. (2001) 'Large UK Plans to get failing grade on social responsibility concerns', *Pensions and Investments*, 29 (15): 14.

Beck, U. (1999) *World Risk Society*. Cambridge, MA: Polity.

Beck, U. (2000) *The Brave New World of Work*. Malden, MA: Polity.

Beckmann, S.C. and Elliott, R.H. (2000) *Interpretive Consumer Research: Paradigms, Methodologies and Applications* (1st edn). Copenhagen: Copenhagen Business School Press.

Beets, S.D. and Souther, C.C. (1999) 'Corporate environmental reports: the need for standards and an environmental assurance service', *Accounting Horizons*, 13 (2): 129–45.

Beishon, J. (1994) 'Consumers and power', in R. John (ed.), *The Consumer Revolution: Redressing the Balance*. London: Hodder and Stoughton, pp. 1–11.

Belk, R.W. (1987) 'ACR Presidential Address: Happy Thought', in Wallendorf and Anderson (eds), *Advances in Consumer Research*, Vol. 14. Provo, UT: Association of Consumer Research, pp. 1–4.

Bellah, R.N., Madsen, R., Sullivan, W.M., Swindler, A. and Tipton, S. (1985) *Habits of the Heart*. Berkeley, CA: University of California Press: p. 292.

Belson, K. (2003) 'Japan builds a recovery on the boom or bust of exports,' *The New York Times*, 1 December, C16.

Bendell, J. (ed.) (2000) *Terms for Endearment: Business, NGOs and Sustainable Development*. Sheffield, UK: Greenleaf.

Bendell, J. (2004) *Barricades and Boardrooms: A Contemporary History of the Corporate Accountability Movement*. Geneva, SZ: UNRISD Publications. www.unrisd.org.

Benjamin, A. (2002) 'Market forces', *The Guardian*, 21 August.

Bentler, P.M. and Chou, C.P. (1987) 'Practical issues in structural modelling', *Sociological Methods and Research*, 16: 78–117.

Berke, S., Milberg, S. and Smith, C. (1993) 'The role of ethical concern in consumer purchase behavior: understanding alternative processes', in L. McAlister and M. Rothschild (eds), *Advances in Consumer Research*, Vol. 20. Provo, UT: Association of Consumer Research, pp. 119–22.

Berle, A.A. and Means, G.C. (1932) *Modern Corporation and Private Property*. New York: Clearing Press.

Berry, J.M. (1977) *Lobbying for The People – The Political Behaviour of Public Interest Groups*. Princeton: Princeton University Press.

Berry, J.M. (1977) *The Interest Group Society*. White Plain, NY: Longman.

Berry, J.M (1989) *The Interest Group Society* (2nd edn). Glenview, Ill: Scott Foresman.

Birchall, J. (1994) *Co-op: The People's Business*. Manchester: Manchester University Press.

Birchall, J. (2003) *Rediscovering the co-operative advantage: poverty reduction through self-help*. Geneva: International Labour Office.

BITC (2003) Report by Business in the Community on August 2003, YouGov/Social Market Foundation poll, at www.bitc.org.uk/news/news_directory/ethicalprods.htm.

Bloom, A. (1987) *The Closing of the American Mind*. New York: Simon and Schuster.

Bloom, P.N. and Stern, L.W. (1978) 'Consumerism in the year 2000: the emergence of anti-industrialism', in N. Kangun and L. Richardson (eds), *Consumerism: New Challenges for Marketing*. Chicago: American Marketing Association.

Blythman, J. (2004) *Shopped: The Shocking Power of British Supermarkets*. London: Fourth Estate.

BNA Occupational Safety and Health Daily (1998) 'Herman says sweatshop label undecided at conclusion of USEU labor symposium', 24 February, [online].

Body Shop (2004) www.thebodyshop.com/web/tbsgl/about.reason.jsp, accessed 8 July 2004.

Boulstridge, E. and Carrigan, M. (2000) 'Do consumers really care about corporate responsibility? Highlighting the attitude behaviour gap', *Journal of Communication Management*, 4 (4): 355–68.

Bourdieu, P. (1984) *Distinction*. London: Routledge.

Bowers, S. and Finch, J. (2003) 'Littlewoods drops ethical code', *The Guardian*, 1 February, 25.

Boyle, D. and Simms, A. (2001) *The Naked Consumer: Why Shoppers Deserve Honest Product Labelling*. London: New Economics Foundation.

Branigin, W. (1999) 'Top clothing retailers labeled labor abusers: sweatshops allegedly run on US territory', *The Washington Post*, 14 January, A14.

Brass, E. and Koziell, S.P. (1997) 'Gathering force, the Big Issue writers, London', cited in W. Grant (2000) *Pressure Groups and British Politics*. Basingstoke: Macmillan, pp. 139 and 148.

Breton, J.R. (2000) World Affairs Social Audit, World Affairs Social Audit, US, http://world-affairs.com/audit.htm, accessed 30 April 2003.

Brimelow, P. and Spencer, L. (1990) 'Ralph Nader, Inc.', *Forbes*, 146 (6): 117–29.

Brock, G., Clavin, B. and Doane, D. (2001) *Ethical Purchasing Index 2001*. Manchester: Co-operative Bank.

Brown, D. (2002) *American Heat: Ethical Problems with the United States Response to Global Warming*. Blue Ridge Summit, PA: Rowman and Littlefield.

Brown, N. and Deegan, C. (1998) 'The public disclosure of environmental performance information – a dual test of media agenda setting theory and legitimacy theory', *Accounting and Business Research*, 29 (1): 21–41.

Brown, S. (1995) *Postmodern Marketing*. New York: Routledge.

Buchan, D. (2001) 'Spinning and pumping: corporate responsibility: Premier Oil publicly makes the case for constructive engagement in Burma in its social performance report', *Financial Times*, 16 May.

Buchanan, P. (2003) CNBC cable, 4 November.

Buchholz, R.A. (1998) 'The ethics of consumption activities: a future paradigm?', *Journal of Business Ethics*, 17 (8): 871–83.

Buckley, W.F. (2003) *Getting it Right*. Washington, DC: Regnery Publications.

Burgess, J., Harrison, C. and Filius, P. (1995) *Making the Abstract Real: A Cross-Cultural Study of Public Understanding of Global Environmental Change*. London: University College.

Burns, M. and Blowfield, M. (1999) 'Approaches to ethical trade, impact and lessons learned', NRET paper, www.nri.org/NRET/burns_final.pdf.

Bussell, M. (2003) 'The pursuit of competitive advantage: the case of Jordan Grand Prix', *Journal of Change Management*, 3 (3): 212–24.

Byrne, P. (1997) *Social Movements In Britain*. Routledge: London.

Cafaro, P. (2001) 'Economic consumption, pleasure and the good life', *Journal of Social Philosophy*, 32: 471–86.

Cafaro, P. (2004) *Thoreau's Living Ethics: Walden and the Pursuit of Virtue*. Athens, GA: University of Georgia Press.

Cafédirect (2004) Cafédirect website, www.cafedirect.co.uk, accessed 6 July 2004.

Cairncross, F. (1991) *Costing the Earth*. London: Business Books and the Economist Books.

Campbell, C. (1998) 'Consuming the goods and the goods of consuming', in D. Crocker and T. Linden (eds), *Ethics of Consumption: The Good Life, Justice and Global Stewardship*. London: Rowman and Littlefield, pp. 139–54.

Carrigan, M. and Attalla, A. (2001) 'The myth of the ethical consumer – do ethics matter in purchase behaviour?', *Journal of Consumer Marketing*, 18 (7): 560–78.

Carrigan, M., Szmigin, I. and Wright, J. (2003) 'Shopping for a better world? An interpretative study of the potential for ethical consumption within the older market', *Journal of Consumer Marketing*, 21 (6): 401–17.

Carsky, M.L., Dickinson, R. and Smith, M.C. (1995) 'Toward consumer efficiency: a model for improved buymanship', *Journal of Consumer Affairs*, 29 (2): 442–59.

236

Caruana, R.J. (2003) *Morality in Consumption: Towards a Sociological Perspective*. Nottingham: International Centre for Corporate Social Responsibility.

Chaharbaghi, K. and Lynch, R. (1999) 'Sustainable competitive advantage: towards a dynamic resource-based strategy', *Management Decision*, 37 (1): 45–50.

Chakraborty, K. (1997) 'Sustained competitive advantage: a resource-based framework', *Advances in Competitiveness Research*, 5 (1): 32–63.

Chappell, T. (1993) *The Soul of a Business: Managing for Profit and the Common Good*. New York: Bantam.

Cheney, G. and Christensen, L.T. (2000) 'Self-absorption and self-seduction in the corporate identity game', in M. Schultz, M.J. Hatch, and M.H. Larsen (eds), *The Expressive Organization: Linking Identity, Reputation, and the Corporate Brand*. Oxford: Oxford University Press, pp. 246–70.

Childs, C. and Whiting, S. (1998) 'Eco-labelling and the Green consumer'. Research paper for the Sustainable Business Initiative, University of Bradford.

Chisnall, P. (2001) *Marketing Research*. London: McGraw-Hill.

Churchill, G.A., Jr (1991) *Marketing Research*. Chicago: Dryden Press.

Cobb, R. (2002) 'Selling responsibility', *Marketing Business*, June: 25–27.

Cohen, L. (2001) 'Citizen consumers in the United States in the century of mass consumption', in M. Daunton and M. Hilton, (eds), *The Politics of Consumption*. Oxford and New York: Berg.

Collini, S. (2003) 'HiEdBiz', *London Review of Books*, 6 November, 3.

Comic Relief (2003) *Fair Measures – For All*! A nation-wide survey.

Commenne, V. (2001) The point of responsible consumers – presentation for the European Network for Responsible Consumption, Brussels.

Cone Communications (1996) 'Cause-related marketing', report available from Cone Communications, Boston, MA.

Consumers International (2004) 'About CI: rights and responsibilities', www.consumersinternational.org/about_CI/default.asp?regionid=135#rights, accessed 15 April 2004.

Co-op America (1989) 'Interview with Ralph Nader in Building Economic Alternatives', Fall: 11.

Co-operative Bank (1997) *Partnership Report*, 31 December. Manchester: Co-operative Bank.

Co-operative Bank (2003) *The Ethical Consumerism Report 2003*. Manchester: Co-operative Bank. Also available at www.neweconomics.org, accessed 16 May 2004.

Co-operative Group (2004) *Shopping With Attitude*. Manchester: Co-operative Group.

Cowe, R. (2001) 'Firms "need forcing" to do the right thing', *The Observer*, 14 October.

Cowe, R. and Williams, S. (2001) *Who Are the Ethical Consumers?* Manchester, UK: Co-operative Bank.

Crane, A. (2000) 'Facing the backlash: green marketing and strategic re-orientation in the 1990s', *Journal of Strategic Marketing*, 8 (3): 277–96.

Crane, A. (2001) 'Unpacking the Ethical Product', *Journal of Business Ethics*, 30: 361–73.

Crane, A. and Desmond, J. (2002) 'Societal marketing and morality', *European Journal of Marketing*, 36 (5/6): 548–69.

Crane, A. and Livesey, S. (2003) 'Are you talking to me? Stakeholder communication and the risks and rewards of dialogue', in J. Andriof, S. S. Rahman, S. Waddock and B. Husted (eds), *Unfolding Stakeholder Thinking 2: Relationships, Communication, Reporting and Performance*. Sheffield: Greenleaf, pp. 39–52.

Crane, A. and Matten, D. (2004) *Business Ethics*. Oxford: Oxford University Press.

Crocker, D. and Linden, T. (eds) (1998) *Ethics of Consumption: The Good Life, Justice and Global Stewardship*. London: Rowman and Littlefield.

CSR (2003a) 'Sainsbury's supermarket fined for child labour', CSR Europe, www.csreurope.org/news/sainsburychildlabour_page4894.aspx, accessed 28 November 2003.

CSR (2003b) 'Wal-Mart accused of employing illegal immigrants', CSR Europe, www.csreurope.org/news/walmartimmigrants_page4892.aspx, accessed 28 November 2003.

Cudeck, R. and Brown, M.W. (1983) 'Cross-validation of covariance structures', *Multivariate Behavioral Research*, 18: 147–57.

CWS (1995) *Responsible Retailing*. Manchester: CWS Ltd.

Daly, H.E. and Cobb, J.B., Jr (1989) *For the Common Good: Redirecting the Economy towards Community, the Environment and a Sustainable Future*. London: Green Print.

Davies, I.A. and Crane, A. (2003) 'Ethical decision-making in fair trade companies', *Journal of Business Ethics*, 45 (1/2): 79–92.

Davis, J.J. (1992) 'Ethics and environmental marketing', *Journal of Business Ethics*, 11: 81–7.

Dawkins, J. (2003) *The Public's Views of Corporate Responsibility 2003*. MORI White Papers.

Dawson, E. (1998) 'The relevance of social audit for Oxfam GB', *Journal of Business Ethics*, 17 (13): 1457–69.

Day, J. and Curry, A. (1998) *Current Population Reports, P20-505, Educational Attainment in the United States: March 1997*. Washington, DC: US Bureau of the Census.

Dempsey, J. (2002) 'Cool, sexy and fair', Radio Netherlands Wereldomroep, www.rnw.nl/development/html/kuyichi021017.html, accessed 8 November 2004.

Denzin, N.K. and Lincoln, Y.S. (1994) 'The fifth moment', in N.K. Denzin and Y.S. Lincoln (eds), *The Handbook of Qualitative Research*. London: Sage, pp. 575–87.

Denzin, N.K. and Lincoln, Y.S. (1998) *Collecting and Interpreting Qualitative Materials*. Thousand Oaks, CA: Sage.

Denzin, N.K. and Lincoln, Y.S. (2003) *Strategies of Qualitative Inquiry* (2nd edn). Thousand Oaks, CA: Sage.

Desmond, J. (1998) 'Marketing and Moral Indifference', in M. Parker (ed.), *Ethics and Organizations*. London: Sage.

Desmond, J. and Crane, A. (2004) 'Morality and the consequences of marketing action', *Journal of Business Research*, 57: 1222–30.

DETR (1998) 'Sustainable business', Department of the Environment, Transport and the Regions, www.environment.detr.gov.uk/sustainable/business/consult/comm.htm, accessed 18 February 1999.

Dey, C.R. (2002) Social bookkeeping at Traidcraft plc: an ethnographic study of a struggle for the meaning of fair trade. Paper presented at 12th CSEAR Research Summer School, Dundee.

DFES (2004) Department for education and skills website, www.standards.dfes.gov.uk, accessed 9 July 2004.

Dickinson, R. (1988) 'Self-interest – some academic perspectives', Macromarketing Annual Conference, 11– 4 August, San Jose, CA.

Dickinson, R. (1996) 'Consumer citizenship: the US', *Business and the Contemporary World*, 8 (3,4): 255–73.

Dickinson, R. and Hollander, S.C. (1991) 'Consumer votes', *Journal of Business Research*, 22: 335–46.

Dickson, M.A. (1999) 'Consumer motivations for purchasing apparel from socially responsible businesses', in N.J. Owens (ed.), *ITAA Proceedings*. Monument, CO: International Textile and Apparel Association. p. 70.

Dickson, M.A. (2000) 'Personal values, beliefs, knowledge, and attitudes relating to intentions to purchase apparel from socially responsible businesses', *Clothing and Textiles Research Journal*, 18 (1): 19–30.

Dickson, M.A. (2001) 'Utility of no sweat labels for apparel consumers: profiling label-users and predicting their purchases', *Journal of Consumer Affairs*, 35 (1): 96–119.

Dickson, M.A. and Littrell, M.A. (1996) 'Socially responsible behaviour: values and attitudes of the alternative trading organisation consumer', *Journal of Fashion Marketing and Management*, 1 (1): 50–69.

Dickson, M.A. and Littrell, M.A. (1997) 'Consumers of clothing from alternative trading organizations: societal attitudes and purchase evaluative criteria', *Clothing and Textiles Research Journal*, 15: 20–33.

Dickson, M.A. and Littrell, M.A. (2003) 'Measuring quality of life of apparel workers in Mumbai, India: quantitative and qualitative data', in M.J. Sirgy, D. Rahtz and A.C. Samli (eds), *Advances in Quality-of-Life Theory and Research*. The Netherlands: Kluwer Academic Publishers, pp. 211–32.

Dillman, D.A. (1978) *Mail and Telephone Surveys: The Total Design Method*. New York: Wiley.

Dixon, D.F. (1992) 'Consumer sovereignty, democracy, and the marketing concept: a macro-marketing perspective', *Revue Canadienne des Sciences de L'Administration*, 2 (June): 116–25.

238

Doane, D. (2001) *Taking Flight: the Rapid Growth of Ethical Consumerism*. London: New Economics Foundation.

DTI (2003) 'Action Single Market – Opening the Door to Europe', www.dti.gov.uk, accessed 10 December 2003.

Duncombe, R. and Heeks, R. (2002) 'Information, ICTs and ethical trade: implications for self-regulation', *Centre on Regulation and Competition Working Paper Series No. 41*, University of Manchester.

Durning, A. (1992) *How Much is Enough? The Consumer Society and the Future of the Earth*. London: Earthscan.

Eagly, A.H. and Chaiken, S. (1993) *The Psychology of Attitudes*. Orlando: Harcourt Brace College Publishers.

EBP (2003) *Ethical Business Support*, Ethical Business Support, India, 30 April.

ECRA (1989a) Campbell's soup boycott 1979–86, *Ethical Consumer*, 2 (May/June).

ECRA (1989b) 'Daily Telegraph personal boycott survey Feb 1989', *Ethical Consumer*, 3 (July/Aug.).

ECRA (1990a) 'Consumer boycotts in the UK – learning the language of success', *Ethical Consumer*, 11 (Dec. 1990/Jan. 1991).

ECRA (1990b) 'Keep peat in bogs', *Ethical Consumer*, 11 (Dec. 1990/Jan. 1991).

ECRA (1993) *The Ethical Consumer Guide to Everyday Shopping*. Manchester: Ethical Consumer Research Association.

ECRA (1993) 'News', *Ethical Consumer*, 25 (July/Aug.).

ECRA (1994) 'Spotlight on Siemens – lobbying for nuclear power', *Ethical Consumer*, 29 (Apr./May).

ECRA (1995a) 'Eco-light bulbs', *Ethical Consumer*, 38 (Nov./Dec.).

ECRA (1995b) *Ethical Consumer*, 37 (Aug./Sept./Oct.).

ECRA (1997) 'Clothes shops: corporate responsibility', *Ethical Consumer*, 50 (Dec. 1997/Jan. 1998): 6–12.

ECRA (1998) *Ethical Consumer*, 51 (Feb./Mar.).

ECRA (1998/99) *Ethical Consumer*, 56 (Dec. 1998/Jan. 1999): 3.

ECRA (2001) 'Manifesto for change', *Ethical Consumer*, 72 (Aug./Sept.).

ECRA (2002a) 'Sweating it out', *Ethical Consumer*, 76 (Apr./May): 12–15.

ECRA (2002b) 'Why buy ethically? An introduction to the philosophy behind ethical purchasing', www.ethicalconsumer.org, accessed 7 November 2003.

ECRA (2002c) 'A world of ethical guides', *Ethical Consumer*, 75 (Feb./Mar.).

ECRA (2002d) 'Product, price or principle?', *Ethical Consumer*, 76 (Apr./May).

ECRA (2002e) 'Peat bogs saved', *Ethical Consumer*, 76 (May/June).

ECRA (2003) 'Tissues', *Ethical Consumer*, 80 (Dec. 2002/Jan. 2003).

Edwards, R. (2002) 'How to take corporate responsibility: just do it', *The Sunday Herald*, Melbourne, 18 August: 4.

Ekins, P. (1992) 'Towards a progressive market', in P. Ekins and M. Max-Neef (eds), *Real-life Economics: Understanding Wealth Creation*. London and New York: Routledge.

Elkington, J. and Hailes, J. (1988) *The Green Consumer Guide*. London: Gollancz.

Ellwood, W. (1984) *Generating Power: A Guide to Consumer Organising*. Penang, Malaysia: IOCU.

Environics (1999) *The Millennium Poll on Corporate Social Responsibility*. New York: Environics International Ltd.

EPA (1995) Products and technology – ministerial orders', Danish Environmental Protection Agency, www.mst.dk/homepage/default.asp?Sub= www.mst.dk/rules/, accessed 10 November 2003.

Estes, R. (1976) 'Standards for corporate social reporting', *Management Accounting*, 58 (November): 19–28.

Etzioni, A. (1988) *The Moral Dimension*. New York: The Free Press.

Eurobarometer (1997) *Survey on Attitudes of EU Consumers to Fair-trade Bananas*. Brussels: European Commission Directorate-General for Agriculture.

EUROPA (2003) *The Law of Sustainable Development – General Principles*. Belgium: EUROPA.

European Fair Trade Association (2001) *Fair Trade in Europe 2001*. Maastricht: EFTA.

Evans, R. (2003) *What is the Ethical Purchasing Index? Co-operative Bank Partnership Report 2002*. Manchester: Co-operative Bank.

Fair Labor Association (2003) 'First annual public report', available from the Fair Labor Association, Washington, DC, www.fairlabor.org.

Fairtrade Foundation (2002) 'Spilling the beans on the coffee trade'. Press release, www.fairtrade.org.uk/pr040502.htm, accessed 28 January 2005.

Fairtrade Foundation (2003) 'Staggering rise in fairtrade sales'. Press release, www.fairtrade.org.uk/ press_releases/pr030303.htm, accessed 28 January 2005.

Fairtrade Foundation (2004a) 'Sales of Fairtrade products in the UK', www.fairtrade.org.uk. accessed 21 June 2004.

Fairtrade Foundation (2004b) www.fairtrade.org.uk, accessed 30 July 2004.

Federal News Service (1994) 'Press conference with Senator Howard Metzenbaum (D-OH) and Senator Byron Dorgan (D-ND)', 28 November available on LexisNexis.

Feldman, S.J., Soyka, A.P. and Ameer, P.G. (1997) 'Does improving a firm's environmental management system and environmental performance result in a higher stock price?', *Journal of Investing*, 6 (4): 87–97.

Festing, H. (1993) 'Is there life after supermarkets?', *New Economics*, 28 (Winter): 8–9.

Fetter, F.A. (1907) *The Principles of Economics*. New York: The Century Company.

Fisher, R.J. (1993) 'Social desirability bias and the validity of indirect questioning', *Journal of Consumer Research*, 20: 303–15.

Flint, G.D. (2000) 'What is the meaning of competitive advantage?', *Advances in Competitiveness Research*, 8 (1): 121–9.

Foot, P. (1978) *Virtues and Vices and Other Essays in Moral Philosophy*. Oxford: Blackwell.

Foot, P. (2001) *Natural Goodness*. Oxford: Oxford University Press.

Forbes, J.D. (1987) *The Consumer Interest*. Beckenham: Croom Helm.

Fournier, S. and Mick, D.G. (1998) 'Paradoxes of technology: consumer cognizance, emotions, and coping strategies', *Journal of Consumer Research*, 25 (2): 123–44.

Foxall, G.R. and Goldsmith, R.E. (1994) *Consumer Psychology for Marketing*. London: Routledge.

Frank, R. (1988) *Passions with Reason*. New York: Norton.

Frankental, P. (2001) 'Corporate social responsibility – a PR invention?', *Corporate Communications*, 6 (1): 18–23.

Friedman, M. (1999a) *Consumer Boycotts*. London: Routledge.

Friedman, M. (1999b) 'Deciding to initiate a consumer boycott: questions of right or wrong', *Consumer Interest Annual*, Vol. 45.

Friends of the Earth (1995) 'Boycott mahogany'. Press release, 13 February 1995, London.

Friends of the Earth (1997) 'Press release: action needed as moors reprieved', 15 December 1997, www.foe.co.uk/resource/press_releases/19971215164751.html.

Friends of the Earth (1998) *The Good Wood Guide*. London: Friends of the Earth Publications.

Friends of the Earth (2004) Corporate Responsibility Coalition website, www.foe.co.uk/campaigns/corporates/core/, accessed 7 July 2004.

FSC (2004) www.fsc.org/fsc/about, accessed 7 July 2004.

Gabriel, Y. and Lang, T. (1995) *The Unmanageable Consumer: Contemporary Consumption and its Fragmentations*. London: Sage.

Galbraith, J.K. (1974) *The New Industrial State* (2nd edn) Harmondsworth: Penguin.

Garrett, D.E. (1987) 'The effectiveness of marketing policy boycotts', *Journal of Marketing*, 52: 46–57.

Genewatch UK (2004) www.genewatch.org/WTO/WTO_default.htm, accessed July 2004.

Gesser, A. (1998) 'Canada's environmental choice program: A model for a "trade-friendly" eco-labeling scheme', *Harvard International Law Journal*, 39 (2): 501–44.

Giddens, A. (1990) *The Consequences of Modernity*. Cambridge, MA: Polity.

Giddens, A. (1991) *Modernity and Self-Identity: Self and Society in the Late Modern Age*. Stanford, CA: Stanford University Press.

Giles, M. and Cairns, E. (1995) 'Blood donation and Ajzen's theory of planned behaviour: an examination of perceived behavioural control', *British Journal of Social Psychology*, 34: 173–88.

Gill, E. (2003) 'Slap on a label', *Green Futures*, 42 (Sept./Oct.).

Gill, J. and Johnson, P. (1991) *Research Methods for Managers*. London: Chapman.

Global Compact (2004) 'What is global compact?', www.unglobalcompact.org/Portal/Default.asp, accessed 10 March 2004.

Global Exchange Website (2003) 'Kraft, activist groups still differ on "fair-trade" coffee', www.globalexchange.org/campaigns/fairtrade/coffee/1165.html, accessed 8 October 2003.

Goffman, E. (1956) *The Presentation of Self in Everyday Life*. Edinburgh: University of Edinburgh Social Sciences Research Centre.

Gordan, W. (1999) *Goodthinking: A Guide to Qualitative Research*. Henley-on-Thames: Admap Publications.

Gorsuch, R.L. and Ortberg, J. (1983) 'Moral obligation and attitudes: their relation to behavioral intentions', *Journal of Personality and Social Psychology*, 44 (5): 1025–8.

Government of Denmark (2003a) Legislation, Natural Resources, Denmark, www.law.du.edu/naturalresources/Individual%20Countries/Denmark.htm, accessed 10 November 2003.

Government of the Netherlands (2003b) 'European Environmental Law', European Environmental Law Homepage – The Netherlands, www.eel.nl/Countries.net.htm, accessed 10 November 2003.

Government of Norway (2003c) 'Norway's Accounting Act: extensive information about the environment in the directors reports in all companies annual reports', The Norwegian Law of Accounts, www.enviroreporting.com/others/norway_act.pdf, accessed 10 November 2003.

Granberg, D. and Holmberg, S. (1990) 'The intention-behavior relationship among U.S. and Swedish voters', *Social Psychology Quarterly*, 53 (1): 44–54.

Grant, W. (2000) *Pressure Groups and British Politics*. Basingstoke: Macmillan.

Gray, R., Owen, D. and Adams, C.A. (1996) *Accounting and Accountability: Changes and Challenges in Corporate Social and Environmental Reporting*. Europe: Prentice-Hall.

Greaves, B.B. (2003) www.libertyhaven.com.

Green, D. (2000) 'Codes of conduct and the ethical trading initiative', CAFOD, London, www.cafod.org.uk/policy/eti.shtml, accessed 4 November 2003.

Green, P.E. (1974) 'On the design of choice experiments involving multifactor alternatives', *Journal of Consumer Research*, 1 (Sept.): 61–8.

Green, P.E. and Srinivasan, V. (1978) 'Conjoint analysis in consumer research: issues and outlook', *Journal of Consumer Research*, 5 (Sept.): 103–23.

Greenpeace (1997) 'International award for ozone friendly fridges'. Press release, 16 September, London.

Greenpeace (2004) 'Greenfreeze: from a snowball to an industrial avalanche', Wolfgang Lohbeck, June 2004, www.eu.greenpeace.org/downloads/climate/ GreenfreezeBackgrounder.pdf.

Greider, W. (1992) *Who Will Tell the People?* New York: Touchstone.

GRI (2002) *GRI Sustainability Reporting Guidelines*. Amsterdam: Global Reporting Initiative.

Groves, R.M. and Couper, M.P. (1998) *Non-response in Household Interview Surveys*. New York: Wiley.

Guardian (2001) Interview with Peter Blackburn, Nestlé CEO. 21 April.

Gussow, J.D. (1991) *Chicken Little, Tomato Sauce and Agriculture: Who will Produce Tomorrow's Food?* New York: Bootstrap.

Hackston, D. and Milne, J.M. (1996) 'Some determinants of social and environmental disclosures in New Zealand companies', *Accounting, Auditing and Accountability Journal*, 9 (1): 77–108.

Haddock, F. (1999) 'Corporate angels', *Global Finance*, 13: 24–33.

Hadeniuus, A. and Uggla, F. (1996) 'Making civil society work', cited in Zadek et al. (1996) *Purchasing Power*. London: New Economics Foundation.

Hair, J.F., Jr, Anderson, R.L., Tatham, R.L. and Black, W.C. (1995) *Multivariate Data Analysis with Readings*. New Jersey: Prentice-Hall.

Hamel, G. and Prahalad, C.K. (1991) 'Corporate imagination and expeditionary marketing', *Harvard Business Review*, 69 (July/Aug.): 81–92.

Hammersley, M. and Atkinson, P. (1995) *Ethnography* (2nd edn). London: Routledge.

Handy, C. (2002) 'What's a business for?', *Harvard Business Review*, 80 (Dec.): 49–55.

Hankins, M., French, D. and Horne, R. (2000) 'Statistical guidelines for studies of the theory of reasoned action and the theory of planned behaviour', *Psychology and Health*, 15: 151–61.

Hanson and Schreder (1997) 'A modern model of consumption for a sustainable society', *Journal of Consumer Policy*, 20 (4): 443–4: 69.

Harper, C.L. (1996) *Environment and Society: Human Perspectives on Environmental Issues*. Upper Saddle River, NJ: Prentice-Hall.

Harrison, D. (2000) 'Survey: Pension Fund Investment: Ethics under the Microscope: Socially Responsible Investment', *Financial Times*, London: 1.

Harrison, R. (2003) 'Corporate responsibility and the consumer movement', *Consumer Policy Review* 13 (July/Aug.): 127–31.

Hartman, L.P. and Wokutch, R.E. (2003) 'Nike, Inc.: corporate social responsibility and workplace standard initiatives in Vietnam', in L.P. Hartman, D.G. Arnold and R.E. Wokutch (eds), *Rising above Sweatshops: Innovative Approaches to Global Labor Challenges*. Westport, CT: Praeger, pp. 145–89.

Hartman, L.P. Wokutch, R.E. and French, J.L. (2003) 'Adidas-Salomon: child labor and health and safety initiatives in Vietnam and Brazil', in L.P. Hartman, D.G. Arnold and R.E. Wokutch (eds), *Rising above Sweatshops: Innovative Approaches to Global Labor Challenges*. Westport, CT: Praeger, pp. 191–248.

Von Hayek, F.A. (1935) *Collectivist Economic Planning*. London: Routledge.

Hearn, J., Roseneil, S. and the British Sociological Association Conference (1999) *Consuming Cultures: Power and Resistance*. New York: St. Martin's Press.

Heeks, R. and Duncombe, R. (2003) 'Ethical trade: issues in the regulations of global supply chains'. Working paper, University of Manchester, Manchester.

Heiskanen, E. and Pantzar, M. (1997) 'Towards sustainable consumption: two new perspectives', *Journal of Consumer Marketing*, 11 (2): 45–54.

Henriques, A. (2000) 'Social audit and quality', *Quality Focus*, 4 (2): 60–4.

Herrmann, R.O. (1993) 'The tactics of consumer resistance: group action and marketplace exit', *Advances in Consumer Research*, 20: 130–4.

Hines, C. (1976) *Food Co-ops: How to Save Money by Getting Together and Buying in Bulk*. London: Friends of the Earth.

Hirschman, A. (1979) *Exit Voice and Loyalty*. Cambridge, MA: Harvard University.

Hirschman, A. (1982) *Shifting Involvements*. Princeton, NJ: Princeton University Press.

Hirschman, A. (1989) 'Reactionary rhetoric', *Atlantic Monthly*, May: 63–70.

Ho, L., Powell, C. and Volpp, L. (1996) '(Dis)assembling rights of women workers along the global assembly line: human rights and the garment industry', *Harvard Civil Rights – Civil Liberties Law Review*, 31 (Summer): 383–414.

Hobson, K. (2002) 'Thinking habits into action: the role of knowledge and process in questioning household consumption practices', *Local Environment*, 8: 95–112.

Hobson, K. (2003) 'Competing discourses of sustainable consumption: does the "Rationalisation of Lifestyles" make sense?', *Environmental Politics*, 11: 95–120.

Hoelter, J.W. (1983) 'The analysis of covariance structure: goodness-of-fit indices', *Social Methods Research*, 11: 325–44.

Holbrook, M. (1998) *Consumer Value: A Framework for Analysis and Research*. London: Routledge.

Holbrook, M. (forthcoming) *Journal of Macromarketing*.

Hollis, M. (1995) *Reason in Action: Essays in the Philosophy of Social Science*. Cambridge: Cambridge University Press.

Holyoake, G. (1872) *The History of Co-operation in Rochdale*. London: Trubner.

Holzner, B. (1973) 'The construction of social actors: an essay on social identities', in T. Luckmann (ed.), *Phenomenology and Sociology*. Kingsport, TN: Penguin.

Hoovers (2004) www.hoovers.com Body Shop International company profile, accessed 21 June 2004.

Hoyle, R.H. and Smith, G.T. (1994) 'Formulating clinical research hypotheses as structural equation models: a conceptual overview', *Journal of Consulting and Clinical Psychology*, 62: 429–40.

Hursthouse, R. (1999) *On Virtue Ethics*. Oxford: Oxford University Press.

Husted, B.W. and Allen, D.B. (2000) 'Is it ethical to use ethics as strategy?', *Journal of Business Ethics*, 27 (1/2): 21–31.

Hutt, W.H. (1934) 'Economic method and concept of competition', *The South African Journal of Economics*, 2 (1): 23.

Hutton, W. (2002) 'Capitalism must put its house in order', *The Observer*, 24 November.

ICC (2004) *International Listing of Corporate Governance Guidelines and Codes of Best Practice*, www.iccwbo.org/CorpGov/Best_Practices_And_Codes.asp, accessed 10 March 2004.

Illich, I. (1973) *Tools for Conviviality*. London: Calder and Boyars.

ILO (2002) International Labour Organization, International Labour Organization, UN, www.ilo.org, accessed 6 November 2003.

INFACT (2004a) 'The nuclear weaponmakers campaign (1984–1993)', www.infact.org, accessed 21 June 2004.

INFACT (2004b) www.infact.org/aboutinf.html, accessed 12 July 2004.

Inglehart, R. (1977) *The Silent Revolution: Changing Values and Political Styles among Western Publics*. Princeton, NJ: Princeton University Press.

Irvine, S. (1989) 'Beyond green consumerism'. Discussion paper no. 1 (Sept.) London: Friends of the Earth.

Jackson, J. (2001) 'Prioritising customers and other stakeholders using the AHP', *European Journal of Marketing*, 35 (7/8): 858–71.

Jackson, T. and Michaelis, L. (2003) 'Policies for sustainable consumption', in the *Annual Report*. London: Sustainable Development Commission.

James, P. (1999) 'Standards in performance data needed', *Financial Times*, London: 10.

Jarvis, C.B., MacKenzie, S.B. and Podsakoff, P.M. (2003) 'A critical review of construct indicators and measurement model misspecification in marketing and consumer research', *Journal of Consumer Research*, 30 (2): 199–218.

John, R. (ed.) (1994) *The Consumer Revolution: Redressing the Balance*. London: Hodder and Stoughton.

Jordan, G. (1998) 'Politics without parties', *Parliamentary Affairs*, 51 (3): 314–28.

Joyner, B.E., Payne, D. and Raiborn, C.A. (2002) 'Building values, business ethics and corporate social responsibility into the developing organization', *Journal of Developmental Entrepreneurship*, 7 (1): 113–31.

Kahneman, D., Knetsch, J. and Thaler, R. (1986) 'Fairness and assumptions of economics', *Journal of Business*, 59: S285–S300.

Kerlinger, F.N. (1986) *Foundations of Behavioral Research*. New York: Holt, Rinehart and Winston.

Kierkegaard, S. and Auden, W.H. (1963) *The Living Thoughts of Kierkegaard*. Bloomington, IN: Indiana University Press.

Kim, S., Littrell, M.A. and Paff Ogle, J.L. (1999) 'Social responsibility as a predictor of purchase intentions for clothing', *Journal of Fashion Marketing and Management*, 3 (3): 207–18.

King, F. and Marcus, R. (2000) *Big Business, Small Hands – Responsible Approaches to Child Labour*. London: Save the Children Fund UK.

Kinnear, T. and Taylor, J. (1995) *Marketing Research: An Applied Approach*. London: McGraw-Hill/Irwin.

Kitson, A. (1996) 'Taking the pulse: ethics and the British Co-operative Bank', *Journal of Business Ethics*, 15 (9): 1021–31.

Kitzinger, J. (1995) 'Introducing focus groups', *British Medical Journal*, 311: 299–302.

Klein, N. (2000) *No Logo*. London: Flamingo/HarperCollins.

Knight, P. and Propper, S. (1999) 'Verifying the verifiers: environment viewpoint: independent auditing of social and environmental performance should not be left to the Big Five accountancy firms', *Financial Times*, London: 18.

Kok, P., Wiele, T., McKenna, R. and Brown, A. (2001) 'A corporate social responsibility audit within a quality management framework', *Journal of Business Ethics*, 31 (4): 285–97.

Korten, D.C. (1995) *When Corporations Rule the World*. West Hartford, Conn: Kumarian.

Kotler, P., Jain, D. and Maesincee, S. (2002) *Marketing Moves: A New Approach to Profits, Growth and Renewal*, cited in M. Scammell (2003). Boston: Harvard Business School Press.

Kozinets, R.J. (2002) 'Can consumers escape the market? Emancipatory illuminations from burning man', *Journal of Consumer Research*, 29 (1): 20–38.

Kozinets, R.V. and Handelman, J.M. (1998) 'Ensouling consumption: a netographic exploration of boycotting behaviour', *Advances in Consumer Research*, 25: 475–80.

Kozinets, R.V. (2001) 'Utopian enterprise: articulating the meanings of Star Trek's culture of consumption', *Journal of Consumer Research*, 28 (June): 67–88.

Kozinets, R.V. (2003) at www.kozinets.com.

Krebs, A.V. (1992) *The Corporate Reapers: The Book of Agribusiness*. Washington, DC: Essential.

Lager, F. (1994) *Ben and Jerry's: The Inside Scoop*. New York: Crown.

Lane Keller, K. (2000) 'Building and managing corporate brand equity', in M. Schultz, M.J. Hatch and M. Holten Larsen (eds), *The Expressive Organization: Linking Identity, Reputation, and the Corporate Brand*. Oxford: Oxford University Press, pp. 115–37.

Lang, T. and Heasman, M. (2004) *Food Wars: The Global Battle for Mouths, Minds and Markets*. London: Earthscan.

Lang, T. and Hines, C. (1993) *The New Protectionism: Protecting the Future Against Free Trade*. London: Earthscan.

Langeland, L. (1998) 'On communicating the complexity of a green message', *Greener Management International*: 25: 81–91.

Langerak, F., Peelen, E. and van der Veen, M. (1998) 'Exploratory results on the antecedents and consequences of Green marketing', *Journal of the Market Research Society*, 40: 323–35.

LaPiere, R.T. (1934) 'Attitudes vs. actions', *Social Forces*, 13: 230–7.

Lasley, P. and Bultena, G. (1986) 'Farmers opinions about third-wave technologies', *American Journal of Alternative Agriculture*, 3 (Summer). Cited in R.T. Libby (1998), *Eco-Wars: Political Campaigns and Social Movements*. New York: Columbia University Press.

Lawrence, F. (2004) *Hard Labour*. London: Penguin.

Lazzarini, S.G. and de Mello, P.C. (2001) 'Governmental versus self-regulation of derivative markets', *Journal of Economics and Business*, 53: 185–207.

Le Grand, J. (2003a) 'Living with the enemy', *The Economist*, 7 August.

Le Grand, J. (2003b) *Motivation, Agency and Public Policy: Of Knights and Knaves, Pawns and Queens*. Oxford: Oxford University Press.

Lerner, M. (1988) 'Firing Line', 24 January.

Lewis, A.T. (2003) 'Pure Baby'. Unpublished research on a new range of organic and fairly traded babywear, Manchester.

Lewis, E. (2003) 'Why giving is good for you', *Brand Strategy*, 170 (Apr.): 26–8.

Li, L. (2001) 'Encouraging environmental accounting worldwide: a survey of government policies and instruments', *Corporate Environmental Strategy*, 8 (1): 55–64.

Libby, R.T. (1998) *Eco-Wars: Political Campaigns and Social Movements*. New York: Columbia University Press.

Liedtka, J. (1999) 'Linking competitive advantage with communities of practice', *Journal of Management Inquiry*, 8 (1): 5–16.

Littrell, M.A. and Dickson, M.A. (1999) *Social Responsibility in the Global Market: Fair Trade of Cultural Products*. Thousand Oaks, CA: Sage.

Littrell, M.A., Ma, Y.J. and Halepete, J. (2004) 'Fair trade market survey summary report'. Unpublished report available from M. Littrell, Colorado State University, Fort Collins, Co.

Livesey, S. (2002) 'The discourse of the middle ground: citizen Shell commits to sustainable development', *Management Communication Quarterly*, 15 (3): 313–49.

Lunt, P. and Livingstone, S. (1992) *Mass Consumption and Personal Identity*. Buckingham: Open University Press.

Ma, H. (1999) 'Anatomy of competitive advantage: a SELECT framework', *Management Decision*, 37 (9): 709–18.

McCracken, G.D. (1988a) *Culture and Consumption: New Approaches to the Symbolic Character of Consumer Goods and Activities*. Bloomington, IN: Indiana University Press.

McCracken, G.D. (1988b) *The Long Interview*. Newbury Park, CA: Sage.

McCrary, D. (2002) 'Green accounting: a new route to corporate transparency?', *California CPA*, 71 (3): 12–15.

McEachern, M.G. and Schröder, M.J.A. (2002) 'The role of livestock production ethics in consumer values towards meat', *Journal of Agricultural and Environmental Ethics*, 15 (2): 221–37.

McEachern, M.G. and Warnaby, G. (2004) 'Retail "quality assurance" labels as a strategic marketing communication mechanism for fresh meat', *International Review of Retail, Distribution and Consumer Research*, 14 (2): 255–71.

McGregor, S. (1999) 'Towards a rationale for integrating consumer and citizenship education', *Journal of Consumer Studies and Home Economics*, 23 (4): 2007–211.

MacIntyre, A. (1984) *After Virtue* (2nd edn). Notre Dame: University of Notre Dame Press.

McMurray, S.E. (2003) 'Corporate compliance with human rights', *Australian Business Law Review*, 31 (4): 265–84.

Maitland, A. (2002a) 'McDonalds responds to anti-capitalist grilling', *Financial Times*, London, 24 July: 1.

Maitland, A. (2002b) 'McDonalds responds to anti-capitalist grilling: corporate social responsibility: the group claims to have listened to its critics on issues of globalisation, nutrition and the environment', *Financial Times*, London, 15 April: 13.

Maitland, A. (2002c) 'Rise in environmental reporting: corporate disclosure pressure to reveal non-financial performance', *Financial Times*, London, 29 July: 4.

Maitland, A. and Mann, M. (2002) 'Challenge to a voluntary preserve: corporate social responsibility: campaign groups want mandatory reporting', *Financial Times*, London, 30 May: 14.

Manstead, A.S.R., Proffitt, C. and Smart, J.L. (1983) 'Predicting and understanding mothers' infant-feeding intentions and behavior: testing the theory of reasoned action', *Journal of Personality and Social Psychology*, 44 (4): 657–71.

Maquila (2003) 'Codes primer', Maquila Solidarity Network, Toronto, Canada, www.maquilasolidarity.org/resources/codes/primer1.htm, accessed 4 November 2003.

Marshall, C. and Rossman, G.B. (1999) *Designing Qualitative Research* (3rd edn). London: Sage.

Marwell, G. and Ames, R. (1981) 'Economists free ride: does anyone else?', *Journal of Public Economics*, 15: 295–310.

Marymount University (1995) 'Garment workers study', report available from Marymount University, Center for Ethical Concerns, Arlington, VA.

Marymount University (1996) 'Garment workers study', report available from Marymount University, Center for Ethical Concerns, Arlington, VA.

Maslow, A. (1987) *Motivation and Personality* (3rd edn). New York: Harper & Row.

Meiklejohn, D. (1998) 'Child labour', *Ethical Consumer*, 51: 30.

Meyer, A. (1999) 'Green and competitive beyond the niche: reflections on green positioning strategies'. Paper presented at Business Strategy and the Environment Conference, University of Leeds.

Middlemiss, N. (2003) 'Authentic not cosmetic: CSR as brand enhancement', *Journal of Brand Management*, 10 (4/5): 353–61.

Miller, A. and Dess, G.G. (1993) 'Assessing Porter's (1980) model in terms of its generalizability, accuracy and simplicity', *Journal of Management Studies*, 30 (4): 553–85.

Miller, D. (1994) *Material Culture and Mass Consumption* (revised reprint edn.). Oxford: Blackwell.

Miller, D. (ed.) (1995) *Acknowledging Consumption*. London: Routledge.

Miller, D. (1998) *A Theory of Shopping*. Cambridge: Polity.

Miller, D. (2001a) *Consumption: Critical Concepts in the Social Sciences*. London: Routledge.

Miller, D. (2001b) 'The poverty of morality', *Journal of Consumer Culture*, 1 (2): 225–43.

Miller, D., Jackson, P., Thrift, N., Holbrook, B. and Rowlands, M. (1998) *Shopping, Place and Identity*. London: Routledge.

Mintel (1994) *The Green Consumer*, Vols 1 and 2. London: Mintel Research.

Mintel (2003) 'Organic foods – UK – November 2003'. Intelligence report. London: Mintel.

Mitchell, A. (1997) 'The power of ethical branding', *Marketing Week*, 22: 26–7.

Mohr, L.A. and Webb, D.J. (2001) 'Do consumers expect companies to be socially responsible? The impact of corporate social responsibility on buying behavior', *Journal of Consumer Affairs*, 35 (1): 45–72.

Monaghan, P. and Beer, J. (2000) 'Warts and all', *Management Accounting*, 78 (6): 28–9.

Monbiot, G. (2000) *Captive State: The Corporate Takeover of Britain*. London: Macmillan.

Morgan, D.L. (1988) *Focus Groups as Qualitative Research*. London: Sage.

MORI (2000) *The First Ever European Survey of Consumers Attitudes Towards Corporate Social Responsibility and Country Profiles*. London: MORI and CSR Europe.

Mulatuli, (1987 [1860]) *Max Havelaar or the Coffee Auctions of the Dutch Trading Company*. Harmondsworth: Penguin.

Murphy, D. and Bendell, J. (2001) 'Getting engaged', in R. Starkey and R. Welford (eds), *The Earthscan Reader in Business and Sustainable Development*. London: Earthscan.

Murray, J.B. and Ozanne, J.L. (1991) 'The critical imagination: emancipatory interests in consumer research', *Journal of Consumer Research*, 18 (2): 129–42.

Murtagh, C. and Lukehart, C. (2001) 'Co-op America's boycott organiser's guide', Washington, DC: Co-op America, www.coopamerica.org/boycotts/boycott_organizer_guide.pdf, accessed November 2003.

Nader, R. (1970) 'Foreword', in J.S. Turner (ed.), *The Chemical Feast: The Ralph Nader Study Group Report on Food Protection and the Food and Drug Administration*. New York: Grossman.

Nader, R. (1991) 'Keynote Speech to the World Consumer Congress'. Hong Kong: International Organisation of Consumers Unions.

Nader, R. and Smith, W.J. (1992) *The Frugal Shopper*. Washington, DC: Center for Study of Responsive Law.

National Consumer Council (1996) *Green Claims: A Consumer Investigation into Marketing Claims About the Environment*. London: NCC.

National Consumer Council (2001) *Consumer Education: Beyond Consumer Information*. London: NCC.

Nelson, D. (1991) 'The seikatsu club consumers' co-operative: activism for alternatives', *World Consumer*, December: 4–5.

Newholm, T. (1999a) 'Considering the ethical consumer'. PhD thesis, Open University, Buckingham.

Newholm, T. (1999b) 'Relocating the ethical consumer', in R. Norman (ed.), *Ethics and the Market*. Aldershot: Ashgate, pp. 162–84.

Newholm, T. (2000) 'Understanding the ethical consumer: employing a frame of bounded rationality'. PhD thesis, Open University, Buckingham.

Nganwa, P.K. (2002) 'Taking on the triple bottom line', *Accountancy SA* (Oct.): 13–14.

Nicholls, A.J. (2002) 'Strategic options in fair trade retailing', *International Journal of Retail and Distribution Management*, 30 (1): 6–17.

Nicholson-Lord, D. (1994) 'Consumerism with a shrunken vision', *The Independent*, 25 May.

Norman, R. (1998) *The Moral Philosophers: An Introduction to Ethics*. Oxford: Oxford University Press.

Norris, F. (2003) 'Consumer dominance hits a 54-year high', *The New York Times*, 1 December: C1.

Norusis, M.J. (1993) *SPSS: SPSS for Windows Professional Statistics Release 6.0*: Chicago, IL: SPSS Inc.

O'Connor, H. and Madge, C. (2003) 'Focus groups in cyberspace: using the internet for qualitative research', *Qualitative Market Research: An International Journal*, 6 (2): 133–43.

OECD (2003) 'Guidelines for multinational enterprises', Organisation for Economic Co-operation and Development, France, www.oecd.org/about/ 0,2337,en_2649_34889_1_1_1_1_1,00.html, accessed 10 November 2003.

Ölander, F. and Thøgersen, J. (1995) 'Understanding of consumer behaviour as a prerequisite for environmental protection', *Journal of Consumer Policy*, 18 (4): 345–85.

Ollman, B. (1998) 'Market mystification in capitalism and market socialist societies', in B. Ollman (ed.), *Market Socialism*. New York: Routledge, pp. 81–122.

O'Riordan, T. (1999) 'Corporate social reporting', *Environment*, 41 (7): 1–2.

Osborn, A. (2003) 'Continents apart', *The Guardian*, 17 November.

O'Shaughnessy, J. and O'Shaughnessy, N. (forthcoming) 'The Rational Choice Model, Fran's Commitment Model, Nozicks's Decision-Value Model and Considerations of Equity in Marketing'.

Oxfam (2002) *Mugged: Poverty in Your Coffee Cup*. Oxford: Oxfam.

Palese, M. and Crane, Y.T. (2002) 'Building an integrated issue management process as a source of sustainable competitive advantage', *Journal of Public Affairs*, 2 (4): 284–92.

Parfit, D. (1984) *Reasons and Persons*. Oxford: Oxford University Press.

Patten, D.M. (1992) 'Intra-industry environmental disclosures in response to the Alaskan oil spill: a note on legitimacy theory', *Accounting, Organizations and Society*, 17 (5): 471–5.

Peattie, K. (1992) *Green Marketing*. London: Pitman.

Peattie, K. (1995) *Environmental Marketing Management: Meeting the Green Challenge*. London: Pitman.

Peattie, K. (1999) 'Trappings versus substance in the greening of marketing planning', *Journal of Strategic Marketing*, 7: 131–48.

Pettit, P. (1991) 'Consequentialism', in P. Singer (ed.), *A Companion to Ethics*. Oxford: Blackwell, pp. 230–40.

Pike, K.L. (1954) *Language in Relation to a Unified Theory of the Structure of Human Behavior*. Glendale, CA: Summer Institute of Linguistics.

Plender, J. (1999) 'Stakeholder power: will social reporting produce meaningful information or will it be just another public relations weapon in the hands of self-interested managements?', *Financial Times*, 15 July: 14.

Pollio, H.R., Henley, T.B. and Thompson, C.J. (1997) *The Phenomenology of Everyday Life*. Cambridge: Cambridge University Press.

Porter, M.E. (1985) *Competitive Advantage: Creating and Sustaining Superior Performance*. New York: Free Press.

Porter, M.E. and van der Linde, C. (1995) 'Green and competitive', *Harvard Business Review*, September–October: 120–34.

Powell, E. (1969) *Freedom and Reality*. Kingswood: Elliot Right Way Books.

Powell, R.A. and Single, H.M. (1996) 'Focus groups', *International Journal of Quality in Health Care*, 8 (5): 499–504.

Pratley, N. (2003) 'Kick them where it hurts', *The Guardian*, 19 December.

Pruitt, S.W. and Friedman, M. (1986) 'Determining the effectiveness of consumer boycotts: a stock price analysis of their impacts on corporate targets', *Journal of Consumer Policy*, 9: 375–87.

Purushothaman, M., Tower, G., Hancock, P. and Taplin, R. (2000) 'Determinants of corporate social reporting practices of listed Singapore companies', *Pacific Accounting Review*, 12 (2): 101–33.

Pusey, M.J. (1956) *Eisenhower, the President*. New York: Macmillan.

Raats, M.M., Shepherd, R. and Sparks, P. (1995) 'Including moral dimensions of choice within the structure of the theory of planned behavior', *Journal of Applied Social Psychology*, 25 (6): 484–94.

Radin, T.J. (2003) 'Levi Strauss and Co.: implementation of global sourcing and operating guidelines in Latin America', in L.P. Hartman, D.G. Arnold and R.E. Wokutch (eds), *Rising above Sweatshops: Innovative Approaches to Global Labor Challenges*. Westport, CT: Praeger, pp. 249–91.

Ramey, J. (1996) 'Reich's sweatshop war goes offshore', *Women's Wear Daily*, 24 September: 29–30.

Rashid, M.Z.A. and Ibrahim, S. (2002) 'Executive and management attitudes towards corporate social responsibility in Malaysia', *Corporate Governance*, 2 (4): 10–16.

Rawls, J. (1972) *A Theory of Justice*. Oxford: Oxford University Press.

Rawvas, M.Y.A. (2001) 'Culture, personality, and morality: a typology of international consumers' ethical beliefs', *International Marketing Review*, 18 (2): 188–209.

Redfern, P. (1913) *The Story of the CWS*. Manchester: Co-operative Wholesale Society.

Redfern, P. (1920) *The Consumers' Place in Society*. Manchester: Co-operative Union.

Reinecke, J., Schmidt, P. and Ajzen, I. (1996) 'Application of the theory of planned behavior to adolescents' condom use: a panel study', *Journal of Applied Social Psychology*, 26 (9): 749–72.

Rhoades, S.B. (1985) *The Economist's View of the World*. Cambridge: Cambridge University Press.

Rice, D. (2002) 'Human rights strategies for corporations', *Business Ethics: A European Review*, 11 (2): 134–6.

Riege, A. (2003) 'Validity and reliability tests in case study research: a literature review with "hands–on" applications for each research phase', *Qualitative Market Research*, 6 (2): 75–86.

Rising Tide (2003) www.risingtide.org.uk/pages/news/no-waract.htm, accessed November 2003.

Roberts, J.A. (1995) 'Profiling levels of socially responsible consumer behavior: a cluster analytic approach and its implications for marketing', *Journal of Marketing Theory and Practice*, 3 (Fall): 97–117.

Roberts, J.A. (1996) 'Will the real socially responsible consumer please step forward?', *Business Horizons*, 39 (1): 79–84.

Roddick, A. (1992) *Body and Soul*. London: Vermilion.

Rose, C. (1997) 'Greenpeace – implementing solutions', Marine Environmental Management Review of Events in 1996, 4 cited in Gray, Tim, S. (1998) 'The changing role of environmental non-governmental organisations in the UK in the 1990s', *Contemporary Political Studies*, www.psa.ac.uk/cps/1999/gray.pdf.

Rose, C. (1998) *The Turning of the Spar*. London: Greenpeace.

Rosen, C.M. (2001) 'Environmental strategy and competitive advantage: an introduction', *California Management Review*, 43 (3): 8–15.

Rosen, E.I. (2002) *Making Sweatshops: The Globalization of the US Apparel Industry*. Berkeley: University of California Press.

Rucht, D. (1996) 'The impact of national contexts on social movement structures' in D. McAdam, J. McCarthy and M. Zald (eds), *Comparative Perspectives on Social Movements*. New York: Cambridge University Press.

Ryan, A. (2003) 'The Way to Reason', *The New York Review of Books*, 4 December: 43–5.

Sanger, E. (2003) 'P. Diddy: I won't stand for sweatshop; rapper says Sean John would terminate its relationship with plant if abuses are confirmed', *Newsday*, 29 October: A12.

Sayer, A. (1999) *Realism and Social Science*. London: Sage.

Sayer, A. (2003) '(De)commodification, consumer culture, and moral economy', *Environment and Planning D: Society and Space*, 21: 341–57.

Scammell, M. (2003) 'Citizen consumers – towards a new marketing of politics?', in J. Corner and D. Pels (eds), *Media and the Restyling of Politics*. London: Sage.

Schilling, D. (2003) 'Small steps toward transformation: changing conditions in Asia's garment factories', Interfaith Centre on Corporate Responsibility (ICCR),www.iccr.org/issue_groups/accountability/feature_codes2.htm, accessed 4 November 2003.

Schlegelmilch, B. (1994) 'Green, Ethical and Charitable', in M. Baker (ed.), *Perspectives in Marketing Management*. Chichester: Wiley, pp. 57–68.

Schlesenger, A. (1986) *The Cycles of American History*. New York: Houghton-Mifflin.

Schor, J. (1999) *The Overspent American: Why We Want What We Don't Need*. New York: HarperPerennial.

Schor, J. and Holt, D.B. (2000) *The Consumer Society Reader*. New York: New Press (distributed by W.W. Norton and Co.)

Scott, P. (2000) 'The truth about verification', *Environmental Finance,* September: 28–9. Also available at www.environmental-finance.com/2000/featsep2.htm, accessed 13 January 2005.

Seanor, D. and Fotion, N. (1988) 'Levels, methods, and points', in D. Seanor and N. Fotion (eds), *Harre and Critics: Essays on Moral Thinking.* New York: Oxford University Press, pp. 1–7.

SEC (2003) Securities and Exchange Commission, US Securities and Exchange Commission, www.sec.gov/, accessed 10 November 2003.

Sen, A. (1987) *On Ethics and Economics.* Oxford: Blackwell.

Sen, A. (2003) *Rationality and Freedom.* Cambridge, MA: Belknap.

Senge, P. and Carstedt, G. (2003) 'Innovating our way to the next industrial revolution', in T.W. Malone, R. Laubacher and M.S. Scott Morton (eds), *Inventing the Organizations of the 21st Century.* Cambridge, MA: MIT.

Seybold, P., Marshak, R. and Lewis, J. (2001) *The Customer Revolution.* New York: Random House.

Shaw, D. (2000) 'Consumed by ethics?: a model building approach to the ethical consumer'. Glasgow Caledonian University, April.

Shaw, D. and Clarke, I. (1999) 'Belief formation in ethical consumer groups: an exploratory study', *Marketing Intelligence and Planning,* 17 (2 and 3): 109–19.

Shaw, D. and Newholm, T. (2002) 'Voluntary simplicity and the ethics of consumption', *Psychology and Marketing,* 19 (2): 167–90.

Shaw, D. and Newholm, T. (2003) 'Consumption simplicity among ethical consumers', in S.P. Shohov (ed.), *Advances in Psychology,* Vol. 20, pp.175–92.

Shaw, D. and Shiu, E. (2003) 'Ethics in consumer choice: a multivariate modelling approach', *European Journal of Marketing,* 37 (10): 1485–99.

Shaw, D. and Thomson, J. (2002) 'Spirituality and ethical consumption', Consumption, Christianity and Creation conference. Sheffield: Hallam University.

Shaw, D., Shiu, E. and Clarke, I. (2000) 'The contribution of ethical obligation and self-identity to the theory of planned behaviour: an exploration of ethical consumers', *Journal of Marketing Management,* 16 (8): 879–94.

Shaw, D., Shiu, E. and Hassan, L. (2004a) 'Modelling values in ethical consumer decision-making', Academy of Marketing Annual conference, 6–9 July, Chelteham: Gloucestershire, UK.

Shaw, D., Grehan, E., Shiu, E., Hassan, L. and Thomson, J. (2004b) 'An exploration of values in ethical consumer decision making', *Journal of Consumer Behaviour,* 4 (1): not yet in print.

Shaw, D.S. and Duff, R. (2002) *'Ethics and social responsibility in fashion and clothing choice.'* Paper presented at the European Marketing Academy Conference, Portugal.

Shiu, E. and Hassan, L. (2002) 'A critical comparison of the use of multiple regression and structural equation modelling on the theory of planned behaviour'. Paper presented at the European Marketing Academy Conference, Portugal.

Silver, S. (2002) 'The banana giant that found its gentle side: corporate social responsibility: partnerships with environmentalists and unions helped Chiquita's reputation, but some former critics are unsure of how close they should get', *Financial Times,* London: 14.

Simms, J. (2002) 'Business: corporate social responsibility – you know it makes sense', *Accountancy,* 130 (1311): 48–50.

Sinclair, U. (1985 [1906]) *The Jungle.* Harmondsworth: Penguin.

Singer, P. (1997) *How are We to Live? Ethics in the Age of Self-Interest.* Oxford: Oxford University Press.

Singer, P. (2002) *One World: The Ethics of Globalization.* New Haven: Yale University Press.

Slote, M. (2000) 'Virtue ethics', in H. LaFollette (ed.), *The Blackwell Guide To Ethical Theory.* Oxford: Blackwell, pp. 325–47.

Smith, A. (1759) *The Theory of the Moral Sentiments.* Edinburgh.

Smith, A. (1937 [1776]) *An Inquiry into the Nature and Causes of the Wealth of Nations.* New York: The Modern Library.

Smith, D. (2000) 'Pension funds to adopt ethical investment policy', *Sunday Times,* London, 25 June: B2.

Smith, K. (2002) 'ISO considers corporate social responsibility standards', *The Journal for Quality and Participation,* 25 (3): 42.

Smith, N.C. (1990a) 'The case study: a useful research method for information management', 5: 123–33.

Smith, N.C. (1990b) *Morality and the Market: Consumer Pressure for Corporate Accountability*. London: Routledge.

Smith, N.C. (1998) 'Ethics and the typology of value', in M. Holbrook (ed.), *Consumer Value*, London: Routledge. p. 152.

Soil Association (2003) 'Food and Farming Report 2003', Executive summary information sheet at www.soilassociation.org. Bristol.

Sparkes, R. (1995) *The Ethical Investor*. London: Zondervan.

Sparks, P. and Guthrie, C.A. (1998) 'Self-identity and the theory of planned behavior: a useful addition or an unhelpful artifice?', *Journal of Applied Social Psychology*, 28: 1393–410.

Sparks, P. and Shepherd, R. (1992) 'Self-identity and the theory of planned behavior: assessing the role of identification with Green consumerism', *Social Psychology Quarterly*, 55 (4): 388–99.

Sparks, P., Shepherd, R. and Frewer, L.J. (1995) 'Assessing and structuring attitudes toward the use of gene technology in food production: the role of perceived ethical obligation', *Basic and Applied Social Psychology*, 16 (4): 267–85.

Stake, R.E. (1995) *The Art of Case Study*. Thousand Oaks, CA: Sage.

Stavropoulos, W.S. (1996) 'Environmentalism's third wave: managing for global competitiveness', *Executive Speeches*, 11: 28–30.

Stern, P. (1986) 'Blind Spots in policy analysis: what economics doesn't say about energy use', *Journal of Policy Analysis and Management*, 5 (2): 200–27.

Strauss, A. and Corbin, J. (1990) *Basics of Qualitative Research*. Newbury Park, CA: Sage.

Strauss, A. and Corbin, J. (1998) *Basics of Qualitative Research: Techniques and Procedures for Developing Grounded Theory*. Thousand Oaks, CA: Sage.

Strong, C. (1997) 'The problems of translating fair trade principles into consumer purchase behaviour', *Marketing Intelligence and Planning*, 15 (1): 32–7.

Sustainability (2004) Sustainability website www.sustainability.com, accessed 7 July 2004.

Svendsen, A. (1998a) 'Social accounting: the state of the art', The Centre for Innovation in Management, Canada, www.cim.sfu.ca/pages/resources_profits.htm, accessed 5 May 2003.

Svendsen, A. (1998b) 'Social audits good for the bottom line', The Centre for Innovation in Management, Canada, www.cim.sfu.ca/pages/resources_social_audits.htm, accessed 5 May 2003.

Svendsen, A., Abbott, R., Boutilier, R. and Wheeler, D. (2001), 'Pathways to competitive advantage', *CA Magazine*, 134: 29–30, 39.

Swanton, C. (2003) *Virtue Ethics: A Pluralistic View*. Oxford: Oxford University Press.

Sweet, C. (2001) 'Designing and conducting virtual focus groups', *Qualitative Market Research: An International Journal*, 4 (3): 130–5.

Swift, T.A. (2002) 'No trust without verification', Amnesty International, UN, www.amnesty.org.uk/business/newslet/autumn02/trust.shtml, accessed 30 April 2003.

Tallontire, A. (2001) 'Challenges facing fair trade: which way now?' Paper for DSA Annual conference. IDPM, Manchester.

Tallontire, A., Rentsendorj, E. and Blowfield, M. (2001) *Consumers and Ethical Trade: A Review of Current Literature*. Chatham: National Resources Institute.

Tanner, C. and Wolfing Kast, S. (2003) 'Promoting sustainable consumption: determinants of Green purchases by Swiss consumers', *Psychology and Marketing*, 20 (10): 883–903.

Targett, S. (2000) 'National news: pensions industry faces close scrutiny', *Financial Times*, London, 21 September: 4.

Taylor, R. (2002) *Virtue Ethics*. Amherst, NY: Prometheus.

Taylor, S. and Todd, P. (1997) 'Understanding the determinants of consumer composting behavior', *Journal of Applied Social Psychology*, 27: 602–28.

Tesch, R. (1990) *Qualitative Research: Types and Research Tools*. London: Falmer.

The Economist (2003) 'Reflecting the views of Julian Le Grand of the London School of Economics', 1 November: 74.

The Independent (1995) Leader Column, 21 June.

Thøgersen, J. (1999) 'The ethical consumer: moral norms and packaging choice', *Journal of Consumer Policy*, 22: 439–60.

Thomas, A. (1998) 'Challenging cases', in A. Thomas, J. Chataway and M. Wuyts (eds), *Finding out Fast*. London: Sage, pp. 307–32.

Thompson, C.J. (1996) 'Caring consumers: gendered consumption meanings and the juggling lifestyle', *Journal of Consumer Research*, 22: 388–407.

Thompson, C.J. (1997) 'Interpreting consumers: a hermeneutical framework for deriving marketing insights from the texts of consumers' consumption stories', *Journal of Marketing Research*, 34 (4): 438–56.

Thompson, C.J. (2003) 'Natural health discourses and the therapeutic production of consumer resistance', *The Sociology Quarterly*, 44 (1): 81–107.

Thompson, C.J., Locander, W.B. and Pollio, H.R. (1989) 'Putting consumer experience back into consumer research: the philosophy and method of existential-phenomenology', *Journal of Consumer Research*, 16 (4): 133–47.

Thompson, D. (1994) *Weavers of Dreams: Founders of the Modern Co-operative Movement*. Davis, CA: Center for Co-operatives/University of California.

Thompson, E.P. (1993 [1971]) 'The moral economy of the English crowd in the eighteenth century', cited in E.P. Thompson (1993). *Customs in Common*. Harmondsworth: Penguin, pp. 185–258.

Thurow, L. (1985) *The New York Review*. 21 November: 37.

Thurow, L. (1986) *The Zero-Sum Solution: Building a World Class American Economy*. New York: Simon and Schuster.

Titus, P.A. and Bradford, J.L. (1996) 'Reflections on consumer sophistication and its impact on ethical business practice', *Journal of Consumer Affairs*, 30 (1): 170–94.

Todd, S. (2003) 'Social auditing as a learning process: new terms of engagement II', Solstice Consulting, Canada, www.cim.sfu.ca/SueTodd.ppt, accessed 30 April 2003.

Todoroki, E. (2002) 'Globilization and corporate social responsibility (CSR)', World Bank Institute, www.people.virginia.edu/~yfy2d/Globilization%20and%20Corporate%20Social%20Responsibility.ppt, accessed 26 November 2003.

Tomolillo, D. and Shaw, D. (2003) 'Undressing the ethical issues in clothing choice', *International Journal of New Product Development and Innovation Management*, June/July: 99–107.

Towell, J. (1998) 'Secondary effects of consumer boycotts' website at www.i-way.co.uk/~jtowell/2bcthome.htm, accessed 21 June 2004.

US Bureau of the Census (1997) *'Current Population Reports, Series P23–194, Population Profile in the United States, 1997'*. Washington, DC: US Government Printing Office.

US Chamber of Commerce (2003) 'Economic sanctions/boycotts don't work!', Washington, DC, April 2003, www.amcham.ch/events/content/downloads03/Economic_sanctions.pdf, accessed 26 November.

US General Accounting Office (1994) 'Garment industry: efforts to address the prevalence and conditions of sweatshops', Washington, DC: US General Accounting Office.

US Green Party (2001) 'Global Greens International Day of Action', 11 July 2001, www.gp.org/articles/exxonmobil.html.

USCIB (1998) USCIB Position Paper on Codes of Conduct, USCIB, US, www.uscib.org/index.asp?documentID=1358, viewed 4 November 2003.

Vallerand, R.J., Deshaies, P., Cuerrian, J.P., Pelletier, L.G. and Mongeau, C. (1992) 'Ajzen and Fishbein's theory of reasoned action as applied to moral behavior: a confirmatory analysis', *Journal of Personality and Social Psychology*, 62 (1): 98–109.

Van Inwagen, P. (1990) *Material Beings*. Ithaca, NY: Cornell University Press.

Varadarajan, P.R. and Menon, A. (1988) 'Cause-related marketing: a coalignment of marketing strategy and corporate philanthropy', *Journal of Marketing*, 52 (July): 58–74.

Varley, P. (1998) *The Sweatshop Quandary: Corporate Responsibility on the Global Frontier*. Washington, DC: Investor Responsibility Research Center.

Varney, R.V. (2002) *Marketing Communication: Principles and Practice*. London: Routledge.

Vidal, J. (1997) *McLibel: Burger Culture on Trial*. London: Pan.

Vogel, D. (1978) *Lobbying the Corporation*. New York: Basic.

von Weizacher, E., Lovins, A. and Lovins, L. H. (1998) *Factor Four: Doubling Wealth, Halving Resource Use*. London: Earthscan.

Wainwright, M. (1998) 'Couples may put embryo on ice to fit career plan', *Guardian*, 17 August.

Walden, W.D. and Schwartz, B.N. (1997) 'Environmental disclosures and public policy pressure', *Journal of Accounting and Public Policy*, 16: 125–54.

Warde, A. (2004) 'Theories of practice as an approach to consumption', ESRC/AHRB *Cultures of Consumption Programme Working Paper* No. 6. Available at www.consume.bbk.ac.uk/publications.html.

Warnock, M. (1967) *Existentialist Ethics*. London: Macmillan.

Weeks, J. (1995) *Invented Moralities: Sexual Values in an Age of Uncertainty*. New York: Columbia University Press.

Wells, P. and Jetter, M. (1991) *The Global Consumer: Best Buys to Help the Third World*. London: Gollancz.

White, A. (1999) 'Sustainability and the accountable corporation', *Environment*, 41 (8): 30–43.

Wiggins, D. (2001) *Sameness and Substance Renewed*. Cambridge: Cambridge University Press.

Wilk, R. (2001) 'Consuming morality', *Journal of Consumer Culture*, 1 (2): 245–60.

Will, R., Marlin, A.T., Corson, B. and Schorsch, J. (1989) *Shopping for a Better World*. New York: Council on Economic Priorities.

Williams, B. (1973) 'A critique of utilitarianism', in J.C.C. Smart and B. Williams (eds), *Utilitarianism For and Against*. Cambridge: Cambridge University Press, pp. 75–150.

Williams, B. (1985) *Ethics and the Limits of Philosophy*. London: Fontana.

Williams, C.J.F. (1992) *Being, Identity, and Truth*. Oxford: Oxford University Press.

Williams, M. (2000) 'Interpretivism and generalisation', *Sociology*, 34 (2): 209–24.

Winward, J. (1993) 'The organized consumer and consumer information co-operatives', in R. Keat, N. Whitely and N. Abercrombie (eds), *The Authority of the Consumer*. London: Routledge, pp. 75–90.

Witkowski, T.H. (1989) 'Colonial consumers in revolt: buyer values and behavior during the nonimportation movement, 1764–1776', *Journal of Consumer Research*, 16 (2) September: 216–26.

Wolfe, A. (1989) *Whose Keeper?: Social Science and Moral Obligation*. Berkeley, CA: University of California Press.

Wong, V., Turner W. and Stoneman, P. (1995) *Marketing Strategies and Marketing Prospects for Environmentally-friendly Consumer Products*. Warwick: The University of Warwick.

Wootliff, J. and Deri, C. (2001) 'NGOs: the new super brands', *Corporate Reputation Review*, 4 (2): 157–65.

Worcester, R. and Downham, J. (eds) (1986) *Consumer Market Research Handbook*. London: McGraw-Hill.

Wright, C. (2003) 'Consuming lives, consuming landscapes: interpreting advertisements for Cafédirect coffees'. Paper presented at British Sociological Association Annual Conference, University of York, UK.

Wright, S. (2001) 'Setting the standard', *Organiclife*, October/November.

WWF UK (2004) www.wwf-uk.org/core/about/whoweare.asp, accessed 5 July 2004.

Yanz, L. and Jeffcott, B. (1999) 'Codes of conduct: from corporate responsibility to social accountability', Maquila Solidarity Network, Toronto, Canada, www.web.net/~msn/5codes1.htm, accessed 4 November 2003.

Yin, R.K. (2003) *Case Study Research: Design and Methods* (3rd edn). Thousand Oaks, CA: Sage.

Young, I.M. (2003) 'From guilt to solidarity: sweatshops and political responsibility', *Dissent*, Spring: 39–44.

Zadek, S., Lingayah, S. and Forstater, M. (1998a) *Social Labels: Tools for Ethical Trade*. London: New Economics Foundation.

Zadek, S., Lingayah, S. and Murphy, S. (1998b) *Purchasing Power – Civil Action for Sustainable Consumption*. London: New Economics Foundation.

Zhongzhi, Z. (2001) 'Ethical and economic evaluations of consumption in contemporary China', *Business Ethics: A European Review*, 10 (2): 92–7.

Znaniecki, F. (1934) *The Method of Sociology*. New York: Farrer and Rinehart.

Zulch, H. (2003) 'Sustainable business solutions', PricewaterhouseCoopers, www.pwcglobal.com/Extweb/service.nsf/docid/50B9FB80FCF4DA3380256B, accessed 10 September 2003.

Zutshi, A. and Adams, C.A. (2004) 'Voluntary guidelines: are they enough to sustain the environment?', *Alternative Law Journal*, 29 (1): 23–6.

Index

FAIR TRADE

ALEX NICHOLLS & CHARLOTTE OPAL

Alex Nicholls *Said Business School, University of Oxford* and
Charlotte Opal *TrainsFair, USA*

'Today, Fair Trade finds itself at a crucial point in its evolution from alternative trading mechanism to a mainstream economic model. As the only certifier in the largest Fair Trade market in the world, TransFair USA has observed the explosive growth in consumer awareness and business interest in Fair Trade certification. New research into the progress of Fair Trade to date and, crucially, its key future directions is urgently needed. **Fair Trade** is therefore a valuable and timely contribution.The range and depth of the book is considerable. It is international in outlook and engages with a broad spectrum of theory and thinking. Its style is approachable yet rigorous. I would strongly recommend it to industry, academics, students, policy-makers and the interested reader in general.' - *Paul Rice, CEO, TransFair USA*

Fair Trade is at a crucial moment in its evolution from alternative trading mechanism to mainstream economic model. This timely and thoughtful book looks at the strategic future for Fair Trade.

Each chapter spearheads a key area of Fair Trade thinking and theory and the political, legal and economic context of Fair Trade is given careful scrutiny. Difficult questions are tackled such as 'What is the role and value of corporate social responsibility?' and 'What is the brand meaning of Fair Trade?' Throughout, readers are supported by:

- Revealing case studies and useful data analysis
- Concise histories of different Fair Trade organisations
- Chapter summeries and conclusions

Contents

The Rise of Fair Trade \ Introduction \ Fair Trade: The Story So Far \ The Economics of Fair Trade \ Supply Chain Ethics \ Fair Trade Operations \ Fair Trade Industry Structures and Business Strategies \ **Whitni Thomas** Financing Fair Trade \ Fair Trade Certification \ The Marketing of Fair Trade \ The Impact of Fair Trade \ The Fair Trade Market \ Measuring Impact \ Fair Trade Futures

June 2005 • 272 pages
Cloth (1-4129-0104-9) £70.00 • Paper (1-4129-0105-7) £21.99